Lecture Notes in Computer Science 12026

More information about this series at http://www.springer.com/series/7409

Slim Kallel · Frédéric Cuppens ·
Nora Cuppens-Boulahia ·
Ahmed Hadj Kacem (Eds.)

Risks and Security of Internet and Systems

14th International Conference, CRiSIS 2019
Hammamet, Tunisia, October 29–31, 2019
Proceedings

Springer

Editors
Slim Kallel (ID)
ReDCAD
University of Sfax
Sfax, Tunisia

Frédéric Cuppens
IMT Atlantique, Lab-STICC
Université Bretagne Loire
Rennes, France

Nora Cuppens-Boulahia
IMT Atlantique, Lab-STICC
Université Bretagne Loire
Rennes, France

Ahmed Hadj Kacem
ReDCAD
University of Sfax
Sfax, Tunisia

ISSN 0302-9743 ISSN 1611-3349 (electronic)
Lecture Notes in Computer Science
ISBN 978-3-030-41567-9 ISBN 978-3-030-41568-6 (eBook)
https://doi.org/10.1007/978-3-030-41568-6

LNCS Sublibrary: SL3 – Information Systems and Applications, incl. Internet/Web, and HCI

This Springer imprint is published by the registered company Springer Nature Switzerland AG
The registered company address is: Gewerbestrasse 11, 6330 Cham, Switzerland

Preface

This volume contains the papers presented at the 14th International Conference on Risks and Security of Internet and Systems (CRiSIS 2019), which was organized in Hammamet, Tunisia, October 29–31, 2019. It continued a tradition of successful conferences: Bourges (2005), Marrakech (2007), Tozeur (2008), Toulouse (2009), Montréal (2010), Timisoara (2011), Cork (2012), La Rochelle (2013), Trento (2014), Mytilene (2015), Roscoff (2016), Dinard (2017), and Arcachon (2018).

The CRiSIS conference constitutes an open forum for the exchange of state-of-the-art knowledge on security issues in Internet-related applications, networks, and systems. Following the tradition of the previous events, the program was composed of high-quality contributed papers. The program call for papers looked for original and significant research contributions in the following topics:

- Analysis and management of risk
- Attacks and defenses
- Attack data acquisition and network monitoring
- Cryptography, biometrics, and watermarking
- Dependability and fault tolerance of Internet applications
- Distributed and embedded systems security
- Empirical methods for security and risk evaluation
- Hardware-based security and physical security
- Intrusion detection and prevention systems
- Privacy protection and anonymization
- Risk-aware access and usage control
- Security and risk assessment and metrics
- Security and dependability of operating systems
- Security and safety of critical infrastructures
- Security and privacy of peer-to-peer system and wireless networks
- Security models and security policies
- Security of new generation networks, VoIP, and multimedia
- Security of e-commerce, electronic voting, and database systems
- Security of social networks
- Security of industrial control systems
- Smartphone security and privacy
- Traceability, metrology, and forensics
- Trust management
- Use of smart cards and personal devices for Internet applications
- Web and cloud security

In response to the call for papers, 64 papers were submitted. Each paper was reviewed by at least three reviewers, and judged according to scientific and presentation quality, originality, and relevance to the conference topics. The Program Committee selected 20 regular papers and 4 short papers. The program was completed with excellent invited talks given by Lotfi ben Othmane (Iowa State University, USA) and Takoua Abdellatif (University of Sousse, Tunisia). Finally, the conference included two tutorials given by Suraj Kothari (Iowa State University, USA) and Reda Yaich (IRT SystemX, France).

It is impossible to organize a successful program without the help of many individuals. We would like to express our appreciation to the authors of the submitted papers, the Program Committee members, and the external referees. We owe special thanks to the Organizing Committee for the hard work they did locally in Hammamet.

November 2019

Slim Kallel
Frédéric Cuppens
Nora Cuppens-Boulahia
Ahmed Hadj Kacem

Organization

General Chairs

Ahmed Hadj Kacem   University of Sfax, Tunisia
Nora Cuppens-Boulahia   IMT Atlantique, France

Program Committee Chairs

Slim Kallel   University of Sfax, Tunisia
Frédéric Cuppens   IMT Atlantique, France

Publicity Chairs

Saoussen Cheikhrouhou   University of Sfax, Tunisia
Reda Yaich   IRT SystemX, France

Organizing Chair

Slim Kallel   University of Sfax, Tunisia

Local Organizing Members

Ismail Bouassida   University of Sfax, Tunisia
Hatem Hadj Kacem   University of Sfax, Tunisia
Nesrine Khabou   University of Sfax, Tunisia
Fairouz Fakhfakh   University of Sfax, Tunisia
Riadh Ben Halima   University of Sfax, Tunisia
Ghislaine Le Gall   IMT Atlantique, France

Program Committee

Takoua Abdellatif   University of Carthage, Tunisia
Esma Aimeur   University of Montreal, Canada
Abderrahim Ait-Wakrime   IRT Railenium, France
Jocelyn Aubert   University of Luxembourg, Luxembourg
Ismail Bouassida   University of Sfax, Tunisia
Anis Bkakria   IMT Atlantique, France
Nora Cuppens-Boulahia   IMT Atlantique, France
Frédéric Cuppens   IMT Atlantique, France
Mohamed Ghazel   IFSTTAR, France
Bogdan Groza   Politehnica University of Timisoara, Romania
Mohamed Jmaiel   University of Sfax, Tunisia

Christos Kalloniatis	University of the Aegean, Greece
Sokratis Katsikas	Norwegian University of Science and Technology, Norway
Igor Kotenko	St. Petersburg Institute for Informatics and Automation, Russia
Marc Lacoste	Orange labs, France
Jean-Louis Lanet	LHS Rennes, France
Wassef Louati	University of Sfax, Tunisia
Mohamed Mosbah	University of Bordeaux, France
Raja Natarajan	Tata Institute of Fundamental Research, India
Roberto Di Pietro	Hamad Bin Khalifa University, Qatar
Kai Rannenberg	Goethe University Frankfurt, Germany
Riadh Robbana	University of Carthage, Tunisia
Michael Rusinowitch	Lorraine University, France
Ketil Stoelen	University of Oslo, Norway
Lingyu Wang	Concordia University, Canada
Reda Yaich	IRT SystemX, France
Akka Zemmari	University of Bordeaux, France

Additional Reviewers

Houssem Aloulou
Hamdi Aloulou
Sourour Ammar
Maissa Ben Jamaa
Jean-Michel Bruel
Mariam Chaabane
Marwa Chaieb
Saoussen Cheikhrouhou
Rustem Dautov
Fairouz Fakhfakh
Tarek Frikha
Enrique Garcia-Ceja
Ikram Garfatta
Amal Gassara
Mohamed Hammi
Angeliki Kitsiou

Sihem Loukil
Fatma Masmoudi
Katerina Mavroeidi
Afef Mdhaffar
Argyri Pattakou
Montida Pattaranantakul
Mouna Rekik
Wael Sellami
Maria Sideri
Stavros Simou
Qipeng Song
Yousfi Souheib
Iraklis Symeonidis
Shukun Tokas
Mouna Torjmen

Contents

Network and Cloud Security

Information Security Policy

Data Protection and Machine Learning for Security

Distributed Detection System and Blockchain

Risk Analysis and Management

pQUANT: A User-Centered Privacy Risk Analysis Framework

Welderufael B. Tesfay[1]([✉]), Dimitra Nastouli[2], Yannis C. Stamatiou[2,3], and Jetzabel M. Serna[1]

[1] Chair of Mobile Business and Multilateral Security, Goethe University Frankfurt, Theodor-W.-Adorno-Platz 4, 60323 Frankfurt am Main, Germany
{welderufael.tesfay,jetzabel.serna}@m-chair.de
[2] Department of Business Administration, University of Patras, Patras, Greece
nastouli@upatras.gr
[3] Computer Technology Institute and Press "Diophantus", 26504 Patras, Greece
stamatiu@ceid.upatras.gr

Abstract. The last few decades have entertained a fast digital transformation of our daily activities. This has brought about numerous benefits as well as unanticipated consequences. As such, on the consequences side, information privacy incidents have become prevalent. This has further raised the concern of users and data protection bodies alike. Thus, quantifying and communicating privacy risks plays paramount role in raising user awareness, designing appropriate technical solutions, and enacting legal frameworks. However, previous research in privacy risk quantification has not considered the user's heterogeneously subjective perceptions of privacy, and her right to informational self determination since, often, the privacy risk analysis and prevention takes place once the data is out of her control. In this paper, we present a user-centered privacy risk quantification framework coupled with granular and usable privacy risk warnings. The framework takes a new approach in that it empowers users to take informed privacy protection decisions prior to unintended data disclosure.

Keywords: Privacy · Privacy risk analysis · Privacy risk communication

1 Introduction

The rapid digitization of society's activities during the last years has contributed to a huge increase in digital information sharing [2]. In particular, the surge of Web 2.0 along with anywhere-anytime internet connected smart devices, fostered the availability of massive amount of information that is useful to better understand and address crucial societal challenges (e.g. transportation or health). Despite its benefits, however, the collection of large amounts of data also presents major threats to individuals' privacy, such as, identity theft or reputation damage resulting from personal data leaks, which in turn, have caused a general

S. Kallel et al. (Eds.): CRiSIS 2019, LNCS 12026, pp. 3–16, 2020.
https://doi.org/10.1007/978-3-030-41568-6_1

increase of users' privacy concerns [15], as shown in recent surveys. Recent surveys indicate that user privacy concerns and the demand to have explicit control over their personal data has increased. For instance, 81% of Europeans feel that they do not have complete control over their personal data online while *69% would like to give their explicit approval before the collection and processing of their personal data* [1]. Thus, with the prevalence of privacy incidents and recurrent leaks, information privacy protection has become a pressing topic not only for users, but also for practitioners and data protection entities.

Information privacy protection is a multidisciplinary task that involves designing privacy protection tools [13], user awareness [23] and enacting supportive legal frameworks [18]. In this regard, quantifying privacy risks also plays an important role in raising user awareness and designing fitting data protection regulations. Moreover, privacy risk communication paradigms should also be incorporated into the solution design [3]. However, despite its importance, previous research in privacy risk quantification has not fully considered the user's heterogeneously subjective perceptions on privacy, and her *right to informational self determination* since, often, the privacy risk analysis and prevention (usually by applying anonymisation techniques) takes place once the data is out of her control. To address this, in this paper, we introduce *p*QUANT, a user-centered privacy risk quantification framework coupled with fine-grained and user friendly information privacy risk warnings. *p*QUANT enables the user to take proactive measures prior to privacy damages. Moreover, it also increase trust and reduce information privacy concerns.

In short, this paper's contributions are summarized as follows:

- Introduce a tool to quantify the privacy risk of user's personal information disclosure by designing user-centered privacy risk quantification framework.
- A privacy risk warning component to effectively inform users and enable them to take conscious decisions regarding their information disclosure, thereby empowering them to exercise their informational self-determination rights. To the best of our knowledge, this is the first generic and user-centred framework to couple privacy risk quantification and warning.

The rest of the paper is structured as follows: Sect. 2 assesses the state of the art in the problem domain. Section 3 describes the theoretical models, and Sect. 4 introduces the system design and components, followed by Sect. 5 presenting the validation results. Finally, Sect. 6 presents the main conclusions and points out future research works.

2   Related Work

2.1   Privacy Risk Quantification

Biega et al. [5] performed an abductive reasoning to compute probabilistic privacy risk. They write down deductive rules with probabilities and use a tool to deduce whether, for instance, a user has some characteristic (e.g. alcoholic) or other. Compared to theirs, our approach does not rely on reasoning like this one, but rather, compute some characteristics of an existing population based on their credentials and then advise a visiting user or citizen of the place whether, for instance, uncovering certain characteristics of hers can lead to privacy risks.

Banerjee et al. [4] quantified the deviation of data collectors practices from what they promise in their privacy policies, as opposed to the user's needs. Wan et al. [24] proposed a game theoretic approach to identifying privacy violations. Although an interesting work, they assume that the attacker must obtain a degree of background knowledge in order to perpetrate their attack. Likewise, Du et al. [10] provided an approach to use background knowledge to the probability of re-identification. The authors used maximum entropy principle to compute the probability of sensitive attributes from a given set of user quasi identifiers. Similarly, Ngoc et al. [16] used probability and entropy to quantify a privacy metric for users in social networking sites. de Montjoye et al. [8] have demonstrated that having large scale of anonymised data sets the probability of uniquely re-identifying users with, for example, only using four spatiotemporal points could reach 90%. In those and many other related works such as Watanabe et al. [25] and Sattar et al. [19], the privacy quantification and analysis is done once the privacy sensitive information of the user leaves the user's device. They present interesting approaches to understand the problem, but less options for user participation in privacy decision making. Thus, our framework takes a step further to involve users in privacy risk prevention through risk warning.

2.2 Privacy Risk Communication

Other (recent) efforts for increasing user awareness on privacy risks in mobile communications have emerged. Similar to our approach, their main goal is to enable users to perform informed decisions with respect to their privacy and personal information disclosure. Yet, many of those approaches such as [3,11] and [12] have focused on monitoring accesses and permissions requested by mobile applications; however, little attention has been given to the information sharing habits from users. Privacy risk communication was also identified as an important challenge by Bal et al. [3]. Authors proposed to graphically communicate to users about benefits and consequences when allowing mobile applications to access device information.

Christin et al. [6] have investigated novel mechanisms to warn users about potential risks of sharing personal information. In particular, the authors proposed a graphical warning approach which displays three level warnings based on user privacy predefined settings. Their results show that more than 70% of the participants reacted and changed their privacy settings after experiencing a picture-based warning. Important to note that this approach did not have any privacy quantification system, but was designed to alert users on potential privacy risks and support better decision making with respect to their privacy settings in participatory sensing applications. This approach is limited to the information obtained by sensor readings in a participatory sensing applications.

3   System Model

3.1   Attribute-Entity Model

In this section we propose a combinatorial, set-theoretical model for attributes that will allow us to state, formally, interesting privacy-related problems. This framework will, also, allow us to formally define and prove statements about large entity populations associated with attributes owners or use algorithms in order to provide evidence for their validity.

Definition 1 *(Credential Representation). A Credential C is an ordered set of m attributes $A_1, A_2, \ldots, A_m$, each taking values from a finite domain $D_{A_1}, D_{A_2}, \ldots, D_{A_m}$. An instance of a Credential C is an ordered tuple of values $(v_1, v_2, \ldots, v_m)$ with $v_i \in D_{A_i}$. Such an instance corresponds to an individual and his/her attribute value pairs.*

We can represent a population U of n individuals in which an attribute scheme have been introduced with attributes $A_1, \ldots, A_m$, by a binary matrix as shown in Table 1: This matrix is composed of m attribute *zones*, where zone i corresponds to attribute A_i, and n columns, where column j corresponds to individual j in the population.

Table 1. Individuals in a population along with their attribute-set

		u_1	u_2	$\cdots$	u_n
	set S_1^1 for $v_1^1 \in D_{A_1}$	X	X	$\cdots$	X
	set S_2^1 for $v_2^1 \in D_{A_1}$	X	X	$\cdots$	X
Zone 1 (Attribute A_1):	$\vdots$	X	X	$\cdots$	X
	set $S_{|D_{A_1}|}^1$ for $v_{|D_{A_1}|}^1 \in D_{A_1}$	X	X	$\cdots$	X
		$\vdots$	$\vdots$	$\cdots$	$\vdots$
	set S_1^i for $v_1^i \in D_{A_i}$	X	X	$\cdots$	X
	set S_2^i for $v_2^i \in D_{A_i}$	X	X	$\cdots$	X
Zone i (Attribute A_i):	$\vdots$	X	X	$\cdots$	X
	set $S_{|D_{A_i}|}^i$ for $v_{|D_{A_i}|}^i \in D_{A_i}$	X	X	$\cdots$	X
		$\vdots$	$\vdots$	$\cdots$	$\vdots$
	set S_1^m for $v_1^m \in D_{A_m}$	X	X	$\cdots$	X
	set S_2^m for $v_2^m \in D_{A_m}$	X	X	$\cdots$	X
Zone m (Attribute A_m):	$\vdots$	X	X	$\cdots$	X
	set $S_{|D_{A_m}|}^m$ for $v_{|D_{A_m}|}^m \in D_{A_m}$	X	X	$\cdots$	X

Within a zone i, or attribute A_i, there is a set of sets (matrix rows), each corresponding to one of the possible values in the domain D_i of attribute A_i.

Thus, zone i has $|D_{A_i}|$ sets (rows), each of them corresponding to one of its possible values. The 1's in each such row correspond to the individuals (columns) who possess this particular value for attribute A_i. Each "X" is either 1 or 0. A "1" in the zone of A_i, for value v_j and column u_k means the following: *user k has attribute value v_j for attribute A_i.* A "0" signifies the opposite. We assume that within each attribute zone, each column contains exactly one "1" since each user is assumed to have one single value for each of the attributes (e.g. one eye color, one profession etc.).

Definition 2. *A set of attributes is called l-identifying if there are values for them such that the cardinality of their coincidence (i.e. number of individuals having these values, for these attributes) is equal to l.*

Thus, refering to the matrix representation of credentials in Table 1, a set of attributes is l-identifying if for each attribute we can find a row such that all the chosen rows have l 1's in the same place (i.e. l individuals possess have the specific values for these attributes) or, equivalently, their intersection size is equal to l. For instance, the ID attribute (identity number) and Health Insurance Number form, each, a set (singleton) of 1-identifying attributes since these numbers normally identify, uniquely, individuals in a population.

3.2 Some Privacy Related Problems

In what follows, based on the attributes entity model we developed in Sect. 3.1, we define a number of problems related to privacy as well as their applications.

Definition 3 (The Max-Coincidence Problem). *Given m sets of sets $S_1, \ldots, S_m$, each consisting of elements over a universe $U = \{u_1, \ldots, u_n\}$, select exactly one set from each of the sets $S_1, \ldots, A_m$ in order to maximize the coincidence of the selected sets.*

In our context, the set S_i represents the attribute A_i by containing all the row sets in zone i as shown in Table 1. In other words, $S_i = \cup_{j=1}^{|D_{A_i}|} S_j^i$.

This problem, in a more general form that allows m to be a varying parameter and, thus, part of the input, was defined in [7] (Problem 1) using the word "intersection" instead of "coincidence". Note that in our model, m (the number of attributes of an entity) is considered a constant since it is unrealistic to be unbounded (e.g. dependent on n) as, in practice, an attribute set includes a relatively small number of attributes.

Since the number m of sets A_i (i.e. attributes) is constant while also the number of sets is constant (i.e. attribute values) contained in each of them, the problem can be solved in polynomial time. We can consider all possible set combinations, one from each of the A_i. There is a total of $|D_{A_1}| \cdot |D_{A_2}| \cdots |D_{A_m}|$ possible combinations, which is not a large number for a customary attribute set each containing a small number of possible values. The time-consuming operation is the set coincidence which is of complexity $O(n)$ i.e. as much as the size of the population which can very large and prohibitive for on-line computations.

However, the maximum coincidence size can be computed periodically, in an off-line fashion, following the variations in the population's attributes (which, in general, is expected to vary smoothly) and offered in public to interested parties.

However, in case a dynamic computation is necessary and n is large one can follow a simple approximation scheme. To this end, we sample each of the sets S by having each of the contained n elements (i.e. individuals) be present in the sampled set with probability p. Thus, each of these sets will contain pn elements, on the average, after sampling. Then, assuming that the coincidence of the initial m sets (one for each of the m attributes) has size s, the coincidence of the sampled sets will contain, approximately, sp^m of these elements. We can compute the maximum coincidence on the sampled sets and, thus, obtain the sampled sets combination which has the larger coincidence size, obtaining an approximation of the maximum coincidence size of the initial sets fast. Moreover, let us assume that $sp^m = x$. Then we can approximate the maximum coincidence size by $s = \frac{x}{p^m}$.

We form each such combination and then compute the coincidence size of the sets. In contrast, the original problem defined in [7] in which m varies, is NP-complete i.e. computationally intractable.

This problem is related to privacy as follows: given a set of attributes for a given population, it asks to find a combination of values for those attributes that maximizes the coincidence, i.e. it maximizes the number of users having these values at the corresponding attributes. Let μ be this maximum value. If such a subset of attribute values is found, then any subset of it forms a set of attribute values whose intersection is no less than the maximum value μ. Observe that if the attributes contain an l-identifying set of attributes, then the maximum value for the coincidence is at least l.

Definition 4 (The Relaxed Max-Coincidence Problem). *Given m sets of sets $A_1, \ldots, A_m$ with elements over a universe $U = \{u_1, \ldots, u_n\}$, is there a family of at least L sets such that all combinations of their sets, one from each set in the family, have coincidence size at least T?*

This version of the previous problem introduces a second optimization factor that removes the requirement that all attributes $A_1, \ldots, A_m$ participate in contributing sets for the coincidence. Now it is sufficient to consider intersections of sets from at least L of the sets $A_1, \ldots, A_m$. This is important in order to avoid trivialities when an attribute set contains l-identifying attributes such as the Identity Number, which is a 1-identifying attribute. If one always includes such an attribute in the intersection, as in the previous problem, then the coincidence size will be always equal to 1. We also, converted the "maximized" statement in the last sentence of the definition of the previous problem to being at least T with no harm to generality (the two versions are equivalent, complexity-theoretic wise).

Definition 5 (The Min-Coincidence Problem). *Given m sets of sets $A_1, \ldots, A_m$ with elements over a universe $U = \{u_1, \ldots, u_n\}$, select exactly one* *set from each of the sets $A_1, \ldots, A_m$ in order to minimize the coincidence of the selected sets.*

This problem asks for a combination of attribute values that is possessed by the least number of individuals. Such an attribute-value combination is considered dangerous since revealing these values for these attributes leads to a small individual set.

Definition 6 (The Relaxed Min-Coincidence Problem). *Given m sets of sets $A_1, \ldots, A_m$ with elements over a universe $U = \{u_1, \ldots, u_n\}$, is there a family of at least L sets such that all combinations of their sets, one from each set in the family, have coincidence size at most T?*

Similarly to the Max-Coincidence Problem, this is a relaxed version of the Min-Coincidence Problem that avoids trivialities when the attribute set contains l-identifying attributes.

Definition 7 (The Cardinality One Problem). *Given m sets of sets $A_1, \ldots, A_m$ with elements over a universe $U = \{u_1, \ldots, u_n\}$, find a family of the m sets such that there exists a set combination, one from each set in the family, whose coincidence is a singleton (i.e. of cardinality 1)?*

This problem asks for a set of attributes that can possibly identify a user (if a certain set of value combinations is revealed).

3.3 Privacy Risks Metrics

The privacy risk scores illustrated in Table 2 are adapted from Dini et al. [9], which were originally introduced by the CNIL (Commission Nationale de l'Informatique et des Libertes)[1] proposal for privacy risk management methodology. We further clustered these risk scores into three levels (cf. Table 2) such that the distinction can easily be communicated to the user. Negligible Risk refers to a risk level when it seems to be hardly possible to identify a user by using her personal data. We say a risk level is Significant when it appears to be relatively easy to identify a user by using her personal data. Finally, a High Risk level indicates it is extremely easy to identify a user by using a single or combination of her personal data. The risk scores are calculated by applying the definitions in Subsect. 3.2 and following the steps below.

Let U be the number of users in the target population. Assume that we specify a tuple of specific values $(c_1, c_2, \ldots, c_m)$ for a credential drawn from the domains of the attributes $A_1, \ldots, A_m$. For "don't care" attributes, i.e. attributes we are not interesting in fixing a value, we set them equal to the special "wildcard" character "*" which matches any value in a domain. Then we denote by $U_{c_1, c_2, \ldots, c_m}$ the set of users whose credentials have the values $(c_1, c_2, \ldots, c_m)$ in

---

[1] CNIL, How to implement the data protection act, (2012). URL http://goo.gl/ jdlw5O, last access, May 2, 2017.

Table 2. Adjusted privacy risk metrics

Privacy risk score	Interpretation
$0 < X < 0.33$	Negligible risk
$0.33 \leq X < 0.66$	Significant risk
$0.66 \leq X \leq 1.0$	High risk

the corresponding attributes. Then we can define the *privacy ratio* of the users belonging to this set as follows:

$$f_{c_1,c_2,\ldots,c_m} = \frac{|U_{c_1,c_2,\ldots,c_m}|}{|U|}. \tag{1}$$

The value of the ratio lies in the interval $[0,1]$. Equation (1) provides a measure to how much privacy is preserved for a specific user when the user discloses the attribute tuple $t = (c_1, c_2, \ldots, c_m)$. A value close to 0 means that privacy is rather at stake while the opposite is true for a value close to 1.

Definition 8. *Let $t = (c_1, c_2, \ldots, c_m)$ and $t' = (c_1', c_2', \ldots, c_m')$ be two tuples of attribute values of a credential. We say t' subsumes t, denoted by $t \subseteq t'$, if for all i, $1 \leq i \leq m$, it either holds $c_i' = c_i$ or $c_i' = *$.*

Then for any two tuples $t = (c_1, c_2, \ldots, c_m)$ and $t' = (c_1', c_2', \ldots, c_m')$, where t' subsumes t, we define the *conditional privacy ratio* as follows:

$$f_{c_1,c_2,\ldots,c_m|c_1',c_2',\ldots,c_m',\subseteq} = \frac{|U_{c_1,c_2,\ldots,c_m}|}{|U_{c_1',c_2'\ldots,c_m'}|}. \tag{2}$$

For $t' = (c_1', c_2', \ldots, c_m') = (*, *, \ldots, *)$, Eq. (2) reduces to Eq. (1). The value of the ratio defined by this equation lies again, in the interval $[0,1]$. This ratio, like that in Eq. (1), measures how much privacy is preserved but this time in a smaller population defined by the condition that the members of the population should include the individual having attribute values $t = (c_1, c_2, \ldots, c_m)$ (as t' subsumes t) and, also, have attribute values defined by $t' = (c_1', c_2', \ldots, c_m')$. In other words, we assess the level of privacy of an individual within the user group defined by $t' = (c_1', c_2', \ldots, c_m')$ to which, also, the user belongs if the user uncovers the values in t for which t' has "*".

Finally, for *any* two attribute tuples $t = (c_1, c_2, \ldots, c_m)$ and $t' = (c_1', c_2', \ldots, c_m')$, we define the following:

$$f_{c_1,c_2,\ldots,c_m|c_1',c_2',\ldots,c_m'} = \frac{|U_{c_1,c_2,\ldots,c_m} \cap U_{c_1',c_2',\ldots,c_m'}|}{|U_{c_1',c_2'\ldots,c_m'}|}. \tag{3}$$

The ratio in Eq. (3) lies, again, in the interval $[0,1]$, gives an estimate of the level of privacy of a user who uncovers the values $t = (c_1, c_2, \ldots, c_m)$ with respect to a population with credential values $t' = (c_1', c_2', \ldots, c_m')$, for any values in the tuples.

4   *p*QUANT Components and Design Goals

To realize the implementation of the framework, we have followed a modular design approach, i.e separating main functional and supplementary components. This approach is useful to further extend the framework. In the following subsections, the design goals, and architectural components are introduced.

4.1   Design Goals

Below we describe three essential Design Goals (DG) relevant to the application of *p*QUANT.

DG1 - Give the user a quantified privacy risk of her PII disclosure. One of the objectives of *p*QUANT is to perform privacy risk analysis for a given user. As such, the framework provides a measured privacy consequence on the revelation of personal information. By doing so, it empowers users with regard to their understanding of privacy consequences as well as their decision making.

DG2 - Provide the user an understandable privacy risk warning. Privacy risk warnings are imperative to encourage users to take precautionary steps to prevent unwanted information disclosure. As such, *p*QUANT presents the risk in granular and easy to understand texts and boards. It also uses coloring to differentiate among the risk levels mentioned in Table 2, such that red is used for high risk scenarios, while yellow is for significant risk, and green is for negligible risk.

DG3 - Enhance privacy protection. The end effect of the framework is to enhance the privacy protection of end users. To do so, it involves users in the loop of the privacy protection process.

4.2   System Components

As depicted in Fig. 1, *p*QUANT's architecture has three main components, as well as other sub-components.

Attribute Selector. The Attribute selector module is the part of *p*QUANT that users use to interact with the system in order to supply the attribute sets. Users have the option to either select from predefined attribute-value pairs, or change the setting to be able to provide values that do not exist within the large default set.

Privacy Risk Estimation Engine. The privacy risk likelihood estimator is the central part of the framework. It gets invoked by the Attribute Selector module, and it provides numeric estimation of privacy risk of individuals with the given attribute sets is in a population. This module mainly implements the probabilistic and set theoretic definitions stated in Sect. 3 above. The computational result of the risk estimation is then mapped to the privacy metrics in Table 2, and consequently communicated to the user.

Privacy Risk Communication Manager. In real world situations, human beings are intrinsically aware of risk and extreme events that cause harm [20]. For example, when people are near a fire, they intend to subconsciously start to move away faster. In the digital world and its associated risks such as privacy, however, the senses and reflexes do not react as such, since recognizing these threats requires awareness, mental effort, and knowledge of the unforeseen and long term side effects. As such, we argue that privacy risk analysis techniques should be coupled with appropriate and user-friendly privacy warning engines. As stated in Sect. 1, one of the framework's strengths is its user-centric approach. As such, the risk communication module implements an effective and user-friendly warning of the risk estimations. This module gets its input from the Risk Estimator component. It further employs granular privacy risk communication (cf. Table 2), in that, it uses different coloring schemes and icons depending on the degree of the privacy risk at hand.

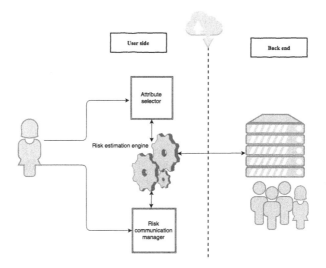

Fig. 1. Simplified and high level architecture

5   Validation and Discussion

To validate pQUANT, we have used the Adult Data Set from UCI machine learning repository [17]. The rationale for choosing this data set is that it contains a multivariate data which represents a sample of real population census. It has 15 attributes[2], namely Age, Gender, Occupation, Education, Workclass, HoursPerWeek, fnlwgt, EducationNum, MaritalStatus, Relationship, Race, CapitalGain, CapitalLoss, Country, and Target.

---

[2] The descriptions of the attributes http://archive.ics.uci.edu/ml/machine-learning-databases/adult/adult.names.

Table 3. Test case

Credential	Attributes set
C_1	$\{Age\}$
C_2	$\{Age, Gender\}$
C_3	$\{Age, Gender, Occupation\}$
C_4	$\{Age, Gender, Occupation, Education\}$
C_5	$\{Age, Gender, Occupation, Education, Workclass\}$
C_6	$\{Age, Gender, Occupation, Education, Workclass, HoursPerWeek\}$

For simplicity, we will assume that a new user holds six attributes (cf. Table 3) and then apply the definitions in Sect. 3 to analyze the possible privacy risks. Furthermore, lets take random attribute-value assignment, i.e., $C_1 = \{(age, 27)\}$; $C_2 = \{(age, 27), (gender, female)\}$; $C_3 = \{(age, 27), (gender, female), (occupation, sales)\}$; $C_4 = \{(age, 27), (gender, female), (occupation, sales), (education, 11th grade)\}$; $C_5 = \{(age, 27), (gender, female), (occupation, sales), (education, bachelors), (workClass, private)\}$; $C_6 = \{(age, 27), (gender, female), (occupation, sales), (education, bachelors), (workClass, private), (hoursPerWeek, 40)\}$. Accordingly, Fig. 2 depicts the initial results after applying pQUANT on the test case. We observe that sharing C_1 or C_2 has negligible privacy risk consequences while disclosing C_3 or C_4 has a low but still considerable privacy risk, where as C_5 and C_6 have high privacy risk therefore it is not advisable to share these attributes. The framework produces alerting messages based on this classifications.

Furthermore, Fig. 3 shows the risk warnings that alert the user in a given scenario (fulfilling the desing goals cf. Sect. 4). Following similar approach to Hogganvik and Stolen [14], we used textual and graphical risk warnings (i.e., warning icons). Graphical warnings help in explicitly conveying the risk and its consequences to the user. Depending on the entries the user selects and the privacy risk level these entries entail, pQUANT produces three types of warning messages (cf. Fig. 3).

Application Areas. There are different scenarios where users (especially privacy aware ones) look for tools like pQUANT to help them analyze privacy risks. E.g., in eHealth patients can give out PIIs that are mandatory for the medical case, while they can decide to lower the privacy risk on unnecessary PIIs disclosure. Another potential application area is when citizens are requested by organizations to participate in "data philanthropy"[3] for different purposes such as scientific studies. After the users have decided on the acceptable risk level, the data receiver can later apply anonymization techniques for second level privacy protection.

---

[3] Data philanthropy is a newly emerging concept in which private sector, or citizens participate in donating data for the public good, cf. http://corporatecitizenship.bc.edu/data-philanthropy.

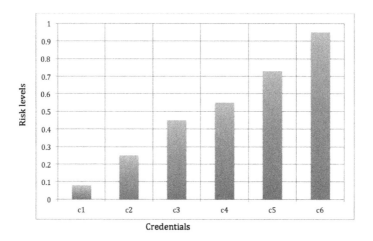

Fig. 2. Sample risk analysis results

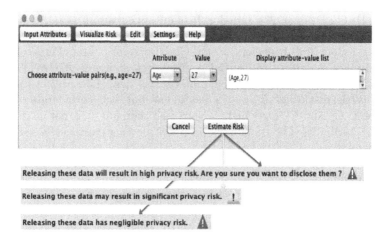

Fig. 3. Risk warning and GUI of pQUANT

6   Summary and Future Work

In this paper, we have proposed a generic user-centered privacy risk quantification framework composed of quantifying unintended information disclosure risks and consequently producing privacy warnings to users. Such a framework has multifaceted benefits to users, i.e empowers them to take informed decisions, gives the control of their personal data disclosure and raise their privacy awareness. Although more enhancements works are required for its maturity and off-shelf functionality, the proposed framework and the validation results indicate the framework provides users an enhanced privacy protection.

As a future work in this line of research, we envision to enhance the framework by adding more functionalities: (1) considering privacy risk impact and PII sensitivity level as additional decision factors; (2) allowing the user to define policies that the framework can automatically use to estimate the risk tailored to the specific user, and also integrating the framework with privacy policy definitions [21,22]; and (3) using information privacy risk detection techniques by building an intelligent agent component (using machine learning) to complement the framework. Furthermore, we also plan to explore the applicability of the framework in personal data marketing scenarios, in that, once the personal data is quantified, it can also be traded with service providers for the economic benefits of the data owners. Last but not least, executing field experiments to assess the adoption of the framework by users is also under consideration for future research.

References

1. The EU data protection reform and big data factsheet. http://www.ec.europa. eu/justice/data-protection/files/data-protection-big-data_factsheet_web_en.pdf. Accessed 07 June 2017
2. Acquisti, A., Brandimarte, L., Loewenstein, G.: Privacy and human behavior in the age of information. Science **347**(6221), 509–514 (2015)
3. Bal, G., Rannenberg, K., Hong, J.: Styx: design and evaluation of a new privacy risk communication method for smartphones. In: Cuppens-Boulahia, N., Cuppens, F., Jajodia, S., Abou El Kalam, A., Sans, T. (eds.) SEC 2014. IAICT, vol. 428, pp. 113–126. Springer, Heidelberg (2014). https://doi.org/10.1007/978-3-642-55415-5_10
4. Banerjee, M., Karimi Adl, R., Wu, L., Barker, K.: Quantifying privacy violations. In: Jonker, W., Petković, M. (eds.) SDM 2011. LNCS, vol. 6933, pp. 1–17. Springer, Heidelberg (2011). https://doi.org/10.1007/978-3-642-23556-6_1
5. Biega, J., Mele, I., Weikum, G.: Probabilistic prediction of privacy risks in user search histories. In: Proceedings of the First International Workshop on Privacy and Security of Big Data, pp. 29–36. ACM (2014)
6. Christin, D., Michalak, M., Hollick, M.: Raising user awareness about privacy threats in participatory sensing applications through graphical warnings. In: Proceedings of International Conference on Advances in Mobile Computing & #38; Multimedia, MoMM 2013, pp. 445:445–445:454. ACM, New York (2013)
7. Clifford, R., Popa, A.: Maximum subset intersection. Inf. Process. Lett. **111**(7), 323–325 (2011)
8. de Montjoye, Y.-A., Radaelli, L., Singh, V.K., Pentland, A.: Unique in the shopping mall: on the reidentifiability of credit card metadata. Science **347**(6221), 536–539 (2015)
9. Dini, G., Martinelli, F., Matteucci, I., Petrocchi, M., Saracino, A., Sgandurra, D.: Risk analysis of android applications: a user-centric solution. Future Gener. Comput. Syst. **80**, 505–518 (2016)
10. Du, W., Teng, Z., Zhu, Z.: Privacy-maxent: integrating background knowledge in privacy quantification. In: Proceedings of the 2008 ACM SIGMOD International Conference on Management of Data, pp. 459–472. ACM (2008)

11. Enck, W., et al.: TaintDroid: an information-flow tracking system for realtime privacy monitoring on smartphones. In: Proceedings of the 9th USENIX Conference on Operating Systems Design and Implementation, OSDI 2010, pp. 1–6. USENIX Association, Berkeley (2010)
12. Fawaz, K., Shin, K.G.: Location privacy protection for smartphone users. In: Proceedings of the 2014 ACM SIGSAC Conference on Computer and Communications Security, CCS 2014, pp. 239–250. ACM, New York (2014)
13. Hansen, M., Berlich, P., Camenisch, J., Clauß, S., Pfitzmann, A., Waidner, M.: Privacy-enhancing identity management. Inf. Secur. Tech. Rep. **9**(1), 35–44 (2004)
14. Hogganvik, I., Stølen, K.: A graphical approach to risk identification, motivated by empirical investigations. In: Nierstrasz, O., Whittle, J., Harel, D., Reggio, G. (eds.) MODELS 2006. LNCS, vol. 4199, pp. 574–588. Springer, Heidelberg (2006). https://doi.org/10.1007/11880240_40
15. Hong, W., Thong, J.Y.: Internet privacy concerns: an integrated conceptualization and four empirical studies. MIS Q. **37**, 275–298 (2013)
16. Ngoc, T.H., Echizen, I., Komei, K., Yoshiura, H.: New approach to quantification of privacy on social network sites. In: 2010 24th IEEE International Conference on Advanced Information Networking and Applications (AINA), pp. 556–564. IEEE (2010)
17. PARTY, A.D.P.W.: UCI machine learning repository adult data set. https://archive.ics.uci.edu/ml/datasets/adult. Accessed 30 Mar 2017
18. Rotenberg, M., Jacobs, D.: Updating the law of information privacy: the new framework of the European Union. Harv. JL Pub. Pol'y **36**, 605 (2013)
19. Sattar, A.S., Li, J., Ding, X., Liu, J., Vincent, M.: A general framework for privacy preserving data publishing. Knowl.-Based Syst. **54**, 276–287 (2013)
20. Slovic, P., Weber, E.U.: Perception of risk posed by extreme events (2002)
21. Tesfay, W.B., Hofmann, P., Nakamura, T., Kiyomoto, S., Serna, J.: I read but don't agree: privacy policy benchmarking using machine learning and the EU GDPR. In: Companion Proceedings of The Web Conference 2018, pp. 163–166. International World Wide Web Conferences Steering Committee (2018)
22. Tesfay, W.B., Hofmann, P., Nakamura, T., Kiyomoto, S., Serna, J.: PrivacyGuide: towards an implementation of the EU GDPR on internet privacy policy evaluation. In: Proceedings of the Fourth ACM International Workshop on Security and Privacy Analytics, pp. 15–21. ACM (2018)
23. Tuunainen, V.K., Pitkänen, O., Hovi, M.: Users' awareness of privacy on online social networking sites-case facebook. In: Bled 2009 Proceedings, p. 42 (2009)
24. Wan, Z., et al.: A game theoretic framework for analyzing re-identification risk. PLoS One **10**, e0120592 (2015). Supporting information. threshold, 7:9
25. Watanabe, C., Amagasa, T., Liu, L.: Privacy risks and countermeasures in publishing and mining social network data. In: 2011 7th International Conference on Collaborative Computing: Networking, Applications and Worksharing (CollaborateCom), pp. 55–66. IEEE (2011)

An Industrial Trial of an Approach to Identification and Modelling of Cybersecurity Risks in the Context of Digital Secondary Substations

Aida Omerovic[1(✉)], Hanne Vefsnmo[2], Oddbjørn Gjerde[2],
Siri T. Ravndal[3], and Are Kvinnesland[3]

[1] SINTEF Digital, Oslo, Norway
aida.omerovic@sintef.no
[2] SINTEF Energy, Trondheim, Norway
{hanne.vefsnmo,oddbjorn.gjerde}@sintef.no
[3] Lyse Elnett, Sandnes, Norway
{siri.ravndal,are.kvinnesland}@lyse.no

Abstract. We have in an earlier study proposed a set of requirements and an approach to identification and modelling of cybersecurity risks and their impacts on safety, within the context of smart power grids. The approach, which consisted of a process and a modelling language, was a partially customized version of the existing "CORAS" risk-analysis approach. As a part of the study, feasibility of the approach was evaluated by applying it on an industrial pilot for so-called self-healing functionality of a smart power grid. The results obtained were promising, but further empirical evaluation was strongly needed in order to further assess usefulness and applicability of the approach in the context of smart power grids. This paper provides a detailed account of results of applying the same approach to cybersecurity risk identification and modelling in the context of another smart grid pilot, namely digital secondary substations. The trial was conducted in a real setting, in the form of an industrial case study, in close collaboration with the major Norwegian distribution system operator that has been running the pilot for about two years. The evaluation indicates that the approach can be applied in a real setting to identify and model cybersecurity risks. The experiences from the case study moreover show that the presented approach is, to a large degree, well suited for its intended purpose, but it also points to areas in need for improvement and further evaluation.

Keywords: Cybersecurity · Digital substations · Cyber risk · Smart power grids · Risk identification · Risk analysis · Risk modelling

1 Introduction

Power grids are being increasingly digitalized, thanks to the evolving maturity and availability of the information and communication technologies (ICT). The digitalization of the electric power grids will include new concepts based on intelligent sensors in the grid and efficient communication between these sensors and the

S. Kallel et al. (Eds.): CRiSIS 2019, LNCS 12026, pp. 17–33, 2020.
https://doi.org/10.1007/978-3-030-41568-6_2

Supervisory Control and Data Acquisition (SCADA) system or distribution management system (DMS) [3]. The modern electric power grids adopting the technologies such as new communication networks, software, hardware, and control systems, are denoted as "Smart Grids". The goal of the energy providers and distributors is to utilize the digitalization in order to meet the needs for flexibility and efficiency of the power grid. Those needs are primarily driven by new power intensive loads due to, for example, electric vehicle charging, thus increasing the peak power demand along with the simultaneous penetration of stochastic renewable energy sources. In this setting, it is crucial to preserve the resilience of such a critical infrastructure that the power grid represents. However, the smart grids are not only enabling better utilization of the power grids, but also increasing complexity of the systems, thus introducing new kinds of risks, including the so-called cybersecurity risks (also known as digital risks). The cybersecurity risks may also lead to risks impacting security of power supply. One example of how adversaries can exploit the new components and technologies, is the cyber-attack against the Ukrainian Power Grid in December 2015, where the outages affected approximately 225000 customers that lost power across various areas [16].

By adding functionality to the power grids, ICT systems also contribute to unwanted incidents. Tøndel et al. [22] argue that power grid reliability will increasingly depend on ICT components and systems. They also claim that the current methods for risk analysis of power systems seem unable to take into account the full array of intentional and accidental threats. In addition, they found few methods and publications on identification of interdependencies between the ICT and power system. The objective of this research has been to provide support for cybersecurity risk analysis that takes into account the specific characteristics of smart power grids and meets the distinct needs within this domain.

A major challenge of the power domain is that the smart grid solutions have been in operation for a very limited period of time. Since the emerging solutions are at their early stages, there is a lack of historical data and operational experiences that could constitute relevant input to the risk models. This uncertainty due to lack of knowledge makes it extremely difficult to identify or predict the unwanted incidents that may occur in the future. Instead, one must focus on identification of the known vulnerabilities that are introduced due to the increasing usage of ICT technologies and their interdependencies with the physical power grid. However, the traditional risk analysis approaches often pre-assume that the nature and impact of the unwanted incidents are known, by demanding specific information on event description and risk quantification. Risk modelling, that is, the modelling of what can go wrong [17], is a technique for risk identification and assessment.

With respect to the state-of-the-art, several tree-based and graph-based notations within risk modelling exist. Fault Tree Analysis [9], Event Tree Analysis [10] and Attack Trees [21] are examples of the former and provide support for reasoning about the sources and consequences of unwanted incidents, as well as their likelihoods. Cause-Consequence Analysis [19], CORAS [17], and Bayesian networks [4] are examples of graph-based notations. CORAS is a tool-supported and model-driven approach to risk analysis that is based on the ISO 31000 risk management standard [13]. It uses diagrams as a means for communication, evaluation and assessment. Markov models [11], CRAMM [2], OCTAVE [1], Threat Modelling [18] and a number of others, have also been applied to support risk analysis. A framework for studying vulnerabilities and risk in the electricity supply, based on the bow-tie model, has been developed and is published for instance in [8, 14, 15].

From a risk analysis perspective smart power grids are characterized by their inherent uncertainties due to both the stochastic nature of generation and load as well as an increased complexity giving rise to new risks which are introduced through the ICT part of the system. Moreover, the interdisciplinary nature of such systems poses requirements on comprehensibility of the design of smart power grids and the corresponding risk models. Hence, a smart grid setting which includes a complex and critical cyber physical system, human in the loop, uncertainty due to lack of knowledge, many dependencies and interdisciplinary aspects, challenges the state-of-the-art on cybersecurity management. In an ideal setting, the risk model can be presented to human in a suitable interface, thereby serving as a useful support for decision making during design and operation. However, as they stand, none of the existing approaches provides the support that takes into account the specific characteristics of smart power grids and meets the distinct needs for cybersecurity risk analysis within this domain. This indicates a need for an approach to cybersecurity risk identification which is customized to address the following **requirements** (the ordering is arbitrary and does not express the relative importance of the requirements):

1. The approach is cost-effective and light-weight, i.e. the benefits of using it are well worth the effort. In particular, the value of gaining the decision support through applying the approach, should significantly outweigh the effort needed.
2. The cyber risk model can be developed and easily understood by the involved actors who represent varying roles and background.
3. The risk model has sufficient expressive power to capture relevant aspects of the cybersecurity risk picture in the context of smart power grids.
4. The risk model facilitates inclusion of the information that is available, while not requesting unrealistic degree of precision.
5. The risk model can visualize the cybersecurity relevant dependencies and sequence of states/events both for the whole context and for the detailed parts of the scope of analysis. This implies the ability of the modelling approach to both address a sufficiently broad scope, as well as to express the necessary details.

We have in an earlier study [20] introduced the above listed requirements to a risk analysis and modelling approach in the context of smart electric power distribution grids. Based on these requirements, this earlier study proposed a customized four-step approach to cybersecurity risk identification and modelling. The feasibility of the approach was evaluated on an industrial pilot for so-called self-healing functionality of a smart grid. The approach, which consisted of a process and a modelling language, was, to a high degree, based on parts of the previously mentioned CORAS method for model-based risk analysis. Compared to CORAS, the process and the modelling approach we have applied are simplified and partially adapted. The results obtained were promising. However, the need for more empirical evaluation in order to further assess usefulness of the approach, was evident. The original requirements to the approach and the approach itself, were therefore suggested to still be relevant and applicable for the next trial, i.e. the study reported in this paper.

This paper provides a detailed account of results of applying the abovementioned previously proposed approach to cybersecurity risk identification and modelling in the context of another smart distribution grid pilot, namely an operational pilot on digital secondary substations. The trial was conducted in a fully realistic setting, in the form of an industrial case study, in close collaboration with a major Norwegian power distribution system operator (DSO) owning the digital secondary substations, which were commissioned in the period 2016–2019. The evaluation indicates that the approach can be usefully applied in a realistic setting to identify and model cybersecurity risks. The experiences from the case study moreover show that the presented approach is, to a large degree, well suited for its intended purpose, but it also points to areas in need for improvement and further evaluation.

The rest of this paper is organized as follows: In Sect. 2 we briefly present the research strategy applied. Our approach for cybersecurity risk identification and modelling is presented in Sect. 3. The setup and the results from the trial of the approach are outlined in Sect. 4. In Sect. 5 we discuss the results, before concluding in Sect. 6.

2 Research Strategy

The research strategy applied is in line with the design science approach [23], and follows the three steps illustrated in Fig. 1. Although Fig. 1 illustrates sequential steps, the research strategy was followed iteratively where some of the steps were revisited during the process. In Step 1, the goal was to identify the requirements for a risk identification and modelling approach that addresses the specific characteristics of the smart grid domain. In Step 2, the goal was to develop a customized approach with respect to the requirements identified in Step 1. Based on the state-of-the-art overview and the lessons learned from the above-mentioned previous trial of the approach, the original five requirements and the approach that were identified and proposed in the previous study, were deemed to still be relevant and applicable. The requirements are listed in Sect. 1, while the approach containing four phases is presented in Sect. 3.

Fig. 1. Research strategy.

Finally, in Step 3 of the research strategy, we evaluated the approach in an industrial setting together with a DSO (i.e. the power distribution system operator that was the use case provider) that is currently operating a pilot on digital secondary substations in their power grid. The evaluation was carried out as follows: First, we established the context and gained a deep understanding of the digital secondary substations, based on reports on state of the practice, dialogue with domain experts who participated in the analysis group, as well as the documentation provided by the DSO. Then, the modelling approach was introduced by the analyst to the domain experts from the DSO. Thereafter, the analyst proposed a preliminary version of the risk model which focused on cybersecurity aspects of reliable energy supply. The preliminary version of the risk model was thereafter revised through several iterations, in close collaboration between the analyst and the domain experts. Once no more of the context documentation or brainstorming in the analysis group was needed for further modelling, a tool (checklist) for IoT security from ENISA [6] was proposed by the analyst and reviewed by the DSO, resulting in a new and complete version of the risk model. Lastly, a verification of the risk model was performed by the DSO putting forward a set of independently developed risk scenarios (originating from a former risk analysis of a similar context, which had been performed independently from ours). The scenarios were then exposed to the risk model in order to seek needs for updates. The model was reviewed against the scenarios during a workshop with the analysis group and two additional domain experts from the DSO who had not been involved in the previous steps of the analysis. The independence of the brought risk scenarios and the two new domain experts, were a means of strengthening the reliability of the validation step. The complete evaluation process, as well as the outcomes of it, are presented in Sect. 4.

3   Approach to Cybersecurity Identification and Modelling

Our approach to cybersecurity risk identification and modelling has been previously proposed and presented in Omerovic et al. [20]. The description of the approach is a core baseline for understanding contents of the trial. Hence, this section contains nearly the same generic description of the approach as the one given in the original source (i.e. the paper reporting on the aforementioned previous study), in order to enable the audience to read this paper independently from the former one. The approach consists of four main phases, inspired by the CORAS method and modelling language, but simplified and customized in order to address our specific requirements listed in Sect. 1. Our approach is assumed to be carried out by an analysis group, consisting of analysts and domain experts, representing competence in risk analysis, cybersecurity, and smart power grids. One individual may cover one or more roles, and several individuals may represent a similar role. Most importantly, the composition of the analysis group needs to include the relevant competence and ensure a sufficient degree of continuity (with respect to attendance of some of the participants) within the group. The four phases of the process include: 1: Context establishment; 2: Risk identification and modelling; 3: Risk model validation; and 4: Follow-up.

The objective of Phase 1 is to characterize the scope and the target of the analysis. Stakeholders that the analysis is being performed on behalf of, time perspective, relevant terminology, assumptions, roles and participants of the analysis group, as well as the information sources, are specified. Assets, that is the values that will drive the focus of the analysis, are also defined. This phase produces descriptions, insights and a common understanding of the target of analysis. The target of the analysis is, moreover,

Table 1. Constructs of the cybersecurity risk modelling language.

Symbol	Name	Simple explaination
$ Text	Direct asset	Something of a value to the stakeholders and needs to be protected. The risks are to be identified with respect to the direct assets.
i Text	Vulnerability	A state or a property that may be exploited.
Text	Threat scenario	A relevant event or a property that does not directly harm an asset.
Text	Unwanted incident	An event that directly harms an asset.
$ Text	Indirect asset	Something of a value to the stakeholders and can be affected by a direct asset.

specified and modelled with respect to capabilities, structure, dataflow, workflow, etc. The existing target specifications (i.e. those which are available prior to the analysis) may be reused or referred to.

The objective of Phase 2 is to identify the relevant risk model elements and develop a risk model. The risk model elements may be of the following types: assets, vulnerabilities, threat scenarios and unwanted incidents. The unwanted incidents are the elements that may harm the assets (which are assumed to be specified during Phase 1). The very first step of this phase is to introduce the types of the model elements to the analysis group. A brief introduction to the modelling constructs and their simple explanations is illustrated in Table 1. The explanations in the last column are simplified wordings inspired by corresponding definitions from CORAS[1]. Thereafter, the identification of risks through a risk modelling activity using the constructs in Table 1, is initiated. The instantiated constructs are, as a part of this process, annotated with descriptive text. The relationships between the instantiated model constructs are expressed with arcs connecting the relevant elements, thus resulting in a risk model shaped as an acyclic directed graph. The analyst shall facilitate the model development by iteratively posing questions on risks that may harm the assets and the possible vulnerabilities and threat scenarios that cause those risks. The analyst shall also contribute with cybersecurity domain knowledge during the risk modelling. The analyst shall, moreover, ensure that the syntax of the risk model is consistent. The domain experts shall, during the risk modelling, contribute with the domain knowledge on power grids. Discussion is facilitated in order to align the different domains and reveal the relevant risks. At the same time, the context description from Phase 1 is actively used. Moreover, if needed, refined descriptions of selected model elements are provided. For some parts of the risk model, it may be appropriate to express uncertainties and assumptions, in form of supplementary information or within the model.

---

[1] Note that the definition of vulnerability from the energy sector is slightly different, namely "Vulnerability is an expression for the problems a system faces to maintain its function if a threat leads to an unwanted event and the problems the system faces to resume its activities after the event occurred. Vulnerability is an internal characteristic of the system" [15].

Phase 3 aims at validating the risk model developed in the preceding phase. That is, the model should be exposed to quality assurance based on various and complementing kinds of empirical input, in order to ensure an acceptable level of uncertainty. The uncertainty may origin from insufficient information or knowledge, or from variability in context, usage, etc. This is followed by adjustments of the model with respect to the structure and the individual elements. Eventually, the model is approved if the evaluation shows that the revised version is sufficiently complete, correct and certain.

The objective of Phase 4 is two-fold, namely communication and maintenance of the results. The specific tasks of this phase include summary of most critical findings, evaluations of validity and reliability of the risk model, recommendations of risk treatments, summary of uncertainties in the findings, as well as communications of the results to the relevant stakeholders. Maintenance of the risk model involves monitoring of assumptions and the context changes that may require updates of the risk model.

4 Trial of the Approach on an Industry Pilot on Future Digital Substations

This section outlines the process undergone during the industrial case, as well as the main properties of the risk model produced. We also summarize the lessons learned.

4.1 Setting of the Case Study

By the introduction of digital secondary substations new sensors and communication technologies provide new measurements and remotely controlled disconnectors in the medium voltage (MV) (1–35 kV) distribution grid. As a result, the digitalization of the secondary substation gives new possibilities for smarter operation and fault- and interruption handling. At the same time these technologies introduce new vulnerabilities to the system. To study these vulnerabilities a case study has been performed together with a Norwegian grid company, in order to study 31 digital secondary substations they own in the south-western part of Norway.

Digital Secondary Substations. The electrical energy must be transported from the power generators to the consumers. On the way, electric power may flow through several substations being transformed between different voltage levels. The secondary substations are the interconnection between the MV and low voltage (LV) distribution grid levels. A digital secondary substation is typically described as an electrical substation where operation is managed between distributed intelligent electronic devices (IEDs) which are interconnected by the communication network. In this specific case study, the secondary substations (31 in total) are equipped slightly differently, but with a lot of common functionality. The first digital secondary substation was commissioned in 2016 and the last one within this pilot, was commissioned in 2019. All 31 secondary substations are equipped with remotely controlled disconnectors at all incoming and outgoing cables. Every cable has also a fault current indicator, annotated with green circles in Fig. 2, that detects both short-circuit fault and earth-fault, and communicates directly to the SCADA-system via remote terminal unit (RTU). For the transformers in

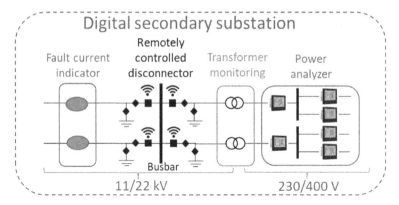

Fig. 2. A sketch of the digital secondary substation indicating the different types of sensors and technologies installed. (Color figure online)

the secondary substation, sensors are installed to monitor the oil pressure, the oil level and the transformer temperature, as indicated within the blue box in Fig. 2. On the LV side of the secondary substation, indicated with orange color in Fig. 2, power analyzers are installed to measure current, voltage, active/reactive power and earth fault. In addition, sensors are installed on the doors to detect whether the door is closed or open, and temperature sensors are installed to measure the room temperature within the substation building. Monitoring of the arc arrester and detection of the SF-6 pressure is, moreover, installed.

The different sensors placed in the digital secondary substation transfer the following parameters to the SCADA system in real-time through secured and encrypted fiber network: temperature (room and transformer); frequency, line voltages; phase voltages, total harmonic distortion (THD) voltages; currents; THD currents; active power (P), reactive power (Q) and apparent power (S); power factor.

Scope of the Analysis. The stakeholder of this risk analysis has been the DSO, owning the 31 digital secondary substations. Their concern is the company reputation, their income (economy), as well as Environment, Health and Safety (EHS). The scope of the analysis has been to protect the asset; the reliability of supply of the electric power system, defined as: "*probability that an electric power system can perform a required function under given conditions for a given time interval.*" (IEV 617-01-01) [12]. This asset may be affected (positively or negatively) by digitizing the secondary substation. On the positive side, the sensors will give warnings for instance of increasing transformer temperature, which may trigger desired maintenance and avoid transformer damage. For instance, a fault current indicator functioning correctly will contribute to localizing the fault faster which will reduce the fault localization time and by that the interruption time and cost. On the other hand, wrong signals from the sensors may lead to wrong decisions, and in worst case lead to longer interruption duration. In addition, remotely controlled disconnectors may potentially be opened by an attacker, and lead to interruption for all customers behind that substation. By adding all these sensors, the system becomes more complex and the consequences of the

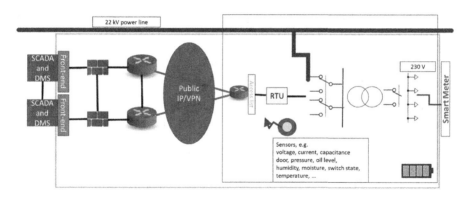

Fig. 3. Sketch of what is within and outside of the analysis. The yellow rectangle shows the boundaries of what is inside the analysis. (Color figure online)

critical events may increase, while the introduction of the ICT-support decreases the consequences of the frequent events [7].

The scope of the analysis comprised all systems and subsystems starting from the front-end at the SCADA-systems and until the LV-side of the secondary substation. The infrastructure for the smart meters and the SCADA-system itself, are outside of the scope. The focus was on the parts within the yellow rectangle in Fig. 3. The figure was developed during the context establishment and was later actively used during the analysis. The frontends are the parts of the SCADA-system which have two-ways communication with all digital secondary substation. The communication link (indicated with red lines) involves firewalls and routers. It uses encryption before sending the information over public fiber network. The routers and the firewalls are duplicated on the SCADA side of the communication link. At the secondary substation, the signals are received by a router which contains an access list. The RTU is the receiver of the information from the SCADA-system. In addition, the RTU is the unit collecting all data from the sensors within the substation. The secondary substations have battery back-up (24 V), which can, in case of interruptions, supply the required power to the RTU and the sensors.

Assumptions and Delimitation of the Industrial Case. The following assumptions were made in the case study as part of context establishment:

- The SCADA system is outside of the scope of this analysis (as indicated in Fig. 3).
- The smart meters (installed at all end-users in Norway from 1st of January 2019) and the belonging infrastructure are outside of the scope.
- Physical security of the secondary substation and human safety are outside of scope of this analysis.

- The purpose has been to carry out a qualitative risk assessment of the digital secondary substation, no quantification has been done.
- The focus is on the 31 secondary substations in south-eastern part of Norway. Any possible additional consequences resulting from an increased number of digitalized secondary substations, are not a part of the analysis.

The main focus has been on the new vulnerabilities and threats introduced by installing the new technology and sensors, especially with establishing the communication link between the SCADA-system and the disconnectors at all secondary substations. Cyber-security, specifically related to the communication infrastructure, is of particular importance. The exclusion of the SCADA system and the smart meters from the scope was a deliberate choice, as primarily the risks introduced by the particularities and new aspects of this specific case study, were focused on.

Background of the Participants Involved in the Analysis. The analysis was performed with a core team of seven people. The risk analysis was performed by one analyst, PhD, with about 16 years of experience in software engineering and cyber-security risk management, and two domain experts with 6–18 years of relevant experience within power system reliability and security of electricity supply. These three participants are affiliated with the research institute. From the grid company a six people in total have been involved in this analysis. The main contributions have been given by a core group consisting of four people; one manager and three domain experts. The three domain experts have the following expertise area; one is a network communication expert; one is a SCADA system expert and one is an information security expert. They each have more than 20 years of experience in their fields. Two additional experts from the grid company participated only in the validation workshop; one expert in planning of the digital secondary substation and the other expert in risk analysis. These two had not been a part of this analysis before and gave useful input in the validation phase.

4.2 Process Outline

The case study was conducted between November 2018 and March 2019, in the form of eight videoconference meetings and one physical meeting. The setting was fully realistic in terms of the context specified, the process undergone, the risk model that was developed, and the participants that were involved. The cybersecurity risks of the secondary digital substations pilot were identified and modelled, with respect to the established context. The case study included trial of primarily the first three phases of the approach presented in Sect. 3.

Table 2 summarizes the process undergone. For each workshop, we list the meeting number, the date, the participants, the meeting type, the meeting length, and the activities which were conducted. Unless otherwise specified, the mentioned activities were conducted during the meeting.

Table 2. The process conducted during the case study.

Meeting number: 1; **Date:** 21.11.2018; **Participants:** analyst, 1 domain expert from the grid company, and one from the research institute, the manager from the grid company; **Meeting type:** video; **Duration:** 1,5 h; **Activities:** Establishment of context, goals, scope and focus for the case study
Meeting number: 2; **Date:** 22.11.2018; **Participants:** analyst, 2 domain experts from the research institute; **Meeting type:** video; **Duration:** 1 h; **Activities:** An introduction to the digital secondary substations and their role in the power grid was given by the domain experts to the analyst
Meeting number: 3; **Date:** 10.12.2018; **Participants:** analyst, one domain expert from the grid company and one from the research institute; **Meeting type:** video; **Duration:** 1.5 h; **Activities:** Further clarifications of the context
Meeting no. 4; **Date:** 12.12.2018; **Participants:** analyst, three domain experts from the grid company and one from the research institute, the manager from the grid company; **Meeting type:** video; **Duration:** 2 h; **Activities.** Further clarifications of the context. High level cybersecurity risk analysis
Meeting number: 5; **Date:** 17.12.2018; **Participants:** analyst, three domain experts from the grid company and one from the research institute, the manager from the grid company; **Meeting type:** video; **Duration:** 2 h; **Activities:** Terminology clarifications. Cybersecurity risk modelling, based on the context and the high level risk analysis
Meeting number: 6; **Date:** 21.01.2019; **Participants:** analyst, three domain experts from the grid company and two from the research institute, the manager from the grid company; **Meeting type:** video; **Duration:** 3 h; **Activities prior to the meeting:** the analyst updated the model remaining by covering the remaining aspects from the high-level analysis. **Activities during the meeting:** the analyst presented the new version of the model. Continued cybersecurity risk modelling
Meeting number: 7; **Date:** 20.02.2019; **Participants:** analyst, three domain experts from the grid company and two from the research institute, the manager from the grid company; **Meeting type:** video; **Duration:** 2 h; **Activities prior to the meeting:** the analyst updated the model with the relevant contents and the grid company had an internal walkthrough of the results. **Activities during the meeting:** the analyst presented the new version of the model. Continued cybersecurity risk modelling
Meeting number: 8; **Date:** 06.03.2019; **Participants:** analyst, one domain expert from the grid company and two from the research institute, the manager from the grid company; **Meeting type:** video; **Duration:** 1.5 h; **Activities prior to the meeting:** the analyst retrieved the ENISA IoT tool [6], processed the contents and annotated potentially relevant parts. The list was then processed by the domain experts from the grid company and the relevant parts were extracted. The risk model was then updated by the analyst and sent to the analysis team. The grid company prepared a set of scenarios (based on an independent earlier risk analysis) to be used for validation of the risk model. **Activities during the meeting:** the analyst presented the new version of the model. Continued cybersecurity risk modelling. A brief intro by the analyst to the ENISA IoT tool and a proposal to process it in order to complement the model with any missing aspects mentioned by the tool

(*continued*)

Table 2. (*continued*)

Meeting number: 9; **Date:** 11.03.2019; **Participants:** analyst, five domain experts from the grid company, the manager from the grid company; **Meeting type:** physical; **Duration:** 4 h; **Activities prior to the meeting:** the analyst retrieved the ENISA IoT tool, processed the contents and annotated potentially relevant parts. The list was then processed by the domain experts from the grid company and the relevant parts were extracted. The risk model was then updated by the analyst and sent to the analysis team. The grid company prepared a set of 19 risk elements and 9 scenarios (based on an independent earlier risk analysis of digitalized secondary substations) to be used for validation of the risk model. **Activities during the meeting:** Validation of the risk model. The analyst first presented the updated model. Thereafter, each one of the scenarios were gone through and a check was made as to whether the contents were already represented by the model. During the processing of the risk elements against the risk model, five vulnerabilities were added – three of them were triggered by one risk element each, and two were triggered by a fourth risk element. During the processing of the nine scenarios, a minor model update was made for the first scenario, no updates were needed for the second and the third scenario, the fourth scenario was found to be outside the scope, one vulnerability was added to the model due to the fifth scenario, no changes were needed due to the sixth scenario, one vulnerability was added to the model due to the seventh scenario, no changes were needed due to the eighth scenario, and three vulnerabilities were added to the model due to the seventh scenario

4.3 Results from the Case Study

A high-level view of the risk model obtained from the above summarized process, is shown on Fig. 4. The figure indicates the size of the final model, and reports on some of the contents. Selected parts of the model (i.e. those model elements that miss a textual annotation) are, for confidentiality reasons, undisclosed. The disclosed details on the figure include a representative selection of the specific vulnerabilities, threat scenarios, the one unwanted incident and the asset, in order to illustrate the abstraction level and the relationships among the elements.

The risk model shown on Fig. 4 contains 14 undisclosed threat scenarios (*TS_01–TS_14*) and 10 disclosed ones, one unwanted incident which is disclosed, and one direct asset which is disclosed. Most of the vulnerabilities are undisclosed and only annotated by a numerical value. The numbers associated with the many vulnerability symbols represent the number of distinct anonymized vulnerabilities in the actual model that lead to the specified threat scenarios. For example, one vulnerability is annotated with the digit 18 and leads to the threat scenario "Insufficient security of SCADA or DMS". This conveys that there are eighteen different vulnerabilities that in our final risk model lead to this threat scenario. Moreover, there are, for instance, two distinct vulnerabilities which in our final risk model lead to **both** threat scenarios *TS_10* and *TS_11*.

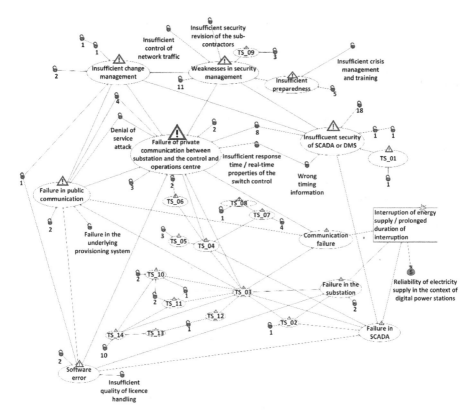

Fig. 4. High level view of the risk model. TS means Threat Scenario. The numbers underneath some of the vulnerabilities indicate the number of the distinct vulnerabilities present in the indicated parts of the model.

4.4 Experiences and Lessons Learned

Upon having completed meeting 5, the grid company wrote a feedback (without any prior request from group members) expressing that the workshop gave a good impression, and that the systematic approach and the graphical representation of the risk model, were appreciated. The second feedback was requested and received upon completion of the case study. The message was: "The process was useful and good. We were not a priori familiar with the approach applied, in particular not with the modelling approach. In addition to the improved competence on methodology for risk analysis, the work will be carried on and used as a baseline for another (specifically named) innovation project."

The group agreed that a thorough understanding of the context is crucial. In fact, a deep understanding of the digital secondary substations was gained by all analysis participants including the analyst, which also enabled the analyst to actively participate in risk modelling and development of the preliminary model. Such a deep insight into the domain is not assumed by the approach, but it was in our case experienced as an enabler of a better progress of the analysis.

Like in the previous trial of the approach, we have observed that regardless of how well the security risk analyst understands the context, it is crucial that the analyst does not develop the risk models alone. Risk identification triggers namely many useful discussions among the analysis participants, and it helps reveal knowledge, risks, inconsistencies and misunderstandings. Such information is crucial for validity of the risk model.

None of the domain experts from the grid company had prior experiences in either CORAS or graphical risk modelling in general. Still, the risk model was gradually updated into new versions through iterative and thorough discussions among all the participants. Our observation is that an adequate level of abstraction was selected, in terms of both the resulting size of the model and the level of detail provided. An important property of the risk model was that it was possible to express all information into one merged model, so that the complexity and the relevant relationships were explicitly reflected in a single comprehensive overview.

5   Discussion

Based on the results presented in Sect. 4, we discuss and evaluate the fulfilment of the requirements defined in Sect. 1. The second part of this section discusses the main threats to validity and reliability of the results.

5.1   To What Degree Are the Requirements Fulfilled?

Requirement 1. To fully justify this requirement, we would have to quantify the benefits, as well as the costs. We have not attempted to do so. However, the feedback which has been received and the experiences gained, at least partially, indicate that the benefit justifies the effort, meaning that our customized approach is reasonably cost effective as well as light-weight. Moreover, our approach does not comprise risk estimation, evaluation and treatment, which are activities that many full-scale risk analysis methods include. This saved significant effort, although benefits of such activities were not realized either.

Requirement 2. As previously mentioned, the participants had rather varying background. Still, after a brief introduction of the approach, they were quickly able to actively contribute to the model development. Moreover, their involvement during the process demonstrated comprehensibility of the modelling approach.

Requirement 3. We were able to express all cybersecurity relevant risk elements and their mutual dependencies that were identified during the process. This suggests that our risk modelling approach has the expressiveness needed to capture relevant aspects of the cybersecurity risk picture in the context of smart power grids.

Requirement 4. As previously mentioned, smart grid concepts and technologies are still relatively immature, as they have not been in operation for a significantly long time. Thus, there is little experience on possible cyber risk incidents and their conse-quences for power system. Our approach has therefore deliberately been designed with simplicity as a goal, and with focus on vulnerabilities instead of the incidents. In the context of this case study, no unavailable information or details of unrealistic precision were demanded by the approach. In cases where such contents were possible and desired to include, the model was capable of adopting them. The analysis group was therefore free to choose the level of granularity in the risk model which is appropriate for expressing the information available.

Requirement 5. The final risk model included the high-level risk picture overview for the whole context. The needed details, such as decomposed vulnerabilities as well as dependencies among the model elements, were also explicitly expressed within the same model. This suggests scalability of the modelling approach in terms of both the ability to address a broad scope and to detail the necessary parts of it. Given its size, our model was readable when printed on a poster of A0-format.

5.2   Threats to Validity and Reliability

The results of the trial indicate feasibility of applying the approach. We have observed and received feedback suggesting that new knowledge about the target of analysis and its security risks was gained, which may suggest usefulness of the approach. However, application of the approach on a specific case such as digital secondary substations has clear limitations in terms of representativeness of the target of the analysis for the aimed smart grid domain. A generalization of the results is therefore not yet possible. For that, far more empirical evidence and multiple trials are needed.

The brainstorming-driven approach to risk modelling which significantly relies on the domain-expert knowledge is a threat in itself, due to the limited structure. Under such circumstances, the ability to ensure that all possible risk model elements have been considered, is limited. The validation step of the approach is therefore crucial.

The validation phase showed that several updates of the model were needed, upon exposure of the model to the independently retrieved risk scenario. Also, the use of the ENISA IoT tool triggered significant number of updates in terms of new model ele-ments. All these steps were performed during some of the final meetings. Hence, we have no evidence that additional empirical sources would not have involved new changes in the risk model. This clearly represents a threat to reliability and validity.

A retrospective evaluation of the model with respect to historical risks would have been of interest, but the industry pilot has not been running for long enough in order to have sufficient empirical baseline. The fact that the analysis group was composed of experienced domain experts, did most likely balance this and contribute to validity of the input. It should be mentioned that the analyst from this case study had a main role in the original design of the customized version of the approach. This may represent a threat to validity of the evaluation of performance of the approach with respect to the five requirements (in Sect. 5.1). As such, it is also a threat to reliability of the evalu-ation results, as we cannot know to what degree another analysis group, without presence of the approach designer, would have obtained the same results.

The follow-up phase of the approach was not tried out, thus leaving another uncertainty in the evaluation. We did, however, show that the model is relatively easy to modify, as well as that if facilitates communication of the risk picture.

6 Conclusions and Future Work

This paper reports on the results of applying an earlier proposed approach to cyber-security risk identification and modelling, on a pilot on digital secondary substations. The trial was conducted in a fully realistic setting, in the form of an industrial case study, in close collaboration with a major Norwegian distribution system operator. We argue that our approach to some extent fulfils the five pre-identified requirements and the results do indicate feasibility and usefulness of the approach. However, there are at the same time, clear limitations in terms of reliability and validity of the results.

The next step will be to perform a postmortem evaluation of both this case study, as well as the previous one that addressed the self-healing pilot. The two case studies as well as their respective postmortems will then be cross-analyzed in order to progress the evaluation. Another next step is to develop specific recommendations, templates and guidelines for cybersecurity risk identification in the smart grid domain, based on our approach.

For future studies it would be of interest also to investigate (1) the importance and possible increased risk (possible single points of failure) related to installing similar equipment in many secondary substations versus the increased complexity and possible interoperability issues if different equipment is selected and (2) the impact on the power distribution system from increased penetration of digital secondary substations (e.g. possible propagation of failure).

Acknowledgements. This paper has been funded by CINELDI - Centre for intelligent electricity distribution [5], an 8-year Research Centre under the FME-scheme (Centre for Environment-friendly Energy Research, 257626/E20). The authors gratefully acknowledge the financial support from the Research Council of Norway and the CINELDI partners. The centre gathers a significant number of the major public and private actors from the energy sector in Norway, and performs research on the future intelligent energy distribution grids.

References

1. Alberts, C., Dorofee, A., Stevens, J., Woody, C.: Introduction to the OCTAVE Approach. Carnegie Mellon University, Pennsylvania (2003)
2. Barber, B., Davey, J.: The use of the CCTA risk analysis and management methodology CRAMM in health information systems. In: Proceedings of the 7th International Congress on Medical Informatics, pp. 1589–1593 (1992)
3. Belmans, R.: Strategic research agenda for Europe's electricity networks of the future - SmartGrids SRA 2035: European technology platform SmartGrids (2012)
4. Ben-Gal, I.: Bayesian networks. Encycl. Stat. Qual. Reliab. **1**, 1–6 (2008)
5. CINELDI (2019). https://www.sintef.no/cineldi. Accessed 2 June 2018

6. ENISA Good practices for IoT and Smart Infrastructures Tool (2019). https://www.enisa. europa.eu/topics/iot-and-smart-infrastructures/iot/good-practices-for-iot-and-smart-infrastructures-tool. Accessed 22 Feb 2019
7. Heegaard, P.E., Helvik, B.E., Nencioni, G., Wäfler, J.: Managed dependability in interacting systems. In: Fiondella, L., Puliafito, A. (eds.) Principles of Performance and Reliability Modeling and Evaluation. SSRE, pp. 197–226. Springer, Cham (2016). https://doi.org/10. 1007/978-3-319-30599-8_8
8. Hofmann, M., Kjølle, G., Gjerde, O.: Development of indicators to monitor vulnerabilities in power systems. In: Proceedings of the 11th International Probabilistic Safety Assessment and Management Conference and the Annual European Safety and Reliability Conference 2012: Curran Associates, Inc., pp. 5869–5878 (2012)
9. IEC: IEC 61025:1990 Fault tree analysis (FTA): International Electrotechnical Commission (1990)
10. IEC: IEC 60300-3-9:1995 Dependability management - Part 3: Application guide - Section 9: Risk analysis of technological systems: International Electrotechnical Commission (1995)
11. IEC: IEC 61165:2006 - Application of Markov techniques: International Electrotechnical Commission (2006)
12. IEC: IEC 60050-617:2009 - Organization/Market of electricity: International Electrotechnical Commission (2009)
13. ISO: ISO 31000: Risk Management - Principles and Guidelines: Geneva: International Organization for Standardization (2009)
14. Kjølle, G., Gjerde, O.: Risk analysis of electricity supply. In: Hokstad, P., Utne, I., Vatn, J. (eds.) Risk and Interdependencies in Critical Infrastructures: A Guideline for Analysis, pp. 95–108. Springer, London (2012). https://doi.org/10.1007/978-1-4471-4661-2_7
15. Kjølle, G., Gjerde, O.: Vulnerability analysis related to extraordinary events in power systems. In: Proceedings of the 2015 IEEE Eindhoven PowerTech, pp. 1–6. IEEE (2015)
16. Lee, R.M., Assante, M.J., Conway, T.: Analysis of the Cyber Attack on the Ukrainian Power Grid: Defense Use Case. Electricity - Information Sharing and Analysis Center, Washington (2016)
17. Lund, M.S., Solhaug, B., Stølen, K.: Model-Driven Risk Analysis: The CORAS Approach. Springer, Heidelberg (2010). https://doi.org/10.1007/978-3-642-12323-8
18. Microsoft Security Development Lifecycle (2018). https://www.microsoft.com/en-us/SDL. Accessed Nov 2018
19. Nielsen, D.S.: The Cause/Consequence Diagram Method as a Basis for Quantitative Accident Analysis, p. 1374. Risø National Laboratory, Roskile (1971)
20. Omerovic, A., Vefsnmo, H., Erdogan, G., Gjerde, O., Gramme, E., Simonsen, S.: A feasibility study of a method for identification and modelling of cybersecurity risks in the context of smart power grids. In: Proceedings of the 4th International Conference on Complexity, Future Information Systems and Risk. vol. 1, pp. 39–51 (2019)
21. Schneier, B.: Attack trees: modeling security threats. Dobb's J. **24**(12), 21–29 (1999)
22. Tøndel, I.A., Foros, J., Kilskar, S.S., Hokstad, P., Jaatun, M.G.: Interdependencies and reliability in the combined ICT and power system: an overview of current research. Appl. Comput. Inform. **14**(1), 17–27 (2017)
23. Wieringa, R.J.: Design Science Methodology for Information Systems and Software Engineering. Springer, Heidelberg (2014). https://doi.org/10.1007/978-3-662-43839-8

Continuous Risk Management for Industrial IoT: A Methodological View

Carolina Adaros-Boye[(✉)], Paul Kearney, and Mark Josephs

Birmingham City University, Birmingham B4 7XG, UK
carolina.adarosboye@mail.bcu.ac.uk
{paul.3.kearney,mark.josephs}@bcu.ac.uk

Abstract. Emergent cyber-attacks and exploits targeting Operational Technologies (OT) call for a proactive risk management approach. The convergence between OT and the Internet-of-Things in industries introduces new opportunities for cyber-attacks that have the potential to disrupt time-critical and hazardous processes. This paper proposes a methodology to adapt traditional risk management standards to work in a continuous fashion. Monitoring of risk factors is based on incident and event management tools, and misbehaviour detection to address cyber-physical systems' security gaps. Another source of information that can enhance this approach is threat intelligence. Risks are calculated using Bayesian Networks.

Keywords: Cybersecurity · Risk monitoring · IoT · IIoT · ICS

1 Introduction

In automated and smart industries, a certain level of cyber-risk is usually accepted, especially if security controls have conflicts with safety, performance, or availability [4]. For example, security updates can compromise reliability of operations [8], defences against brute force attack can lock out valid users in the middle of a crisis, and control flow integrity checks can present throughput overheads [15]. Finding methods to monitor cybersecurity risks continuously is relevant to allow better preparedness in the case of cyber-threats, particularly in cases of risks with a low likelihood but a high impact.

Many companies are engaging in Industry 4.0, or connecting their existing Operational Technologies (OT) to their information systems. This paradigm, also known as the Industrial Internet of Things (IIoT), is used in various business domains including industries such as electrical, utilities, transport, manufacturing, and building management, among others. These systems differ from typical IT because their core functionalities are based on cyber-physical systems. Industrial operations have requirements that introduce challenges in the application of security controls and many legacy cyber-physical systems were

S. Kallel et al. (Eds.): CRiSIS 2019, LNCS 12026, pp. 34–49, 2020.
https://doi.org/10.1007/978-3-030-41568-6_3

not originally designed having security in mind [5,15]. Limitations on memory and processing capabilities plus real-time response requirements restrict having strong authentication or encryption. The attack surface is also larger than in traditional IT because of the additional communication and information processing layers. Multiple access points, and numerous nodes make difficult to monitor and control all the devices connected to the network and who accesses them. They also work with specific purpose communication protocols which are unknown to traditional network security tools [7]. Some widely used protocols, such as Modbus, Profinet, and Bacnet, among others, do not consider basic security controls such as authentication and data integrity checking.

Compensating controls such as rigorous physical security, network segmentation, and continuous monitoring can counteract the lack of built-in security in Industrial Control Systems (ICS) [2]. However, access points enabled for maintenance, configuration and support activities performed by external or internal personnel can also be a threat vector for an incident either malicious or unintended. However, even if rigorous security controls are in place, organisations still will need to assume a certain level of risk, since it is impossible to cover all the possible flanks of attack. Therefore, the main objective of our research is to find mechanisms to continuously monitor security risks and increase cyber-situational awareness in IIoT. Our key questions are: What information do you need to know in order to monitor security risks in ICS? How can that information be derived from what you can actually measure? How can existing cyber-risk management frameworks be adapted for a more dynamic risk monitoring? How can these modifications be introduced?

In a previous paper we presented a proposal for a continuous risk assessment method for ICS/IIoT [1]. Detection of anomalies or misbehaviour in the system's physical measurements is considered as a mean to fill gaps left by typical intrusion detection methods. The present paper proposes a process oriented view of this approach based on workflow and descriptions of activities with their expected inputs and outputs. Through this perspective, we identify which activities are covered by a traditional risk management process and which need to be defined. Using the ISO/IEC 27005 [11] standard as a reference, workflows are presented together with a blueprint of how to integrate standard cyber-risk management frameworks with a continuous risk assessment paradigm.

2   Why Continuous Risk Management for ICS?

Risk management deals with the fact of not being able to control all aspects of a situation. Often decisions need to be made with incomplete information. Internal and external conditions are always changing, and so is the availability and accuracy of information. Thus, monitoring risks can help to validate assumptions and to check if a risk is becoming more likely to materialise than initially thought, or even transforming into an imminent issue. A cybersecurity programme addressing known vulnerabilities should help avoiding to become an easy target and deter opportunistic attackers, but not those who might go the extra mile to develop elaborate exploit mechanisms. Examples of this are targeted ICS malware such as Stuxnet, TRITON, and LockerGoga. In the case of ICS, a cyber-attack can cause material or environmental damage and even compromise human lives and safety. Abuse of privileges from an insider is also considered an important threat in ICS.

Monitoring risks is "maintaining ongoing awareness of an organisation's risk environment, risk management program, and associated activities to support risk decisions" [3]. Typically this is done as a periodic and discrete activity that is not integrated with operational processes. We propose that risk monitoring should make use of near-real time operational data. Signs of an attack in IIoT can be discovered by monitoring not only network and software related variables, but also sensor's data. Then, if traditional cybersecurity controls are bypassed, the status of physical variables can give signs that an unusual situation is happening.

Figure 1 proposes an architecture to support a continuous risk monitoring and re-assessment methodology. A risk calculation engine updates key risk indicators based on different sorts of inputs, some of them are updated in a continuous stream and others on a batch basis. The effect of different events on the risk scores is determined by a Bayesian Network which is defined in a setup process establishing relationship between different events. The data capture and processing and alert generation are performed by a SIEM (Security Information and Event Management) tool which is fed by different sources of data. The approach also applies anomaly and misbehaviour detection techniques to physical variables in order to provide independent evidence of possible security issues.

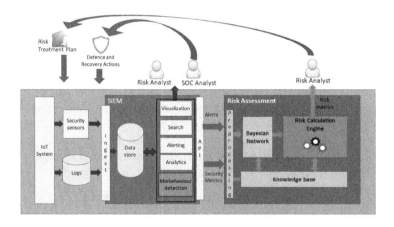

Fig. 1. Architecture of the approached proposed.

A combination of expert's knowledge and machine learning techniques is used to model the system's behaviour. For example, an operations expert should provide business rules and functional requirements, including forbidden states and safety considerations, a control and automation expert should know particularities of the programming language of controllers, their memory handling mechanisms, and communication protocols. This would enable the definition of what is normal and abnormal for parameters in different components of a system. Suspicious events in the IT components such as unusual logs, brute force attack access, and malicious code can be identified by a cybersecurity operations expert and monitored by regular off the shelf tools. Continuous updates aim for a better integration of operational processes, risk management, and security processes. This should allow shortening response times. A more detailed description of our ideas on continuous risk assessment for ICS can be found on our previous paper [1].

3   Users, Relevant Stakeholders, and Related Processes

The methodology is designed for risk analysts. However, as shown in Fig. 1, the results can be shared with the Security Operations Centre (SOC) or equivalent area. Therefore, some of the alerts generated by the continuous risk assessment should be forwarded to them. Any suspicious event or behaviour that changes normal trends or any abrupt changes should be also escalated to the appropriate stakeholders, such as process owners.

Risk management processes in practice are often defined and performed by a separate area from the one dealing with security operations. This has different reasons including that often risk analysts work at a more strategic level and security analysts at a tactical level. Nevertheless, cybersecurity standards regard risk management as an integral part of a cybersecurity management system [8, 10, 11]. Lack of integration between security risks and operations management can take away the purpose of doing a risk assessment in the first place. Figure 2 represents how cybersecurity risk management should not just overlap but contain security operations management. Updated security metrics can reduce the levels of uncertainty involved in a risk analysis. In our approach, we define three categories of indicators depending on the degree of confidence they can give to predict an attack: Indicators of Risk (IoR), which can modify the estimation of likelihood of an attack, Indicators of Compromise (IoC), which are a type of IoR that can reveal a possible breach in any of its stages, and alerts, that indicate with a high degree of certainty an imminent issue.

Fig. 2. Indicators hierarchy in a cybersecurity management system

Frequent updates of risks can also support decision-makers to make informed and rational choices. Think on a manufacturing company where plant A uses legacy systems, and plant B uses new generation IIoT with built-in security. Plant B is more efficient so they are evaluating to use the same technology in plant A, but the capital expenditure is high. Quantitative information about reduction of cybersecurity risks can contribute in supporting the business case for the migration by increasing the return on the investment calculation.

4   Related Work

Given the need of having a better visibility in ICS, it is not surprising to see work proposing continuous assessment methods for cyber-physical security risks. The work done in [14] and [9] propose real-time risk analysis methods based on the human immune system. However, their focus is mostly on network security rather than addressing all the layers of the system, which is required in order to consider all possible cybersecurity risks.

Original approaches have been proposed, as well, to detect anomalies in IoT systems based on their behaviour by analysing sensor data and correlating events [4,13] and detecting invalid or "prohibited" states of the system [16]. Their work is highly related to the ideas we are proposing and confirms that monitoring risk factors in cyber-physical systems (IoT, IIoT, ICS) in operational or near real time is not a misbegotten idea, despite the practical challenges it may offer.

Among other related research that we have taken into account is the work done in [7] and [5] which highlights challenges and requirements and describe techniques for intrusion detection in industrial cyber-physical systems. Work has been done in this regard by proposing methods to generate dynamic security metrics, including risk metrics in order to help deciding or automatically choose among alternatives for countermeasures [6]. Some of these even go further and suggest ways to deal with unknown threats [12]. This is also a consideration taken in our methodology. Some of these approaches can provide potentially useful techniques and methods to capture real-time security metrics which will be key inputs for our risk calculations. An example of this is the use of Bayesian Networks [18] and fuzzy logic [12,18]. Nonetheless, many of them cannot be considered as an holistic cyber-risk assessment either by their limited scope [9,14] or lack of consideration of the context and business impact [18].

To the best of our knowledge, this is the first paper to present a methodological view which, as well adapts the traditional risk management process to continuous operation. This does not contradict the fact that, overall, our work gathers ideas already presented in different publications that have been reviewed as part of the state of the art and that were mentioned in this section.

5   The Continuous Risk Assessment Methodology

Industry standards do not define processes for a continuous risk assessment. However, we found that our approach does not have fundamental contradictions with the contents of frameworks such as IEC 624433, ISO 270005, NIST 800-37, or OG86. Most Risk Management models describe risk assessments as a PDCA cycle (Plan-Do-Check-Act) where risk monitoring (check) has the purpose of identifying changes in risk factors in an early stage [11]. For this, an organisation should identify the reassessment frequency and triggering criteria for cyber-risks where the period reflects the fast-changing nature of cyber security [10]. Rather than re-defining the traditional risk management process we propose to extend it to support methods that work on a continuous basis.

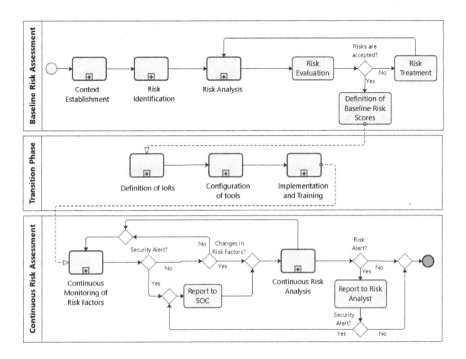

Fig. 3. Macro-process of the methodology.

Our approach proposes three phases: the baseline (initial) risk assessment phase, the transition phase, and the continuous risk assessment phase, performed during normal operation. The baseline risk assessment follows a standard process, as defined by the ISO/IEC 27005 standard. However, additional activities and work products are added as a preparation for the continuous risk assessment. In particular, information needed to model the system's functional behaviour under normal operation is gathered during the Context Establishment. In the transition phase the metrics that will be gathered during the continuous risk assessment are defined and the supporting tools for the continuous risk assessment are configured. In the continuous risk assessment phase the information from the baseline risk analysis gets updated based on operational data. Risk scores are modified when a significant change is detected. Figure 3 shows a work-flow of the "macro-process" of the methodology. A modified version of BPMN, which is a widely-used notation for workflow modelling, is used to represent in separate lanes which activities are covered by the ISO/IEC 27005 standard and which are added by us. This is done just for modelling and representation purposes with the understanding that lanes are originally meant to separate roles. In the following sub-sections different sub-process are described for each phase.

5.1 Baseline Risk Assessment

In this phase a risk analysis is undertaken to generate baseline risk scores. Figure 4 shows the different sub-processes involved. In the context establishment all the information relevant to risk management is gathered [11]. This is critical for the success of any risk assessment since it sets the priorities, methods, and risk tolerance level. As it is not feasible to analyse all the possible risks, a scope needs to be defined to focus in the most critical assets, also known as "crown jewels" [2]. Involvement of experts is crucial to define the variables of the system that can be monitored in the continuous phase, and to model their behaviour. The availability of operational data of the system under normal conditions is also important to model the system's behaviour. Characteristics of the infrastructure, network architecture, business rules, and configuration of the controllers need to be known. Outputs of the Context Establishment added in our approach are a list of sources of data to identify risk factors including online and batch automatic input feeds, as well as manual ones. This information will be used later to define the IoRs.

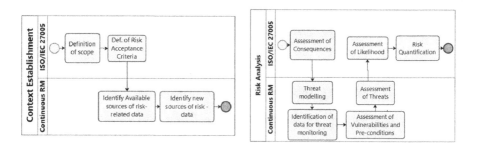

Fig. 4. Sub-processes of the baseline risk assessment.

The following step is the risk identification, which is not shown in Fig. 4, since it is exactly as in ISO/IEC27005, which means it encompasses the identification of assets, threats, security controls, vulnerabilities, and impacts. In the Risk Analysis process, a threat model should be developed to describe different possible attacks. An attack taxonomy specific to cyber-physical systems needs to be considered, such as the one proposed in [17]. This taxonomy differentiates a "change" which is an effect at a system level from an "impact", which is the implication for the business. Changes that relate to each threat are used to define IoRs, IoCs and alerts. The likelihood of a risk is estimated based on available data such as pentesting results and CVSS scores, for quantification of the vulnerability level, and threat intelligence sources to estimate levels of threat. A Bayesian Network is used to link the dependencies between different factors and their likelihood of occurrence given a series of conditions.

In the Risk Evaluation process, risks are prioritised and categorised. The risks above the acceptable level must be considered for further review and treatment. Risk acceptance should only happen when risks are below a defined threshold. When a risk is reduced to an acceptable level instead of being eliminated it is known as a "residual" risk. In exceptional cases, the organisation might decide to accept a risk that is higher than their accepted level. It must be noted that to acknowledge a high level of risk and accepting it is totally different, in principle, from underestimating a risk. Optimism bias is common when risks are not properly analysed, and can lead to an organisation to be unprepared to deal with security issues when they arise. On the other hand, accepting a risk implies that there is awareness about its potential consequences, but a decision to accept it is formally made. In these cases, risk monitoring becomes a compensating control that allows actions to be taken promptly if there is evidence that the risk is rising to become an issue. In the cases where the risk treatment plan, or parts of it, requires more time to be put in place or to show results, the risk scores will remain over the threshold until the controls are effectively working on reducing it. The Risk Evaluation and Risk treatment processes that we define do not have major variations from the ISO/IEC 27005 standard. The definition of baseline risk scores, provides a benchmark that is based on the available information of the condition of the system in a certain point of time. For this reason, this methodology considers the results of the initial risk assessment not a definitive evaluation but just the setting of initial scores for the continuous risk assessment.

5.2 Transition Phase

In this phase the variables that will be monitored in continuous risk assessment are linked to the risks analysed in the previous stage. The attack model done during the risk analysis should provide a record of the means of detection or inferring possible changes that different elements of the system can suffer in different stages of an attack, as well as the pre-conditions that can allow a certain attack method to be executed. Each change and precondition can be related to a risk metric that termed an IoR.

For indicators related to physical variables, a misbehaviour detection model needs to be defined to address specific needs of ICS. Commonly used means of detection will usually not be sufficient to alert of changes in physical variables. Analysing data from sensors and actuators can allow to detect physical effects of cyber attacks. This is highly relevant, since insiders present important threats in ICS [2] and, as these actors will have valid access, they can bypass traditional security controls. Tools need to be configured, including firewalls, Intrusion Detection Systems (IDS), malware detection, network monitoring, log monitoring, as well as misbehaviour detection. A SIEM will be used to process information and handle alerts. The modules that need to be setup and configured for the next phase are the misbehaviour detection module, the pre-processing of risk metrics and calculation of IoRs.

The transition phase can be complex considering the amount of tools, variables, and methods that the methodology comprises. To overcome this, it is possible to approach it as a project where incremental changes are applied at different stages. For example, start with a reduced scope (e.g. only critical processes and systems). A training period will be necessary for users, as well as for detection algorithms. Tools settings and parameters will need to be adjusted, and calibrated in order to maximise accuracy, and minimise false positives.

5.3   Continuous Risk Assessment

The main processes that interact in this phase are the Continuous Monitoring of Risk Factors, the Continuous Risk Analysis and the generation and report of security and risk alerts. The difference between a security alert and a risk alert is that while the first requires immediate action, the other might not. Figure 5 shows the continuous risk monitoring process where inputs are monitored in order to identify significant changes. At this stage there might be conditions that trigger immediately a security alert that is reported to the SOC, prior to the risk analysis as shown in Fig. 3.

Significant changes reported during the continuous risk monitoring process will lead to new values of IoRs and IoCs, and to trigger alerts, if applicable. Adjustments can be either because previous assumptions have been proven inaccurate or biased, or because of internal and external changes. Awareness about relevant changes will be provided by continuous processing and analysis of data from different sources including security sensors and logs, and threat and vulnerability intelligence sources. The use of a SIEM will allow an important amount of the data used for monitoring is supplied in near real time, or in a batch modality, but automatically. However, manual inputs, such as uploading data files and manually changing parameters in absence of the adequate tools, can also be considered. For example, when there is information from a zero-day vulnerability coming from another source this can make it necessary to make manual modifications to some parameters.

Figure 6 shows the continuous risk analysis, where indicators are mapped with their corresponding risk scores whose values are consequently updated. The risk calculation engine recalculates risk scores every time that a condition in the system requires an IoR to change its value. As conditions are monitored continuously, risk scores can be updated at any moment. If any updated risk score exceeds the acceptable level "risk alert" is triggered. As it is not possible to capture all the possible attack mechanisms in the threat modelling, a special risk score will be defined to represent unknown or zero-day attacks. Combinations of IoRs that cannot be linked to a known risk will be linked to this score.

All alerts get reported to the risk analyst to be analysed in order to consider the implementation of additional security and risk mitigation measures. In the

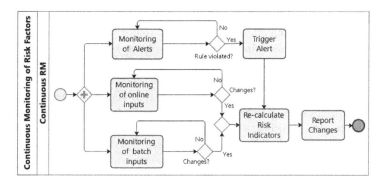

Fig. 5. Continuous risk monitoring

case of security alerts and risk alerts that are judged to require some sort of immediate reaction the SOC analyst is informed. Security alerts can be raised automatically by rules managed by the SIEM, by the results of the risk calculations or by the risk analyst. While this approach does not deal with any of the processes related to the SOC operations, it contributes on giving an instance of collaboration between risk management and security operations.

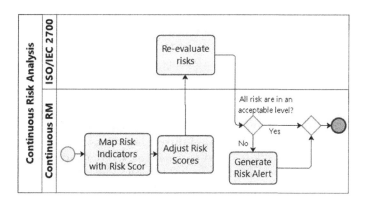

Fig. 6. Continuous risk analysis

6   Using Bayesian Networks in Risk Estimations

The initial risk quantification is based on Bayesian Network whose nodes represent events that can lead to one or more risks. An incidence matrix indicates whether or not there is a relationship between nodes. In the graphical representation of the network the nodes are linked by arrows. For each existing relationship a table of conditional probabilities is defined to calculate the likelihood of an event "A" given the occurrence of an event "B". The overall likelihood of a risk is estimated based on a chain of events. An analogous process is done to link the IoRs to each action allowing to update likelihoods in the presence of IoRs during the continuous risk analysis.

In [1] an example of a temperature control in a Data Centre, supervised and controlled by a Building Management System (BMS) is used as use case to explain continuous risk assessment. A BMS controls environmental variables such as temperature, pressure, and humidity, and it could also monitor variables related to the use of the building such as perimeter security and access control, and utilities consumption, among others. In some contexts the environmental control of the building can be critical, for example in a chemical or nuclear plant. In data centres the environmental control system is used to keep temperature and humidity within levels that allow the servers to perform at their best capacity, and to prevent overheating and other unsafe conditions. In the case of temperature this is usually 25 °C.

In this example it is assumed that the temperature setting may be changed from a small number of privileged accounts, which may be accessed remotely. ICS tend to have restricted remote access or to be isolated from corporate and public access networks either physically or through the configuration of a DMZ (demilitarised zone). Nevertheless, it can be the case that remote access enabled for a system's administrator [2]. It is also often that cyber-hygiene measures that are considered to be basic in IT systems are not be implemented in ICS because they conflict with the availability, integrity and even safety of an operation. For example, a typical defence against brute force attacks is locking access to the system after a number of failed login attempts. However, in an emergency situation which can be time-critical, locking an ICS system because of human mistake such as a forgotten password could be riskier than exposing the system to a brute force attack.

Figure 7 shows a simplified representation of a Bayesian Network to quantify cyber-risks for this case study. Two possible attacks on the temperature control allow an attacker to achieve the goal of disturbing the normal operation of the data centre. The first attack is based on changing the temperature setting to a considerably higher value than the acceptable limit, which is 30 °C. The second attack consists of disabling the temperature control. All nodes have states that depend on the achievement of certain goals by the attacker. In each node, the conditional probabilities of an attacker's goal been achieved is registered in a table given each of the possible combination of states of the previous nodes. When a change is observed, then the likelihood of a possible estate can increase which will means that the estimation of the probabilities that certain attacker's goal can be achieved increases, as well. This will be computed and, if applicable, presented to the user as an IoR. An attack goal can be associated to more than one IoR and each IoR can be associated with more than one attack goal. Hence, an IoR by itself is not conclusive to detect a certain type of attack, but by having a combination of them the level of uncertainty can be reduced.

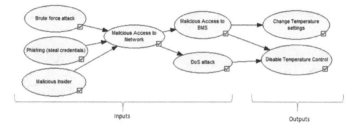

Fig. 7. Example of bayesian network

In Fig. 7 the nodes represent different attack goals and the figure represents a combination of possible kill-chains. The arrows indicate that the probability that the destination action has been performed is directly influenced by whether the source action has been performed. In Fig. 8, the nodes on the left hand side of each diagram are associated with actions (as in Fig. 7), but the nodes in the right are associated with observations (termed IoR). The arrows denote that the probability that the relevant phenomenon has been observed depends directly on whether the action has been performed. Inferencing is "forward" in Fig. 7, and "backward" in the two diagrams of Fig. 8, so that in the initial risk analysis inputs nodes are the actions and output nodes the likelihood of a risk and in the continuous risk analysis the input nodes are the IoRs which allow calculating the likelihood of particular actions in a kill chain taking place as well as the associated risks.

Not all means of detection are deterministic and Bayesian Networks allow calculation of the probability of an action being detected. An IoR is not necessarily related to a single action, but can be a symptom of several causes. A Bayesian Network can help inferring a set of possible malicious actions and the likelihood of each one of them taking place. If we take as an example "traffic from an unusual location" as an IoR, from the diagram at the left in Fig. 8 it can be observed that it is related to three nodes. So if traffic from an unusual location is detected, this could be evidence of a brute force attack to gain access, or of malicious access, and also could be indicative of a Denial of Service attack (DoS) in its early stages. Nevertheless, when this indicator is correlated with other indicators it can give a more precise information. For example, if there are also multiple failed access attempts followed by a successful one this increases the probability that unauthorised access was gained through a successful brute force attack.

In the case of an insider attack, a different approach needs to be taken since in this scenario an agent that can be either malicious, or coerced to act maliciously, will have valid access credentials. This means that there will be no anomalies at a network or software level. For these cases, it is necessary to count on IoRs that can detect a functional misbehaviour in the system. The diagram at the right in Fig. 8 shows a Bayesian network for different IoRs that are calculated through misbehaviour detection. In a sophisticated attack it could be possible that the

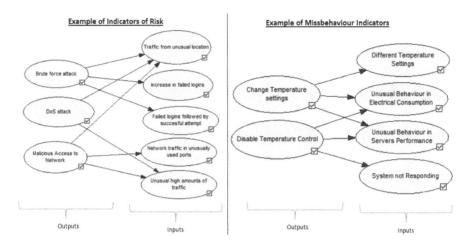

Fig. 8. Link between changes and Indicators of Risk (IoR)

attacker tampers with the temperature values displayed in the BMS preventing alerts being triggered directly by the change in the temperature values or settings. An example of this is the case of Stuxnet where normal operational values were replayed in the system while the frequency of the motor drives of the nuclear centrifuges was changed. To address this, anomalies in other variables, such as unusual behaviour in electrical power consumption or in server's performance, could raise an alert concerning the temperature.

A key challenge of risk management is trying to quantify what you do not know. Sometimes there is enough information to identify and analyse a risk by making plausible assumptions. However, at other times there is no prior information at all. This is the case of zero-day attacks. As it is not possible to identify all possible risks in the baseline risk assessment, it is important to consider a likelihood of an undesirable event with undefined characteristics. To address this, every IoR will have among its possible causes an unknown or undefined cause as shown in Fig. 9. This has not been included explicitly in previous figures for simplicity of presentation. When a combination of IoRs cannot be mapped to any known risk, the likelihood of an unknown risk unfolding is increased. One or more nodes could also be defined to represent non-cybersecurity related triggers for an IoR.

7   Future Work

As the present paper provides just a conceptual approach, considerable work needs to be done to prove specific methods can work under the proposed framework. Future work will focus on further demonstration of the methodology using different use cases related to ICS and IIoT. One of our goals is to explore the correlation of data from physical variables (sensor and actuator data) to reveal

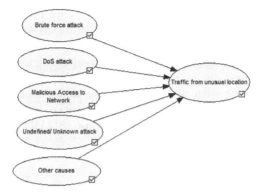

Fig. 9. Addressing unknown attacks

information about the physical system that is not directly observable and that an attacker might be trying to obfuscate.

Due to the breadth and complexity of our proposal, several challenges need to be addressed including proving the potential scalability of the approach. Selecting appropriate methods, rules, and training mechanisms to detect misbehaviour and avoid false positives is another challenge for which a good level of understanding about the expected normal behaviour of the system is required. It is proposed to formalise expert knowledge during the initial risk assessment where context and business rules should be captured. This should include specifications about normal behaviour of key processes of the system, a list of relevant variables to be monitored and availability of monitoring mechanisms. Possible correlations between physical variables should be identified and analysed, such as temperature and pressure. Additionally, machine learning techniques can be used to model patterns of behaviour that cannot be defined mathematically by experts. It must be noted that when data is gathered to model the normal behaviour of the system, this is done under the assumption that it has not yet been compromised.

Minimising cyber-security risks requires being up to date with new threats and vulnerabilities, as well as with new cyber-security tools and methods for prevention, detection, response, and recovery. As the methodology aims to be technology agnostic, it should be possible to introduce new monitoring and detection tools after the initial implementation.

In many industries cyber-security in ICS and IIoT systems has been neglected and there is lack of personnel equipped to deal with it. The continuous monitoring of cyber-risks should help increase cyber-security awareness and identify cybersecurity weaknesses. This also should include processes, people and training, since not all risks are technical since cybersecurity vulnerabilities can also be related to processes and procedures.

An more advanced approach will be to define the likelihood in terms of a distribution rather than a single point estimation, using Monte Carlo techniques. This can give a more realistic view of the uncertainty level than single point probabilities. The specific technique and algorithm used to calculate the baseline risk scores should be defined during the context establishment. This methodology is general enough to work with different emerging approaches and ideas. Examples of this are deep learning and artificial intelligence, threat intelligence, and Security Orchestration, Automation and Response (SOAR).

8   Conclusions

Methods to maintain continuous cyber-risk awareness can support rational and well informed decisions as well as improve times and effectiveness of reactions in the event of an incident. The methodology proposed links detection mechanisms with risk assessment by using security metrics to calculate risk indicators in real time. Through this, we postulate the idea that integrating risk management with the security operations should enable a better prioritisation of security resources and more timely reactions. Current availability of off-the-shelf tools for real time data analytics also can constitute a powerful resource to make this approach feasible.

This paper regards continuous risk management as an extension of ISO/IEC 27005 in alignment with IEC 62443 and other frameworks rather than defining it as a totally different process. Because each ICS will have its own requirements, it is not possible to generate a one-size-fits-all solution. However, defining steps for each organisation to develop their own continuous risk assessment strategy can serve as a guideline that can be used broadly across different systems. Expert knowledge and contextual information are captured during initial assessment and transition phases. It is not possible to provide a general answer to some of our questions since our risk analysis approach needs to be tailored to the particularities of each system.

As in many cases the data gathered from security controls and IT elements of the system does not tell the whole story, and may itself be compromised by an attacker. Anomaly and misbehaviour detection techniques based on physical variables, such as temperature and power consumption, address this gap which can help to overcome different challenges in ICS cybersecurity, such as detection of physical attacks, detection of malicious insiders, and detection of unknown threats and zero day attacks.

Cybersecurity and OT operations, including safety management, have been developed on totally separate tracks. However, much of the knowledge in the field of control engineering and safety can be useful in the implementation of cybersecurity controls, as well as in the development of a future continuous risk assessment paradigm.

References

1. Adaros Boye, C., Kearney, P., Josephs, M.: Cyber-risks in the industrial internet of things (IIoT): towards a method for continuous assessment. In: Chen, L., Manulis, M., Schneider, S. (eds.) ISC 2018. LNCS, vol. 11060, pp. 502–519. Springer, Cham (2018). https://doi.org/10.1007/978-3-319-99136-8_27
2. Cyber-X Labs: 2019 Global ICS and IIoT Risk. A data-driven analysis of vulnerabilities in our industrial and critical infrastructure. Technical Report, Cyber-X Labs (2018)
3. Dempsey, K., et al.: Information Security Continuous Monitoring (ISCM) for Federal Information Systems and Organizations. National Institute of Standards and Technology (NIST) Special Publication 800–137 (2012)
4. Desnitsky, V., Kotenko, I., Nogin, S.: Detection of anomalies in data for monitoring of security components in the internet of things. In: 2015 XVIII International Conference on Soft Computing and Measurements (SCM), pp. 189–192. IEEE (2015)
5. Ding, D., Han, Q.L., Xiang, Y., Ge, X., Zhang, X.M.: A survey on security control and attack detection for industrial cyber-physical systems. Neurocomputing **275**, 1674–1683 (2018)
6. Gonzalez-Granadillo, G., et al.: Dynamic risk management response system to handle cyber threats. Future Gener. Comput. Syst. **83**, 535–552 (2018)
7. Han, S., Xie, M., Chen, H.H., Ling, Y.: Intrusion detection in cyber-physical systems: techniques and challenges. IEEE Syst. J. **8**(4), 1052–1062 (2014)
8. Health and Safety Executive (HSE): Cyber Security for Industrial Automation and Control Systems (IACS) OG86. Technical Report, UK Government (2018)
9. Huang, H., Xie, D.: Real-time network risk evaluation paradigm-inspired by immune. In: 2015 11th International Conference on Natural Computation (ICNC), pp. 786–790. IEEE (2015)
10. International Electrotechnical Commission: IEC 62443 2–1: Establishing an industrial automation and control system security program (2011)
11. ISO/IEC: ISO/IEC 27005:2011. Information security risk management (2011)
12. Kotenko, I., Saenko, I., Ageev, S.: Countermeasure security risks management in the internet of things based on fuzzy logic inference. In: 2015 IEEE Trustcom/BigDataSE/ISPA. vol. 1, pp. 654–659. IEEE (2015)
13. Kotenko, I.V., Levshun, D.S., Chechulin, A.A.: Event correlation in the integrated cyber-physical security system. In: 2016 XIX IEEE International Conference on Soft Computing and Measurements (SCM), pp. 484–486. IEEE (2016)
14. Liu, C., Zhang, Y., Zeng, J., Peng, L., Chen, R.: Research on dynamical security risk assessment for the internet of things inspired by immunology. In: 2012 8th International Conference on Natural Computation, pp. 874–878. IEEE (2012)
15. McLaughlin, S., et al.: The cybersecurity landscape in industrial control systems. Proc. IEEE **104**(5), 1039–1057 (2016)
16. Sicard, F., Zamai, E., Flaus, J.M.: Filters based approach with temporal and combinational constraints for cybersecurity of industrial control systems. IFAC-PapersOnLine **51**(24), 96–103 (2018)
17. Yampolskiy, M., Horváth, P., Koutsoukos, X.D., Xue, Y., Sztipanovits, J.: A language for describing attacks on cyber-physical systems. Int. J. Crit. Infrastruct. Prot. **8**, 40–52 (2015)
18. Zhang, Q., Zhou, C., Tian, Y.C., Xiong, N., Qin, Y., Hu, B.: A fuzzy probability bayesian network approach for dynamic cybersecurity risk assessment in industrial control systems. IEEE Trans. Ind. Inform. **14**(6), 2497–2506 (2018)

Systematic Asset Identification and Modeling During Requirements Engineering

Nazila Gol Mohammadi$^{(\boxtimes)}$, Roman Wirtz$^{(\boxtimes)}$, and Maritta Heisel

University of Duisburg-Essen, Duisburg, Germany
{nazila.golmohammadi,roman.wirtz,maritta.heisel}@uni-due.de

Abstract. Risk management primarily targets the treatment of threats which might harm the assets of a system. Therefore, identifying such assets of a system and documenting them systematically in an asset model are the key activities in any risk management approach. Based on the ISO/IEC 27005 standard, the consideration of assets consists of two major activities: (i) asset identification, and (ii) asset valuation. However, despite the crucial role of asset identification and asset documentation, such documentation is often neglected during software development. In this paper, we aim to support security analysts in identifying and analyzing assets in the earliest stages of software development, i.e., during requirements engineering. Our contribution is two-fold: We first provide a conceptual model for assets that allows us to classify assets and to express the relations between assets. Second, we propose a method for a systematic identification of system assets and their documentation in an asset model. Our method is based on the functional requirements of software which are expressed by means of problem diagrams. We illustrate and evaluate our proposed approach by applying it to an application example from the smart home sector.

Keywords: Risk management · Requirements engineering · Problem frames · Asset modeling · Security

1 Introduction

Risk management describes a set of activities: (i) to identify threats for an asset, (ii) to estimate the risk for the asset due to the identified threats, and (iii) to reduce the risk by applying suitable controls [1]. However, before identifying threats, it is necessary to define the assets to be protected, i.e., anything of value for a stakeholder and should be protected. Following the principle of security-by-design, risk management should take place as early as possible, i.e., during requirements engineering. The identification of assets in such an early stage is a major task during the risk management. Based on these assets, other steps in the risk management are affected, e.g., identifying threats, vulnerabilities and controls. Despite the central role of assets identification in risk management,

© Springer Nature Switzerland AG 2020
S. Kallel et al. (Eds.): CRiSIS 2019, LNCS 12026, pp. 50–66, 2020.
https://doi.org/10.1007/978-3-030-41568-6_4

systematic identification and documentation of assets are hardly addressed in the literature.

Assets exist within the system boundary and are under the system's protection. Therefore, the system needs to be properly described, and from that description assets need to be identified and documented systematically. Furthermore, it is necessary to provide a reasoning for the asset's value to later on decide about existing risks. The reasoning about an asset's value can be determined with respect to the requirements, i.e., how important an asset is for fulfilling a system requirement.

In this paper, we provide a systematic and model-based identification and documentation of assets during requirements engineering. The functional requirements for the software serve as the initial input, which we describe with a problem-based approach [2]. Using our approach, assets are documented explicitly through an asset model, together with their relation to the system requirements. Our approach supports risk analysts of the system in the decision-making process about the protected assets and their values. We provide an asset model that proposes different hierarchical asset classes. Our model makes the relations between different asset classes explicit, and we establish relations between the description of the functional requirements and the asset classes. Based on the asset model, we introduce a step-wise method to identify assets from functional requirements. The method first enhances the requirements model with necessary security-related aspects and then helps to systematically identify and categorize assets. We document the assets and their relations, by instantiating our asset model.

The resulting asset model serves as the starting point to identify threats that might harm the assets, thus leading to some value loss. Since we document the relations between functional requirements and assets, we support traceability and consistency of risk management artifacts, e.g., which assets need to be protected for which reason, which threats may threaten the asset under consideration, which control has been selected and realized for protecting the respective asset.

The remainder of the paper is organized as follows: Sect. 2 describes the underlying concept of problem diagrams. In Sect. 3, we introduce our conceptual asset model and our method to identify assets. We exemplify the application of our method in Sect. 4 and provide an example for an asset model. Section 5 discusses related work. We conclude our paper in Sect. 6 with a summary and an outlook on future research directions.

2 Background

To model requirements, we make use of problem diagrams as proposed by Jackson [2]. To model those diagrams, we use UML class diagrams as proposed by Côte et al. [3]. For each element of a problem diagram, there is a class in the underlying model to which an appropriate stereotype is applied.

A problem diagram consists of domains and a requirement. Each domain represents entities of the real world that are related to the problem. There are the following types: *biddable domains* (e.g., people and companies), *causal domains* (e.g., technical equipment), *machines* (representing the piece of software to be developed), and *lexical domains* (data representations). A *display domain* is a special kind of causal domain used to show some information to a stakeholder. A *connection domain* makes a connection between domains (e.g., a network) explicit.

To model the relations between domains, there are interfaces between domains which share a set of phenomena. There are *symbolic phenomena*, representing some kind of information or state, and *causal phenomena*, representing events, actions and so on. Each phenomenon is controlled by exactly one domain (indicated by $A!\{...\}$, where A is an abbreviation for the controlling domain) and can be observed by other domains. A phenomenon controlled by one domain and observed by another is called a shared phenomenon between these two domains.

A functional requirement is an optative statement that describes how the environment should behave when the machine is integrated. Each problem diagram contains at least one requirement and the problem domains which are related to the requirement.

There are references between requirements and problem domains. Such references can be either *constrains* or *refers to* references, which are annotated with phenomena. The constrained phenomena describe desired characteristics of the domain when the machine has been integrated. Examples of the use of problem diagram are provided in Sect. 4 (cf. Figs. 4 and 5).

The notation used for problem diagrams is also used for a more precise domain knowledge elicitation by setting up knowledge domain diagrams [4]. By using domain knowledge diagrams, further information about systems' context can be made explicit, e.g., assumptions about indirect stakeholders of a system. An example of the use of domain knowledge model can be found in Fig. 6.

3   Asset Identification Approach

In this section, we describe our contribution in the form of an asset identification approach. First, we state requirements on asset identification which we derived from the ISO 27005 standard [1]. Second, we propose a conceptual model for asset classes and their relations. We developed the conceptual model based on the concepts of the ISO 27005 standard and asset classes from the existing risk management approaches (e.g., [5,6]). Third, we introduce a method for the identification of assets based on functional requirements of software.

3.1   Requirements on Asset Identification

Before describing our method for the asset identification, we present the requirements on our method based on the ISO 27005 standard [1].

The ISO 27005 standard provides guidelines for risk management with regard to information security. According to the standard, the objective of risk identification is to identify assets, threats, existing controls, vulnerabilities, and consequences. Assets are anything of value, thus requiring protection by controls against threats. Establishing the context prior to risk identification serves as the initial input for identifying assets and risks. During requirements engineering, the context can be defined by functional requirements for the software from which assets can be derived. With regard to ISO 27005, there are two categories of assets: (i) primary assets, i.e., information and business processes; (ii) supporting assets on which the primary assets rely. The asset identification shall capture all assets and shall categorize them according to the standard.

For the context establishment we require the functional requirements of software by means of problem diagrams (cf. Sect. 2). From the problem diagrams, the assets shall be identified and documented systematically in an asset model.

After identifying all assets, the asset valuation shall be supported by the resulting asset model. The value assigned to an asset depends on the importance of that asset to fulfill the goals of stakeholders, e.g., how important the contribution of an asset is to satisfy stakeholders' requirements.

In the following, we provide an asset model and asset identification method to satisfy the above-mentioned requirements.

3.2 Conceptual Model and Asset Classes

In this subsection, first, we present our conceptual model (shown in Fig. 1) that is underlying our method. Note that the white colored concepts are based on the ISO 27005 standard and existing asset classes in the state of art. We describe the elements under "Conceptual Model". Then, we present the mapping of the asset classes to the concepts from problem diagrams (gray colored). The gray colored concepts are described under "Mapping to Requirements Model".

Conceptual Model. To categorize assets that can be identified during requirements engineering, we provide a conceptual model (shown in Fig. 1). The ISO 27005 standard [1] distinguishes between *primary assets* and *supporting assets*. Each asset has an *asset owner* who not necessarily has property rights, but who is responsible for the asset, e.g., for its maintenance.

As primary assets, the standard considers *Information* and *Business processes*. There are three types of security protection goals for a piece of information: (i) confidentiality, protection against unauthorized disclosure of the asset, (ii) integrity, protection against unauthorized manipulation of asset, and (iii) availability, ensuring access to asset for authorized entities.

The ISO 27005 standard specifies the *relies on* relation between a primary asset and its supporting assets. Primary assets rely on supporting assets. The following asset classes belong to the category of supporting assets: *Location, Network, Stakeholder, Hardware*, and *Software*.

The location denotes the physical location for the asset, e.g., a company's building. As network assets, we consider the underlying infrastructure that is responsible for information exchange between different entities.

Surridge and Wilkinson further refine stakeholders to *Human* and *Organization* [5], which is similar to the classification of the ISO 27005 standard.

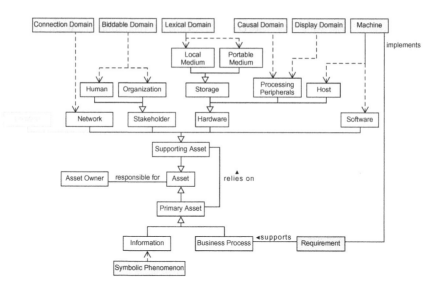

Fig. 1. Conceptual model for asset classes and mapping to requirements model

Storage, Processing Peripherals, and *Hosts* are hardware assets. For storage, we distinguish between *Local Medium*, e.g., databases, and *Portable Medium*, e.g., USB sticks. Since information is a primary asset which can be stored, both types are crucial points with regard to security. Processing peripherals describe external technical equipment such as printers or displays. Hosts are strongly related to software. Software describes the implementation of specific function-alities, thus implementing the functional requirements, and hosts describe the underlying hardware on which software shall later be deployed.

Mapping to Requirements Model. As described in Sect. 2, we use domains, phenomena, and statements to document functional requirements and domain knowledge of a system. In the following, we map these elements (from problem diagrams) to the different asset classes. In Fig. 1, we visualize the mapping and highlight the elements of the requirements model in gray color.

In problem diagrams, we make use of symbolic phenomena for a piece of information. Hence, we map a symbolic phenomenon to the primary asset class of information. Requirements support business processes and are implemented by machines.

The asset class location is greyed out. There is no element in problem dia-grams that makes the location explicit. Machine domains describe a piece of software to be developed, thus belonging to the asset classes software and hosts. Since causal and display domains represent technical equipment, we map them to the class of processing peripherals. Lexical domains can represent either a local or a portable storage medium. Biddable domains describe domains with an unpredictable behavior, and therefore are mapped to both human and orga-nization asset classes. Connection domains make connections between domains explicit and belong to the asset class network.

We further refine the *relies on* relation from ISO 27005 to specify in more detail the relation between a primary asset and its supporting assets. We show that refinement in Fig. 2. For supporting assets which belong to the classes *Software*, *Host* or *Processing Peripherals*, we define the relation *processed by*. For the class of local and portable storage mediums, we refine the relation to *stored at*, and for stakeholders there is a relation called *available for*. We use the relation *located at* to relate a primary asset to a location, and for networks, we use the relation *transmitted via*.

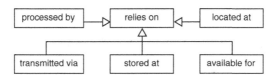

Fig. 2. Refinement for *relies on* relation

To annotate the asset classes at the domains and phenomena, we make use of a UML profile that defines a stereotype per asset class and per relation. An example of a model using the UML profile is given in Fig. 9.

3.3   Our Method for Systematic Asset Identification

Figure 3 provides an overview of our method showing the six steps to be performed as well as input and output of these steps. In the following, we describe each step in detail.

(1) Create problem diagrams. During context establishment, we suggest creating problem diagrams for each functional requirement. Problem diagrams, for the software under development, include the entities of the environment and their relations to the machine in a structured manner. Therefore, these diagrams serve as a good starting point for our asset identification method.

(2) Identify connection domains. With regard to security, network communications are a crucial point since they are unreliable connections between domains. Connection domains can be used to make those connections explicit in problem diagrams. Faßbender et al. propose a method to systematically identify relevant connection domains with regard to security [7]. Connection domains can be used to describe network assets. In this step, we use the proposed method by Faßbender et al. to extend our problem diagrams (from Step 1) to make network assets explicit.

(3) Elicit domain knowledge. Problem diagrams initially only capture the domains and stakeholders that are part of the description of a functional requirement. However, especially for security, an accurate consideration of domain knowledge is necessary. To do so, we use questionnaires proposed by Meis to elicit relevant domain knowledge [4]. For each domain contained in a problem diagram, there are questions to identify indirect stakeholders or so-called hidden behavior, e.g., personal communication between stakeholders. Indirect stakeholders are those stakeholders who are not directly related to functionalities, but who influence the system. Using domain knowledge diagrams (e.g., Fig. 6), which are similar to problem diagrams, further stakeholders and behavior can be documented (which are ignored in problem diagrams). Since indirect stakeholders can also have influence on the system's security, we complement our requirements model with domain knowledge.

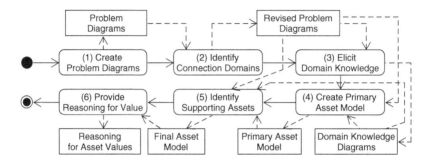

Fig. 3. Method overview

(4) Create asset model for primary assets. In this step, we use our conceptual model to create an asset model that includes primary assets. As shown in Fig. 1, there are two types of primary assets: "Information" and "Business Process". We use symbolic phenomena to express some information in the problem diagrams. Therefore, symbolic phenomena are candidates for primary assets of the category "Information". For each of those candidates which are considered as an asset, it is necessary to define the asset owner in the form of a reference to the corresponding stakeholder. Business processes are not part of problem diagrams directly. However, business processes can be derived from requirements that are part of problem diagrams. The outcome of this step is the asset model capturing all primary assets.

(5) Identify supporting assets. In this step, we use our conceptual model to identify supporting assets of primary assets from Step 4. These identified supporting assets will be included in the asset model. Vulnerabilities of supporting assets may be misused to harm a primary asset, i.e., domains of the system that process information considered as an asset. To assist this step, we create an information flow graph as proposed by Wirtz et al. [8]. Such a graph (e.g., Fig. 8) is directed and depicts which information represented as a phenomenon is available at which domain. The authors suggest inspecting the interfaces between domains of the problem diagrams and domain knowledge diagrams to create that graph. When both domains share an asset-related phenomenon, it means that the information is available at both domains. We limit the information flow graph to the analysis of those phenomena that have been identified as primary assets.

As supporting assets, we consider those domains on which a primary asset is available, and we classify the domains according to the defined asset classes in the conceptual model.

(6) Provide reasoning for value. As the last step, we use the asset model (output of Step 5) to provide a reasoning for asset values. That reasoning supports security analysts in identifying consequences and risk estimation.

The reasoning for the value of each primary asset or supporting asset is done by providing details about why it is of value. For this purpose, we annotate which of the assets have impact on satisfying the requirements and consequently on related business processes. In case of supporting assets, we further consider how important the supporting asset is in preserving the security of the related primary asset.

The reasoning can be documented in natural language or with a reference to the corresponding requirement. The output of this step, together with the generated asset model can be used later on to determine qualitative and quantitative scales to express an asset's value.

4   Application Example

To exemplify our method, we apply it on a smart grid scenario. A smart grid is an intelligent power supply network which enables an energy supplier to control and maintain the power supply at a customer's home remotely. Additionally, a customer is able to communicate with the energy supplier, e.g., with regard to invoicing. At the customer's home, there is a gateway called *Communication Hub* for which software shall be developed. Smart meters that measure the actual power consumption are connected to the gateway. The measured data can be used to automatically generate invoices. Here, we focus on the following three functional requirements:

FR1: Customers can edit their personal data, e.g., name and invoice address that are stored at the communication hub.

FR2: In given intervals, smart meters transmit their measured data to the communication hub.

FR3: Each month, the communication hub generates invoices based on the customer data and the measured data. The invoice is sent to the customer via e-mail.

In the following, we describe the application of our method step-by-step and show the corresponding output.

(1) Create problem diagrams. We create a problem diagram for each functional requirement. Note that the corresponding diagrams (shown in Figs. 4 and 5) already contain the identified connection domains resulting from the second step.

- FR1: Figure 4 shows the problem diagram for the first functional requirement. It contains three domains: *Customer* (biddable domain), *Communication Hub* (machine), and *Customer Data* (lexical domain). A customer sends the command to edit the data to the machine which then changes the data. This functional requirement refers to the command of the customer and constrains the customer data.
- FR2: In Fig. 4, we also show the problem diagram for the second functional requirement. There is a causal domain *Smart Meter* which transmits data to the machine *Communication Hub*. The lexical domain *Meter Data* represents the internal database of the communication hub to store the data. This functional requirement refers to the phenomenon of the smart meter and constrains the phenomenon of the lexical domain.
- FR3: For the third requirement, we present the problem diagram in Fig. 5. The communication hub request data from both lexical domains, *Meter Data* and *Customer Data*. After generating the invoice, the machine sends the invoice via e-mail. We make use of a display domain as representation for the e-mail. This functional requirement refers to the phenomena of both lexical domains and constrains the representation of the display domain.

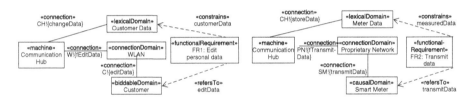

Fig. 4. Revised problem diagrams for FR1 (left side) and FR2 (right side)

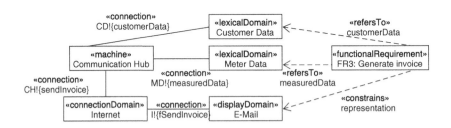

Fig. 5. Revised problem diagram for *FR3: Generate invoice*

(2) Identify connection domains. Using the approach of Faßbender et al., we identified the following connection domains: (i) The customer uses WLAN to connect to the communication hub (see Fig. 4); (ii) A smart meter uses a proprietary network to communicate with the communication hub (see Fig. 4); (iii) The communication hub sends the e-mail via the Internet (see Fig. 5). The corresponding connection domains are added to the problem diagrams.

(3) Elicit domain knowledge. Using the domain knowledge elicitation questionnaires, we elicited the following domain knowledge, represented as assumptions (A):

– A1: The customer reads the e-mail sent from the communication hub.
– A2: The energy supplier maintains the communication hub locally. In case of a problem in this communication hub, it will be replaced with a new one by the energy supplier. However, by replacing the communication hub with a new one, it is possible that the energy supplier may get a copy of data stored at the damaged communication hub.
– A3: The internet connection is maintained by an internet service provider who has access to the connection.

We show the corresponding domain knowledge diagrams in Fig. 6.

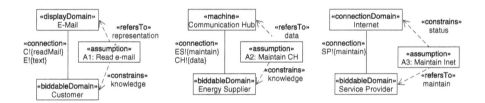

Fig. 6. Domain knowledge

(4) Create asset model for primary assets. As primary assets, we consider *measured data* and *personal data*. The measured data are required by the energy supplier to generate the corresponding invoices for the customer. Therefore, the energy supplier is the asset owner. For personal data, we define the customer as asset owner since he/she maintains the data at the communication hub. As relevant business process, we consider the invoicing for which the energy supplier is the owner. The functional requirements *FR2: Transmit data* and *FR3: Generate invoice* support that process.

In Fig. 7, we show the corresponding asset model using a UML class diagram with stereotypes.

(5) Identify supporting assets. Figure 8 shows the generated information flow graph based on the functional requirements and the elicited domain knowledge. For each domain, we annotate the available asset, e.g., at the customer domain the personal data is available. Using the graph, it is now possible to identify supporting assets for the primary assets *personalData* and *measuredData*. Each

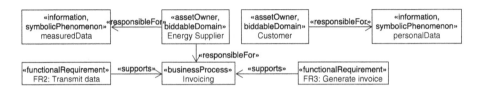

Fig. 7. Model for primary assets

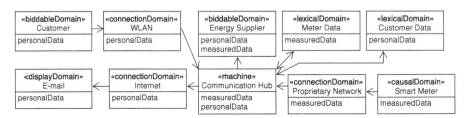

Fig. 8. Information flow graph

domain at which a primary asset is available is considered as a supporting asset for the primary one.

For *personalData*, we identified seven supporting assets that are listed on the following page. We further map these supporting assets to specific asset classes and identify the corresponding asset owner. For a biddable domain, the asset owner is the domain itself.

1. *Customer* is a human stakeholder.
2. *WLAN* is a network for which the customer is responsible, e.g., its configuration.
3. *Energy Supplier* is a stakeholder of type "organization".
4. *Communication Hub* is the piece of software to be developed, thus being a host and software. The energy supplier is responsible for the hub.
5. *Customer Data* is an internal database of the communication hub. Therefore, the energy supplier is the responsible asset owner.
6. *E-mail* contains the invoice address and name of the customer data. As the asset owner, we consider an external service provider.
7. *Internet* transfers the invoice. Again, the responsible asset owner is a service provider.

For the asset *measuredData*, we identified five supporting assets as follows:

1. *Energy Supplier* as defined in number 3 of the previous list.
2. *Communication Hub* as defined in number 4 of the previous list.
3. *Meter Data* as an internal database of the communication hub, thus the energy supplier is the responsible owner.
4. *Proprietary Network* is a network used by the communication hub to connect to smart meters. Therefore, the energy supplier is the responsible asset owner.

5. *Smart Meter* is considered as a peripheral according to our defined asset classes, and the energy supplier is the responsible asset owner.

In Fig. 9, we show our final asset model for the supporting assets in the UML class diagram notation with appropriate stereotypes.

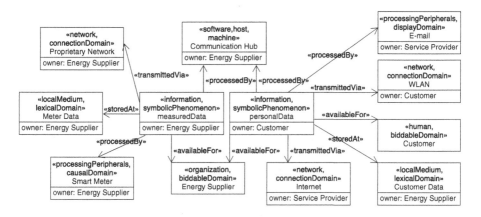

Fig. 9. Final asset model with supporting assets

(6) Provide reasoning for value. In the following, we document the reasoning for each primary asset and its supporting assets. There are two primary assets:

– *personalData*: Disclosing the personal data may harm for the customer with regard to her/his privacy. The integrity and availability of the data is important for the energy supplier to generate the invoices correctly.
– *measuredData*: The measured data documents the customer's power consumption. Therefore, integrity and availability of the *measuredData* are of value to generate the invoices correctly.

There are ten supporting assets:

– *Customer Data* belongs to the asset class of local storage medium. The related database stores the primary asset *customer data* persistently and is, therefore, of high importance. This asset is involved in addressing the requirements *FR1: Edit personal data* and *FR3: Generate invoice*.
– *Meter Data* belongs to the asset class of local storage medium. The related database stores the primary asset *measuredData* persistently and is, therefore, of high importance. This asset is involved in addressing the requirements *FR2: Transmit data* and *FR3: Generate invoice*.
– *Customer* belongs to the asset class of human stakeholders. He/she can edit the stored primary asset *personalData* and is, therefore, of importance. This asset is involved in addressing the requirement *FR1: Edit personal data*.

- *Energy Supplier* belongs to the asset class of organizational stakeholders. It is a supporting asset for both primary assets since it can replace the communication hub for maintenance reasons. The communication hub stores both primary assets persistently.
- *Internet* belongs to the asset class of networks. It is responsible for transmitting the invoices containing both primary assets. This asset is involved in addressing the requirement *FR3: Generate invoice*.
- *Proprietary Network* belongs to the asset class of networks and transmits the measured data to the communication hub for further processing. This asset is involved in addressing the requirement *FR2: Transmit data*.
- *WLAN* belongs to the asset class of networks and transmits the personal data to the communication hub for being stored persistently. This asset is involved in addressing the requirement *FR1: Edit personal data*.
- *Smart Meter* is a supporting asset of the class processing peripherals. It measures the power consumption and is, therefore, responsible to provide the initial data of the primary asset *measuredData*. This asset is involved in addressing the requirement *FR2: Transmit data*.
- *E-mail* belongs to the asset class of supporting peripherals. It processes both primary assets to provide the invoice to the customer, thus being of importance for both primary assets, too. This asset is involved in addressing the requirement *FR3: Generate invoice*.
- *Communication Hub* belongs to the asset classes "software" and "host". It is a crucial domain since it processes both primary assets. The software implements the functional requirements based on the underlying hardware. This asset is involved in addressing the requirements *FR1: Edit personal data, FR2: Transmit data*, and *FR3: Generate invoice*.

The resulting asset model can be used in the following steps of the risk identification, i.e., in the next step threats will be identified that may harm the assets. The documentation of the asset owner allows to assign responsibilities with regard to the security for an asset.

5 Related Work

The ISO 27005 standard [1] considers three major steps for risk identification and treatment: (i) identifying assets, (ii) identifying threats and evaluate their risks for the assets, and (iii) identifying controls to protect the assets against threats. Existing risk management methods mostly do not consider explicitly documenting and modeling the assets of the system under consideration.

Lund et al. [6] propose the CORAS method that defines a model-based risk management process. Wirtz et al. [8] extend the CORAS method for an application during requirements engineering. Therein, problem diagrams are also used to describe the requirements of software. However, there is no systematic method to capture assets, hence our method can improve the presented works.

There are few related contributions employing asset models in risk assessment approach, e.g., by developing a tool that makes it possible to set up an asset model [5,9]. Surridge et al. [9] present a risk management method. This method supports the automated identification of threats and controls based on an asset model. Although the approach is promising, it suffers from the limitations of considering system requirements, and it does not have a link to system requirements. We consider the asset classes defined by the authors in other works [5,9] for our conceptual model. Furthermore, their tool is commercialized and an independent use of setting up an asset model for the system under consideration is not possible. With our approach independently of which risk assessment approach will be used later on, one can identify the assets with a systematic consideration of the system requirements and its context. Furthermore, we provide a systematic method for identifying assets and documenting them in a model.

Asnar et al. [10] propose a methodology, namely the Goal-Risk framework, to analyze and model security problems. The methodology relies on the SI* requirements modeling language to capture stakeholders' goals, risks that might threaten the goals, and countermeasures required to mitigate the unacceptable risks. In another work, Asnar et al. [11] extend SI* with the possibility of specifying relationships on resources. In our work, we extend this work by adding an asset model to identify assets of the system. However, we consider problem-based requirements engineering instead of using goal models. Our approach, unlike these approaches, supports a systematic identification and documentation of assets and reasoning on assets' values, thus providing a valuable input (i.e., asset model) to these frameworks in order to perform further risk assessment.

There are several works that aim to consider risk assessment in early stages of the development life-cycle by providing security requirements engineering [12]. Among goal-oriented approaches, van Lamsweerde proposed a dual model composing goals and anti-goals to elaborate security requirements using KAOS [13]. Haley et al. [14] document goals of attackers for quantifying harm. The authors also use problem diagrams as input for their approach. Elahi et al. [15] enrich goal models in i* notation by including attackers and vulnerabilities. Liu et al. [16] propose also an extension of the i* framework to identify attackers, and analyze vulnerabilities through actor's dependency links. They consider all actors as potential attackers; hence, they analyze possible damages caused by actors. Matulevičius et al. [17] extend the Secure Tropos language [18] to support modeling of security risks and their countermeasures. All these approaches could use our asset model as an input for considering security requirements. Therefore, our method can be used complementary to these approaches during requirement engineering. We discuss in the present paper that an asset model should be added and linked to the requirements.

Salehie et al. [19] propose an approach to document the changes to the assets and assets' values during run-time. These changes might occur because of adding new assets to the system. Although they consider asset variability as a source of risk (e.g., by new vulnerabilities) at run-time, they do not consider a systematic modeling or identification of assets. Few other efforts on risk-adaptive solutions have also been performed (e.g., [9,20–23]). Our asset model can provide an input for their run-time consideration of assets. However, our approach does not consider detecting assets at run-time, but it allows a systematic and model-based documentation of assets at design-time. These well-structured design-time asset model provides useful information for considering adaptive risk assessment during run-time.

6   Conclusions and Future Work

In this paper, we proposed a model-based approach to create an asset model during requirements engineering. Our contribution is two-fold: First, we introduce a conceptual model to categorize assets and to express relations among different assets and stakeholders. We derived the asset classes from the ISO 27005 standard [1] and further refined those based on existing asset classes from the literature (e.g., [5,9]). To document and model assets of a system under development with a link to requirements of the system, we made use of a problem-based approach. We mapped the different elements of problem diagrams to the defined asset classes in our conceptual model.

Second, we describe a systematic method to identify assets based on the functional requirements for the software to be developed. The method includes steps for: (i) modeling of functional requirements; (ii) the elicitation of domain knowledge; (iii) the adjustment of problem diagrams; (iv) the identification of assets with regard to our conceptual model; and (v) the reasoning about valuation of assets. The final outcome of the method can be used in risk management processes that currently lack of a systematic identification of assets, e.g., the ProCOR method [8]. The model-based approach ensures consistency and traceability between the different steps of our method and the next steps of a risk management process.

We partially provide a tool that supports the application of our method, e.g., in generating the information flow graph automatically. We plan further extensions based on the defined asset model. For example, candidates for primary assets can be suggested, and the supporting assets can be identified with the existing algorithm for automated generation of the information flow graph. By integrating the conceptual model as an underlying meta-model in the tool, the supporting assets can also be classified automatically. Manual effort is still required for creating the problem diagrams, to elicit and document domain knowledge and to provide reasoning for asset values. However, the automatically generated artifacts provide guidance.

As future work, we plan to incorporate quality requirements such as privacy or reliability as an additional input for the asset identification. Since the asset valuation is an important aspect to estimate risks that need to be treated by controls, we also plan to extend our method with regard to this aspect. Furthermore, we will extend the method to identify context-dependent assets such as location, as well.

Acknowledgment. This work received funding from the EU's Horizon 2020 research and innovation programme under grant agreement 731678 (RestAssured).

References

1. ISO 27005:2011: Information technology – Security techniques – Information security risk management. Standard (2011)
2. Jackson, M.: Problem Frames: Analyzing and Structuring Software Development Problems. Addison-Wesley, Boston (2001)
3. Côté, I., Heisel, M., Schmidt, H., Hatebur, D.: UML4PF - a tool for problem-oriented requirements analysis. In: 19th IEEE International Conference on Requirements Engineering, pp. 349–350 (2011)
4. Meis, R.: Problem-based consideration of privacy-relevant domain knowledge. In: Hansen, M., Hoepman, J.-H., Leenes, R., Whitehouse, D. (eds.) Privacy and Identity 2013. IAICT, vol. 421, pp. 150–164. Springer, Heidelberg (2014). https://doi.org/10.1007/978-3-642-55137-6_12
5. RestAssured Consortium: D7.1 - RestAssured Security and Privacy Engineering Methodology (2018). https://restassuredh2020.eu/wp-content/uploads/2018/07/D7.1.pdf
6. Lund, M.S., Solhaug, B., Stølen, K.: Model-Driven Risk Analysis - The CORAS Approach. Springer, Heidelberg (2011). https://doi.org/10.1007/978-3-642-12323-8
7. Faßbender, S., Heisel, M., Meis, R.: Functional requirements under security PresSuRE. In: 9th International Conference on Software Paradigm Trends, pp. 5–16 (2014)
8. Wirtz, R., Heisel, M., Meis, R., Omerovic, A., Stølen, K.: Problem-based elicitation of security requirements - the ProCOR method. In: 13th International Conference Evaluation of Novel Approaches to Software Engineering, pp. 26–38 (2018)
9. Surridge, M., Nasser, B., Chen, X., Chakravarthy, A., Melas, P.: Run-time risk management in adaptive ICT systems. In: International Conference on Availability, Reliability and Security, pp. 102–110 (2013)
10. Asnar, Y., Li, T., Massacci, F., Paci, F.: Computer aided threat identification. In: 13th IEEE Conference on Commerce and Enterprise Computing, pp. 145–152 (2011)
11. Asnar, Y., Giorgini, P., Mylopoulos, J.: Goal-driven risk assessment in requirements engineering. Requirements Engineering 16(2), 101–116 (2011)
12. Crook, R., Ince, D., Nuseibeh, B.: Security requirements engineering: when anti-requirements hit the fan. In: Proceedings of the IEEE Joint International Conference on Requirements Engineering, pp. 203–205 (2002)
13. van Lamsweerde, A.: Elaborating security requirements by construction of intentional anti-models. In: 26th International Conference on Software Engineering, pp. 148–157 (2004)
14. Haley, C., Laney, R., Moffett, J., Nuseibeh, B.: Security requirements engineering: a framework for representation and analysis. IEEE Trans. Softw. Eng. 34(1), 133–153 (2008)
15. Elahi, G., Yu, E., Zannone, N.: A vulnerability-centric requirements engineering framework: analyzing security attacks, countermeasures, and requirements based on vulnerabilities. Requir. Eng. 15(1), 41–62 (2010)
16. Liu, L., Yu, E., Mylopoulos, J.: Security and privacy requirements analysis within a social setting. In: 11th IEEE International Conference on Requirements Engineering, pp. 151–161 (2003)
17. Matulevičius, R., Mouratidis, H., Mayer, N., Dubois, E., Heymans, P.: Syntactic and semantic extensions to secure tropos to support security risk management. J. Univ. Comput. Sci. 18(6), 816–844 (2012)

18. Mouratidis, H., Giorgini, P.: Secure tropos: a security-oriented extension of the tropos methodology. Int. J. Softw. Eng. Knowl. Eng. **17**(2), 285–309 (2007)
19. Salehie, M., Pasquale, L., Omoronyia, I., Ali, R., Nuseibeh, B.: Requirements-driven adaptive security: protecting variable assets at runtime. In: 20th IEEE International Conference Requirements Engineering, pp. 111–120 (2012)
20. Mann, Z.Á., et al.: Secure data processing in the cloud. In: Mann, Z., Stolz, V. (eds.) ESOCC 2017. CCIS, vol. 824, pp. 149–153. Springer, Heidelberg (2017). https://doi.org/10.1007/978-3-319-79090-9_10
21. Gol Mohammadi, N., Mann, Z.Á., Metzger, A., Heisel, M., Greig, J.: Towards an end-to-end architecture for run-time data protection in the cloud. In: 44th Euromicro Conference on Software Engineering and Advanced Applications, pp. 514–518 (2018)
22. Cheng, P., Rohatgi, P., Keser, C., Karger, P.A., Wagner, G.M., Reninger, A.S.: Fuzzy multi-level security: an experiment on quantified risk-adaptive access control. In: IEEE Symposium on Security and Privacy, pp. 222–230 (2007)
23. Covington, M.J., Long, W., Srinivasan, S., Dey, A.K., Ahamad, M., Abowd, G.D.: Securing context-aware applications using environment roles. In: 6th ACM Symposium on Access Control Models and Technologies, pp. 10–20 (2001)

Access Control and Permission

Inference Control in Distributed Environment: A Comparison Study

Adel Jebali[1,2(✉)], Salma Sassi[3], and Abderrazak Jemai[1,4]

[1] Faculty of Mathematical Physical and Natural Sciences of Tunis,
SERCOM Laboratory, Tunis El Manar University, 1068 Tunis, Tunisia
adel.jbali@fst.utm.tn
[2] ESPRIT School of Engineering, Tunis, Tunisia
[3] Faculty of Law Economics and Management of Jendouba, VPNC Laboratory,
Jendouba University, 8189 Jendouba, Tunisia
salma.sassi@fsjegj.rnu.tn
[4] Polytechnic School of Tunisia, SERCOM Laboratory, INSAT, Carthage University,
1080 Tunis, Tunisia
abderrazekjemai@yahoo.co.uk

Abstract. Traditional access control models aim to prevent data leakage via direct accesses. A direct access occurs when a requester performs his query directly into the desired object, however these models fail to protect sensitive data from being accessed with inference channels. An inference channel is produced by the combination of a legitimate response which the user receives from the system and metadata. Detecting and removing inference in database systems guarantee a high quality design in terms of data secrecy and privacy. Parting from the fact that data distribution exacerbates inference problem, we give in this paper a survey of the current and emerging research on the inference problem in both centralized and distributed database systems and highlighting research directions in this field.

Keywords: Access control · Inference control · External knowledge · Data distribution · Secrecy and privacy

1 Introduction

Access control models protect sensitive data from direct disclosure via direct accesses, however they fail to prevent indirect accesses [19]. Indirect accesses via inference channels occur when a malicious user combines the legitimate response that he received from the system with metadata (see Fig. 1). According to [20], external information to be combined with data in order to produce an inference channel could be database schema, system's semantics, statistical information, exceptions, error messages, user-defined functions and data dependencies. Detecting and removing inference in database systems guarantee a high quality

© Springer Nature Switzerland AG 2020
S. Kallel et al. (Eds.): CRiSIS 2019, LNCS 12026, pp. 69–83, 2020.
https://doi.org/10.1007/978-3-030-41568-6_5

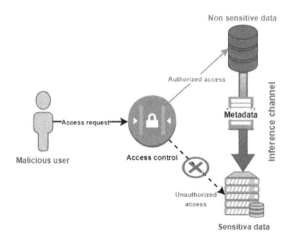

Fig. 1. Bypass access control with inference channels

design in terms of data secrecy and privacy since the latter is considered as a new vision of the inference problem [46]. Absolutely, this diversity of techniques to bypass access control mechanisms with inference channels has attracted considerable attention in recent years. A growing body of literature has examined the inference problem but no one of those proposed solutions seemed to be a viable method to resolve the problem. In reality, for each of the underlying techniques a specific solution has been proposed for handling each particular attack. There is consensus among security community that data distribution exacerbates inference problem. This is why several attempts have been done in the last two decades to address this problem. This paper investigates current and emerging research on the inference control in centralized database systems, then it highlights inference in distributed environment. The reminder of this paper is organized as follows: Sect. 2 gives a trade-off between access control and inference control. Section 3 provides a brief description of research efforts on controlling inference in centralized database systems. In Sect. 4, we review works on the inference control in distributed environment. Research directions are given in Sect. 5. Finally, we conclude in Sect. 6.

2   Access Control vs Inference Control

Traditional access control models aim to prevent data leakage via direct accesses. A direct access occurs when a requester poses his query directly on the desired object. However, these models fail to protect sensitive data from being accessed via indirect accesses [19]. To deal with such situation, several works have augmented access control mechanisms with an inference engine in order to control both direct and indirect accesses. Although access control and inference control share the same goal of preventing data from unauthorized disclosure, they differ in several fundamental aspects [27]. We give in Table 1 the major differences between them. According to our comparison Table 1, we can note that access control is more preferable than inference control from a complexity perspective. Consequently, several researchers have attempted to replace inference control engines with access control mechanisms. We refer the interested reader to [7, 8, 27]. The discussion of these approaches is out of the scope of this paper.

Table 1. Access control vs inference control

Access control	Inference control
Direct access control	Indirect access control
Deterministic	Related to stochastic channels
Static: through a set of rules	Dynamic: vary through time and influenced by user action and queries
Normal expensive	More expensive then access control
Computational efficiency and high accuracy of security control	Efficiency and accuracy less than access control
Modular: can cover distributed environment	Adaptability to data distribution requires complicated techniques

3 Inference Control in Centralized Database Systems

Classical access control models have not been designed to protect data from inference. These models have been only designed to protect data from direct accesses. An inference problem (also called inference aggregation problem) occurs when a user deduces sensitive information from a sequence of innocuous information in the database. It has been widely investigated in the literature since 1987 with the emergence of multilevel database systems. The first works in this field are presented in [30, 39, 42].

In [42], authors have augmented the relational database with an inference engine, this module acts as an intermediary between the queries and the database. The inference engine resorts to first order logic to represent queries, security constraints, environment information and real world information. Hence, the current query is converted into a first order logic expression by the inference engine and then compared against the database constraints to determine if the query could lead to security constraint violation. If this is the case, and the query is identified as suspicious, then it will be rejected. Otherwise it will be converted to relational algebra and forwarded to the DBMS for execution. Results returning from the database are assigned a classification label to ensure the absence of unauthorized disclosure.

Morgenstern [30] presents a framework for inference analysis and detection during design and classification of data in multilevel database. The proposed methodology aims to anticipate the inference channels in order to classify data.

Hence, the author introduced the classification process as a constraint satisfaction, then he provided a concept called sphere of influence (SOI) to restrict the scope of possible inferences. In order to prevent these inference channels (consisting of a set of objects) from being achieved, he presented the following solutions: safety classification level which consists of increasing the security clearance of an inferred object to an appropriate classification. Besides, a data sanitization process which consists of imposing aggregation classification on the set and classifies the aggregation in a way that the whole aggregate cannot be inferred from the individual values given to a lower level user. Furthermore, a third solution was introduced aiming to disturb the inference channels and prevent precise inference from being revealed by adding noise data.

The work in [39] investigates the inference problem due to functional dependencies (FD) and multivalued dependencies (MVD) in multilevel relational databases with attributes and records classification schemes. For inference channels produced by functional dependencies, authors proposed a level adjustment algorithm to adjust attributes level with minimum information loss so that FD compromises are avoided. In the case of inference channels with MVD, authors introduced a level adjustment algorithm that adjusts security levels of tuples in relation instance to eliminate MVD compromises. However, there are some shortcomings to mention in this work. Firstly, the inference algorithms are given for each type of dependency separately but not when they are present together. Secondly, authors consider only two types of dependencies, FD and MVD. Thirdly, the access control granularity is restricted to tuple level and single-attribute level. Finally, since their solution for eliminating a detected inference channel is based on increasing the classification level of individual attributes, it restricts the availability of data.

3.1   Inference Attacks

According to [19], there are three types of inference attack:

- **Statistical attacks:** it is considered with statistical databases. The security breaches occur when confidential information about an individual is obtained by correlating different statistics while the security requirement is to provide access to statics about groups of entities while protecting the confidentiality of the individual entities [17].
- **Semantic attacks:** they aim to produce inference channels to bypass an access control model. In this type of attack, semantic relationship between data is used to infer sensitive information. There exist three ways to produce a semantic inference attack including: inference from constraints on queries, inference resulting from the combination of data with metadata and inference from value constraints (constraints defined over data).
- **Inference due to data mining:** data mining is considered as one of the most used techniques for knowledge discovery and process. Nevertheless, it is considered as a double-edged weapon. From the one hand there is a consensus for the importance of data mining in data engineering and knowledge

discovery. On the other hand, through its mining algorithms, data mining can produce inference channels if the privacy of users is not respected.

For each of the mentioned techniques, researchers have devoted a lot of efforts to deal with inference problem. For statistical attacks, techniques like *Anonymization* and *Data-perturbation* have been developed to protect data from indirect access. For security threats based on data mining, techniques like *privacy-preserving data mining* and *Privacy-preserving data publishing* was carried out. Furthermore, a lot of works have investigated the semantic attacks [10, 12, 28, 39].

3.2   Inference Prevention Methods

There exist in the literature more than one criteria to classify approaches that deal with inference. One proposed criteria is to classify these approaches according to data level and schema level [50]. In such classification, inference constraints are classified into schema constraints level and data constraints level. Another criteria could be according to the time when the inference control techniques are performed. According to this criteria, the proposed approaches are classified in three categories: design time, query run time and at update time.

Design time approaches are considered as proactive techniques. They argue that since the inference problem is a resources consuming task, it is better to achieve all consuming processing offline before the system is executed. Moreover, since the inference is examined at a conceptual level in this approaches, detecting an inference channel is called second path detection (characterized as multiple paths between two attributes such that the path's security levels are inconsistent). In fact, these approaches exploit semantic relationship between data and graphs to detect the second path (the inference channel). When an inference channel is detected, either the classification level of the inferred attributes is increased or the database schema is modified to block the inference channel from being achieved. Approaches that deal with inference at design time are found in [16, 24–26, 28, 32, 33, 39, 40, 47].

Run time inference control techniques belong to reactive categories. These approaches aim to detect and block inference channel at query run time. For this purpose, the DBMS should be augmented with an inference engine to control the queries executed by the users against the database. The run time approaches are history-based since they combine the query executed by the user with the set of queries previously executed by the same user in addition to a set of semantic constraints to determine if the current query could lead to an inference channel. Several approaches supporting run time have been developed in the past [4, 10, 12, 41, 42]. It is important to note that users can collaborate to produce an inference channel based on the query sequences of collaborators. This problem was addressed in [13] where the authors have developed a query-time inference violation detection model to evaluate collaborative inference based on the query sequences of collaborators and their task-sensitive collaboration levels. Besides, the work in [20] presents a database inference controller in the presence of probabilistic dependencies. Authors of [20] have developed a formal language called ATKLOG providing an expressive and concise way to represent attacker's beliefs during their interaction with the system. By leveraging to this formal language, they developed AGERONA a secure inference controller mechanism to prevent the disclosure of sensitive information in presence of probabilistic dependencies.

In addition to design time and query run time categories, inference control can be performed at update time. To the best of our knowledge this problem was only tackled in [43]. In this work, authors have built on [10] to introduce a Dynamic Disclosure Monitor to prevent illegal inferences via database constraints at update time while maximizing data availability. The authors have developed a module called *Update Consolidator* which uses the user's history file in addition to database updates and database constraints to produce a new history file that does not contain any outdated data values. Then by resorting to *Update Consolidator* and *Disclosure Monitor*, the proposed approach guarantees completeness and soundness properties of the inference algorithm (data security and data availability) in the presence of updates. Furthermore, the authors show through the experimental results how their framework can handle collaborative inference.

3.3   Discussion of the Inference Prevention Methods

The purpose of inference control at design time is to detect inference channels from earliest stage and eliminate them. These approaches provide a better performance for the system since no monitoring module is needed when the users query the database, by consequence improving query execution time. Nevertheless, design time approaches are too restrictive and may lead to over classification of the data. Besides, it requires that the designer has a good concept of how the system will be utilized. On the other hand, run time approaches provide data availability since they monitor the suspicious queries at run time. However, run time approaches lead to performance degradation of the database server since every query needs to be checked by the inference engine. Furthermore, the inference engine needs to manage a huge number of log files and users. As a result, this could induce slowing down query processing. In addition, run time approaches could induce a non deterministic access control behavior (users with the same privileges may not get the same response).

By the end, we can conclude that the main evaluation criteria of these techniques is a trade-off between availability and system performance. Some works have been elaborated to overcome these problems especially for run time approaches. Example in [49] a new paradigm of inference control with trusted computing was developed to push the inference control from server side to client side in order to mitigate the bottleneck on the database server. Furthermore, in [38] the authors have developed a run time inference control techniques while retaining fast query processing. The idea behind this work was to make query processing time depends on the length of the inference channel instead of user query history. We assert that the distribution of the data exacerbates the inference and privacy problems. In the next section we investigate the inference problem in distributed environment.

4   Inference Control in Distributed Environment

Inference control in distributed environment have been investigated from early 2000 until now. This field of study has received the intention from researchers in database security, due to the fact that distribution aggravates inference problems and privacy concerns. In this section, we start by investigating research efforts on inference prevention in distributed database systems, then we introduce how inference channels occur in data integration systems through a case study and review different works for mitigating inference in such architecture. We survey inference problem in data integration systems through the *Mediator/Wrapper* architecture for the reason that this is the most suitable design to access distributed, heterogeneous and autonomous data sources. Additionally, we highlight inference prevention methods in data outsourcing scenario. We note that inference attacks and prevention methods destined for centralized database systems remain applicable for distributed environment.

4.1   Inference Control in Distributed Database Systems

In [11], the authors have considered the inference problem where the data is combined from distributed database and released to the final users. In this situation of data dissemination, problem arises when non-sensitive attributes compromise sensitive attributes. According to presented work, one technique to mitigate inference is by modifying the non-sensitive data in the database. Nevertheless, even with this modification, sensitive attributes still deducible when data from other databases is incorporated. For example, consider a database containing an attribute aids classified as sensitive. In addition, consider another database containing information about drug abuse, one can deduce from the two databases that drug abuser's injections may lead an individual to contract aids. As a result, the history of drug injection (which is considered non-sensitive), allows to infer with a higher chance if a user is contracted with aids or not even the diagnosis has not been released. In order to mitigate the occurrence of inference, the authors proposed a mechanism called *Relational Downgrader* that exploits Bayesian network to reason about probabilistic dependencies relationships among attributes of the distributed database systems. The Downgrader is composed of three components: the GUARD, the Decision Maker and the Parsimonious Downgrader. The main idea behind this framework is to not release certain non-sensitive information that can lead to probabilistic inference about the sensitive information while minimizing the loss of functionality. Consequently, the outputs of the Downgrade are records that have been modified in order to anonymize sensitive attributes.

The authors of [44] have built on [11] to develop a work turning around inference prevention in distributed database systems. They proposed an inference prevention approach that enables each of the database in a distributed system to keep track of probabilistic dependencies with other databases and by consequence use that information to help preserve the confidentiality of sensitive data. The methodology is called "Agent-based" because every node in the distributed system is augmented with an agent to keep track of other nodes so that single point of failure and communication bottleneck are avoided. The principle of this framework is the following: in the first phase a *Rule Generator* is developed to reflect the probability dependency relationship among the databases by the construction of a *Bayesian Network* that preserves the individual database dependencies and take into consideration dependencies between autonomous databases. Then, a set of rules are derived from the trained Bayesian Net by analyzing the inference of the sensitive target attributes. In the next phase, an agent (which is considered as a downgrader) is attached to each machine in the distributed system. This agent blocks the inference in the local machine and the inference from several distributed machines by keeping track of these machines. However, this approach have some limits. It treats the case where the distributed databases are overlapped (similar or have common attributes). Moreover, it assumes that the records in the distributed databases share the same keys constraints.

Inference problem have been also investigated in Peer-to-Peer environment through the work in [29]. The authors pinpoint the inference that occurs in homogeneous peer agent through distributed data mining and call this process peer-to-peer agent-based data mining systems. They assert that performing Distributed Data Mining (DDM) in such extremely open distributed systems exacerbates data privacy and security issues. As a matter of fact, inference occurs in DDM when one or more peer sites learn any confidential information (model, patterns, or data themselves) about the dataset owned by other peers during a data mining session. The authors firstly classified inference attacks in DDM in two categories:

- **Inside Attack Scenario:** it occurs when a peer try to infer sensitive information from other peers in the same mining group. Depending on the number of attackers the authors distinguishes single attack (when one peer behaves maliciously) and coalition attack (when many sites collude ta attack one site). Moreover, a probe attack was introduced by the authors, which is independent of the number of peers participating in the attack.
- **Outside Attack Scenario:** it takes place when a set of malicious peer try to infer useful information from other peers in a different mining group. In this case eavesdropping channel attack is performed by malicious peers to steal information from other peers.

After identifying DDM inference attacks, the authors propose an algorithm to control potential attacks (inside and outside attacks) to particular schema for homogeneous distributed clustering, known as *KDEC*. The main idea behind this algorithm is to reconstruct the data from the kernel density estimates since a malicious peer can use the reconstruction algorithm to infer non-local data. However, the algorithm proposed by the authors need to be improved from an accuracy point to expose further possible weakness of the KDEC schema.

4.2   Inference Control in Data Integration Systems

Inference control in data integration systems have been investigated in the last decade through the work of [22,34,36]. In such systems, a mediator is defined as a unique entry point to the distributed data sources. It provides to the user a unique view of the distributed data. From a security point of view, access control is a major challenge in this situation. two major security issues has been studied in this field: access control policies integration [1,2,6,14,15,21,31,35] and inference problem [22,34,36]. In the former, researchers aim to enforce a global security policy which is deduced from the back-end data sources in addition to possibly enforcing additional security properties. In this situation, the global policy must comply with the source policies. Figure 2 reports that complying with source policies means that a prohibited access at the source level should be also prohibited at the global level. [22,34,36] have demonstrated that despite the generation of a global policy at the mediator level that synthesizes and enforces the back-end data sources policies, security breaches still possible via inference channel produced by semantic constraints (data dependencies). The problem is that the system (or the designer of the system) cannot anticipates the inference channels that arise due to the dependencies that appear at the mediator level. To the best of our knowledge, all the works that deal with inference problem in data integration systems are performed at query run time or at the global policy design time.

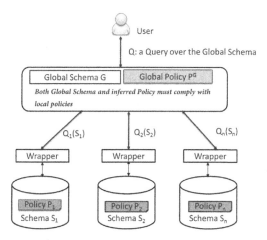

Fig. 2. Secure data integration system

The first work attempting to control inference in data integration systems was introduced in [22]. The authors propose an incremental approach to prevent inference with functional dependencies. The proposed methodology includes three steps:

- **Synthesizing global policies:** derives the authorization rule of each virtual relation individually by the way that it preserves the local authorization of the local relations involved in the virtual relation.
- **Detection phase:** by resorting to a graph based approach, this step aims at identifying all the violations that could occur using functional dependencies. Such violation is called violating transaction consisting of a series of innocuous queries when it is achieved leads to violation of authorization rule.
- **Reconfiguration phase:** in this phase the author proposes two methods to forbid the completion of each transaction violation. The first one uses a historic-based access control by keeping track of previous queries to evaluate the current query (this method is considered as a run-time approach). The second one proposes to reconfigure the global authorization policies at the mediator level in a way that no authorization violation will occur (this method is considered at design-time of the global security policy).

In this work, the authors have discussed only semantic constraints due to functional dependencies. Neither inclusion nor multivalued dependencies was investigated. Besides, other mapping approaches need to be discussed such as LAV and GLAV approaches.

The authors of [36] have been inspired by [22] to propose an approach aiming to control inference in data integration systems. The proposed methodology resorts to formal concept analysis as a formal framework to reason about authorization rules and functional dependencies as a source of inference. The authors adopt an access control model with authorization views and propose an incremental approach with three steps:

- **Generation of the global policy, global schema and global FD:** this step takes as input a set of source schema together with their access control policies and starts by translating the schema and policies to formal contexts. Then, the global policy is generated in a way that the source rules are preserved at the global level. Next the schema of the mediator (virtual relations) is generated from the global policy to avoid useless attributes combination (every attributes in the mediator schema is controlled by the global policy). Finally, a global FD is considered from the source FD as a formal context.
- **Identifying disclosure transactions:** by resorting to FCA as a framework to reason about the global policy, the authors identifies the profiles to be denied from accessing sensitive attributes at the mediator level. Then, they extract the violating transaction by reasoning about the Global FD.
- **Reconfiguration phase:** this step is achieved by two ways. At design time with a policy healing consisting to complete the global policy with additional rules in order that no violating transaction is achieved. At query run time with a monitoring engine to prohibit suspicious queries.

In [34] the authors have examined inference that arise in the web through RDF store. They propose a fine-grained framework for RDF data, then they exploit close graph to verify the consistency propriety of an access control policy when inference rules and authorization rules interact. Without accessing the data (at policy design-time), the authors propose an algorithm to verify if an information leakage will arise given a policy P and a set of inference rules R. Furthermore, the authors demonstrate the applicability of the access control model using a conflict resolution strategy (most specific takes precedence).

4.3 Inference and Data Outsourcing

The Inference problem was not only investigated in previous distribution scenarios but also in data outsourcing. In this case, data owners place their data among cloud service providers in order to increase flexibility, optimize storage, enhance data manipulation and decrease processing time. Nonetheless, data security is widely recognized as a major barrier to cloud computing and other data outsourcing or Database-As-a-Service arrangements. Users are reluctant to place their sensitive data in the cloud due to concerns about data disclosure to potentially untrusted cloud providers and other malicious part [48]. It is from this perspective that inference problem was investigated in [9,45].

In [9] authors resort to a Controlled Query Evaluation strategy (CQE) to detect inference based on the knowledge of non-confidential informations contained in the outsourced fragments and priori knowledge that a malicious user might have. Regarding that CQE relies on logic-oriented view on database systems, the main idea of this approach is to model fragmentation logic-oriented too allowing for inference proofness to be proved formally even the semantic database constraints that an attacker may hold. Besides, vertical database fragmentation technique was considered by authors in [45] to ensure data confidentiality in presence of data dependencies among attributes. Those dependencies allow unauthorized users to deduce informations about sensitive attributes. In this work, three types of confidentiality violations that can be caused by data dependencies were defined: firstly when a sensitive attribute or association is exposed by the attributes in a fragment. Secondly, if An attribute appearing in a fragment is also derivable from some attributes in another fragment, thus enabling linkability among such fragments, and thirdly when an attribute is derivable (independently) from attributes appearing in different fragments, thus enabling linkability among these fragments. To tackle these issues, authors reformulate the problem graphically through an hyper-graph representation and then compute the closure of a fragmentation by deducing all information derivable from its fragments via dependencies to identify indirect access. Nevertheless, the major limit of this approach is that it explores the problem only in single relational database.

5   Research Directions

Since the discussed works are recent, there are a number of concepts associated to security policies, privacy, data distribution and semantic constraints which could be considered to ensure better security and prevent inference from occurring in distributed environment. Hence, there are many research directions to pursue:

- Absence of modularity in data integration systems: in the case where a new source joins the system it is necessary to revise the global schema and the global policy. This is not suitable for distributed environment where the source joins and leaves the system continuously (e.g. Mobile environment).
- Authors deal only with semantic constraints represented by functional dependencies and probabilistic dependencies as a source of inference. However, other semantic constraints, example inclusion dependencies, join dependencies and multivalued dependencies should be considered as sources of inference.
- In data integration scenario, all approaches aim to handle inference at query run time by keeping track of the history of user queries and the current query. In the case where the system deals with a large volume of data and users number, run time approaches will lead to performance degradation by slowing down query processing, consequently, this may push the server (mediator) to bottleneck. Hence, design time approach should be adopted to overcome these problems since it is performed offline.
- Another weakness in these approaches is the negligence of collaborative inference. In fact, authors propose to block a sequence of violating transaction from being achieved to prevent the inference channel, but, what if this violating transactions results from a combination of a set of queries from more than one user?
- Functional dependencies should be considered as a source of inference in data outsourcing scenario. Although data dependencies may resemble functional dependencies, they model a different concept. In future work, we will present a study aiming to prevent inference from occurring in distributed cloud database. Our approach is graph-based that firstly detects inference channels caused by functional dependencies and secondly breaks those channels by exploiting vertical database fragmentation while minimizing dependencies loss.

6   Conclusion

This paper has surveyed the inference problem from two perspectives: centralized and distributed design. We first gave a review of current and emerging research about the inference control in centralized database systems, we have introduced different inference attacks and their prevention methods and discussed the trade-off between them. Furthermore, an insightful discussion about inference control in distributed environment was provided. We also pinpoint potential issues that are still unresolved. These issues are expected to be addressed in future work.

References

1. Akeel, F., Fathabadi, A.S., Paci, F., Gravell, A., Wills, G.: Formal modelling of data integration systems security policies. Data Sci. Eng. 1(3), 139–148 (2016)
2. Akeel, F.Y., Wills, G.B., Gravell, A.M.: Exposing data leakage in data integration systems. In: 2014 9th International Conference for Internet Technology and Secured Transactions (ICITST), pp. 420–425. IEEE (2014)

3. An, X., Jutla, D., Cercone, N.: Auditing and inference control for privacy preservation in uncertain environments. In: Havinga, P., Lijding, M., Meratnia, N., Wegdam, M. (eds.) EuroSSC 2006. LNCS, vol. 4272, pp. 159–173. Springer, Heidelberg (2006). https://doi.org/10.1007/11907503_12

4. An, X., Jutla, D., Cercone, N.: Dynamic inference control in privacy preference enforcement. In: Proceedings of the 2006 International Conference on Privacy, Security and Trust: Bridge the Gap Between PST Technologies and Business Services, p. 24. ACM (2006)

5. Bahloul, S.N., Coquery, E., Hacid, M.S.: Access control to materialized views: an inference-based approach. In: Proceedings of the 2011 Joint EDBT/ICDT Ph. D. Workshop, pp. 19–24. ACM (2011)

6. Bahloul, S.N., Coquery, E., Hacid, M.S.: Securing materialized views: a rewriting-based approach. In: 29emes Journées BDA, pp. 1–25 (2013)

7. Biskup, J., Embley, D.W., Lochner, J.H.: Reducing inference control to access control for normalized database schemas. Inf. Process. Lett. **106**(1), 8–12 (2008)

8. Biskup, J., Hartmann, S., Link, S., Lochner, J.-H.: Efficient inference control for open relational queries. In: Foresti, S., Jajodia, S. (eds.) DBSec 2010. LNCS, vol. 6166, pp. 162–176. Springer, Heidelberg (2010). https://doi.org/10.1007/978-3-642-13739-6_11

9. Biskup, J., Preuß, M., Wiese, L.: On the inference-proofness of database fragmentation satisfying confidentiality constraints. In: Lai, X., Zhou, J., Li, H. (eds.) ISC 2011. LNCS, vol. 7001, pp. 246–261. Springer, Heidelberg (2011). https://doi.org/10.1007/978-3-642-24861-0_17

10. Brodsky, A., Farkas, C., Jajodia, S.: Secure databases: constraints, inference channels, and monitoring disclosures. IEEE Trans. Knowl. Data Eng. **12**(6), 900–919 (2000)

11. Chang, L.W., Moskowitz, I.: A study of inference problems in distributed databases. In: Gudes, E., Shenoi, S. (eds.) Research Directions in Data and Applications Security. ITIFIP, vol. 128, pp. 191–204. Springer, Boston, MA (2003). https://doi.org/10.1007/978-0-387-35697-6_15

12. Chen, Y., Chu, W.W.: Database security protection via inference detection. In: Mehrotra, S., Zeng, D.D., Chen, H., Thuraisingham, B., Wang, F.-Y. (eds.) ISI 2006. LNCS, vol. 3975, pp. 452–458. Springer, Heidelberg (2006). https://doi.org/10.1007/11760146_40

13. Chen, Y., Chu, W.W.: Protection of database security via collaborative inference detection. In: Chen, H., Yang, C.C. (eds.) Intelligence and Security Informatics. SCI, vol. 135, pp. 275–303. Springer, Heidelberg (2008). https://doi.org/10.1007/978-3-540-69209-6_15

14. Clifton, C., et al.: Privacy-preserving data integration and sharing. In: Proceedings of the 9th ACM SIGMOD Workshop on Research Issues in Data Mining and Knowledge Discovery, pp. 19–26. ACM (2004)

15. Cuzzocrea, A., Hacid, M.S., Grillo, N.: Effectively and efficiently selecting access control rules on materialized views over relational databases. In: Proceedings of the Fourteenth International Database Engineering & Applications Symposium, pp. 225–235. ACM (2010)

16. Delugach, H.S., Hinke, T.H.: Wizard: a database inference analysis and detection system. IEEE Trans. Knowl. Data Eng. **8**(1), 56–66 (1996)

17. Domingo-Ferrer, J.: Advances in inference control in statistical databases: an overview. In: Domingo-Ferrer, J. (ed.) Inference Control in Statistical Databases. LNCS, vol. 2316, pp. 1–7. Springer, Heidelberg (2002). https://doi.org/10.1007/3-540-47804-3_1

18. Fan, W., Geerts, F., Li, J., Xiong, M.: Discovering conditional functional dependencies. IEEE Trans. Knowl. Data Eng. **23**(5), 683–698 (2011)
19. Farkas, C., Jajodia, S.: The inference problem: a survey. ACM SIGKDD Explor. Newslett. **4**(2), 6–11 (2002)
20. Guarnieri, M., Marinovic, S., Basin, D.: Securing databases from probabilistic inference. In: 2017 IEEE 30th Computer Security Foundations Symposium (CSF), pp. 343–359. IEEE (2017)
21. Haddad, M., Hacid, M.S., Laurini, R.: Data integration in presence of authorization policies. In: 2012 IEEE 11th International Conference on Trust, Security and Privacy in Computing and Communications (TrustCom), pp. 92–99. IEEE (2012)
22. Haddad, M., Stevovic, J., Chiasera, A., Velegrakis, Y., Hacid, M.-S.: Access control for data integration in presence of data dependencies. In: Bhowmick, S.S., Dyreson, C.E., Jensen, C.S., Lee, M.L., Muliantara, A., Thalheim, B. (eds.) DASFAA 2014. LNCS, vol. 8422, pp. 203–217. Springer, Cham (2014). https://doi.org/10.1007/978-3-319-05813-9_14
23. Hale, J., Shenoi, S.: Catalytic inference analysis: detecting inference threats due to knowledge discovery. In: Proceedings of the 1997 IEEE Symposium on Security and Privacy, pp. 188–199. IEEE (1997)
24. Hinke, T.H.: Inference aggregation detection in database management systems. In: Proceedings of the 1988 IEEE Symposium on Security and Privacy, pp. 96–106. IEEE (1988)
25. Hinke, T.H., Delugach, H.S.: AERIE: an inference modeling and detection approach for databases. In: Sixth Working Conference on Database Security, p. 187 (1992)
26. Hinke, T.H., Delugach, H.S., Wolf, R.P.: Protecting databases from inference attacks. Comput. Secur. **16**(8), 687–708 (1997)
27. Katos, V., Vrakas, D., Katsaros, P.: A framework for access control with inference constraints. In: 2011 IEEE 35th Annual Computer Software and Applications Conference (COMPSAC), pp. 289–297. IEEE (2011)
28. Landwehr, C., Jajodia, S.: The use of conceptual structures for handling the inference problem (1992)
29. de Mantaras, R.L., Saina, L.: Inference attacks in peer-to-peer homogeneous distributed data mining. In: 16th European Conference on Artificial Intelligence, ECAI 2004, 22–27 August 2004, Valencia, Spain: Including Prestigious Applicants [sic] of Intelligent Systems (PAIS 2004): Proceedings, vol. 110, p. 450. IOS Press (2004)
30. Morgenstern, M.: Controlling logical inference in multilevel database systems. In: Proceedings of the 1988 IEEE Symposium on Security and Privacy, pp. 245–255. IEEE (1988)
31. Nait-Bahloul, S., Coquery, E., Hacid, M.-S.: Authorization policies for materialized views. In: Gritzalis, D., Furnell, S., Theoharidou, M. (eds.) SEC 2012. IAICT, vol. 376, pp. 525–530. Springer, Heidelberg (2012). https://doi.org/10.1007/978-3-642-30436-1_43
32. Qian, X., Stickel, M.E., Karp, P.D., Lunt, T.F., Garvey, T.D.: Detection and elimination of inference channels in multilevel relational database systems. In: Proceedings of 1993 IEEE Computer Society Symposium on Research in Security and Privacy, pp. 196–205. IEEE (1993)
33. Rath, S., Jones, D., Hale, J., Shenoi, S.: A tool for inference detection and knowledge discovery in databases. In: Spooner, D.L., Demurjian, S.A., Dobson, J.E. (eds.) Database Security IX. IAICT, pp. 317–332. Springer, Boston (1996). https://doi.org/10.1007/978-0-387-34932-9_20

34. Sayah, T., Coquery, E., Thion, R., Hacid, M.-S.: Inference leakage detection for authorization policies over RDF data. In: Samarati, P. (ed.) DBSec 2015. LNCS, vol. 9149, pp. 346–361. Springer, Cham (2015). https://doi.org/10.1007/978-3-319-20810-7_24

35. Sellami, M., Gammoudi, M.M., Hacid, M.S.: Secure data integration: a formal concept analysis based approach. In: Decker, H., Lhotská, L., Link, S., Spies, M., Wagner, R.R. (eds.) DEXA 2014. LNCS, vol. 8645, pp. 326–333. Springer, Cham (2014). https://doi.org/10.1007/978-3-319-10085-2_30

36. Sellami, M., Hacid, M.-S., Gammoudi, M.M.: Inference control in data integration systems. In: Debruyne, C., et al. (eds.) OTM 2015. LNCS, vol. 9415, pp. 285–302. Springer, Cham (2015). https://doi.org/10.1007/978-3-319-26148-5_17

37. Shafer, G.: Detecting inference attacks using association rules (2001)

38. Staddon, J.: Dynamic inference control. In: Proceedings of the 8th ACM SIGMOD Workshop on Research Issues in Data Mining and Knowledge Discovery, pp. 94–100. ACM (2003)

39. Su, T.A., Ozsoyoglu, G.: Controlling FD and MVD inferences in multilevel relational database systems. IEEE Trans. Knowl. Data Eng. **3**(4), 474–485 (1991)

40. Thuraisingham, B.: Handling security constraints during multilevel database design. In: Burns, R. (ed.) Research Directions zn Database Securt (v, IV, Mitre Technical report, M92B0000 118, Mitre Corp., McLean, Va (1992)

41. Thuraisingham, B., Ford, W., Collins, M., O'Keeffe, J.: Design and implementation of a database inference controller. Data Knowl. Eng. **11**(3), 271–297 (1993)

42. Thuraisingham, M.: Security checking in relational database management systems augmented with inference engines. Comput. Secur. **6**(6), 479–492 (1987)

43. Toland, T.S., Farkas, C., Eastman, C.M.: The inference problem: maintaining maximal availability in the presence of database updates. Comput. Secur. **29**(1), 88–103 (2010)

44. Tracy, J., Chang, L., Moskowitz, I.S.: An agent-based approach to inference prevention in distributed database systems. Int. J. Artif. Intell. Tools **12**(03), 297–313 (2003)

45. di Vimercati, S.D.C., Foresti, S., Jajodia, S., Livraga, G., Paraboschi, S., Samarati, P.: Fragmentation in presence of data dependencies. IEEE Trans. Dependable Secure Comput. **11**(6), 510–523 (2014)

46. Wang, H., Liu, R.: Privacy-preserving publishing microdata with full functional dependencies. Data Knowl. Eng. **70**(3), 249–268 (2011). https://doi.org/10.1016/j.datak.2010.11.002, http://www.sciencedirect.com/science/article/pii/S0169023X10001291

47. Wang, J., Yang, J., Guo, F., Min, H.: Resist the database intrusion caused by functional dependency. In: 2017 International Conference on Cyber-Enabled Distributed Computing and Knowledge Discovery (CyberC), pp. 54–57. IEEE (2017)

48. Xu, X., Xiong, L., Liu, J.: Database fragmentation with confidentiality constraints: a graph search approach. In: Proceedings of the 5th ACM Conference on Data and Application Security and Privacy, pp. 263–270. ACM (2015)

49. Yang, Y., Li, Y., Deng, R.H.: New paradigm of inference control with trusted computing. In: Barker, S., Ahn, G.-J. (eds.) DBSec 2007. LNCS, vol. 4602, pp. 243–258. Springer, Heidelberg (2007). https://doi.org/10.1007/978-3-540-73538-0_18

50. Yip, R.W., Levitt, E.: Data level inference detection in database systems. In: 1998 Proceedings of 11th IEEE Computer Security Foundations Workshop, pp. 179–189. IEEE (1998)

MAPPER: Mapping Application Description to Permissions

Rajendra Kumar Solanki[1](✉), Vijay Laxmi[1](✉), and Manoj Singh Gaur[1,2](✉)

[1] Malaviya National Institute of Technology Jaipur, Jaipur, India
rajendra.kr.solanki@gmail.com, vlgaur@gmail.com, gaurms@gmail.com
[2] Indian Institute of Technology Jammu, Jammu, India

Abstract. Android operating system has seen phenomenal growth, and Android Applications (Apps) have proliferated into mainstream usage across the globe. Are users informed by the developers about everything an App does when they consent to install an App from Google's Play Store? In this paper, we propose a technique called MAPPER which aggregates the App permissions with the textual description for more precise App permissions enumeration. We focus on whether the application description fully describes permissions an App will ask and whether the user is made aware of those possible capabilities to take informed decision to install or not to install the App. We investigate permissions inferred from application descriptions and permissions declared in the Android manifest files of 1100+ Android applications. MAPPER prototype finds a large number of Apps live on Google's Play Store which do not inform users about permissions, more than three-fourths of them are over-privileged from this perspective, and their application descriptions need revision. Our work can be used by App developers also to educate users in a better way.

Keywords: Android · Application description · Over-privileged · Permissions

1 Introduction

In the recent decade or so, the third platform has become a default choice for service delivery. Users have adopted mobile phones as a primary device for accessing applications [1]. A vast majority of credit is can be attributed to the phenomenal growth and commercial success of Android operating system since 2009 [2,3]. Android-powered devices have outnumbered offerings from other players in the mobile platform operating system [4]. With this growth, Android platform has also become an easy target for malware writers who have published Potentially Harmful Applications (PHAs). Recent data breaches [5] and incidents like Facebook-Cambridge Analytica [6] show that organizations are not doing enough to protect user's Personally Identifiable Information (PII). Many organizations are forced to update their Privacy Policy [7] due to push by regulations such as Global Data Protection Regulation (GDPR). GDPR regulates how

© Springer Nature Switzerland AG 2020
S. Kallel et al. (Eds.): CRiSIS 2019, LNCS 12026, pp. 84–98, 2020.
https://doi.org/10.1007/978-3-030-41568-6_6

user's personal data is collected, stored, and processed. GDPR also mandates giving control to users over their personal data [8].

It is not trivial to classify an Android App as leaking Personally Identifiable Information (PII) or written with malicious behaviour or developed as a genuine application for the target audience with the intended purpose only. It is well documented in the literature that malicious Apps over-declare permissions in Android Apps [16]. Every Android App on Play Store [31] has a full description displayed on the website. This App description at Play Store describes what an App can do when it executes. Since Google does not provide a formal execution specification for an Android App, we use this Application Description as a proxy for Execution Specification of an Android App. Android App should describe all its capabilities, and in Android, they are governed by the permission-based security model [19–22]. A novice user may not know or understand the nuances of Android permissions and permission groups while installing an App. Not all user can judge or decide upon all permissions an App is interested in when they consent to all permissions being asked for. Informed users will deny specific

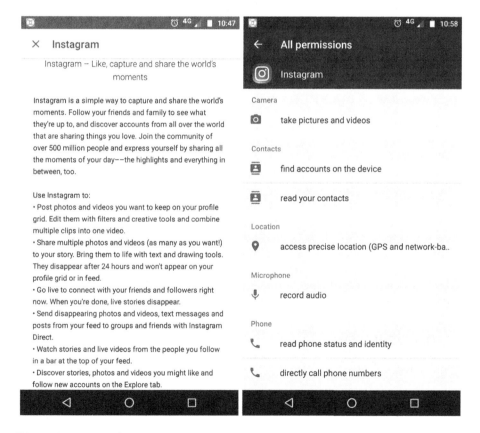

Fig. 1. Instagram App asking permission "directly call phone numbers" without any mention in its Application Description

permissions if they know what the App is asking for [16,17]. A majority of users are most likely to trust what an App says - what it can do when it executes. This App Description can help potential users to make an informed decision about not to install or to install and be aware of the risk involved. We advocate for a more dependable and usable application description to assist a permission-based security model.

In this work, we study Application Description of Android Apps live on Play Store and permissions declared inside Android Manifest file [23] in their APK file. We find that some of the most popular Apps on the Play Store (see Fig. 1) are not making it explicit about all permissions they are declaring. Developers or malware writers may use these extra-permissions for malicious purposes. In this example, Instagram App has not made it explicit that it may "directly call phone numbers". Our prototype MAPPER can be used to signal such excess permissions declared by Apps on Play Store.

The remainder of this paper is organized as follows. In Sect. 2, we present the detailed design of our prototype MAPPER, how data was collected and processed. In Sect. 3, we describe how the MAPPER prototype is evaluated, and the results are presented. In Sect. 4, we discuss a few case studies, limitations and future directions. Finally, Sect. 6 concludes the work.

2   MAPPER Design

2.1   Overview of MAPPER

We propose the MAPPER prototype to map application description to permissions. Fig. 2 provides an overview of MAPPER. There are four components in MAPPER - App Description Scrapper (parser), Semantic Rule Engine, Rule Interpreter, and Manifest Interpreter. App Description Scrapper parses application description, App category, and package name from Play Store. Semantic Rule Engine stores rules for VERB and NOUN pairs and a corresponding set of permissions. Rule Interpreter finds a model set of permissions M from application description with the help of Semantic Rule Engine. Manifest Interpreter creates a set of permissions D from Manifest XML file inside APK archive of the App. Further, Rule Interpreter in MAPPER reports an App over-privileged if $M \subset D$. These MAPPER components are discussed further in this section below.

2.2   Data Collection

Various phases of MAPPER Data Collection are described below.

URL Extraction. To get a list of URLs from Play Store, we take an intuitive approach to how a web crawler works. We start with a seed URL of the form "https://play.google.com/store/apps/details?id=" followed by a package name of the App. Now, we open this URL using Chrome Driver [18] and put the URL

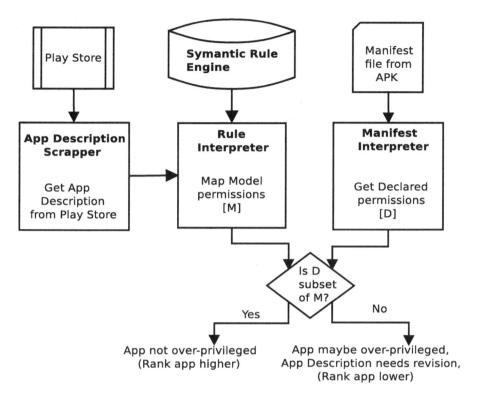

Fig. 2. MAPPER Framework: Model permissions inferred from Application Description are compared with Declared permissions from Manifest file for every App to find out if there are extra permissions and Application Description needs revision.

in the URL_LIST. We find the first similar App on the web page opened by this URL and open the corresponding URL of the same App. We add this new URL in URL_LIST if this is not present already. We repeat this with 11 different seed URLs and collect 7970 URLs. This list has duplicates and we are left with 4485 unique URLs after removing duplicates. Thus, we create an extensive list of URLs to be explored at Play Store.

As we observed, similar Apps may not belong to the same App category. Hence, we use multiple seed URLs to collect more URLs, and this gives us duplicate URLs which are removed later. Also, the similar Apps list is a finite list of suggested Apps.

Getting Application Description. The App Description Scrapper component uses Phantomjs headless browser to open the Play Store URL of an App. With the help of Beautiful Soup and HTML parsers, we obtain an application description. We collect App metadata from Play Store: package name, category, along with Application description, and capture extracted information in a JSON format for every App.

Collect APKs. We have collected URLs from Play Store in URL Extraction phase. From each of these URLs, we find the package names of Android Apps. Using these package names, we download more than 2700 APK files from APK Pure website [26]. We can not get all 4485 Apps because of paid category Apps and some Apps being in non-English languages (Russian, Chinese, Tamil, Urdu, etc.). Further, we group these APK files as per application category. To obtain an application category from APK file, we use AAPT tool [28]. We rename these APK files to their package names so that processing them is simpler subsequently.

2.3   Application Description to Permission Modeling

Application description of Apps is a textual description comprising sentences in the English language. In a sentence, the context of the noun defines how it is used, and this is evident from the verbs in the sentence. Semantic Rule Engine stores stemmed verb and stemmed noun pairs. For every such pair, it stores a subset of likely Android permissions. Stemming is the process of reducing derived words in the text to their root or base forms. For stemming, Lancaster stemmer is used. We create such 480 rules to be used by MAPPER, and a sample subset is shown in Table 1.

Table 1. Permissions from stemmed VERB and NOUN pairs

Verb	Noun	Stemmed Verb	Stemmed Noun	Permissions
share	photo	shar	photo	INTERNET, ACCESS_NETWORK_STATE
follow	friends	follow	friend	READ_CONTACTS, INTERNET, ACCESS_NETWORK_STATE
live	video	liv	video	CAMERA, RECORD_AUDIO, WRITE_EXTERNAL_STORAGE, INTERNET
edit	offline	edit	offlin	READ_EXTERNAL_STORAGE, WRITE_EXTERNAL_STORAGE
can	call	can	cal	CALL_PHONE, READ_PHONE_STATE

2.4   Processing Applications

Rule Interpreter performs pre-processing on the application description text and creates a model set of permissions from this text. For extracting permissions from application description, the following steps are required:

1. We segment text into sentences.
2. Find root words (stemming) from VERB and NOUN tokens in each sentence.

3. For every sentence, create pairs of stemmed VERB and stemmed NOUN. For Part-Of-Speech (POS) tagging - to find NOUN or VERB, we use Spacy [24] libraries.
4. We match pairs of stemmed VERB and stemmed NOUN with stored rules by Semantic Rule Engine and get likely permissions for those pairs.
5. Next, we construct a list of permissions obtained from application description for all sentences and remove duplicates.

To get permissions from individual App manifest files, Manifest Interpreter uses AAPT tool [28] and constructs a list of permissions obtained from App manifest and duplicates are removed.

Further, Rule Interpreter compares both the set of permissions and finds extra-permissions not inferred from application description.

3   Evaluation

In this section, we present the evaluation of MAPPER prototype. Using MAPPER, for Android Apps, we can find out the correspondence between the set of permissions inferred from application description and the set of permissions declared in App manifest file. Further, we attempt to answer the following research questions:

- **RQ1**: What are the statistical parameters - precision, recall, accuracy, and F-Score of MAPPER prototype while reasoning about *over-privileged* Apps?
- **RQ2**: What are the numbers of *over-privileged* and *not-over-privileged* Apps reported by MAPPER?
- **RQ3**: How effective MAPPER prototype is to scale to all Android permissions?
- **RQ4**: Has Android framework been able to contain any permission misuse by App developers or MAPPER finds all permissions as extra permissions in equal measures?

3.1   Evaluation Setup

We consider 1166 randomly chosen active Apps on Play Store from Social, Tools, Education, and Communication category. We consider these four categories as Apps from these categories are used more often than others [1]. Out of 1166 Apps, 112 Apps were manually analyzed to understand application description better and update rules for Semantic Rule Engine.

We choose Android permissions as discussed in Table 2 for analysis related to (a) user's data privacy, (b) an App costing money, and (c) privileged access.

Table 2. Permissions considered for evaluation

Objective	Permissions	Description
Data privacy	ACCESS_NETWORK_STATE,	View network connections
	READ_CONTACTS,	Read your contacts
	READ_CALENDAR,	Read calendar events and details
	READ_CALL_LOG,	Read call log
	GET_ACCOUNTS,	Find accounts on the device
	READ_EXTERNAL_STORAGE,	Read the contents of SD card
	CAMERA	Take pictures and videos
	READ_SMS	Read SMS
Costing money	INTERNET,	Have full network access
	CALL_PHONE	Directly call phone numbers
Privileged access	WRITE_CONTACTS,	Modify your contacts
	WRITE_CALENDAR,	Add or modify calendar events
	WRITE_CALL_LOG,	Modify or delete call log
	WRITE_EXTERNAL_STORAGE	Modify or delete SD card content

We use our MAPPER prototype on these Apps and compute the number of true positives *(TP)*, false negative *(FN)*, false positive *(FP)*, and true negative *(TN)* as follows:

1. TP = Permission identified from application description and present in the manifest file
2. FN = Permission NOT identified from application description and present in the manifest file (missed)
3. FP = Permission identified from application description and NOT present in the manifest file (extra)
4. TN = Permission NOT identified from application description and NOT present in the manifest file

Further, we discuss precision, recall [29], accuracy, and F-score of MAPPER. Precision is defined as the ratio of the number of true positives *(TP)* to the total number of Apps for whom permission was identified (*TP* and *FP*) from the application description. Recall is defined as the ratio of the number of true positives *(TP)* to the total number of Apps for whom permission was present (*TP* and *FN*) in the manifest file. Accuracy is the ratio of the sum of true positives *(TP)* and true negatives *(TN)* to the total number of Apps studied. F-score is the weighted average of two other parameters - precision and recall.

Higher the precision, recall, accuracy, and F-score, higher the effectiveness of permissions inferred from application description by MAPPER. Precision is seen as a measure of quality, while recall is seen as a measure of completeness. Hence, the low values of recall clearly show that application description needs revision as it missed to inform permissions against declaration in App manifest file. We compute precision, recall, accuracy and F-score of MAPPER to find out permissions from application description as follows:

1. $Precision = \frac{TP}{TP+FP}$

2. $Recall = \frac{TP}{TP+FN}$

3. $Accuracy = \frac{TP+TN}{TP+FN+FP+TN}$

4. $F-score = \frac{2*Precision*Recall}{Precision+Recall}$

We categorize an App as *over-privileged* if and only if there is at least one permission that is in App manifest file and not in the set of permissions inferred from application description. An App is categorized as *not-over-privileged* if set difference of these two is empty.

Let **M** be the set of model permissions from application description, **D** be the set of declared permissions from the App Manifest XML file. MAPPER reports an App *over-privileged* if $\mathbf{M} \subset \mathbf{D}$. Also, App is *not-over-privileged* if $\mathbf{D} \cap \mathbf{M} = \mathbf{D}$. Set $\mathbf{D} \setminus \mathbf{M}$ denotes extra permissions that are not mentioned in the application description.

3.2 Results

Here, we describe evaluation results and statistical data from our work.

RQ1: What are Precision, Recall, Accuracy, and F-Score of MAPPER? Table 3 shows results of permissions evaluated. Column "Permission" shows permission under consideration, columns TP, FN, FP, and TN denote the number of true positives, false negatives, false positives, and true negatives respectively. Finally, columns Prec, Rec, Acc, and F# show precision, recall, accuracy, and F-score computed as defined above. The table shows average Precision, Recall, Accuracy, F-score as 74.5%, 49.8%, 82.5%, and 59.7% respectively for 1166 Apps from four different categories analyzed for 14 permissions. The average accuracy of 82.5% is impressive, with only 10% of Apps analyzed manually.

Table 4 shows results of the same permissions evaluated for Apps from Social category alone. This table shows average Precision, Recall, Accuracy, and F-score as 78.6%, 73.5%, 83.4%, and 76.0% for 98 Apps from Social category analyzed for 14 permissions.

RQ2: What are the Numbers of *Over-Privileged* and *Not-over-Privileged* Apps Reported by MAPPER? A large number of Apps are reported with one or more extra permissions. Out of 1166 Apps, 161 Apps (see Fig. 3) did not have any extra permissions, i.e. 14% of Apps studied are *not-over-privileged*. Hence, potential *over-privileged* Apps outnumber *not-over-privileged* Apps on Play Store. Also, we see from this Fig. 3 that the number of extra permissions being declared is mostly below 10 or so. In other words, a large number

Table 3. Results for permissions evaluated

Permission	TP	FN	FP	TN	Prec	Rec	Acc	F#
INTERNET	662	440	20	44	97.1	60.1	60.5	74.2
ACCESS_NETWORK_STATE	643	426	36	61	94.7	60.1	60.4	73.5
CALL_PHONE	47	41	116	962	28.8	53.4	86.5	37.4
READ_CONTACTS	73	85	128	880	36.3	46.2	81.7	40.7
READ_CALENDAR	5	27	6	1128	45.5	15.6	97.2	23.2
READ_CALL_LOG	5	22	11	1131	15.4	8.3	97.2	10.8
WRITE_CONTACTS	13	68	36	1049	26.5	16.0	91.1	20.0
WRITE_CALENDAR	2	28	4	1132	33.3	6.7	97.3	11.2
WRITE_CALL_LOG	0	14	0	1152	0	0	98.8	0
GET_ACCOUNTS	36	173	32	925	52.9	17.2	82.4	26.0
READ_EXTERNAL_STORAGE	204	269	144	549	58.6	43.1	64.6	49.7
WRITE_EXTERNAL_STORAGE	295	383	118	370	71.4	43.5	57.0	54.1
CAMERA	137	136	74	819	64.9	50.2	82.0	56.6
READ_SMS	0	27	0	1139	0	0	97.7	0
Total	2119	2139	725	11341	74.5	49.8	82.5	59.7

Table 4. Results for Apps from Social category

Permission	TP	FN	FP	TN	Prec	Rec	Acc	F#
INTERNET	92	4	2	0	97.9	95.8	93.9	96.8
ACCESS_NETWORK_STATE	91	4	3	0	96.8	95.8	92.9	96.3
CALL_PHONE	8	4	7	79	53.3	66.7	88.8	59.3
READ_CONTACTS	27	10	23	38	54.0	73.0	66.3	62.1
READ_CALENDAR	4	3	0	91	100	57.1	96.9	72.7
READ_CALL_LOG	2	0	1	95	66.7	100	99.0	80.0
WRITE_CONTACTS	3	9	18	68	14.3	25.0	72.4	18.2
WRITE_CALENDAR	1	5	0	92	100	16.7	94.9	28.6
WRITE_CALL_LOG	0	0	0	98	0	0	100	0
GET_ACCOUNTS	10	27	7	54	58.8	27.0	65.3	37.0
READ_EXTERNAL_STORAGE	42	20	21	15	66.7	67.7	58.2	67.2
WRITE_EXTERNAL_STORAGE	49	28	11	10	81.7	63.6	60.2	71.5
CAMERA	32	16	5	45	86.5	66.7	78.6	75.3
READ_SMS	0	0	0	98	0	0	100	0
Total	361	130	98	783	78.6	73.5	83.4	76.0

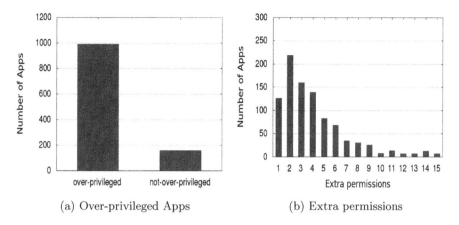

(a) Over-privileged Apps (b) Extra permissions

Fig. 3. Number of Apps categorized as over-privileged and not-over-privileged (a). Extra permissions being declared v/s Number of Apps (b)

of Apps have 10 or less extra permissions declared. This includes 3rd-party permissions that cannot be inferred from application description. Therefore, we conclude that the number of extra permissions declared by a majority of the Apps is much less compared to a total of all dangerous and normal Android permissions combined.

RQ3: How Effective MAPPER Prototype is to Scale to All Android Permissions? We analyze 1166 application descriptions of live Android Apps and a total of 4,29,574 VERB and NOUN pair comparisons are made. These are checked against 480 rules in Semantic Rule Engine.

The average accuracy of 82.5% reported by MAPPER demonstrates the usability of MAPPER prototype and further manual analysis of more Apps can improve this on the higher side. While we analyze 14 permissions mentioned in Table 2, we believe that a more extensive set of dangerous and normal permissions can be analyzed and Semantic Rule Engine can be updated with more rule definitions for these new permissions.

Some Apps have a concise application description. We find 16 Apps with applications description less than 80 characters long, which is a limit for a short description of App on Play Store. This character length is short for an application description compared to permissions being asked by the App. For example, App Multiple Accounts (com.excelliance.multiaccounts.b64) has 174 characters long application description, and this App is asking for 207 permissions. This example confirms that an App may be feature-rich or may have more interactive features, and App developers are not making the permissions explicit to its unsuspecting users.

There are a few Apps that request too many permissions. 152 Apps out of a total of 1166 Apps have more than 25 permissions declared in their manifest files, and 7 Apps have more than 100 permissions declared. For instance,

App Multiple Accounts (com.excell-iance.multiaccounts.b64) that allows multiple WhatsApp accounts, has 207 permissions declared in its manifest file. Samsung App Galaxy Watch Plugin (com.-samsung.android.geargplugin) has 182, Gear S Plugin (com.samsung.android.gearoplugin) has 182 and Gear Fit2 Plugin (com.samsung.android.gearfit2plugin) has 154 permissions declared in their respective manifest files. These examples show MAPPER identifies such outliers, and this reflects in reduced recall rate.

RQ4: Is Android Ecosystem Helping to Curb Permission Misuse?
Commercial Android releases have been around for more than a decade, and so is the permission-based security model of Android. Introduction of run-time permissions in Android 6.0 compared to the original install time all-or-none permissions has helped users to review permissions using dialog boxes. This is true for subsequent App updates as well. Second big leap was Project Strobe [5] updates. In the aftermath of Project Strobe, more permission dialog boxes were added for fine-grained control of access to users' data. It reduced the number of use-cases of account access through Google Apps (Gmail, Drive, etc.), and reduced Apps' ability to ask for CALL_LOG and SMS related permissions. MAPPER confirms the reduction in the permissions READ_SMS, READ_CALL_LOG and WRITE_CALL_LOG being requested (see Table 3) compared to all other permissions. Less than 2% Apps of all Apps studied asked for these three permissions. This fact demonstrates that permission control is possible when it comes to users privacy and access to data.

A lot needs to be done for other permissions. MAPPER asserts the fact many Apps ask for Internet, account, and storage related permissions without informing users explicitly. Play Store should limit excess permissions asked by App developers, which in turn will help the Android ecosystem.

4   Discussions and Future Work

Google Play Store has a very dynamic set of Apps available. We observed close to 110 Apps were removed from the Play Store, while we were collecting application description in March-to-May, 2019. This removal may be due to Google's policy after project strobe [5], where they have taken some actions to limit access to 3rd-party APIs, and developers may be no longer be updating Apps. Frequently removal of Apps on the Play Store makes our task a bit challenging as we do not work on offline application descriptions.

MAPPER does not perform well for some randomly chosen Apps when the length of the application description is minimal, less than 250 characters. However, this also confirms that in the absence of sufficient text description, neither developers can inform users in a better way about App capabilities nor users get adequate information. This direction has been the main focus of our work.

4.1 Limitations

MAPPER prototype demonstrates a lightweight approach to find over-privileged Apps. However, it has its own few limitations as discussed below.

POS Tagging: MAPPER relies on state-of-the-art Part Of Speech (POS) tagging by Spacy [24]. However, this may not lead to correct tagging of verbs in some cases. For example, Spacy does not identify VERB if a sentence starts with a VERB. Instead, it may identify it as a NOUN and MAPPER may miss this VERB to pair with applicable NOUN in the sentence. For instance, in the sentence, *Grant access to record and send voice messages to partner*, "record" is identified as a NOUN instead of a VERB. Such cases bring down recall rate.

Auxiliary Verbs: We do not consider the primary auxiliary verbs in English: be, do, and have; also the modal auxiliary verbs can, could, may, might, must, shall, should, will, and would are not considered in general while creating pairs with nouns. This omission is not a limitation per se, and they were only considered with manual inspection of Apps, if required.

Linguistic Concerns: Our work focuses on context-aware permission usage (verb in this case), and it does not cover the grammatical relationship between different words in a sentence. We do not work on English linguistic issues and sentiment analysis of the sentences used in the application description.

No Text for Certain Permissions: MAPPER cannot find some dangerous permissions from application description. For instance, READ_PHONE_STAT, READ_PHONE_NUMBERS, WRITE_CALL_LOG, SYSTEM_ALERT_WIND OW, READ_SMS, etc. This set may be larger than permissions we mentioned and requires us to analyze more Apps for more permissions manually. Because of a humongous effort needed to analyze English sentences in application description, we could not cover all permissions, and we restricted our analysis to specific permissions.

Deprecated or Non-existing Permissions: While looking at permissions, we consider Android API level 23 and above. There are cases wherein we find deprecated or non-existing permissions used in App manifest file. These are ignored and not considered as extra permissions.

4.2 Future Work

We have made an effort to take 1166 random Apps from Play Store, and we cover four categories of Android Apps. We would like to scale this to all 32 categories of Apps, and six categories of games as Android Apps are categorized broadly. Manual analysis of Apps at scale is imperative to learn more from a textual description since we are dealing with sentences in the English language. One may explore dependency of the verb (context in which it is used) with other parts of speech in the sentences; this will further improve precision and recall rates. Contributions from English grammar analysis and sentiment analysis may help take this work to a new dimension.

Further, we would like to prepare a mapping of permissions to API calls for a few recently released Android versions or API levels 25 and later as the previous work in this direction is obsolete [9,11]. We can use this mapping for a better fine-grained analysis of application behaviour and find sensitive or protected APIs provided by Android. Google or Android developer website does not present any such list of permissions to API mapping. Such information is useful for behaviour analysis of binary programs. Towards this, we will use Android source at different API levels with the Atlas framework and extend plugin-ins available [32].

5 Related Work

The closest related work by Pandita et al. [12] used Stanford Typed Dependency Parser [33,34] to determine the relationship between words or tokens in the sentence and showed if the sentence is a permission sentence. Their work evaluated less than 10,000 sentences of 581 Apps for only three permissions to read the calendar, read contacts, and record audio (microphone). Unlike our work, they did not look into App manifest information and focused on language issues and NLP.

Gorla et al. [13] extracted representational words from the textual description and categorized Apps into clusters using K-means clustering. They demonstrated permission outliers in each App cluster by API usage. To detect malware, Gorla et al. used the sensitive API list from Felt et al. [9].

Felt et al. proposed Stowaway, which used automated testing tools on the Android API checks in the code to build the permission map. Stowaway evaluated 940 Android Apps and detected one-third Apps as over-privileged. This mapping of permissions (Android 2.2) to the sensitive API is obsolete now.

Wei et al. [15] analyzed permission text itself over "top paid business" category Apps for six permissions. Their approach based on word frequency count in permission sentences revealed only one permission prediction of more than 80% accuracy.

Wijesekara et al. [16] used survey questionnaires to show that informed users would deny certain permissions and how Apps violate contextual integrity if they are not explicitly asking permissions from users when they install Apps. This concern is partly addressed with Android moving from all-or-none install-time permissions to run-time permissions from Android API level 23, and with multiple dialogue boxes being displayed to users.

The above described previous works do little towards finding a correspondence between information from application description and information from App manifest file. MAPPER is the first prototype to establish this correspondence.

6 Conclusion

In this paper, we show how application description can be used to infer permissions. We presented the MAPPER prototype and demonstrated that a majority of Android Apps are not making it clear to the user about what all an App can do. This includes permissions related to the privacy of user data, App costing money, and privileged access App may request. This poses a potential risk to contextual integrity of application behaviour and to what a user consents while installing an App. We conclude that any App not making its capabilities explicit does not conform to its execution specification as mentioned on the App's web-page on Play Store. Future work in this direction is proposed to prepare a mapping of permissions to API calls for a fine-grained analysis of permissions focusing on more recent Android API levels.

Acknowledgments. We acknowledge reviewers and researchers at MNIT Jaipur, who helped us to refine the problem statement, and provided valuable inputs during discussions. We acknowledge assistance from Shaikh Mamun Hoque, a sophomore at IIT Jammu who helped us in two scripts for getting lists of URLs and downloading APK files. We thank Marcello Lins for his insight on how a web-based App crawler works and how to build an extensive URL list.

References

1. Usage of Apps. https://mindsea.com/app-stats/. Accessed 01 May 2019
2. Android Open Source Project. https://source.android.com
3. Number of Android Apps. https://www.statista.com/statistics/276623/number-of-apps-available-in-leading-app-stores/. Accessed 01 May 2019
4. Gartner Report (2018). https://www.gartner.com/newsroom/id/3859963
5. Project Strobe by Google. https://www.blog.google/technology/safety-security/project-strobe/. Accessed 01 May 2019
6. Facebook-Cambridge Analytica Data Scandal. https://en.wikipedia.org/wiki/Facebook%E2%80%93Cambridge_Analytica_data_scandal. Accessed 01 May 2019
7. Organizations updating Privacy Policy. https://www.popsci.com/gdpr-privacy-policy-update-notices. Accessed 01 May 2019
8. GDPR. https://eugdpr.org/
9. Felt, A.P., Chin, E., Hanna, S., Song, D., Wagner, D.: Android permissions demystified. In: Proceedings of the 18th ACM Conference on Computer and Communications Security (CCS 2011), Chicago, Illinois, USA, pp. 627–638 (2011)
10. Vidas, T., Christin, N., Cranor, L.F.: Curbing Android permission creep. In: W2SP 2011, CMU, USA (2011)
11. Au, K.W.Y., Zhou, Y.F., Huang, Z., Lie, D.: PScout: analyzing the Android permission specification. In: Proceedings of the 2012 ACM Conference on Computer and Communications Security (CCS 2012), Raleigh, North Carolina, USA, pp. 217–228 (2012)
12. Pandita, R., Xiao, X., Yang, W., Enck, W., Xie, T.: WHYPER: towards automating risk assessment of mobile applications. In: Proceedings of 22nd USENIX Security Symposium, pp. 527–542 (2013)
13. Gorla, A., Tavecchia, I., Gross, F., Zeller, A.: Checking app behavior against app descriptions. In: Proceedings of the 36th International Conference on Software Engineering (ICSE 2014), Hyderabad, India, pp. 1025–1035 (2014)
14. Geneiatakis, D., Fovino, I.N., Kounelis, I., Stirparo, P.: A permission verification approach for Android mobile applications. Comput. Secur. **49**, 192–205 (2014)

15. Wei, M., Gong, X., Wang, W.: Claim what you need: a text-mining approach on Android permission request authorization. In: 2015 IEEE Global Communications Conference (GLOBECOM), San Diego, CA, USA (2015)
16. Wijesekera, P., Baokar, A., Hosseini, A., Egelman, S., Wagner, D., Beznosov, K.: Android permissions re-mystified: a field study on contextual integrity. In: Proceedings of the 24th USENIX Security Symposium, pp. 499–514 (2015)
17. Gerber, P., Volkamer, M., Renaud, K.: The simpler, the better? Presenting the COPING Android permission-granting interface for better privacy-related decisions. J. Inf. Secur. Appl. **34**(Part 1), 8–26 (2017)
18. Chrome Driver. http://chromedriver.chromium.org/
19. Manifest Permissions. https://developer.android.com/reference/android/Manifest.permission.html. Accessed 30 Apr 2019
20. Permission Groups. https://developer.android.com/reference/android/Manifest.permission_group. Accessed 30 Apr 2019
21. Protection Levels. https://developer.android.com/guide/topics/manifest/permission-element.html. Accessed 30 Apr 2019
22. Requesting Permissions. https://developer.android.com/training/permissions/requesting. Accessed 30 Apr 2019
23. AOSP source for Manifest XML. https://github.com/aosp-mirror/platform_frameworks_base/blob/master/core/res/AndroidManifest.xml
24. Spacy. https://spacy.io/usage/linguistic-features
25. NLTK. https://www.nltk.org/
26. APK Pure Archive. https://apkpure.com
27. APK Tool for reverse engineering APK files. https://ibotpeaches.github.io/Apktool
28. Android Asset Packaging Tool (AAPT). https://elinux.org/Android_aapt
29. Precision and Recall. https://en.wikipedia.org/wiki/Precision_and_recall
30. AndroGuard. https://github.com/androguard
31. Google Play Store. https://play.google.com/store
32. Android Essentials Toolbox from EnSoft. https://github.com/EnSoftCorp/android-essentials-toolbox
33. Stanford typed dependency. https://nlp.stanford.edu/software/stanford-dependencies.html. Accessed 18 May 2019
34. de Marneffe, M.-C., Manning, C.D.: The Stanford typed dependencies representation. In: Proceedings of the Workshop in COLING 2008, pp. 1–8 (2008)
35. Android API 23 changes. https://developer.android.com/sdk/api_diff/23/changes/android.Manifest.permission.html. Accessed 01 May 2019

Secure Embedded Systems

Delegation of Computation Using FV Cryptosystem

Amina Bel Korchi[1,2(✉)] and Nadia El Mrabet[1]

[1] Mines Saint-Etienne, CEA-Tech, Centre CMP, Departement SAS,
13541 Gardanne, France
`nadia.el-mrabet@emse.fr`
[2] Kontron, La Garde, France
`Amina.BelKorchi@kontron.com`

Abstract. Homomorphic encryption is a very promising cryptosystem for industrial. However, it is impossible to take a decision based on homomorphic cipher texts comparison. In this paper we provide a method to do a comparison between homomorphic cipher texts, using a secure element. We give a detailed description of an IoT use case where homomorphic encryption is used to ensure security, privacy, anonymity, and aggregation. This use case shows the necessity of cipher texts comparison to turn a real use case in an IoT environment.

Keywords: IoT use case · Cloud security · Anonymity · Homomorphic encryption

1 Introduction

Nowadays, data security has become a very important subject for the industries to improve business. They need to manipulate data while ensuring data protection, privacy, and anonymization. Homomorphic encryption responds to this challenge and enables computations, without decryption, on encrypted data. Let $E(a)$ and $E(b)$ be the encryption of a and b using an homomorphic cryptosystem, $E(a)$ and $E(b)$ verify the following properties: $E(a) \oplus E(b) = E(a + b)$ and $E(a) \otimes E(b) = E(a \times b)$. Homomorphic encryption allows to perform comparison on homomorphic ciphertexts. However, the result of the comparison is encrypted, so we cannot send alerts and perform conditional branching.

1.1 Contribution

In this paper, we give a practical method to enable taking decisions when comparing two homomorphic ciphertexts. We provide a detailed use case of homomorphic encryption, where taking decisions and sending alerts is necessary. Our method consists in decrypting ciphertexts in a secure environment and comparing the plaintexts. The main constraint of the secure element is the memory size, and to with this limitation, we give a detailed method to delegate computation in the CPU.

© Springer Nature Switzerland AG 2020
S. Kallel et al. (Eds.): CRiSIS 2019, LNCS 12026, pp. 101–112, 2020.
https://doi.org/10.1007/978-3-030-41568-6_7

1.2   Related Work

Two variants of homomorphic encryption exist: Fully Homomorphic Encryption (FHE) and Somewhat Homomorphic Encryption (SWHE). FHE is a fully homomorphic encryption allowing the evaluation of an arbitrary circuit, as to SWHE, it can evaluate circuits of constant depth. The circuit depth is the number of multiplication that can be performed using a given scheme. Exceeding this depth, decryption cannot be done correctly due to the noise that appears during the encryption of plaintexts. This noise grows after every ciphertext multiplication until we reach a level where we can not decrypt correctly.

Gentry [10] has invented the first FHE cryptosystem in 2009 using a bootstrapping [10] procedure to transform a SWHE cryptosystem into a FHE cryptosystem. The security of Gentry's scheme is based on ideal lattices [16]. The bootstrapping technique transforms a ciphertext resulting from a circuit to a new ciphertext with a noise similar to the one in a ciphertext freshly encrypted. Numerous schemes have been proposed following Gentry's cryptosystem [7,11, 19], basing their security on different hardness assumptions.

Before the apparition of the technique to turn bootstrapping in less than 0.1 s [8], the inconvenient of FHE schemes was the time to turn the boostrapping, this is the reason why different SWHE schemes as [5,6,9] have been developed with practical depths to use homomorphic encryption in practice. Those practical security schemes are based on LWE [17] (Learning with errors) and RLWE [14] (Ring Learning with Errors) problems.

1.3   Outlines

In the first section of the paper, we define the use case. Then, in the second section, we describe the FV cryptosystem. In the third section, we describe existing implementations of FV, and finally, we provide our method to take decisions when comparing homomorphic FV ciphertexts, and the description of the algorithm to delegate computations to the CPU.

2   IoT Use Case

Homomorphic encryption is a solution to solve the main problems of IoT [1]: security, storage, and computations.

Let's picture a use case in IoT where we have different devices, several gateways and a cloud that holds a secure element and multiple servers to store and manage data. Each gateway receives several messages from sensors, encrypts messages homomorphically and sends them to the cloud. For our case, the cloud should store and enables all the operations on ciphertexts, as the addition, multiplication and taking decision based on the comparison of collected data at different times and in various geographies. Using the secure element, the cloud can compare collected data and sends alerts to the administrator machine. To compare two homomorphic ciphertexts, the secure element will decrypt those ciphertexts and compare the plaintexts.

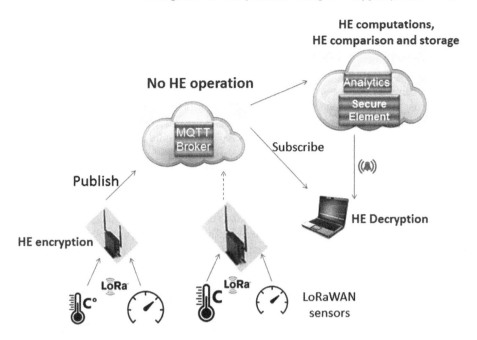

Fig. 1. IoT use case: the Edge/Cloud solution.

The protocol used for sending messages from sensors to the gateway is LORA [3] (Long Range Wireless Protocol). The cloud includes a MQTT [2] server(Publish/Subscribe protocol). To store data in the cloud, the gateway sends a publish command, and to receive data from the cloud, the calculation server sends a subscribe command. This scenario is shown in Fig. 1.

Let's picture a use case in transport and trains. We have several trains of multiple companies, one gateway by a train and several devices for each train car, each gateway receives messages from devices, encrypts them and sends them to the Cloud. The Cloud will aggregate data and enable computing and taking decisions on aggregated data. This use case could be used to verify the water level in each car toilet. Devices send systematically the level of water to the cloud via the gateway. Inside the cloud, the secure element compares the water level to the minimum acceptable level and sends alerts the administrator machine in case of lack of water in a toilet.

Let's take a scenario where different supermarkets of different companies need to store and compute the number of product sales in the context of stock management. The goal of these companies is to store in the cloud the encryption of this data without revealing their identities due to the competition. In the cloud we can compute the sum of sales of each product and compare it, using the secure element, to the number of products in the stock to supply the stock of supermarkets if necessary.

Let's picture a use case in seaports to accelerate the shipments of products through customs by expecting enough trucks to transport the goods. Shipping companies need to verify in real time the transported merchandise without revealing information about the clients. Shipowners are engaged with clients to protect professional secrecy. The companies will verify the value of goods, their overall cost, their content and the weight of goods in order to anticipate the arrival of goods to the seaport, the trucks or train to transport the merchandise and the passage of customs. In this use case, each company has several ships and containers, each ship owns a gateway, and each container holds a sensor. Containers send data to the gateway which will encrypt them and sends them to the cloud. In practice when the cloud receives data we can compute the sum of containers holding products of some companies in the seaport by incrementing the number of containers. We can compute the value of goods of those containers, and the sum of weights of containers before loading them on ships by doing several additions. Moreover, we can compute the currency conversion of goods prices by computing the price of each product and the country currency. This calculation needs one level of multiplication.

Homomorphic encryption will ensure confidentiality, privacy, and anonymization of container origin while allowing publishing an aggregate figure.

We choose to use the homomorphic cryptosystem FV in the use cases above because it is well suited for circuits of small depth. Many libraries [13,18] implement the FV cryptosystem, but they are not portable in the gateway. the size of SEAL library is 5 Mbytes, which has no external dependencies, FV-NFLIB library uses the NFLIB library, and to turn it inside the gateway we need the full module of 5 Mbytes. We choose to implement our API to be embedded in the gateway, the cloud, and the administrator machine.

3   FV Cryptosystem

3.1   Notations

The algebraic structure used by Fan and Vercauteren scheme is the polynomial ring $R = Z[x]/f(x)$, where $Z[x]$ describes the polynomial ring with coefficients in Z and $f(x)$ is a cyclotomic polynomial of degree d. In practice $f(x) = x^d + 1$ and $d = 2^n$. Elements of R are polynomials of degree less than d and coefficients in Z. Let q denotes coefficients modulus, $R_q[x] = Z_q[x]/f(x)$ where $Z_q[x]$ is the polynomial ring with coefficients modulo q. Elements of $R_q[x]$ are polynomials of degree less than d and coefficients modulo q.

Elements of the ring $R_q[x]$ are noted in lowercase ($a \in R_q[x]$), we denote by $[a]_q$ the elements in R obtained by computing all its coefficients modulo q.

For $x \in R_q$ we denote by $\lfloor x \rceil$ rounding to the nearest integer, $\lceil x \rceil$, and $\lfloor x \rfloor$ rounding up and down. Let D denotes a distribution, the notation $x \leftarrow D$ is used to sample randomly x from the distribution D, and $x \xleftarrow{\$} D$ is used to sample uniformly x from D.

3.2   Definition of FV

The cryptosystem of Fan and Vercauteren (FV) [9] is a somewhat homomorphic encryption scheme, developed in 2012, its security is based on the hardness of the RLWE problem [17].

Let λ denotes the security parameter, $q > 1$ denotes the coefficients modulus used to define the polynomial ring R_q, and $t > 1$ an integer used to denote the plaintext modulus, where $t < q$. R_q is the ciphertext space and the plaintext space is R_t.

Let χ be a Gaussian distribution over R with a standard deviation σ. We will use two distributions χ_{err} and χ_{key} to sample errors and the secret key of the scheme. The distributions χ_{err} and χ_{key} are B bounded distributions where $B = 10 \cdot \sigma$. In practice we can choose χ_{key} as the ring R_2, $\sigma = 3.1$, and χ_{err} is a Gaussian distribution bounded by $B = 31$. We denote by $params$ the set of the scheme parameters, $params = (R, d, q, t, \chi_{err}, \chi_{key})$.

KeyGen($params$):
FV cryptosystem is a public key scheme, the generation of keys will return a public key p_k and a secret key s_k. Let's start by generating the secret key which is a polynomial in χ_{key}, $s_k \leftarrow \chi_{key}$ is randomly sampled from χ_{key} , in practice we choose $\chi_{key} = R_2$ and s_k a polynomial of degree less than d with binary coefficients. To compute the public key we need to sample a from the ring R_q $a \xleftarrow{\$} R_q$, and a random error e from χ_{err} $e \leftarrow \chi_{err}$. The public key p_k is a couple of two polynomials,

$$p_k = ([-(a \cdot s_k + e)]_q, a).$$

Let rlk be the relinearization key used to reduce the size of ciphertext after multiplication.

For $i = 0 \ldots l$ we sample a_i from R_q $a_i \xleftarrow{\$} R_q$, e_i from χ_{err} $e_i \xleftarrow{\$} \chi_{err}$, and compute $rlk = ([-(ai \cdot s_k + e_i) + T^i \cdot s^2]_q, a_i)$, where T is a random integer independent from the plaintext modulus t and $l = \lfloor log_T(q) \rfloor$.

Encryption($m, params, p_k = (p_0, p_1)$):
To encrypt a message $m \in R_t$, we start by computing $\delta = \lfloor \frac{q}{t} \rfloor$, we sample $u \leftarrow \chi_{key}$, and $e_1, e_2 \leftarrow \chi_{err}$.
The encryption of m is a ciphertext of two polynomials defined as follows:

$$E(m) = ([p_0 \cdot u + e_1 + \delta \cdot m]_q, [p_1 \cdot u + e_2]_q). \tag{1}$$

One can notice that the ciphertext is a couple of data, where we can see the first element as the ciphertext, and the second as the noise.

Decryption($C, params, s_k$):
To compute the decryption of a ciphertext $C = (c0, c1)$ we evaluate the following equation:

$$D(C) = [\lfloor \frac{t \cdot [c[0] + c[1] \cdot s_k]_q}{q} \rceil]_t.$$

Addition($c[1]$, $c[2]$):
The addition of two ciphertexts $c[1] = (c[1][0], c[1][1])$ and $c[2] = (c[2][0], c[2][1])$ is achieved by computing the addition of polynomials of ciphertexts with modulo reduction.

The result of addition is

$$c[1] + c[2] = ([c[1][0] + c[2][0]]_q, [c[1][1] + c[2][1]]_q) \tag{2}$$

The following equations shows that the addition of two ciphertexts is equal to the encryption of the addition of ciphertexts.

$$[c[1][0] + c[2][0]]_q = ([p_0 \cdot (u_1 + u_2) + (e_1 + e_1') + \delta \cdot (m_1 + m_2)]_q,$$

$$[c[1][1] + c[2][1]]_q = [p_1 \cdot (u_1 + u_2) + (e_2 + e_2')]_q).$$

Multiplication($c[1]$, $c[2]$):
The multiplication of two ciphertexts $c[1]$ and $c[2]$ consists in computing the tensor product of $c[1] = (c[1][0], c[1][1])$ and $c[2] = (c[2][0], c[2][1])$ and scaling by t/q. The multiplication will increase the ciphertext length.

We can simply define

$$(c[1][0], c[1][1]) \cdot (c[2][0], c[2][1]) = (ct_0, ct_1, ct_2)$$

where

$$ct_0 = [\lfloor \frac{t \cdot (c[1][0] \cdot c[2][0])}{q} \rceil]_q,$$

$$ct_1 = [\lfloor \frac{t \cdot (c[1][0] \cdot c[2][1] + c[1][1] \cdot c[2][0])}{q} \rceil]_q,$$

$$ct_2 = [\lfloor \frac{t \cdot (c[1][1] \cdot c[2][1])}{q} \rceil]_q.$$

To transform this ciphertext of three elements (ct_0, ct_1, ct_2) into a ciphertext of two elements (ct_0', ct_1'), we have to use the relinearization technique.

Relinearization($params, rlk, (ct_0, ct_1, ct_2)$):
The relinearization step reduces the number of ciphertext elements by transforming a ciphertext of three elements to a ciphertext of two elements, we call the relinearization step after each multiplication. First we write ct_2 in the base T, $ct_2 = \sum_{i=0}^{l} c[2]^{(i)} T^i$ where $c[2]^{(i)} \in R_T$, and we use the relinearization key to compute the new ciphertext (ct_0', ct_1').

$$ct_0' = [ct_0 + \sum_{i=0}^{l} rlk[i][0] \cdot c[2]^{(i)}]_q,$$
$$ct_1' = [ct_1 + \sum_{i=0}^{l} rlk[i][1] \cdot c[2]^{(i)}]_q.$$

The noise of the ciphertext grows after the relinearization step, and we can avoid this step if the circuit depth is one, by keeping the ciphertext as (ct_0, ct_1, ct_2) and computing the decryption directly using this ciphertext $D(ct_0, ct_1, ct_2) = [\lfloor \frac{t \cdot [ct_0 + ct_1 \cdot s_k + ct_2 \cdot s_k^2]_q}{q} \rceil]_t.$

3.3   Parameters

In this paragraph we will give some practical parameters for FV cryptosystem and their corresponding circuit depth L. In Table 1 we present the sizes of the coefficient q with the degree of the polynomial d according to the security level and the depth we want to achieve. The depth is the maximum number of multiplication that can be performed on an homomorphic ciphertext before the noise makes the decryption step impossible.

Table 1. Parameters of the scheme to encrypt plaintexts of 16 bits.

Depth	Security Level	d	Size of q in bits
0	128	1024	29
	192	2048	39
1	128	2048	56
	192	4096	77
2	128	4096	110
	192	8192	153

4   Existing Implementations:

4.1   FV-NFLlib Library

FV-NFLlib [18] is a software library implementing FV cryptosystem, developed in 2016 in C++, and based on NFLlib [15], a library specially designed for ideal lattices cryptography.

4.2   SEAL Library

SEAL [13] is an Open source library, developed in 2015 in C++ and C# by a Microsoft team. It implements FV cryptosystem with no external library dependencies.

In SEAL, the user chooses the security level: 128 or 192, the plaintext modulus (no limit for the choice) and the degree: 1024, 2048, 4096, 8192 or 16384. The library returns the coefficents modulus size and the noise budget to know if we can make another computation or not.

4.3   SEAL-RNS Library

RNS version of FV: The RNS variant [4] of FV cryptosystem is an improvement of the FV scheme, which enables RNS representation of coefficients. It represents each element of the ring R_q as a vector of several elements in R_{q_i}, where q_i are small modulus. This technique allows the optimization of coefficients storage and the acceleration of computations.

The RNS representation consists of the composition of the coefficients modulus q into a product of multiple small co-prime moduli.

Let q be a product of q_i, $q = q_1 * q_2 * ... * q_n$, and c_k be the coefficient of index k of a polynomial in R_q. Using the CRT theorem c_k can be represented as below:

$$c_k = \begin{cases} c_i' & \mod q_i \\ & ... \\ c_n' & \mod q_n \end{cases}$$

SEAL-RNS library: This version of SEAL [12] implements the FullRNS [4] variant of FV cryptosystem. In this version the coefficients modulus are replaced with several small moduli, to accelerate computations and to optimize the storage of coefficients. It uses the same parameters as the initial version of SEAL.

4.4   Comparison of Libraries

In SEAL and SEAL-RNS, the decryption of a multiplication result can be done by two different methods. The standard method, where we multiply two ciphertexts, we relinearize and decrypt, and the second method which consists in decrypting directly the result of a multiplication. Let $(c[0], c[1], c[2])$ be the product of two ciphertexts and s a secret key, to decrypt this ciphertexts product compute $c[0] + c[1] \cdot s + c[2] \cdot s^2$. The first method is used when the circuit depth is one and the second method is used when we need to evaluate a circuit of more than one multiplication.

We note that FV-NFLIB library is faster than SEAL libraries, but FV-NFLIB does not support circuits with high levels, the maximum level supported by this library is 6. Thus we recommend to use FV-NFLIB for small circuits, and to use SEAL to evaluate large circuits.

For our use case, we need to use the FV cryptosystem to protect data and perform computations on encrypted data. In practice, one of those libraries will be embedded inside the gateway and the cloud, but due to their size (5 Mbytes), they cannot be handled by the gateway (Intel(R) Atom(TM) CPU E3845 1.91 GHz). This is the reason why we developed our own implementation of FV.

5   Delegation of Computation

5.1   Description of Our Method

One of the main limitations of homomorphic encryption is the comparison, the result of homomorphic ciphertexts comparison is encrypted, and we cannot take a decision inside the cloud to send an alert if necessary. In this work, we provide a method to enable In this work, we provide a method to enable sending alerts, when comparing homomorphic ciphertexts encrypted using FV cryptosystem. It is a general method independent of the FV parameters. This method is based on the decryption of ciphertexts inside a secure element, the comparison of plaintexts, and then sending alerts if necessary.

The decryption function $D(C) = [\lfloor \frac{t \cdot [c[0] + c[1] \cdot s_k]_q}{q} \rceil]_t$ will be embedded in the secure element, and we need to avoid computing the product $(c[1] \cdot s_k) \mod q$, which requires an important memory resources and execution time. We propose to do this product inside the CPU, without revealing the secret key. Let's generate inside the secure element a random polynomial $Random \in R_2$ with binary coefficients. We compute the mask of the secret key $M(s_k) = (s_k \oplus Random) \mod q$, which is the sum coefficient by coefficient of the polynomials s_k and $Random$. We send the mask $M(s_k)$ and the polynomial $c[1]$ to the CPU. The CPU will compute $(c[1] \cdot M(s_k)) \mod q$ and sends the result to the secure element. The secure element retrieves the random part from the CPU result, by computing $[(c[1] \cdot M(s_k)) \mod q - (c[1] \cdot Random) \mod q)] \mod q = (c[1] \cdot s_k) \mod q$.

Table 2. The execution time of functions

Operation	Execution time
Time to generate the secret key (ms)	0.041
Generation of the public key (ms)	56.59
Encryption (ms)	69.52
Decryption of a normal ciphertext (ms)	6.52
Decryption of a ciphertext with 3 elements (ms)	62.177
Addition (ms)	0.031
Multiplication (ms)	146.704
Secure element decryption using the delegation method (ms)	59.55
Product in CPU (ms)	76.75

We note that computing the product $(c[1] \cdot Random) \mod q$ requires less memory comparing to $(c[1] \cdot s_k) \mod q$. Algorithm 1 presents the method to delegate the product to the CPU. The line 2, 3, 4, and 5 of the algorithm are executed only once when running the secure element, and the same random polynomial and secret key mask are used each time we delegate the product to the CPU .

5.2   Security Analysis

To enable sending securely the secret key, we proposed above to send the mask $M(s_k) = s_k \oplus Random$ to the CPU. Each coefficient of $M(s_k)$ is computed by adding the corresponding coefficient of the secret key s_k and the random polynomial $Random$, $M(s_k)[i] = (s_k[i] \oplus Random[i]) \mod q$. The value of each $M(s_k)[i]$ is ether $s_k[i]$ or $s_k[i] + 1$, because $Random[i] \in \{0, 1\}$, then the exhaustive attack on $M(s_k)[i]$ is equivalent to the attack on a polynomial of degree d with binary coefficients. As d is equal or greater than 1024, the brute force attack on the mask is not possible.

Algorithm 1. Algorithm to delegate the polynomial product to the CPU

Input $(c[1], s_k)$.
Output $c[1] \cdot s_k$.

1: **function** DELEGATION$(c[1], s_k)$
2:     The secure element generates one random polynomial $Random \in R_2$.
3:     The secure element computes $A = c[1] \cdot Random$.
4:     The secure element computes $M(s_k) = s_k \oplus Random$.
5:     The secure element sends $M(s_k)$ to the CPU.
6:     The CPU computes $B = c[1] \cdot M(s_k)$.
7:     The CPU sends the result B to the secure element.
8:     The secure element computes $B - A = c[1] \cdot s_k$.
9: **return** $c[1] \cdot s_k$

5.3   Implementation and Performances

We implement the FV cryptosystem and the delegation function in C language to be embedded in IoT modules: the client machine, the gateway, the secure element, and the cloud. This implementation is portable, self-contained and independent from other libraries. It can be considered as a proof of concept where we only use the standard mathematics library $math.h$ without SIMD-parallelism and multi-core processing.

We use a set of practical parameters, to enable the evaluation of circuits of one level, a security level of 128 bits, a degree 2048 for the cyclotomic polynomial and 56 bits for the polynomials coefficients. We choose those parameters because they are the smallest that enable to do one multiplication. The scheme enables one level of multiplication and encrypts plaintexts of 16 bits.

The code is embedded and run under an administrator machine, which holds an Intel Core i5 processor at 2.4 GHz. Table 2 presents the performances of our implementation under different platforms.

We implement the FV scheme described below without relinearization, we add some functions to decrypt a ciphertext of three elements and to do addition between ciphertexts.

$Decrypt(s_k, c[1], c[2], c[3])$: This function computes the decryption of a ciphertext resulting from a multiplication and return

$$D(c[1], c[2], c[3]) = [\lfloor \frac{t \cdot [c[1] + c[2] \cdot s_k + c[3] \cdot s_k^2]_q}{q} \rceil]_t.$$

$Addition(c[1], c[2], c[3], c[1]', c[2]')$: This function does the addition of a ciphertext of three elements $(c[1], c[2], c[3])$ and a normal ciphertext $(c[1]', c[2]')$:

$$(c[1], c[2], c[3]) + (c[1]', c[2]') = (c[1] + c[1]', c[2] + c[2]', c[3]). \tag{3}$$

Addition$(c[1], c[2], c[3], c[1]', c[2]', c[3]')$: This function does the addition of ciphertexts of three elements.

$$(c[1], c[2], c[3]) + (c[1]', c[2]', c[3]') = (c[1] + c[1]', c[2] + c[2]', c[3] +, c[3]'). \quad (4)$$

6 Conclusion

In this work, we provide a method to enable taking decisions based on homomorphic ciphertexts comparison. This method consists in decrypting FV ciphertexts and comparing the plaintexts in a secure element. Using our contribution, running the decryption function inside the secure element becomes possible, we proposed to delegate the polynomial multiplication to the CPU. We give a complete use case of homomorphic encryption in the Seaport to encrypt data of containers in the gateways and compute inside the cloud, the weighted sum of containers, the weight of containers before loading them on the ship, or to do currency conversion of goods. We described also a use case in the context of stock management where comparison is necessary to supply the stock of supermarkets.

References

1. Internet of things (IoT). https://internetofthingsagenda.techtarget.com/definition/Internet-of-Things-IoT
2. MQTT (MQ Telemetry Transport). https://internetofthingsagenda.techtarget.com/definition/MQTT-MQ-Telemetry-Transport
3. what is lora? https://www.semtech.com/lora/what-is-lora
4. Bajard, J.-C., Eynard, J., Hasan, M.A., Zucca, V.: A full RNS variant of FV like somewhat homomorphic encryption schemes. In: Avanzi, R., Heys, H. (eds.) SAC 2016. LNCS, vol. 10532, pp. 423–442. Springer, Cham (2017). https://doi.org/10.1007/978-3-319-69453-5_23
5. Bos, J.W., Lauter, K., Loftus, J., Naehrig, M.: Improved security for a ring-based fully homomorphic encryption scheme. In: Stam, M. (ed.) IMACC 2013. LNCS, vol. 8308, pp. 45–64. Springer, Heidelberg (2013). https://doi.org/10.1007/978-3-642-45239-0_4
6. Brakerski, Z.: Fully homomorphic encryption without modulus switching from classical GapSVP. In: Safavi-Naini, R., Canetti, R. (eds.) CRYPTO 2012. LNCS, vol. 7417, pp. 868–886. Springer, Heidelberg (2012). https://doi.org/10.1007/978-3-642-32009-5_50
7. Brakerski, Z., Gentry, C., Vaikuntanathan, V.: (Leveled) fully homomorphic encryption without bootstrapping. In: Goldwasser, S., (ed.) Innovations in Theoretical Computer Science 2012, Cambridge, MA, USA, 8–10 January 2012, pp. 309–325. ACM (2012)
8. Chillotti, I., Gama, N., Georgieva, M., Izabachène, M.: Faster fully homomorphic encryption: bootstrapping in less than 0.1 seconds. In: Cheon, J.H., Takagi, T. (eds.) ASIACRYPT 2016. LNCS, vol. 10031, pp. 3–33. Springer, Heidelberg (2016). https://doi.org/10.1007/978-3-662-53887-6_1
9. Fan, J., Vercauteren, F.: Somewhat practical fully homomorphic encryption. IACR Cryptology ePrint Archive 2012:144 (2012)

10. Gentry, C.: A fully homomorphic encryption scheme. Ph.D. thesis, Stanford University (2009)
11. Gentry, C., Sahai, A., Waters, B.: Homomorphic encryption from learning with errors: conceptually-simpler, asymptotically-faster, attribute-based. In: Canetti, R., Garay, J.A. (eds.) CRYPTO 2013. LNCS, vol. 8042, pp. 75–92. Springer, Heidelberg (2013). https://doi.org/10.1007/978-3-642-40041-4_5
12. Huang, Z., Jalali , A., Chen, H., Han, K., Laine, K.: Simple encrypted arithmetic library - seal (v2.3.0). Online
13. Chen, H., Laine, K., Player, R.: Simple encrypted arithmetic library - seal (v2.2)
14. Lyubashevsky, V., Peikert, C., Regev, O.: On ideal lattices and learning with errors over rings. J. ACM $60(6)$, 43:1–43:35 (2013)
15. Aguilar-Melchor, C., Barrier, J., Guelton, S., Guinet, A., Killijian, M.-O., Lepoint, T.: NFLLIB: NTT-based fast lattice library. In: Sako, K. (ed.) CT-RSA 2016. LNCS, vol. 9610, pp. 341–356. Springer, Cham (2016). https://doi.org/10.1007/978-3-319-29485-8_20
16. Melchor, C.A., Castagnos, G., Gaborit, P.: Lattice-based homomorphic encryption of vector spaces. In: Kschischang, F.R., Yang, E.-H., (eds.) 2008 IEEE International Symposium on Information Theory, ISIT 2008, Toronto, ON, Canada, 6–11 July 2008, pp. 1858–1862. IEEE (2008)
17. Regev, O.: The learning with errors problem (invited survey). In: Proceedings of the 25th Annual IEEE Conference on Computational Complexity, CCC 2010, Cambridge, Massachusetts, USA, 9–12 June 2010, pp. 191–204. IEEE Computer Society (2010)
18. Shoup, V., Halevi, S.: Design and implementation of a homomorphic-encryption library. https://researcher.watson.ibm.com/researcher/files/us-shaih/he-library.pdf
19. van Dijk, M., Gentry, C., Halevi, S., Vaikuntanathan, V.: Fully homomorphic encryption over the integers. In: Gilbert, H. (ed.) EUROCRYPT 2010. LNCS, vol. 6110, pp. 24–43. Springer, Heidelberg (2010). https://doi.org/10.1007/978-3-642-13190-5_2

Hardware Optimization on FPGA for the Modular Multiplication in the AMNS Representation

Asma Chaouch[1,3](✉), Yssouf Fangan Dosso[1], Laurent-Stéphane Didier[1],
Nadia El Mrabet[2](✉), Bouraoui Ouni[3], and Belgacem Bouallegue[3]

[1] IMATH, Université de Toulon,
Toulon, France
{asma-chaouch,dosso,didier}@univ-tln.fr
[2] Mines Saint-Etienne, CEA-Tech, Centre CMP, Departement SAS,
13541 Gardanne, France
nadia.el-mrabet@emse.fr
[3] EµE, Faculty of Sciences of Monastir, University of Monastir,
Monastir, Tunisia
ouni_bouraoui@yahoo.fr, belgacem_bouallegue@yahoo.fr

Abstract. This paper describes our results of the AMNS modular multiplication algorithm for efficient implementations of ECC over $\mathbb{F}_p$ on the Hardware/Software (HW/SW) implementation in FPGA. We provide both arithmetic operators and computation architectures optimized for high speed. We also compare our results with the implementation of the CIOS method for modular multiplication.

Keywords: Arithmetic operators · Modular multiplication · Software implementation · Hardware implementation · Embedded systems · Adapted Modular Number System

1 Introduction

Due to their high efficiency power in combination with forcefulness energy, Field Programmable Gate Arrays (FPGAs) provide very efficient implementation of arithmetic operators. As conception for FPGA hardware give the frequently proclaimed productivity gap, a move to higher basic levels has been done. High-Level Synthesis (HLS) background have actually matured to be a substantially alternative to hand designed (RTL) Register Transfer Level designs, always providing significant efficiency gains at an equal quality of results [1].

However, the available tools are still very complex and cannot be seen as a substitute for detailed knowledge of the underlying hardware. Modular arithmetic is one of the key point for efficient and secure cryptography applications. A challenge is to obtain a number system which permits fast modular computations over large integers. In this paper, we present a hardware IP for modular

© Springer Nature Switzerland AG 2020
S. Kallel et al. (Eds.): CRiSIS 2019, LNCS 12026, pp. 113–127, 2020.
https://doi.org/10.1007/978-3-030-41568-6_8

multipliers for the finite field $\mathbb{F}_p$ where p is a prime integer, with C-based HLS to help designers in the conception of hardware accelerators for implantation of elliptic (ECC) and Hyper-elliptic curve cryptography (HECC) on embedded systems. All these systems require an efficient finite field multiplication. Different algorithms have been proposed in the literature [4,5,12,15,17].

In 2004, Bajard et al. proposed a new number system called the Adapted Modular Number System (AMNS) in order to speed-up the modular operations [2]. The main characteristic of the AMNS is that its elements are polynomials. This system is of particular interest. Indeed, it is shown in [6] that the modular multiplication in AMNS is more efficient than the classical Montgomery modular multiplication. In this work, we provide the first hardware implementation of the multiplication in AMNS. Although the presented modular multiplication algorithm is foremost targeted at the Vivado HLS framework from Xilinx [10], the presented work is applicable to C-based high-level synthesis in general.

This work is organized as follows. In Sect. 2, we give the essential background about the CIOS variant of the Montgomery modular reduction method we use in this paper, we also give an overview on the AMNS representation. Additionally, we explain the usage of FPGA for our implementations of both the CIOS and the modular multiplication in the AMNS; along with an introduction about the HLS. The Sect. 3 is about the hardware implementation of the CIOS algorithm and the AMNS modular multiplication. In Sect. 4, we give implementation results with some comparisons. We finally conclude in Sect. 5.

2 Background

2.1 Coarsely Integrated Operand Scanning (CIOS) Method for Montgomery Modular Multiplication

Let's consider a k-bit processor architecture. Let p be an integer such that n k-bit words are required to represent the elements of $\mathbb{Z}/p\mathbb{Z}$.

When the modulus p does not belong to a special family of numbers like that of Mersenne, the best method to perform the modular multiplication is due to Montgomery [12]. This method allows to perform the modular reduction with division by only a power of two. Since such a division is very cheap, this method is fast. It costs $3n^2$ small multiplications (with an equivalent amount of small additions). In [7], Dussé and Kaliski improve this modular multiplication by reducing the number of small multiplications to $2n^2 + n$.

In [11], Koc et al. analyze and compare five variants of the Montgomery modular multiplication algorithm. These variants are: the Separated Operand Scanning (SOS), the Coarsely Integrated Operand Scanning (CIOS), the Finely Integrated Operand Scanning (FIOS), the Finely Integrated Product Scanning (FIPS) and the Coarsely Integrated Hybrid Scanning(CIHS). All of them take advantage of the improvement in [7]. They mainly differ on two aspects. The first aspect is how the multiplication and the steps are combined. They are either Separated (S) or Coarsely Integrated (CI) or Finely Integrated (FI). The second aspect is how the multiplication of two (big) integers is done. It can be an Operand Scanning (OS), where an outer loop moves through words of one of the operands or a Product Scanning (PS), where the loop moves through words of the product itself. For the CIHS, Hybrid means a mix of OS and PS for multiplication.

In [11], the authors obtain that the CIOS variant is the best variant among the five, especially on a general-purpose processor; see Sect. 9, and Tables 1 & 3 of that paper. It costs $2n^2 + n$ small multiplications, $4n^2 + 4n + 2$ small additions plus some reads and writes operations. This explains the choice of this variant in this paper. For the Montgomery method to work efficiently, the modulus p must be odd in order to have division by only power of two in the reduction step. Assuming that $p = (p_0, \ldots, p_{n-1})$ in the little-endian representation (i.e, the less significant value in the tuple is stored first), we have that p_0 is invertible modulo $W = 2^k$. So, the integer $g = -p_0^{-1} \pmod{W}$ exists. This integer is necessary for all the variants described in [11].

Algorithm 1 is the CIOS variant. In this algorithm, we assume that the inputs are big integers represented as k-bit word array of size n. That is, if $a \in \mathbb{Z}/p\mathbb{Z}$, then $a = (a[0], \ldots, a[n-1])$. Also, the little-Endian representation is used. This algorithm requires an array t of size $n + 2$. Its output is the $n + 1$ first elements of t; i.e, $(t[0], \ldots, t[n])$.

2.2   The Adapted Modular Number System

The Adapted Modular Number System (AMNS) is a number system introduce in 2004 by Bajard et al. [2] in order to speed-up modular arithmetic. The main characteristic of the AMNS is that its elements are polynomials. This characteristic gives to the AMNS many advantages for both efficiency and safety. In [6], Didier et al. show how to generate many AMNS for any prime integer in order to perform modular operations efficiently. They present software implementation (in C language) results which show that the AMNS allows to perform modular multiplication more efficiently than well known libraries like GNU-MP and OpenSSL. In this section, we give an overview on this number system and see how to perform modular operations in it.

Because of the restriction on the number of pages, we do not deal here with the generation process of the AMNS. This generation process requires a consequent mathematical background and is quite long. For the generation process, one should read the works done in [2,6].

The AMNS is a subclass of the Modular Number System (MNS). So, we start by first presenting the MNS.

Definition 1. *Let $p \geqslant 3$ be a prime integer. A modular number system (MNS) is defined by a tuple $\mathcal{B} = (p, n, \gamma, \rho)$, such that for every integer $0 \leqslant x < p$, there exists a vector $V = (v_0, \ldots, v_{n-1})$ such that:*

$$x \equiv \sum_{i=0}^{n-1} v_i \gamma^i \pmod{p},$$

with $|v_i| < \rho$, $\rho \approx p^{1/n}$ and $0 < \gamma < p$.

Algorithm 1. Montgomery CIOS [11]

Require: $a \in \mathbb{Z}/p\mathbb{Z}$ and $b \in \mathbb{Z}/p\mathbb{Z}$

Ensure: $t = ab \pmod{p}$

1: $t \leftarrow (0, \ldots, 0)$ # the array t (also the output) should be set to 0 initially.
2: **for** $i = 0 \ldots n - 1$ **do**
3:     $C \leftarrow 0$
4:     **for** $j = 0 \ldots n - 1$ **do**
5:         $(C, S) \leftarrow t[j] + a[j] * b[i] + C$
6:         $t[j] \leftarrow S$
7:     **end for**
8:     $(C, S) \leftarrow t[n] + C$
9:     $t[n] \leftarrow S$
10:     $t[n + 1] \leftarrow C$
11:     $m \leftarrow g * t[0] \pmod{W}$
12:     $(C, S) \leftarrow t[0] + m * p[0]$
13:     **for** $j = 1 \ldots n - 1$ **do**
14:         $(C, S) \leftarrow t[j] + m * p[j] + C$
15:         $t[j - 1] \leftarrow S$
16:     **end for**
17:     $(C, S) \leftarrow t[n] + C$
18:     $t[n - 1] \leftarrow S$
19:     $t[n] \leftarrow t[n + 1] + C$
20: **end for**
21: return t # $(t[0], \ldots, t[n])$.

In this case, we say that the polynomial $V(X) = v_0 + v_1 X + \cdots + v_{n-1} X^{n-1}$ is a representative of x in $\mathcal{B}$ and we notate $V \equiv x_{\mathcal{B}}$.

For a MNS to be an AMNS, the parameter γ should meet a requirement which is essential for arithmetic operations.

Definition 2. *An Adapted Modular Number System (AMNS) is defined by a tuple $\mathcal{B} = (p, n, \gamma, \rho, E)$ such that (p, n, γ, ρ) is a MNS and γ is a root modulo p of the polynomial $E(X) = X^n - \lambda$, with λ a very small nonzero integer (for instance, $\lambda = \pm 1, \pm 2$ or ± 3).*

Like usual number systems, the main arithmetic operations in the AMNS are the addition and the multiplication. Since elements are polynomials in the AMNS, the addition is the simple polynomial addition and the multiplication is the simple polynomial multiplication. However, in order to have the result of the these operations in the AMNS, additional operations have to be done. We explain below why.

Let $x, y \in \mathbb{Z}/p\mathbb{Z}$ be two integers. Let $V \equiv x_\mathcal{B}$ and $W \equiv y_\mathcal{B}$ be their representatives in $\mathcal{B}$. The polynomial $T = VW$ satisfies $T(\gamma) \equiv xy \pmod{p}$. However, T might not be a valid representative of xy in $\mathcal{B}$ because its degree could be greater than or equal to n. To keep the degree lower than n, the product VW has to be computed modulo the polynomial E. This operation is called the *external reduction*. Notice that since $E(\gamma) \equiv 0 \pmod{p}$ and $T = VW \pmod{E}$, we have $T(\gamma) \equiv xy \pmod{p}$ and $\deg(T) < n$.

Even if $\deg(T) < n$, T might not be a representative of $xy \pmod{p}$ in $\mathcal{B}$, because its coefficients could be greater than or equal to ρ. To have the result in $\mathcal{B}$, a specific primitive called the *internal reduction* has to be applied.

The polynomial $S = V + W$ satisfies $S(\gamma) \equiv (x+y) \pmod{p}$ and $\deg(S) < n$. Here also, S might not be a valid representative in $\mathcal{B}$, since its coefficients could be greater than or equal to ρ. Hence, an internal reduction might be required to retrieve the result in $\mathcal{B}$.

Some Notations and Conventions. Before presenting the arithmetic operations algorithms with the reduction methods, we need to establish some notations and conventions for simplicity and consistency.

For consistency, we will assume that: $p \geqslant 3$ and $n, \gamma, \rho \geqslant 1$.

$\mathbb{Z}_n[X]$ denotes the set of polynomials in $\mathbb{Z}[X]$ which degrees are lower than n:

$$\mathbb{Z}_n[X] = \{C \in \mathbb{Z}[X], \text{ such that: } \deg(C) < n\}.$$

Let $C \in \mathbb{Z}[X]$ be a polynomial. $C \bmod (E, \phi)$ denotes the polynomial reduction $C \bmod E$ where the coefficients of the result are computed modulo ϕ.

The External Reduction. The *external reduction* is a polynomial modular reduction. The goal of this operation is to keep degree of the AMNS representatives lower than n. Let $C \in \mathbb{Z}[X]$ be a polynomial. This operation consists in computing a polynomial R such that:

$$R \in \mathbb{Z}_n[X] \text{ and } R(\gamma) \equiv C(\gamma) \pmod{p}.$$

The Euclidean division of C by E computes Q and R so that:

$$C = Q \times E + R,$$

with $\deg(R) < n$ and $Q \in \mathbb{Z}[X]$. Since $E(\gamma) \equiv 0 \pmod{p}$, one has $R(\gamma) \equiv C(\gamma) \pmod{p}$. So, the external reduction is done as: $R = C \bmod E$. The polynomial E is called the *external reduction polynomial*.

Let $A \in \mathbb{Z}_n[X]$ and $B \in \mathbb{Z}_n[X]$. Let $C = AB$ be a polynomial. Then, $\deg(C) < 2n - 1$. Since $E(X) = X^n - \lambda$, with λ very small, the external reduction can be done very efficiently. RedExt (Algorithm 2), proposed by Plantard in [14] (see Algorithm 28, Sect. 3.2.1), can be used to perform this operation.

Algorithm 2. RedExt (External reduction) [14]

Require: $C \in \mathbb{Z}[X]$ with $\deg(C) < 2n - 1$ and $E(X) = X^n - \lambda$

Ensure: $R \in \mathbb{Z}_n[X]$, such that $R = C \bmod E$

  1: **for** $i = 0 \ldots n - 2$ **do**

  2:     $r_i \leftarrow c_i + \lambda c_{n+i}$

  3: **end for**

  4: $r_{n-1} \leftarrow c_{n-1}$

  5: return R # $R = (r_0, \ldots, r_{n-1})$

The Internal Reduction. The aim of the *internal reduction* is to ensure that the coefficients of polynomials are lower (in absolute value) than ρ. Let $C' \in \mathbb{Z}_n[X]$ be a polynomial, with $\|C'\|_\infty \geqslant \rho$. This operation consists in computing a polynomial R such that $R \in \mathcal{B}$ and $R(\gamma) \equiv C'(\gamma) \pmod{p}$.

Several methods have been proposed to perform this operation [2,3,13]. If the value of the modulus p is not imposed but only its approximate bit-size, then the proposal in [2] might achieve the best efficiency. However, if the value of p is already given, then the proposal in [13] is currently the best one and it is the one we focus on in this paper.

In [13], Negre and Plantard propose a Montgomery-like reduction method to perform the internal reduction. In their proposal, they combine the multiplication operation with their Montgomery-like internal reduction (see Algorithm 1 of that paper). In this paper, we split the multiplication process from the internal reduction, because the internal reduction is also essential for others operations like the addition and the conversions from $\mathbb{Z}/p\mathbb{Z}$ to the AMNS (and vice versa). RedCoeff (Algorithm 3) corresponds to the internal reduction process included in Algorithm 1 of [13].

Algorithm 3. RedCoeff (Coefficient reduction) [13]

Require: $\mathcal{B} = (p, n, \gamma, \rho, E)$, $V \in \mathbb{Z}_n[X]$, $M \in \mathcal{B}$ such that $M(\gamma) \equiv 0 \pmod{p}$, $\phi \in \mathbb{N} \setminus \{0\}$ and $M' = -M^{-1} \bmod(E, \phi)$.

Ensure: $S(\gamma) = C'(\gamma)\phi^{-1} \pmod{p}$, with $S \in \mathbb{Z}_n[X]$

  1: $Q \leftarrow C' \times M' \bmod (E, \phi)$

  2: $R \leftarrow (C' + (Q \times M) \bmod E)$

  3: $S \leftarrow R/\phi$

  4: return S

It can be seen that this Montgomery-like reduction method requires three additional parameters: a non-zero integer ϕ and two polynomials M and M'. These polynomials are such that: $M \in \mathcal{B}$, $M(\gamma) \equiv 0 \pmod{p}$ and $M' = -M^{-1} \bmod(E, \phi)$. Since this algorithm involves many reductions modulo ϕ (line 1) and many exact divisions by ϕ (line 3), it is necessary to take ϕ as a power of two for this algorithm to be efficient. However, taking ϕ as a power of two while ensuring the existence of the polynomials M and M' is not obvious. In [13], the authors do not provide a generation process which allows that. In [8], El Mrabet and Gama give such a generation process but for the special case $E(X) = X^n + 1$.

In [6], Didier et al. propose a generation process which ensures this requirement for $E(X) = X^n - \lambda$, with $\lambda \in \mathbb{Z} \setminus \{0\}$. In the same paper, they also give a generation process for all the others parameters along with a complete set of algorithms to perform arithmetic and conversion operations in the AMNS. Here, we only present the multiplication algorithm since it is the purpose of this paper. One should read the works done in [6] for more details.

The Modular Multiplication. As said above, the authors in [13] propose a modular multiplication method which includes the Montgomery-like reduction method. Algorithm 4 corresponds to their proposal, except that it is split here in a set of algorithms.

Algorithm 4. Modular multiplication in AMNS [13]

Require: $A \in \mathcal{B}$, $B \in \mathcal{B}$ and $\mathcal{B} = (p, n, \gamma, \rho, E)$

Ensure: $S \in \mathcal{B}$ with $S(\gamma) \equiv A(\gamma)B(\gamma)\phi^{-1} \pmod{p}$

1: $C \leftarrow A \times B$

2: $V \leftarrow \text{RedExt}(C)$

3: $S \leftarrow \text{RedCoeff}(V)$

4: return S

In [13], Negre and Plantard show that if the parameters ρ and ϕ are such that:

$$\rho \geqslant 2n|\lambda|\|M\|_\infty \text{ and } \phi \geqslant 2n|\lambda|\rho$$

then, the output S of the Algorithm 4 is such that $\|S\|_\infty < \rho$ (i.e $S \in \mathcal{B}$).

This requirement is assumed in the Algorithm 4.

In [6], the authors prove that it is always possible to generate an AMNS for any prime integer $p \geqslant 3$ where the parameter E is such that $E(X) = X^n - \lambda$, with $\lambda = \pm 2^i$. This makes the internal and the external reductions faster since these operations involves many multiplication by λ. As already said, ϕ should be a power of two; i.e: $\phi = 2^t$, with $t \in \mathbb{N} \setminus \{0\}$.

Let's consider a k-bit processor architecture, then the basic arithmetic computations are performed on k-bit words. The cost of the modular multiplication is given in Table 1 with $\lambda = \pm 2^i$ and $\phi = 2^t$. This cost is expressed as a function of the number of k-bit integer multiplications, additions and shifts. In that table, $\mathcal{M}$ and $\mathcal{A}$ respectively denote the multiplication and the addition of two k-bit integers. We also respectively denote $\mathcal{S}_l^y$ and $\mathcal{S}_r^y$ a left shift and a right shift of y bits.

Table 1. Theoretical cost of the modular multiplication, where $E(X) = X^n \pm 2^i$ and $\phi = 2^t$.

Simple polynomial multiplication	$n^2\mathcal{M} + (2n^2 - 4n + 2)\mathcal{A}$
External reduction	$2(n - 1)\mathcal{A} + (n - 1)\mathcal{S}_l^i$
Internal reduction	$2n^2\mathcal{M} + (3n^2 - n)\mathcal{A} + n\mathcal{S}_r^t$
Total cost	$3n^2\mathcal{M} + (5n^2 - 3n)\mathcal{A} + (n - 1)\mathcal{S}_l^i + n\mathcal{S}_r^t$

2.3   FPGA

In our modular multiplication we use the CIOS algorithm (for coarsely integrated operators scanning) and the AMNS (Adapted modular number system) algorithm. Due to its regularity and simplicity, this algorithms can be easily implemented in the DSP slices of FPGAs.

Most of the proposed solutions in the literature use complex and expensive algorithms to release these data dependencies and improve computing performance in multipliers implanted. Due to the complexity of these algorithms, the corresponding fast modular multipliers often consume a significant amount of FPGA hardware resources. Thus, we can find in the literature examples of FPGA implementations of modular multipliers within ECC cryptosystems using several hundred DSP slices (see for example [9]). We believe that such a consumption of resources is not reasonable for material implementations of embedded cryptosystems. We have therefore decided to propose a different solution based on architectural optimization rather than algorithms.

Our constraint is to implement a high level security of cryptographic (128 or 256, 512 and 1024) in FPGA, knowing that the hardwired control units are not big enough for cryptographic sizes. In our target FPGAs, DSP slices are 18×25 bits units. Then processing each $\mathbb{F}_p$ element would require many parallel BRAMs and DSP slices. But using many BRAMs is useless since the number of intermediate $\mathbb{F}_p$ elements is small in ECC and HECC (up to 10 and 20 respectively). To allow an efficient hardware design area and frequency on FPGA, we have decompose p-bit elements into a world wide of w-bit which is multiple of 18. The choice can reduce the number of slice DSP used in the design. We denote n the number of coefficient of w-bit necessary for each operand with $p = nw$.

2.4   Description of High-Level Synthesis

High-Level Synthesis (HLS) is also known as C Synthesis or Electronic System Level synthesis (ESL synthesis). It allows hardware designers to efficiently build and verify their design hardware implementations by choosing the best directive to optimize their design architecture and allowing one to describe the design in a higher abstract level. Generally, its overall process consists of control and datapath extraction and RTL generation.

The applicability and reliability of the HLS are discussed in [16]. Tambara et al. analyzed the performance and utilization of HLS-based optimization methods, for example the function inlining, pipelining and loop unrolling. These techniques are used in the advanced encryption standard (AES).

For hardware implementation, we used Xilinx HLS for High-Level Synthesis and Xilinx VIVADO 2016.1 for implementation target. All strategy for high-level synthesis in HLS and implementation in VIVADO is set to default parameters. The following and Fig. 1 are our implementation flow.

(1) Design conform encryption in C-code.
(2) Generate and check the RTL with HLS from C-code design.implementation area and latency.
(3) Optimize with directive.
(4) Check RTL with C/RTL co-simulator.
(5) Generate block design of entire ZYNQ-7000 evaluation board including the conform encryption RTL.
(6) Execute synthesis and implementation and check implementation area from implementation report.
(7) Generate program device and target bit-stream file.
(8) Verify generated IP design with ZYNQ-7000.

3   Implementation of the Modular Multiplication Algorithms

The ZedBoard Zynq-7000 FPGA development kit [18] was used in this study. Zynq-7000 is different from standard FPGAs in that it contains Artix-7 FPGA and ARM Cortex-A9 processor on the same chip together. In a FPGA card having two parts of component, the parts which holding intense computations are achieved on FPGA and the control parts not contain computations can be executed on the processor by using software.

Zynq consists of two parts:Programmable Logic and Processing System. Processing System (PS) works like a traditional processor since it contains structures such as ARM Cortex-A9, Floating Point Unit, Memory Controller, Gigabit Ethernet Controller and USB Controller. Programmable Logic part, on the other hand, contains all the structures of a standard FPGA. The communication between PS and PL parts is provided by high performance data-paths [19]. The specification of ZYNQ-7000 XC7Z020 is summarized as follows and shown in Table 2.

The objective of our algorithm is to do it simple while being able to generate a competitive result. The clarity will help us for efficient implementation in the hardware.

3.1   Implementation of CIOS

We wish to help hardware implementation designers in asymmetric encryption to explore various compromises algorithms/number representations/architectures. In this section, we only deal with the reduction modulo p. We will present an example with $p = 128$ and $w = 32$. in this way, we will have $n = 4$ (number of coefficient).

Table 2. Specification of ZYNQ-7000 XC7Z020

CPU	ARM Cortex-A9 32bit processor 886 MHz	
F P G A	Programmable Logic Cells	85K Cells
	Look-Up Tables	53200
	Flip-flops	106400
	Block RAM	560 KB
	Logic Slice	13300

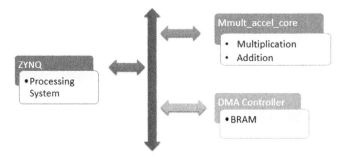

Fig. 1. Architecture with its main units (arithmetic and memory), internal communication system, and control

The top operation is the Modular multiplication CIOS. There are hierarchical dependencies between needed operations:

– we need a function to bring back the coefficient in the Montgomery domain.
– Basic point operations: right shift, left shift.
– Operations over $\mathbb{F}_p$: multiplication, subtraction, addition and inversion of large integers modulo a large prime number.

In this section, we describe the method used during hardware design. Figure 1 represents the flow diagram of the design phases.

The first step is developed with VIVADO HLS 2016.4 to creates an RTL implementation from our C code which is detailed in Algorithm 1. The synthesizer transforms each line in the C code into an hardware operation and insert those operations into clock cycles. Using the information of the clock period and device delays, it places into a single clock cycle, many operations as possible. The design created by Vivado HLS can be optimized. The optimization were used to reduce the total of clock cycles needed. For example, we have used #pragma HLS PIPLINE IT = 1 for using the parallelism between loop iterations. The modular multiplication CIOS core generated with Vivado HLS is connected by the AXI4-Stream interfaces to the DMA controller. Address generation, burst formatting and scheduling of the memory transaction are handled by the AXI DMA IP.

The second step, and after the generating of our IP and after identifying the time-consuming for our function, we have build a basic embedded system and we added our accelerator IP with the VIVADO 2016.4. To make our design functional, we have including two AXI interconnects, the DMA controller: one for the control registers, the other for Accelerator Coherency Port (ACP), the timer subsystem, which will be used for giving very precise hardware timing measurements. Then we have generate a Tcl scripts to completing the necessary process of making connection. The generated design is presented in te Fig. 2.

The Final step, and after setting address and after the validation of our design, we have verified the result of the hardware accelerator with our software only solution with (SDK) platform 2016.4, which should meet the same results.

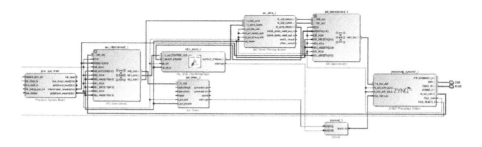

Fig. 2. Block design

3.2   Implementation of AMNS

In this section, we describe our hardware IP for AMNS. Figure 3 represents the flow diagram of the design phases. We have implemented a different architecture for a different width of word, such as $w = 32, 36, 54$ and for different size of p (128, 256, 512, 1024). We present the different steps of implementation for $p = 128$, which will be the same structure of all the different security levels. We divide the AMNS modular multiplication in four steps:

- A function to extract the coefficient of the polynomial result of the multiplication of A by B.
- Internal reduction algorithm.
- External reduction algorithm.
- Basic point operations: right shift, left shift.

The external reduction is detailed in Algorithm 2. Its hardware design is presented in Fig. 4. We used the cell $Mult$ to perform the external step. The input of the cell $Mult$ are: C_i and C_{i+n} provided by the previous step ($C = A \times B$). The output of the cell $Mult$ is C'[i]: the coefficient of the reduced polynomial provided to the next step.

The internal reduction is detailed in Algorithm 3. Figure 5 corresponds to its hardware design. It is composed of three steps:

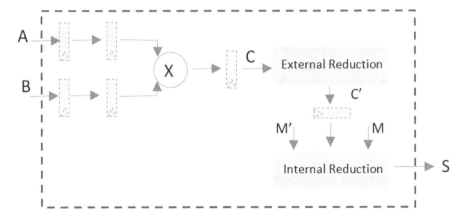

Fig. 3. AMNS architecture

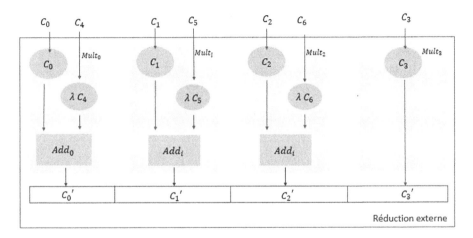

Fig. 4. External reduction

- The first step is the line 1 in Algorithm 3. We have as inputs the coefficients of C' and M'. The cell $Mult$ is used to perform the external step. The outputs are the coefficients of the polynomial Q, which will be given to the next step.
- The second step is the line 2 in Algorithm 3. The inputs are the coefficients of the polynomials Q and M. The cell $Mult$ is used to perform the external step. The cell Add is used to generate the coefficients of the polynomial R, which will be provided in the next step, the C'_i is from the previous step.
- The final step is the line 3 in Algorithm 3. The input of the cell $shiftright$ is provided by the previous step, S is the output of the Algorithm 3.

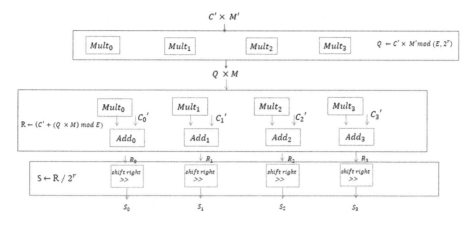

Fig. 5. Internal reduction

4   Implementation Results

We start by comparing the results of the different modular reduction algorithms (CIOS, AMNS) for different sizes of prime integers. The designs were described in a High-Level Synthesis (HLS) and synthesized for the Zedboard Zync-7000 XC7z020 of Xilinx FPGAs. Table 3 shows the results for combinations of directives of optimization that we have tested. In order to check the correctness of our result, we have compared the results given by the FPGA with the python code. The AMNS design offers the possibility to be used in various applications with different bit lengths like ECC, HECC. As it is shown in Table 3, we have an interesting result for our AMNS design in the fact that the number of cycle are independent of the word bit size. We also implement the CIOS version of the Montgomery multiplication in order to make a fair comparison. Indeed, our implementations are homogeneous and if most efficient implementation of the CIOS algorithm exists, it implies that the AMNS multiplication could also be improved.

Table 3. Comparison of our architecture.

	CIOS	AMNS					
p size bit	128	128			256		512
w bit	**32**	**32**	**36**	**54**	**36**	**64**	**64**
Freq (Mhz)	115.6	114.8	118.06	115.6	118.06	118.063	118.06
Cycle	246	497	267	193	926	457	1637
Speed μs	2.12	4.32	2.26	1.66	7.84	3.87	13.86
Slice DSP	60	18	51	106	48	96	96
Slice LUT	5681	3048	3617	4799	2585	3576	4250
BRAM	0	2	10	11	12	16	20

We could notice that, considering difference size of the elementary words which is denoted here w, the AMNS results are better then the CIOS results, considering every point of comparison; the number of clock cycles and the number of slice. Considering the frequency used, for $p = 128$ if we compare the result of CIOS and AMNS with world width 32, we find that the AMNS require less number of DSP and slice then the CIOS design.

5   Conclusion

In this paper, we have built two IP hardware designs with the High-Level Synthesis (HLS), such as the CIOS method of Montgomery application Algorithm and the Adapted Modular Number System (AMNS) over large prime characteristic finite fields F_p. Our motivation was to provide a fair comparison between hardware implementation of the AMNS multiplication with the classical Montgomery's multiplication. We give the results of our two IP designs after routing and placement using a Zedboard Zync-7000 XC7z020 Xilinx FPGAs. Our architecture can be used with different security levels: 128, 256 or 512. We have implemented the first design of AMNS modular multiplication, with the goal of optimizing the design with co-design architecture. Certainly we can have a better result. Our conclusion is that AMNS could be more efficient than Montgomery's CIOS multiplication. In order to improve the performance of our AMNS design, which is the first implementation that is made for AMNS in the FPGA, it could be interesting to provide a VHDL implementation.

References

1. Abid, M.: System-level hardware synthesis of dataflow programs with HEVC as study use case. Ph.D. thesis, Bretagne Loire University, France (2016)
2. Bajard, J.-C., Imbert, L., Plantard, T.: Modular number systems: beyond the mersenne family. In: Handschuh, H., Hasan, M.A. (eds.) SAC 2004. LNCS, vol. 3357, pp. 159–169. Springer, Heidelberg (2004). https://doi.org/10.1007/978-3-540-30564-4_11
3. Bajard, J.C., Imbert, L., Plantard, T.: Arithmetic operations in the polynomial modular number system. In: 17th IEEE Symposium on Computer Arithmetic (ARITH-17) 2005, Cape Cod, MA, USA, pp. 206–213 (2005). https://hal-lirmm.ccsd.cnrs.fr/lirmm-00109201/document
4. Barrett, P.: Implementing the Rivest Shamir and Adleman public key encryption algorithm on a standard digital signal processor. In: Odlyzko, A.M. (ed.) CRYPTO 1986. LNCS, vol. 263, pp. 311–323. Springer, Heidelberg (1987). https://doi.org/10.1007/3-540-47721-7_24
5. Blakely, G.R.: A computer algorithm for calculating the product AB modulo M. IEEE Trans. Comput. $\mathbf{C}-\mathbf{32}$(5), 497–500 (1983). https://doi.org/10.1109/TC.1983.1676262
6. Didier, L.S., Dosso, F.Y., Véron, P.: Efficient modular operations using the adapted modular number system (2019). https://arxiv.org/abs/1901.11485

7. Dussé, S.R., Kaliski, B.S.: A cryptographic library for the Motorola DSP56000. In: Damgård, I.B. (ed.) EUROCRYPT 1990. LNCS, vol. 473, pp. 230–244. Springer, Heidelberg (1991). https://doi.org/10.1007/3-540-46877-3_21

8. El Mrabet, N., Gama, N.: Efficient multiplication over extension fields. In: Özbudak, F., Rodríguez-Henríquez, F. (eds.) WAIFI 2012. LNCS, vol. 7369, pp. 136–151. Springer, Heidelberg (2012). https://doi.org/10.1007/978-3-642-31662-3_10. Kindly check and confirm the updated details are correct in Ref. [9].

9. Alrimeih, H., Rakhmatov, D.: Fast and flexible hardware support for ECC over multiple standard prime fields. IEEE Trans. Very Large Scale Integr. (VLSI) Syst. **22**, 2661–2674 (2014)

10. Hrica, J.: Floating-point design with Vivado HLS. https://www.xilinx.com/support/documentation/application_notes/xapp599-floating-point-vivado-hls.pdf

11. Koc, C.K., Acar, T., Kaliski, B.S.: Analyzing and comparing montgomery multiplication algorithms. IEEE Micro **16**(3), 26–33 (1996)

12. Montgomery, P.L.: Modular multiplication without trial division. Math. Comput. **44**(170), 519–521 (1985)

13. Negre, C., Plantard, T.: Efficient modular arithmetic in adapted modular number system using lagrange representation. In: Mu, Y., Susilo, W., Seberry, J. (eds.) ACISP 2008. LNCS, vol. 5107, pp. 463–477. Springer, Heidelberg (2008). https://doi.org/10.1007/978-3-540-70500-0_34

14. Plantard, T.: Arithmétique modulaire pour la cryptographie. Ph.D. thesis, Montpellier 2 University, France (2005)

15. Takagi, N.: A radix-4 modular multiplication hardware algorithm for modular exponentiation. IEEE Trans. Comput. **41**(8), 949–956 (1992). https://doi.org/10.1109/12.156537

16. Tambara, L.A., et al.: Analyzing reliability and performance trade-offs of HLS-based designs in SRAM-based FPGAS under soft errors. IEEE Trans. Nucl. Sci. **64**(2), 874–881 (2017)

17. Taylor, F.: Large moduli multipliers for signal processing. IEEE Trans. Circuits Syst. **28**(7), 731–736 (1981)

18. Xilinx: Zynq evaluation and development (hardware user's guide) (2014). http://zedboard.org/sites/default/files/documentations/ZedBoard_HW_UG_v2_2.pdf

19. Xilinx: Zynq-7000 SoC data sheet: overview (2018). https://www.xilinx.com/support/documentation/data_sheets/ds190-Zynq-7000-Overview.pdf

A Semantic Framework with Humans in the Loop for Vulnerability-Assessment in Cyber-Physical Production Systems

Yuning Jiang[1]([✉])[ID], Yacine Atif[1][ID], Jianguo Ding[1][ID], and Wei Wang[2][ID]

[1] School of Informatics, University of Skövde, Skövde, Sweden
{yuning.jiang,yacine.atif,jianguo.ding}@his.se
[2] School of Engineering Science, University of Skövde, Skövde, Sweden
Wei.Wang@his.se

Abstract. Critical manufacturing processes in smart networked systems such as Cyber-Physical Production Systems (CPPSs) typically require guaranteed quality-of-service performances, which is supported by cyber-security management. Currently, most existing vulnerability-assessment techniques mostly rely on only the security department due to limited communication between different working groups. This poses a limitation to the security management of CPPSs, as malicious operations may use new exploits that occur between successive analysis milestones or across departmental managerial boundaries. Thus, it is important to study and analyse CPPS networks' security, in terms of vulnerability analysis that accounts for humans in the production process loop, to prevent potential threats to infiltrate through cross-layer gaps and to reduce the magnitude of their impact. We propose a semantic framework that supports the collaboration between different actors in the production process, to improve situation awareness for cyberthreats prevention. Stakeholders with different expertise are contributing to vulnerability assessment, which can be further combined with attack-scenario analysis to provide more practical analysis. In doing so, we show through a case study evaluation how our proposed framework leverages crucial relationships between vulnerabilities, threats and attacks, in order to narrow further the risk-window induced by discoverable vulnerabilities.

Keywords: Cyber-physical production system security ·
Human-in-the-Loop · Vulnerability assessment · Semantic model ·
Reference model

1 Introduction

Industry 4.0 is the current trend of automation in manufacturing sector. Cyber-physical systems (CPSs) are the main driver of the fourth industrial revolution trend, which is evolving as an interaction between ICT systems and

This research has been supported in part by the EU ISF Project A431.678/2016 ELVIRA (Threat modeling and resilience of critical infrastructures), coordinated by Polismyndigheten/Sweden.

S. Kallel et al. (Eds.): CRiSIS 2019, LNCS 12026, pp. 128–143, 2020.
https://doi.org/10.1007/978-3-030-41568-6_9

control elements used to operate a physical process in order to achieve production objectives. A cyber-physical production system (CPPS) is supported by CPS controls to respond to changing conditions, and anticipate changes in physical processes [1]. However, the increasing connectivity facilitated by communication links within and across CPS networks, could prompt an adversary to exploit vulnerabilities along those communication links to create cyber-attacks. For instance, in the year of 2017, the "WannaCry" ransomware attack occurred in several manufacturing plants and caused production to stop [2], incurring substantial business losses.

Meanwhile, dynamic and complex production processes involve multi-domain enterprise management procedures, which may result in communication gaps throughout interconnected application-specific sub-systems of the overall production fabric [1]. Consider Numerical Controllers or NC machining part as an example, which describes a production system typically across four stages, namely part-design that defines its Product and Manufacturing Information (PMI) data, process planning that creates the detailed NC machining process data, part machining that runs this process data on Computer Numerical Controller or CNC machines and the tool condition data to monitor the production process, as well as quality-inspection that involves quality-assessment data. Groups of application-specific staff are responsible for design, machining, and inspection activities within the production process, such as designer, process planner, CNC machine operator and quality inspector. Software administrators are mainly responsible for operational and maintenance tasks to ensure capabilities of Software-as-a-Service (SaaS) within the cloud-based environment, to enable the services of software programs such as computer aided design (CAD) and computer-aided manufacturing (CAM) programs. Therefore, a concrete model should be based on multiple sources of heterogeneous data [3] which needs to be transformed into a common semantic representation [4], and in a machine readable format, to improve a common view of situation awareness.

However, current vulnerability instance response mechanisms in complex CPPS are faced with challenges to bridge the knowledge gap between cybersecurity techniques, industrial control system (ICS) expertise, and socio-technical management procedures, that involve human actors in the production lifecycle. A successful attack that propagates without notice could result in severe impact, due to lack of communication through manufacturing networked-layers and related operators such as network administrators, application-specific engineers and security managers. However, in current manufacturing management structures, the communication between different groups is limited due to inherent differences in working contents. Therefore, it appears vital to set up a common framework to provide a unified understanding from different views, in order to prevent potential threats to infiltrate through cross-layer gaps and to reduce the magnitude of their impact.

In this paper, a semantic framework of vulnerability-assessment with human-in-the-loop is proposed to facilitate a greater level of automation in vulnerability assessment and support a greater level of communication between vulnerability-handling stakeholders. The rest of this paper is organised as follows: In Sect. 2, we explore the state of the art and compare current research approaches against our method. In Sect. 3, we introduce the background of CPPS, with emphasis on topological structures and functional dependencies. In Sect. 4, we propose our vulnerability-assessment framework to set up semantic mapping between threat, vulnerability and attack instances, and leverage use cases via actors involved in the production process through which such infiltration and evolution may occur. In Sect. 5, we provide a case study to present and evaluate an application of our vulnerability-assessment framework in CPPS from different perspectives. In Sect. 6, we provide some concluding remarks and discuss some future research directions.

2   Related Works

Qualitative Vulnerability-assessment models primarily address relationships among vulnerability and risk, to express vulnerability observations based on qualitative data, such as those employed in security-risk management frameworks like SECTEC [8]. In these works, an ontology is used for system implementation as a vocabulary basis consisting of facts (both abstract facts and entity facts), constraints, types and attributes of the system, in order to adopt a common semantic information for knowledge base construction, and to support modelling of security applications. However, these frameworks focus on risk-management fragment on an abstract level, and do not address the details of other security elements, such as how a vulnerability could be exploited by a threat and further materialise into an attack. Therefore, these frameworks suffer from being vague and ultimately subjective. Some works take into consideration the complex and dynamic attributes of CPS [7]. For instance, Quality Control (QC)-based taxonomies are setup by a taxonomy of attack types on CPPSs to improve quality control [10]. Still, these works mostly concentrate on risk-management and/or vulnerability-management from a management perspective, and do not consider the complex and dynamic attack behaviours and exploit patterns.

Some other related works concentrate on attack modelling, such as the metamodel based architecture pwnPr3d (referring to an attack-graph-driven probabilistic threat-modelling approach) [9], which highlights the need for automatic attack-graphs generation to mitigate cyber-attacks. However, these models focus on attack-steps and corresponding prerequisites in vulnerabilities instead of the vulnerable nature of the system. That is they focus on defining attack vectors that model attack-patterns, more than exploit vectors that represent vulnerability patterns. Both patterns are used to model cyberthreat patterns though. The complex structure of CPPSs and the limited computing capability embedded sensing devices lower the protection degree to withstand these cyberthreats, and thus contribute to increasing their vulnerability degree. Such vulnerabilities emerge from specific features of CPPS that are not well addressed in previous works. Furthermore, these works mostly focus on attack modelling and mitigation techniques, while neither works contribute to bridging security controls across CPPS management perspectives.

One missing point in the previous approaches is to take into account the stakeholders to contribute to vulnerability assessment, which can be further combined with attack-scenario analysis to provide more practical security-assessment. Stakeholders with knowledge about CPPS can provide valuable information about vulnerability-exploitability with varying degrees of impact-severity, and are important to be involved in the assessment cycle to support analytics-based decision-making processes to protect critical infrastructures. Our approach proposes a semantic framework to support communication between risk managers, cybersecurity engineers, and also domain-specific operators. This approach also illustrates the connections between different vulnerability instances, threat instances, and attack instances in CPPS, to extract threat, vulnerability and attack (TVA) patterns that support CPPS vulnerability evaluation.

3   Cyber-Physical Production System Security and Human Actors

Conceptually, a cyber-physical system includes a cyber, a control and a physical process layer [5]. In smart manufacturing or CPPS, the control layer includes a network of microprocessor-controlled physical objects, such as programmable logic controllers (PLCs), which interface with physical process sensors. The physical process consists of a production-flow regulated by workstation machines and other manufacturing equipments. Thus, the control layer relays measurements from sensors that interact with field devices such as milling machines and drilling machines, to remote control centres, as illustrated in Fig. 1.

In the physical layer, engineers or operators could locally maintain workstations using local stations or Human Machine Interfaces (HMIs). In the control-layer, Operating Technology or OT administrators, engineers or operators could remotely maintain workstations using remote stations or through a virtual private network (VPN), to optimise production operations. Then, engineers use control and command servers to process these data to support operational production decisions, and to synchronise their operations. The top cyber-layer expresses decision-support analytics to manage the underlying control-system operations, in an enterprise platform of application servers and data-store. The application-servers provide various application services, containing CAD server, software-update server, operation-system server, time-unit server, web server, etc., The datastore includes process-data server, historian-database, and domain-controller. Specifically, design engineers use CAD program to design product through application servers and store the corresponding 3D-model files in data-store servers. Software administrators use software-update server to update outdated firmware or system software, with the support from historian-database. The process-data server stores and transmits design-, process- and manufacturing-data from production-flow, which supports file transfer between data analysers. The historian-database stores historical-data from application servers, which is queried by operators to monitor production processes. The

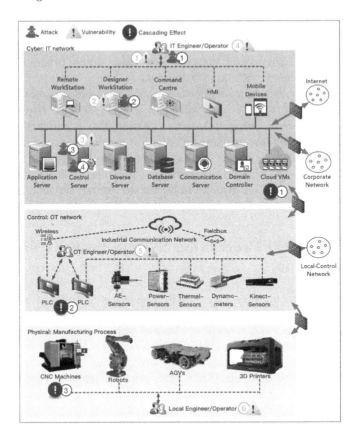

Fig. 1. Cyber-physical production system and involved human actors

domain-controller reserves user-information, and supports corresponding authorisation maintained by administrators.

An advanced persistent threat (APT) might be materialised by an attacker using vulnerability-chain[1], whereby exploits on one particular component may give access to another exploit on another set of components, as illustrated in Fig. 1. *V-x* refers to different vulnerabilities, while *A-x* refers to different attacks. *V-1 (default password setting)* of an application-engineer's account might be exploited by an attacker to compromise this account in Attack *A-1*, which might be followed by another Attack *A-2* by trying to compromise a correlated designer workstation using compromised accounts. If the designer-workstation has *V-2 (weak authentication management)*, then *A-2* might have a higher success probability. Furthermore, another attack *A-3* might be triggered by the threat agent to gain access to a database server through a compromised designer-workstation. A potential vulnerability *V-3 (weak access control)* might allow *A-3* to happen,

---

[1] http://cwe.mitre.org/documents/glossary.

which might let the threat agent further trigger another attack *A-4* to manipulate certain geometry CAM programmes in the control server.

The previous successful attacks of the CAM programme code manipulation may stay unnoticed due to *V-4 (insufficient communication between CAM-engineers and security officers)*, which gives time to the attacker to compromise the whole IT network. Normally, IT department and OT department are distributed in different locations and may have *V-5 and V-6 (communication gaps between IT-personnel, OT-personnel and local operators)*. In this case, the manipulated CAM file might reach PLC without any correction, and further triggers wrong movement track in NC or CNC machines. This can result in a severe consequence in the production process due to communication gaps.

4   Cyber-Security Conceptual Framework

To prevent threat-induced anomalies or intrusion attempts, vulnerabilities need to be rooted out from CPPS infrastructure and assessed to enumerate and rank their severity. This assessment involves modelling vulnerability to account for salient features, as well as identifying critical-component of CPPS infrastructure to weigh vulnerabilities, while accounting for CPPS actors who may be contributed to threat vectors. The component-model in Fig. 2 shows our proposed concept unified modelling language (UML) framework of CPPS cybersecurity taxonomic links across *System*-Objects, *CPPS*-Objects, as well as *Actor*-Objects. Ontological method is adopted to tie eliminate ambiguity and support consistency checking. This semantic framework could support vulnerability-driven cybersecurity analysis across CPPS environments. We also provide an user-interaction model in Fig. 3 that reveals related semantic relationships of contributing stakeholders, based on which we involve different actors into the vulnerability assessment process. The proposed vulnerability assessment methods are later evaluated in the context of CPPS case study.

(A) Component Model for System-Induced Vulnerability Analysis

The component model represents two concepts and related information, *Security-Object*, and *CPPSObject*. A vulnerability could be regarded as an emergent property of an asset within CPPS. Differentiating intrinsic-properties and emergent-properties of an asset could support the detection of abnormal behaviours. Confidentiality, integrity and availability are intrinsic metrics of impact property, while confidentiality-weakness, integrity-weakness, and availability-weakness measure emergent-properties. Vulnerability-assessment evaluates a potential *asset* disruption prospect. Combining *Criticality* of vulnerable asset, and *Severity* of all the emerged *Vulnerability* in this vulnerable asset, we could further compute *Vulnerability Index* at the asset level.

SecurityObject accumulates TVA (Threat, Vulnerability and Attack) information and related relationships. Vulnerabilities may be exploited by an *Attacker*

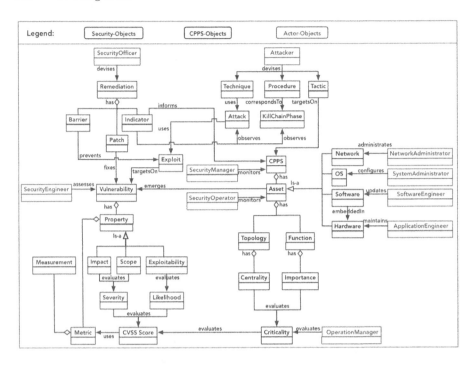

Fig. 2. Vulnerability-driven CPPS security component model

(i.e. threat agent) in different ways using *Exploits*. An *Attacker* may further trigger an attack in different ways. Each vulnerability instance has specific impact, scope and exploitability properties. Each *Exploit* may be used to disrupt a targeted component in *CPPS* infrastructure in different ways. A vulnerability-assessment process mainly involves the identification, definition and evaluation of how exploits trigger attacks, and the magnitude of those attacks i.e. *Impact*. Furthermore, our framework uses cybersecurity-attributes in the form of value-pairs, and could provide a multidimensional view of vulnerabilities, to further support a quantitative analysis using scoring mechanisms such as the industrial standard Common Vulnerability Scoring System (CVSS)[2] to evaluate the severity of each identified vulnerability, and to support risk analysis.

CPPSObject aggregates CPPS assets and related components. Systems and softwares components of various assets in the digitalised industry are interconnected. Vulnerabilities emerge due to these interconnections. Considering the nature of CPPS, we define an asset component to be either a software (e.g. a CAD program), a hardware (e.g. a milling machine), an Operating System (OS), or a network (e.g. a TCP/IP protocol). A software is embedded in a hardware, to form the asset that drives a physical process, for instance electricity supply. Vulnerabilities could be initially categorised based on corresponding types of

---

[2] https://nvd.nist.gov/vuln-metrics/cvss/v3-calculator.

assets. Different vulnerabilities might contribute to threats that bring different levels of impact, measured through levels of losses in confidentiality, integrity and availability (CIA) triad as well as in view, control and/or communication of the physical process. For example, a CPPS hardware may be vulnerable by having no physical-access protection, which might be used by an attacker to gain unauthorised physical access through USB, that could be unknowingly introduced by other legitimate CPPS actors.

(B) User Interaction Model for Human-Induced Vulnerability Management

Dynamic and cooperating vulnerability analysis allows mitigations to occur within the time interval that span the discovery and disclosure of vulnerabilities, and giving time for vulnerability patches to become available and deployed before the time whereby exploits are made public. In our user-interaction model as illustrated in Fig. 3, *ActorObject* includes *CPPS-Staff*, and *Attacker*. Each instance of *ActorObject* may further have a profile including identity information (i.e. role and label) and character (i.e. grouping and sophistication). *Attacker* has specific *Technique*, *Procedure* and *Tactic* used to trigger attack instances.

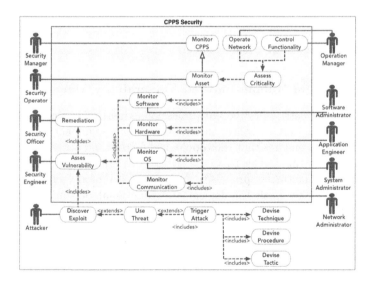

Fig. 3. CPPS security user interaction model

CPPS-Staff instantiates *SecurityOfficer, SecurityManager, SecurityOperator, SoftwareAdministrator, ApplicationEngineer, NetworkAdministrator*, etc., textitSecurityOperator monitors corresponding *Assets*. *SecurityManager* monitors CPPS *Indicators*. Conceptually, *SecurityOfficer* needs to gauge budget investments through adopting an expert-system interpretation of numerical vulnerability-indicators to carry out mitigation decisions like vulnerability-patching. *SecurityEngineer* rank assets by using following vulnerability-indicators: (a) their *Criticality* evaluated by *OperationManager*, (b) their vulnerability exploitability *Likelihood* identified by *SystemAdministrator*, *SoftwareAdministrator*, and *NetworkAdministrator*, as well as (c) the impact *Severity* of threats defined by *ApplicationEngineer* [6]. By distributing dynamic vulnerability-management tasks throughout CPPS organisation, we argue that it improves the level of communication between vulnerability-handling stakeholders.

5 Vulnerability Analysis with Human-In-The-Loop

In the following sections, we provide a thorough case study that involves actor roles in our simplified manufacturing workstation, to illustrate instances of vulnerability-management cooperation in a common industrial-production environment, followed by experiments to evaluate our immersive-analysis framework. In the experiments section, we retrieve CPPS vulnerability reports from cross-linked online vulnerability-repositories to analyse existing vulnerability instances, and produce a qualitative evaluation at CPPS-asset vulnerability level. We also reveal experiment results from our streamlined approach that involves stakeholders to quantitatively assess vulnerability scores. These scores provide statistical information for practical attack-graph generation, which delivers valuable information for security management.

5.1 Case Study of Human-Induced Vulnerability Management

We interviewed industrial-production professionals and operators of a vehicles manufacturing company, to collect information about manufacturing networks structure. This step ensures that the topological factors and other settings of the network structure proposed in this case study could reflect an actual scenario of industrial manufacturing processes. Our proposed model contains around 700 components, 1000 both topological and functional dependencies, as well as around 100 data-flows exchanged across network applications and around 90 involved actors. In this study, we report a simplified account of the manufacturing structure as a reference model that focuses on key functionalities, to emphasise some key functional connections and data-flows, which are illustrated in Fig. 4. Different layered blocks illustrate interdependencies across CPPS smart manufacturing networks, namely cyber-layer, control-layer, and physical-layer. Each layer incorporates different functional sections or zones of CPPS networks. There are four types of connections, namely network connections in blue lines, physical connections in brown lines, data connections in dashed blue lines, and user interaction in dashed orange lines.

We demonstrate how to enhance CPPS security through cross-organisation cooperation involving multilayered-CPPS stakeholders. Usually, groups of application-specific staff are collaborating to complete the production process,

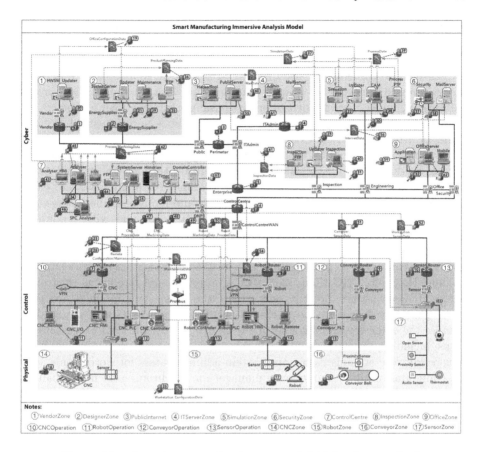

Fig. 4. Manufacturing network reference model (Color figure online)

while having separate roles. For a simplified smart manufacturing that contains only one CNC machine, one robot, and one conveyor, 63 user-roles are needed to attend the whole process, as illustrated in Fig. 4. These 63 technical personnel include 10 network-administrators (labelled 1 to 10 in the figure), 5 CNC or PLC programmers (labeled 11 to 15), 3 application-engineers (labelled 16 to 18), 8 software-administrators (labelled 19 to 26), 8 system-administrators (labelled 27 to 34), 7 manufacturing engineers (labelled 35 to 41), 10 data engineers or operators(labelled 42 to 52), 2 operation managers (labelled 53 to 54), and 9 security engineers or domain-control officers (labelled 55 to 63). Here each staff's role refers to one user account, which might be owned by the same user or different users. Therefore, access-control management is vital to ensure different users have different privileges, in order to prevent privilege escalation threats.

The physical layer contains a CNCZone (or CNC used to automate machining tools), a RobotZone (to program robots performing specific tasks in a production process), a ConveyorZone (to route material across machineries) and distributed SensorZones (to capture various measurements used to achieve basic production purposes). On each manufacturing equipment such as a CNC machine or a Robot, sensors are embedded to collect machining data. While some specific sensors and cameras are also distributed across the shop floor and used by workstations to collect motion and environmental data. In the physical layer, application-engineers are needed to ensure basic workstation maintenance.

In the control layer, typically both CNC machines and industrial Robots consist of drives, Numerical Control or NC kernels, remote input and out (I/O) and personal computer (PC) based controllers. These equipments are connected with each other, and can be reached through PLCs through an internal communication bus such as the process field bus Profibus. Normally CNC and PLC controllers communicate through a master-slave mechanism, namely a master device that initiates queries, and slave devices that respond with requested data to complete transactions. In our scenario, the CNC_PLC is selected as the master device. Meanwhile, CNC_PLC, Robot_PLC and some other intelligent devices are connected to routers through a local communication network such as Modbus. However, CNC_Controller, PLC_Controller, and intelligent electronic devices (IEDs) that are directly connected to the physical equipments, are usually not directly joined in the control network. Certain user-roles are needed optimise the efficiency and to monitor the security of the physical process operations, including network-administrators for local area network (LAN) administration, software-administrators and system-administrators for workstation system configuration update, operation-manager for synchronisation maintenance, CNC-operator and Robot-operator for remote machining and monitoring the process on human-machine interfaces (HMIs), and PLC-programmers that code optimal production-flow operational instructions to field devices.

The cyber layer basically contains a ControlCentre for machining process monitoring, a SimulationZone for machining process planning and simulation, an InspectionZone for quality inspection, an OfficeZone for operations management, an ITAdmin-Zone for network domain administration, a DesignerZone for product models design, a VendorZone for software support, and a SecurityZone for security operation. Generally, designers in the DesignerZone use CAD software to create 3D models with Product and Manufacturing Information (PMI) data and transfer them to the SimulationZone. CAM-engineers receive the CAD files and conduct process planning and simulations, and further creates G/M-codes files (i.e programming instructions that tell CNC machines what to do) out of the ProcessData. Data-engineers query the SimulationDatastore from the ControlCentre, and then further divide queried Process/MachiningData into CNCMachiningData and CNCProcessData to CNC machines for production purpose. Meanwhile, ProcessData and MachiningData from the workstation are sent back by CNC PLC and CNC Controller separately, under the request of data-operators in ControlCentre. These data would be used by CAM-engineers to analysis the machining process.

Dynamic vulnerability-management involves cooperation between IT-operators, application-specific engineers and managers throughout production processes. Different working groups contribute their professional expertise to vulnerability-management from operational, management and executive levels.

5.2 Experiments on CPPS Vulnerability Patterns and Attack Patterns

The following sessions include three parts, namely (a) vulnerability pattern and threat pattern analysis based on statistical data retrieved from multiple online vulnerability repositories, (b) vulnerability quantification involving stakeholders' knowledge, and (c) attach pattern analysis with prerequisite vulnerability setting.

(A) Statistical CPPS Vulnerability Patterns Analysis

We demonstrate our system-induced vulnerability analysis method through an analysis of Human-Machine Interface (HMI) in Supervisory Control and Data Acquisition (SCADA) control and monitoring system. HMI is a key CPPS asset where programmers transmit optimal production-flow operational instructions to actuators to implement these changes onto field devices, or where engineers monitor process/machining data.

By querying the vulnerability repository National Vulnerability Database (NVD) that discloses Common Vulnerability and Exposures (CVE) reports, we obtained 141 reported vulnerability instances related to HMI. According to the documentation of CVSS, we mapped each CVSS version 2 base-score of HMI vulnerability instances to the qualitative severity rating scale, and concluded that more than half (73 out of 141) of these vulnerability instances are evaluated as *High* severity of vulnerability instances, as illustrated in Part (a) of Fig. 5. In order to investigate on the corresponding threat patterns, we also correlated CVE reports against the threat categorisation provided in www.cvedetails.com, and found out the most typical threats that target HMIs are *Code Execution* and *Overflow*, as shown in Part(b) of Fig. 5. Both threat patterns and vulnerability patterns can provide statistic likelihood value for attack-occurrence and attack success rates.

Considering CPPS asset configurations, we retrieved detailed component information for each reported vulnerability through crosschecking our CVE findings with Common Platform Enumeration (CPE) repository. Based on CPE naming specification, we further acquire detailed information of vulnerable components, such as component type, vendor, component name, component version, etc. We sum up all the vulnerable instances and get 276 vulnerable application software instances, 9 vulnerable operating system instances, and 5 vulnerable hardware instances in HMIs. Based on retrieved results, we build a specific dictionary to store HMI vulnerable component versions. We further expand the dictionary by relating each CVE report to the disclosed time and the affected vendors. The most affected HMI vendors and the amount of reported vulnerability instances per year from 2008 till 2019 for each vendor are illustrated in Part(c) of Fig. 5. We also show the short-term situation from Aug 2018 to Jul 2019 in Part(d) of Fig. 5. The vendor-related information is valuable when

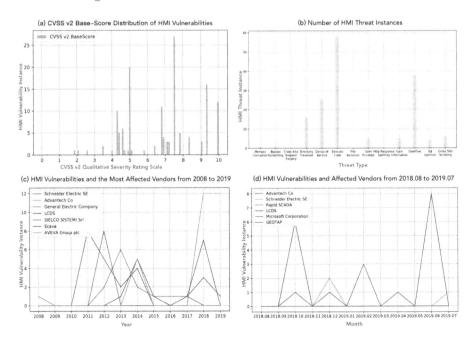

Fig. 5. Vulnerability instance amounts of affect human-machine-interface vendors

an operation manager needs to update configuration settings or to choose from products from different vendors.

(B) Quantitative Assessment Involving Stakeholders

Each vulnerability instance is associated to one or more specific properties, which could be measured across a range of values using vulnerability property-related metrics by security engineers. We adopt CVSS Version 2 to calculate scores for vulnerability instances. For instance, the exploitability property of a vulnerability is based on the possibility, difficulty and complexity of exploiting a vulnerable asset, and could be quantitatively evaluated by security operators using inputs from software administrators, application engineer and network administrator. The impact property of a vulnerability measures the consequences resulting from exploiting the vulnerability, which could cause losses in CIA-triad of the corresponding asset. The impact property of vulnerability could be evaluated by application engineers, as well as network and software administrators.

SecurityOperator, SecurityManager and *OperationManager* are also involved to measure temporal or environmental metrics. For example, vulnerability instance *CVE-2015-0997* has a CVSS v2.0 Base-Score of 3.3. According to the v2 documentation[3], relevant actors are involved in the analysis process, as shown

---

[3] https://www.first.org/cvss/v2/guide.

in Fig. 6. Taken into consideration of the given temporal and environmental measurements, a final CVSS v2 score of 3.2 is assigned. Application specialists can also provide valuable information such as potential costs for system recovering once success attacks happen.

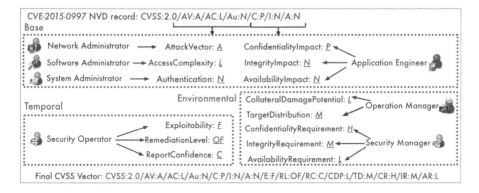

Fig. 6. Quantitative vulnerability assessment involving stakeholders

(C) CPPS Attack-Graph Based on Prerequisite Vulnerability Setting

Based on the manufacturing network reference model in and organisational staff management in Fig. 4, as well as the statistical vulnerability patterns and threat patterns for each asset collected beforehand, we generate attack graphs for different attack instances. In current stage, our model is built using securiCAD[4] which is based on probability Bayesian Network [9] to simulate attack-occurrence and propagation instances. Vulnerability may impact multiple asset instances, and vulnerable assets can be impacted by more than one vulnerability instance. In CPPS, hardware, software, OS and network assets are assembled and used in different ways within CPPS fabrics, which might create various binaries with potential backdoors. Meanwhile, human errors or mistakes could expose new vulnerabilities in both access-control and transferred data. The propagation of an attack is reasoned by statements that check asset dependencies. Here we illustrate an attack scenario of DesignerZone network being compromised, and how this successful attack can trigger SimulationZone network to be compromised as well, then finally end up compromising the ControlServer in ControlCentre, as discussed before in Fig. 1. The generated attack graph in Fig. 7 shows how the vulnerabilities in CPPS and how compromised user-accounts contribute to the attack propagation from DesignerZone to the ControlCentre. The thickness of arrows represent the likelihood values of this attack success rate, which is given by the results in previous experiments.

---

[4] https://www.foreseeti.com/securicad/.

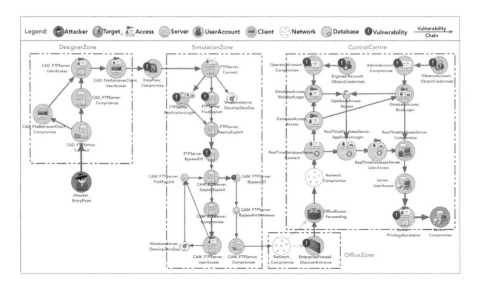

Fig. 7. Attack scenario illustration in manufacturing network

6   Conclusion and Future Works

CPPS networks generate a growing traffic of data, which is highly sensitive to cyberthreat vulnerabilities. Understanding and pinpointing vulnerabilities in such networks are difficult tasks, yet vital for cybersecurity purposes of production processes. In this paper, we proposed a framework to map CPPS components against Threat, Vulnerability and Attack instances, which can reduce the effect of their occurrences. Threats are triggered through vulnerability exploits from malicious agents' behaviour that could result into a cyber-attack instance which can lead to disruption in production infrastructure operations. Our proposed framework also bridges the connection from CPPS system to different actors in the production process through collaborations between security and operation personnel stakeholders, to enable situation awareness that supports vulnerability intelligence, in order to stay on top of potential threats. We also provided a detailed evaluation of our framework through a case study through a manufacturing network reference model, which demonstrates organisational access control and cooperation. We also illustrate the processes of vulnerability information retrieval and analysis through experimental analysis, to show how we combine statistical pattern analysis with quantitative assessment and attack-graph generation for practical security assessment. Further on, we plan to extend our framework into an automatic vulnerability assessment system for CPPSs as part of our future work.

References

1. Wu, D., et al.: Cybersecurity for digital manufacturing. J. Manuf. Syst. **48**, 3–12 (2018)
2. Mohurle, S., Patil, M.: A brief study of Wannacry Threat: Ransomware attack 2017. Int. J. Adv. Res. Comput. Sci. **8**(5) (2017)
3. Välja, M., Lagerström, R., Franke, U., Ericsson, G.: A framework for automatic it architecture modeling: applying truth discovery (2018)
4. Rahm, E., Bernstein, P.A.: A survey of approaches to automatic schema matching. VLDB J. **10**(4), 334–350 (2001)
5. Humayed, A., Lin, J., Li, F., Luo, B.: Cyber-physical systems security-a survey. IEEE Internet Things J. **4**(6), 1802–1831 (2017)
6. Kure, H., Islam, S., Razzaque, M.: An integrated cyber security risk management approach for a cyber-physical system. Appl. Sci. **8**(6), 898 (2018)
7. Jiang, Y., Jeusfeld, M., Atif, Y., Ding, J., Brax, C., Nero, E.: A language and repository for cyber security of smart grids. In: 2018 IEEE 22nd International Enterprise Distributed Object Computing Conference (EDOC), pp. 164–170. IEEE (2018)
8. Hafner, M., Breu, R., Agreiter, B., Nowak, A.: SECTET: an extensible framework for the realization of secure inter-organizational workflows. Internet Res. **16**(5), 491–506 (2006)
9. Johnson, P., Vernotte, A., Gorton, D., Ekstedt, M., Lagerström, R.: Quantitative information security risk estimation using probabilistic attack graphs. In: Groß-mann, J., Felderer, M., Seehusen, F. (eds.) RISK 2016. LNCS, vol. 10224, pp. 37–52. Springer, Cham (2017). https://doi.org/10.1007/978-3-319-57858-3_4
10. Elhabashy, A.E., Wells, L.J., Camelio, J.A., Woodall, W.H.: A cyber-physical attack taxonomy for production systems: a quality control perspective. J. Intell. Manuf. **30**(6), 1–16 (2018)

Network and Cloud Security

A Complete and Generic Security Approach for Wireless Sensors Network

Imen Bouabidi[1] and Pr. Mahmoud Abdellaoui[2(✉)]

[1] National Engineer School of Sfax, WIMCS Research Team,
Sfax University, Sfax, Tunisia
imenba1989@gmail.com
[2] National Engineer School of Electronic and Communication,
WIMCS Research Team, Sfax University, Sfax, Tunisia
mahmoudabdellaoui4@gmail.com

Abstract. Wireless communication-random deployment-resources limitations are the main characteristics of wireless sensors networks that make them vulnerable to attacks. Indeed, sensors nodes and transmitted data are not protected. So, data privacy and integrity are essential to secure the transmitted information and to protect the various nodes. In this context, we have presented in this paper a complete and generic security solution adapted to the WSN constraints. This approach is based on the crossing between the three layers: physical layer, data link layer and network layer through the implementation of a secure MAC protocol and an intrusion detection system. As well as, the development of a new cryptographic solution grouping the modified AES encryption algorithm in CTR mode and a new key management protocol. The simulations results have proved on the one hand, the efficiency of our solution in WSN metrics term namely: mobility rate (from a network size 200, the mobility rate completes 99%), loss packets rate (LPR), energy consumption (does not exceed $0.512\,\mu j$ for the case of our encryption scheme and $142\,mj$ for the case of our MAC protocol SXMachiavel), data freshness (40.79%), control overhead (2.4), etc. On the other hand, it's resistance to the most dangerous attacks in the WSN: eavesdropping attacks, node capture attack, DOS attacks and spoofing attacks.

Keywords: Data privacy · Secure MAC protocol · Authentication · Cryptographic solution · Malware and attacks detection · WSN

1 Introduction

Recent advances in wireless communications and computer technologies have resulted in small, low-cost devices. Many of these devices are deployed in nature to create a wireless sensors network for both control and monitoring purposes. However, the application of a dense wireless sensors network is limited by a number of technical difficulties arising from the constraints imposed by the reduced

Supported by WIMCS Research Team.

capabilities of the sensors nodes: low power, reduced communication capacity and limited storage capacity [1]. The security issue in these networks is schematized as follows (Fig. 1):

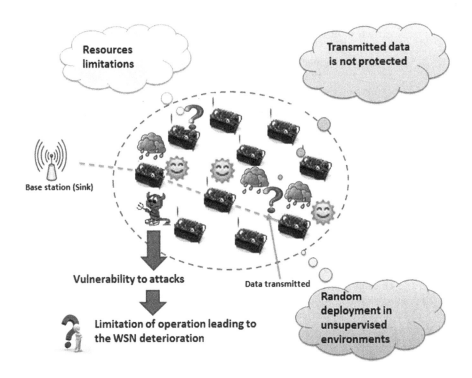

Fig. 1. Security issues in the WSN

To provide end-to-end security in WSNs and in order to ensure a complete security solution that meets the requirements of sensors networks and resists all types of attacks, we used the crossing between layers. Our solution is based on the interaction between the three layers (cross-layers): network layer, data link layer and physical layer. So, the proposed generic solution is effective in most areas of applications starting from E-Health, home automation, smart agriculture, smart cities, industrial control, etc. Also, with objective to guarantee comfort to the users, the sensors must be mobile. Sensor mobility is therefore related to WSN deployments in different applications. For example, in the medical field, the sensor nodes are integrated in the body of the patient who is still moving. In this case, the mobility rate is high. Otherwise and in order to overcome these difficulties, we must develop new algorithms specific to wireless sensors networks reducing energy consumption and ensuring the security of these networks [2]. The proposed solution is based on the use of the cross layers strategy by crossing the three layers: network layer, data link layer and physical layer. It includes two main contributions. The first one concerns the development of a secured and efficient MAC protocol and an intrusion detection system to protect network against jamming attacks. The originality of our first solution is the combination between the security and the energy conservation themes which does not exist in the literature works. The second contribution consists of implementing a novel cryptographic approach based on grouping the encryption algorithm AES modified and adapted with CTR mode and our own key management protocol ESKMS. The originality of our second solution is to obtain a high security level with regard to a minimal resources use (storage only three keys whatever the network density). Our goal is to secure communications between nodes and insure the data privacy and integrity in WSN. We choose AES for many reasons. Firstly, AES is very efficient in terms of speed. Then, its memory resources needs are very low. Also, it is easy to implement which induces a wide variety of platforms and applications. However, AES is a CFB block cipher algorithm. It is based on the use of an initialization vector (IV) with the key. In addition to the key and the encryption algorithm, this IV must be saved in memory. This requires additional storage space. Whereas, in wireless sensors networks the nodes have limited resources. To solve this problem, the CTR mode appeared. In this mode, the key flow is obtained by encrypting the successive values of a counter. This mode combines many advantages because it allows the encryption by flow. In addition, it allows random access to data; it uses only the encryption function. The counter used is a pseudo-random sequence. This mode is one of the most interesting in the framework of the WSN. Indeed, unlike other encryption modes, only the encryption algorithm will need to be implemented in the node, resulting in saving the storage space. Consequently, the resources use is minimized. For these reasons, we chose in our solution this operation mode. All details are found in our article [3].

Our paper is structured as follows: the second section presents a taxonomy of existing security solutions. The third section describes our proposed solution based on a two contributions: the development of an Inter-layered security approach by implementing an energy-efficient MAC protocol and an IDS for the mobile WSN and the implementation of a novel cryptographic solution based on the AES/CTR and a new key management protocol. The fourth section shows the performance evaluation of our solution in WSN metrics. While the fifth section illustrates the behavior of our security approach against the most famous attacks for WSNs. Finally, we complete our work with a conclusion and some prospects.

2 Existing Security Approaches

Security is an essential element to protect a WSN. Thus, few works dealing with the security problem in the WSNs are presented in the literature. These approaches are classified according to several categories: some of them are interested in layer level security protocol, others are concerned with securing the network against specific attacks such as jamming attack or wormhole, etc. Since existing solutions are incomplete and do not meet the specific requirements of the

WSN, we have chosen to classify them according to the following four functional blocks: key management, routing security, data aggregation security, access security channel.

Key Management: Key management includes the establishment, distribution and renewal of cryptographic keys. To secure a cryptographic system, each user must have a set of secret keys. Subsequent work tried to provide solutions for the key management theme [4].

The majority of symmetric cryptosystems require pairwise key storage in all sensors nodes prior to deployment (during the pre-distribution phase) or post-deployment through an effective key management system: for a network size of N nodes, each node is pre-loaded with N-1 secret keys. Each key is known by this node and one of the N-1 other nodes. Thus, each node stores in its memory N-1 keys. As a results, for a large network size (N very high), the memory storage will be increased especially when the keys size are large (for example: N = 1000 nodes, key size = 128 bits. So, memory storage = 128000 bits = 16 kilo bytes).

Routing Security: The network layer is the module responsible for correctly routing data from one point in the network to another. We distinguish three levels of solutions to data routing attacks in WSN that are:

- Solution 1: A first solution using cryptography called SecLEACH protocol [5]. It considered as a cryptographic security solution for the LEACH protocol.
- Solution 2 called "reputation-based approach". The reputation can be defined as the participation level of a node in the retransmission operation. One example using this technique is the Watch dog. It is used locally by each node to control the retransmission operation by each node in the routing path. These mechanisms are also vulnerable because they can be threatened by an attacker.

Data Aggregation Security: Data aggregation is divided into two techniques which are: aggregation based on data in clear and aggregation based on encrypted data. However, aggregation security is an insufficient solution to protect the WSN. One solution interested in this axis is presented in work [6].

Channel Access Security: Each layer of the protocol stack is vulnerable to attacks. As a result, some works are moving towards the protection of these layers against particular attacks. We distinguish two different solutions that are: mono-layer strategies and multi-layers (cross layers) strategies. The crossing between the layers presents an interesting solution to remedy the security problem while guaranteeing a reduced consumption of resources. The integration of the cross-layers approach into the design of the WSN remains a very recent field.

Intrusion Detection System (IDS): The authentication and the cryptography are the best known mechanisms to combat security threats. However, these solutions are sometimes expensive and they can not predict the different types of attacks knowing that new attacks appear constantly. Therefore, it is obvious to implement a second line of defense to improve the security level in the network.

Thus, Intrusion detection systems (IDS) are developed. The work [7] presents the implementation of an IDS in the WSN.

According to our bibliographic study of existing security techniques in the WSN, we deduct that, each security solution is characterized by its own needs and constraints to achieve the desired level of security. Indeed, existing security solutions are expensive in energy and memory space. In addition, the majority of works are based on the assumption that the WSN is static. To overcome these limitations and in order to enhance the security level in the WSN, some of them can be corrected and improved to make a complete solution. It is the cross layers approach. In this context, our solution is installed. It consists of a cross between the three layers: network layer, data link layer and physical layer to provide a fully secure and mobile WSN. A detailed description of our security approach is explained in the next section.

3   Our Proposed Solution

The design of a WSN faces a number of technical difficulties arising from the constraints imposed by them. In fact, recharging the batteries in a WSN is difficult because of the nodes location. For this reason, the energy consumption is considered as an important metric for their performance evaluation because the recharging batteries is difficult; In the other hand, the WSNs are deployed in unsupervised environments; so, there are vulnerable to attacks, consequently the security of these networks is necessary. For thus, the originality of the proposed approach consists to combine these two themes of security and energy conservation into a cross of the three layers: physical layer, data link layer and network layer. Thus, our solution is divided into two contributions detailed in the following subsections.

3.1   Inter-layered Security Approach by Implementing an Energy-Efficient MAC Protocol and an IDS for the Mobile WSN

Our first contribution is divided into two main stages which are: the development of a secure and energy-efficient MAC protocol called SXMachiavel and the implementation of an intrusion detection system at the Sink level to protect the physical layer against jamming attacks.

The data link layer and especially the media access control (MAC) sublayer is mean subject of the first step. The MAC sublayer handles the management of shared media access between the different nodes. Specifically, it determines when a node should transmit or receive data or listen to the channel to ensure reliability, scalability, low latency and throughput. Indeed, sensors nodes are unable to send or receive data at the same time. All neighboring nodes of a source node are listening to shared media. In absence of prevention mechanisms, this medium will be vulnerable against attacks and more exactly denial of sleep attacks. The adequate solution to fight against these attacks is the duty cycling technique. The basic idea is to place the node's radio module in sleep mode as often as possible. In the literature, most energy saving solutions focus on this technique. Among the existing solutions we are interested in the XMachiavel protocol, because according to the studies made and validated by the simulations [8], it is the most economical in energy. However, this protocol has two weak points that are: first, it supports a low mobility and then it is insecure. So, we tried to overcome these two problems by increasing the mobility rate and introducing a security mechanism through the implementation of an authentication mechanism, a hash function and the AES encryption algorithm. The following algorithm details our approach.

Algorithm 1. The proposed security algorithm

Step 1: Each node calculates the AuthNum using the function $g(n) = (p-1)*(q-1)$.

Step 2: If node i want to communicate with node j: it sends firstly a P0 packet containing AuthNum and encrypted by AES algorithm.

Step 3: Destination node after decrypted the packet, extract the p and q values.

Step 4: Destination node sends ACK containing the p and q values.

Step 5: The source node after decrypted the packet, verifies the AuthNum, if verification is successful it authenticate the destination.

Step 6: Node i determines $H_s = H(Data)$.

Step 7: All intermediate nodes and the destination verifies H_s to check the packet integrity.

Step 8: The node that detects that the two hash values (received and calculated) are different broadcast an alert.

Step 9: The destination node verifies the AuthNum and authenticate the source.

In the second step, we focus on ways to ensure physical layer security. The physical layer is the lowest layer of the OSI model. Its main role is to transmit and receive the unstructured bits stream on a physical medium. The physical channel of sensors networks is distinct from traditional networks. For example, the fluctuations caused by an unstable wireless channel are more serious. These features are considered as limitations that must be overcome in the implementation of these networks. Hence, the security of the physical layer represents an interesting attitude. Existing security solutions are often implemented in the upper layers. Remember that this layer is vulnerable to attacks and more particularly to jamming attacks. In jamming mode, the nodes do not have access to the medium and can not communicate due to radio interference. This radio interference will have a direct influence on the values of several network parameters. Subsequently, increasing or decreasing the values of these parameters will be an indication of the existence of a jamming attack. Existing works use the combination of two, three, or up to four parameters. In our solution, we have increased the number of parameters to five. These parameters are: PDR, PSR, LPR, ECA and CST [8]. Each node performs the calculation of each parameter for a given period and sends these values to the base station which compares these values to the different thresholds. We have added a new P3 packet containing the values of these parameters. Each node must encrypt the packet using AES before sending it to the base station. Although, IDS are expensive in energy and the WSN is characterized by low memory capacity and limited power, we chose to apply this IDS only at the sink node. This node is responsible for detecting the anomaly, then informing other nodes of the existence of the intrusion using a broadcast message.

In the next subsection, we will detail our second contribution to secure wireless sensors networks which is interested in the key management and encryption/decryption issues in the WSNs.

3.2 A Novel Cryptographic Solution Grouping a Modified AES/CTR and a New Efficient-Scalable Key Management Protocol

In this subsection, we are interested in the network layer and more precisely in the encryption/decryption process. Existing cryptographic solutions present a compromise between security and resources use. These solutions present specific examples for particular applications. Whereas, our approach is generic and adapted to all WSN architectures and applications. Our solution aims to develop a completely secure WSN by grouping a new dedicated and adapted key management protocol, named Efficient and Scalable Key Management Scheme: "ESKMS", and a modified AES encryption algorithm with CTR mode. Our ESKMS protocol is summarized in the next algorithm.

Recall that our objective is to have a wireless sensors network completely secure, fully mobile and dense. To achieve this goal, our ESKMS key management protocol need to be resistant to the scaling factor while maintaining an acceptable resources consumption. This is the main advantage of ESKMS over other existing key management approaches. To have a complete study and to check the behavior of ESKMS in the face of the network increase, we have planned the extension of the WSN from I to M nodes with $M > I$. The step of adding new nodes is summarized as follows:

1. When a new node joins the network, it sends a joint request message (JM) to the base station containing its identity.
2. When receiving this message, the base station (BS) checks in the network nodes identities list the last ID. If the new node is an attacker then the JM message does not contain an identity or it contains an identity unknown by the base station. However, if the new node is legitimate then its identity will be close to the identities of the nodes that are in NL.
3. BS adds the new identity to the list of network nodes identities.

Algorithm 2. The proposed ESKMS algorithm

Step 1: Before deployment, all nodes and BS are loaded by the PK key. Then, after deployment, the base station randomly generates two nonces N_1 and N_2.

Step 2: The BS broadcasts the following Key Discovery Message "KDM":

$$BS \rightarrow * : \{ID_{BS}||N_1||N_2||MAC_{PK}(N_1||N_2)||KUT + \mu||NL\}_{PK} \quad (1)$$

Step 3: Upon receiving the KDM message, each node responds as follows:

Step 4: Maintains a timer T, then decrypts the message using the pre-loaded key PK.

Step 5: Extracts the nonces N_1 and N_2 and checks the MAC of two nonces: It calculates a new MAC and compares it with the received MAC.

Step 6: If both MAC values are equal. Then, the node accepts the message. Otherwise, the node rejects it.

Step 7: Calculates the CK key:

$$CK = H_{PK}((N_1 \oplus PK) \vee (N_2 \oplus PK)) \quad (2)$$

Step 8: Calculates the BK keys:

$$BK = H_{CK}((CK \oplus PK) \vee (N_1 \wedge N_2) \vee CK) \quad (3)$$

Step 9: When the timer reaches the KUT value, the base station calculates CK and BK according to Equ. 2 and Equ. 3. Then, deletes the two nonces N_1 and N_2 and generates two new nonces N'_1 and N'_2. Also, BS broadcasts the Key Update Message "KUM":

$$BS \rightarrow * : \{ID_{BS}||N'_1||N'_2||MAC_{PK}(N'_1||N'_2)||\mu||NL||IL\}_{BK} \quad (4)$$

Step 10: Each node that receives KUM proceeds as follows:

Step 11: Decrypts the message with the key BK. Then, extracts the new nonces N'_1 and N'_2 and Checks the MAC (Same as in the key establishment step).

Step 12: If the MAC is verified, the node accepts the packet. Then, it deletes BK and CK (if t= KUT+μ).

Step 13: Calculates the new key CK' as follows

$$CK' = H_{PK}((N'_1 \oplus PK) \vee (N'_2 \oplus PK)) \quad (5)$$

Step 14: Calculates the new key BK'

$$BK' = H_{CK'}((CK' \oplus PK) \vee (N'_1 \wedge N'_2) \vee CK') \quad (6)$$

---

4. BS loads the new node with the PK key. Then, it sends the message KUM if the reception time of JM (trecp) is greater than or equal to KUT. But, if the

reception time of JM by the base station is less than KUT, the BS sends the new node the message KDM.
5. When the new node receives KUM or KDM, it proceeds in the same way as an old node.

The encryption scheme is defined by the triple of the algorithms: key generator algorithm, encryption algorithm and decryption algorithm. We use ESKMS as a key generator algorithm and AES/CTR as encryption/decryption algorithm.

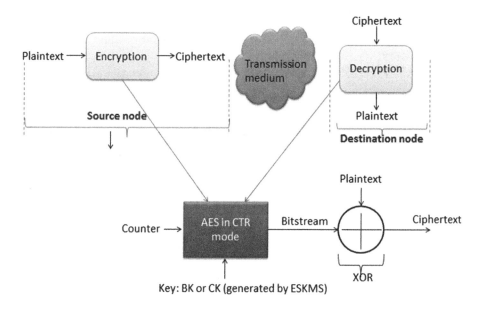

Fig. 2. Our AES/CTR and ESKMS approach

AES takes the encryption key BK or CK (generated by own ESKMS protocol) and a counter as input to produce a bit stream. The bit stream is then XORed with the plain text to produce the cipher text. The encryption is done on 10 rounds composed of 4 stages. When receiving the cipher text, the destination node executes the reverse process to recover the plain text. As result, both the transmitter and the receiver must share the same encryption key which is BK or CK. Figure 2 presents our AES/CTR and ESKMS approach. While the next print screen shows a part of the developed C++ code.

```
//1.Initialization of key data
void InitKey(byte* key, size_t size) {
    for ( size_t i = 0; i < size; ++i ) {
        key[i] = rand();
    }
}
void main()
{
    //Initialize common key and IV with appropriate values
    byte key[CryptoPP::AES::DEFAULT_KEYLENGTH];
    byte counter[CryptoPP::AES::BLOCKSIZE];

    // Initialize common key and IV with appropriate values
    InitKey(key, sizeof(key));
    InitKey(counter, sizeof(counter));

    string plainText = "modified AES in CTR mode";
    cout << "Plain Text : " << plainText << endl;
    //Create an encrypted object
```

4   Performance Evaluation of Our Security Solution

4.1   Implementation Under OMNet++

To implement our project under OMNet++, we have added two new MAC modules that are: the XMachiavel module and the SXMachiavel module and a new physical module for the implementation of the intrusion detection system and two network modules for the ESKMS key generator algorithm and the AES/CTR encryption algorithm. For these modules to operate properly, it is necessary to add the corresponding files. These files are:

- The ".ned file" that describes the network architecture, in our case we created a new file named WSN.ned.
- The ".cc and .h" files that describe the C++ code of our program. We have created four files that are respectively: XMachiavel.cc, XMachiavell.h, SXMachiavel.cc, SXMachiavel.h, ESKMS.cc, ESKMS.h.
- The ".ini file" which contains the initialization parameters of various nodes as well as the simulation parameters. In our project, this file is named "WSN.ini". This file corresponds to the "WSN.ned" file.
- The ".msg file" which contains a description of the messages exchanged between the different elements of the network.

The "WSN.ned" is shown in the next print screen.

```
network WSN extends BaseNetwork
{
    parameters:
        @display("bgb=$playgroundSizeX,$playgroundSizeY,white,,;bgp=10,50");
        int numMOBILEHosts = 9; // total number of weak hosts in the network
        int numSINKHosts = 1; // total number of strong hosts in the network

    submodules:
        ISMChannel: ConnectionManager {
            parameters:
                @display("p=121,0;i=abstract/multicast;is=s");
        }
        SINKNode[numSINKHosts]: PhyMacHost {
            parameters:
                numHosts = numSINKHosts;
                @display("p=248,91;b=42,42,rect,green;i=device/wifilaptop");

        }
        MOBILENode[numMOBILEHosts]: PhyMacHost {
            parameters:
                numHosts = numMOBILEHosts;
                @display("p=70,91;b=42,42,rect,white;i=device/palm");

        }
    connections allowunconnected:
                    // all connections and gates are to be generated dynamically
```

Table 1. Simulation parameters

Parameter	Value
Network coverage	500 m * 500 m/1000 m*1000 m
Nic type	Nic XMachiavel; Nic SXMachiavel
Mobility type	ConstSpeedMobility
Mobility speed	2 ms
Carrier frequency	2.4 GHZ
Header size	24 bits
Routing protocol type	Wise route
Simulation time	150 s
Throughput	15360 bps
Number of mobile nodes	Variable (from 0 to 200)

In order to achieve our goals and especially to make good simulations, some parameters need to be adjusted. WSN.ini file and the previous table summarize the characteristics of these parameters.

In our network model, we first used a 500 m*500 m topology, for the case of the first contribution, and later a 1000 m * 1000 m topology, for the case of the second contribution, with a random deployment of mobile nodes. All sensors nodes are similar power and have limited capabilities for communicating and storing data. Exceptionally, the BS called Sink has high energy resources relative to the all various nodes. These nodes may be fixed or mobile nodes.

After each simulation duration (equal to 150 s), we incremented the number of nodes (up to 200 nodes) and we calculated the different metrics.

4.2   WSN Metrics

Simulation Results of the First Contribution

Our first contribution is based on Inter-layered security approach by implementing an Energy-Efficient MAC Protocol and an IDS for the mobile WSN. To prove the performance of this solution, we have evaluated three metrics among the existing metrics which are: mobility rate, energy consumption and loss packets rate.

(a) Mobility rate

Recall to: the mobility rate is the report between the number of mobile nodes and the total number of nodes in the network. The results of our simulation are presented in Fig. 3.

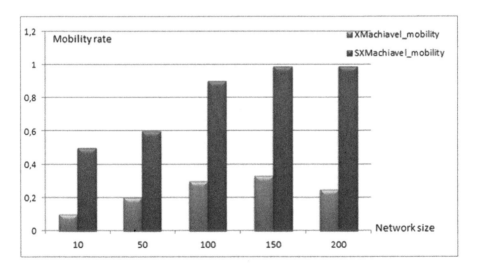

Fig. 3. Mobility rate

According to the simulation results, we noticed that the mobility rate is different for the two protocols. The main goal of our proposition is to provide a totally mobile wireless sensors network. For this reason, we have increased after each simulation duration (=150 s) the total number of mobile nodes. From a network size 200, all the nodes will be mobile except the sink which remains fixed. So, the mobility rate reached 99%. Also, we have implemented a routing protocol in mobile nodes to efficiently remove data. But, it doesn't the case for XMachiavel protocol. In this protocol, the number of fixed nodes is more than the number of mobile nodes (which doesn't exceed 50 nodes). Thus, only fixed nodes participate in routing operations.

In the real case and with the demands of technological progress, sensor mobility is related to WSN deployments in different applications. The sensor module in the intrinsic state is fixed; but in general case, it can be implemented in mobile environments namely in the medical field, the sensor nodes are integrated into the body of the patient who is still moving. In this case, the mobility rate is high. However, in other applications such as environmental monitoring the sensors are embedded in fixed locations. So, mobility is low.

(b) Energy Consumption

Remember that the total energy consumption is the sum of transmission energy, processing energy and energy consumed by units. We notice that the processing energy and the energy consumed by units are neglected. Thus, we consider that the transmission energy presents the total of energy consumption. The results of our simulation are presented in Fig. 4.

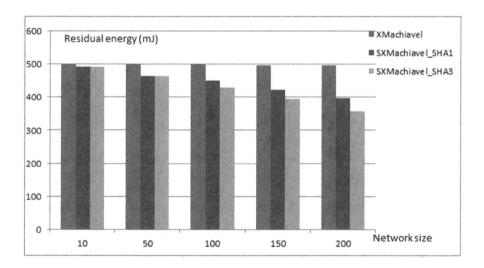

Fig. 4. Variation of residual energy according to network size

When the sensors nodes do not have data to transmit or to receive, they enter in sleep mode to conserve its energy. However, nodes are vulnerable to sleep denial attacks. To fight against these attacks, we proposed a secure and energy efficient MAC protocol: "SXMachiavel". In the existing protocol XMachiavel, the information is sent in clear, it can be intercepted by the attackers forcing them to stay active all the time and therefore the energy consumption is hugely. For this, we have encrypted all communications within the network.

According to this figure, we concluded that the existing unsecure protocol XMachiavel present less energy consuming; due to the absence of security mechanisms in this protocol. However, the energy consumption is higher for the case of SXMachiavel with SHA3 than with SHA1. This is resulting in the addition of several security mechanisms which increase the total energy consumption, namely: an authentication process, a hash function and an encryption algorithm. Consequently, it's possible to exhaust the energetic resources of the nodes. Unfortunately, there is always a trade-off between efficiency and energy consumption.

(c) Loss packets rate (LPR)
The loss packets rate is the report between the number of lost frames and the total number of sent frames. The simulation results of this metrics are summarized in the Table 1.

Table 2. LPR for a network size equal to 200

Protocol	Loss packets rate
XMachiavel	0.28
SXMachiavel	0.17

The loss packets rate increases with the number of nodes in the network. For a dense network size (200 nodes), our proposed approach provides the best results. Our network is completely secured (implementation of three security mechanisms as follow as: authentication process - hash and encryption mechanisms. Then, the risk of intrusion appearance is low (Table 2).

Simulation Results of the Second Contribution
Remember that our second contribution is interested in implementing a novel cryptographic solution grouping the modified AES/CTR and the new key management protocol ESKMS. Table 3 present the simulation results.

In our second contribution, we chose to evaluate six metrics from existing metrics which are: energy efficiency, throughput, loss packets rate, data freshness, network overhead control and PSR. Firstly, we have compared our solution to existing protocols [9,10]. Secondly, and to show the importance of adding security mechanisms in the protection of the WSN, we compared our encryption solution with the WSN without security.

From the simulations results, we found that: firstly, our solution and the Skipjack protocol have a similar energy consumption $(0.512\,\mu j)$, while the Puffin scheme has a high energy consumption value $(13.7\,\mu j)$. This proves that our solution minimizes energy consumption. Secondly, our cryptographic solution has a higher throughput than the existing solution (45177 bps). These results are due to the growth of the exchanged data. Between the nodes as the network density becomes vast. Thirdly, the loss packets rate increases with the growth in the network size. The LPR is lower for the case of our secured network, which proves its resilience to the scaling factor. Also, the total network overhead is high for data without security (18.09)and lower for data with security (2.45). As a result, our cryptographic solution significantly reduces network overhead.

Table 3. Simulation results of the second contribution

Protocol	Metric	Value
Sckipjack	Energy consumption	0.059 µj
Puffin	Energy consumption	013.7 µj
Proposed solution	Energy consumption	0.512 µj
Existing solution	Average throughput	19500 bps
Proposed solution	Average throughput	45177 bps
Network without security	Loss packets rate	0.4
	Control overhead	18.09
	Data freshness (%)	5.5
	PSR (%)	5.52
Network with security	Loss packets rate	0.9
	Control overhead	2.45
	Data freshness (%)	40.79
	PSR (%)	41.09

Consequently, increasing the available bandwidth and minimizing power consumption. In addition, our secure network offers better data freshness (40.79%) and better PSR (41.09%) compared to an unsecured network. This is due to the addition of a robust encryption system to attacks grouping the AES/CTR encryption protocol and the new ESKMS scheme. In the other hand and concerning the behavior of our proposed solution against attacks, we analyze in the next section the resilience of our cryptographic solution against the majority of attacks against the WSN.

5 Behavior of Our Proposed Solution Against Attacks

This section analyzes the resilience of our security approach against the majority of attacks against the WSN. These attacks are:

Nodes capture attack: after having captured nodes, the attacker can recover the secret keys stored in the sensors. To solve this problem, we used a periodic keys update: the node deletes the keys BK and CK from its memory if the timer reaches the value $KUT + \mu$. However, for a time $t < KUT + \mu$ there is a probability that the malicious node will access BK or CK. In order to solve this problem, we have reduced the value of $KUT + \mu$.

Eavesdropping attack: in our two contributions, the transmitted data is encrypted by the secret key (CK, BK or Ks) and the encryption algorithm AES (or the modified AES/CTR). The attacker can not recover the collected data by applying an encryption to the transmitted cryptogram without knowing the key and the decryption process.

Injection of false data: in our SXMachiavel protocol, the encrypted text transmitted is protected by the authentication number, which can only be calculated by the sensors located on the routing path. The attacker can not inject false data to interfere with the transmission without knowing the authentication secret.

Spoofing attack: to protect the WSN from spoofing attacks, we have applied SHA1 and latter SHA3 function at the data packet level. This makes it possible to check if the messages are altered or modified during their transmission.

DOS attacks: to fight against these attacks, we have defined a threshold, if a sensor node receives a number of messages greater than the threshold so it means the existence of a DOS attack. Thus, the node that detects the presence of DOS in the network blocks all messages received and broadcasts an alert to all nodes of the network.

6   Conclusion

The work, proposed by this paper, presents a complete and generic security solution of the WSN. The originality of our approach is manifested by the balance between the resources use and the efficiency in terms of security; and that through the combination of the security and the energy conservation themes while being content to use only three encryption keys regardless of the network density. This solution entails two main contributions namely: the implementation of an energy-secure MAC protocol and an effective system of intrusion detection (IDS) and fight-protection-resistance against jamming attack. As well as, the development of a cryptographic solution through the arrangement of the AES encryption algorithm modified in CTR mode and a new key management protocol entitled "ESKMS". The simulation results showed the efficiency of our security solution in terms of mobility rate (99%), loss packets rate, power consumption, network overload control (2.45), the data freshness (reaches 40.79%) and the PSR. On the other hand, the security analysis has proved the resistance of our approach against attacks (eavesdropping, DOS, spoofing, etc.) threatening the WSN. Although our solution has shown its effectiveness and performance against existing approaches, it can be enriched by adding multivariate cryptography to our key management process.

References

1. Abdellaoui, Pr.M.: Multitasks-Generic-Intelligent-Efficiency-Secure WSNs and theirs Applications, Part 3: Secure Wireless Sensors Network, pp. 142–185. LAMBERT Academic Publishing LAP, Geneva (2017). ISBN: 978-3-330-04707-5. Printed book (330 pages, 4 Parts)
2. Bouabidi, I., Abdellaoui, Pr.M.: Hierarchical organization with a cross layers using smart sensors for intelligent cities. Adv. Sci. Technol. Eng. Syst. J. (ASTESJ) textbf2(1), 97–107 (2017). ISSN: 2415–6698
3. Bouabidi, I., Abdellaoui, Pr.M.: A novel cryptographic solution to secure mobile wireless sensors networks. Int. J. Secur. Netw. **14**(4), 1–18 (2019)

4. Athman, S., Bilami, A., Boubiche, D.: EDAK: an efficient dynamic authentication and key management mechanism for heterogeneous WSNs. Future Gener. Comput. Syst. **92**, 789–799 (2019)
5. Boliveira, L.: SecLEACH- a random key distribution solution for securing clustered sensor networks. In: Fifth IEEE International Symposium on Network Computing and Applications (NCA 2006), pp. 1–8 (2006)
6. Lathaa, A., Prasannab, S., Hemalathac, S., Sivakumar, B.: A harmonized trust assisted energy efficient data aggregation scheme for distributed sensor networks. Cogn. Syst. Res. **56**, 14–22 (2019)
7. Agarkhed, J., Kalnoor, G., Patil, S.R.: Intrusion detection system using pattern matching techniques for wireless sensor networks. In: Saini, H.S., Sayal, R., Govardhan, A., Buyya, R. (eds.) Innovations in Computer Science and Engineering. LNNS, vol. 32, pp. 411–418. Springer, Singapore (2019). https://doi.org/10.1007/978-981-10-8201-6_46
8. Kuntz, R.: Medium access control facing the dynamics of wireless sensor networks. Thesis, Strasbourg University, pp. 1–189 (2010)
9. Zhang, X., Heys, M.H., Li, C.: Energy efficiency of symmetric key cryptographic algorithms in wireless sensor networks. In: 25th symposium on communication, Kingston, ON, Canada, 12–14 May 2010, pp. 168–172 (2010)
10. AnandaKrishna, B., Madhuri, N., Koteswara, M.R., VijaySekar, B.: Implementation of a novel cryptographic algorithm in wireless sensor networks. In: 2018 Conference on Signal Processing And Communication Engineering Systems (SPACES), Vijayawada, India, 4–5 January 2018, pp. 149–153 (2018)

WPA3 Connection Deprivation Attacks

Karim Lounis$^{(\boxtimes)}$ and Mohammad Zulkernine

Queen's Reliable Software Technology Lab, School of Computing,
Queen's University, Kingston, ON, Canada
{lounis,mzulker}@cs.queensu.ca

Abstract. After the KRACK (Key Reinstallation AttaCK) attack on WPA2 (Wi-Fi Protected Access 2) in Fall 2017, the Wi-Fi Alliance started developing WPA3 which was announced in Summer 2018. WPA3 is a certification that adds protection mechanisms to its predecessor WPA2, such as dictionary attack resistance, management frame protection, and forward secrecy. In April 2019, researchers discovered a set of vulnerabilities in WPA3. These vulnerabilities allow an attacker to perform different types of attacks, varying from denial of service to network-password cracking. This has worried the community including organizations and device vendors who have already started implementing WPA3 on their devices. In this paper, we present three possible denial of service attacks on WPA3. We start by presenting the WPA3-SAE (Simultaneous Authentication of Equals) mechanism. Then, we analyze the mechanism and show the existence of specification flaws in WPA3 protocol. An attacker exploits these flaws to generate attacks on Wi-Fi availability to deprive legitimate devices from connecting to WPA3 networks. We experimentally show the feasibility of these attacks and propose possible countermeasures to mitigate the attacks and direct device vendors to better implement security in their future devices.

Keywords: Wi-Fi security · WPA3-SAE · WPA3 security · Wi-Fi attacks

1 Introduction

Wi-Fi technology has provided a number of security mechanisms to guarantee security services, i.e., authentication, confidentiality, integrity, and availability. The first mechanism, ratified in 1999, was WEP (Wired Equivalent Privacy). It applies the RC4 (Ron's Code 4) stream cipher algorithm along with an encryption key and uses the CRC-32 (Cyclic redundancy check 32-bit) algorithm to generate a code for data integrity. Few years later, WEP was completely broken. Serious vulnerabilities were found and the security of WEP became nonsense [1–5]. The IEEE (Institute of Electrical and Electronics Engineers) started proposing the 802.11i framework [6] which promised stronger security mechanisms for authentication, encryption, and data integrity. Due to pressure from the market, the Wi-Fi Alliance rashly (in April 2003) started certifying devices

© Springer Nature Switzerland AG 2020
S. Kallel et al. (Eds.): CRiSIS 2019, LNCS 12026, pp. 164–176, 2020.
https://doi.org/10.1007/978-3-030-41568-6_11

based on a draft version of 802.11i under the name of WPA (Wi-Fi Protected Access). WPA uses the TKIP (Temporal Key Integrity Protocol) encryption that adopts RC4 with longer keys and the Michael algorithm for data integrity. Finally, in June 2004, the final version implementing the 802.11i specification was ratified under the name of WPA2 (Wi-Fi Protected Access 2). WPA2 uses the CCMP (CTR with CBC-MAC Protocol) encryption mechanism that adopts AES (Advanced Encryption Standard) for encryption and AES-CBC-MAC (Cipher Bloc Chaining-Message Authentication Code) algorithm for data integrity.

Despite some security vulnerabilities, mostly related to denial of service attacks [7–12], discovered on WPA2 during the last decade, the protection mechanism has provided an acceptable security level. The community has since then believed that WPA2 is the most secure mechanism that is nowadays available in the market. Nonetheless, in Fall 2017, researchers demonstrated an attack, known as KRACK (Key Reinstallation AttaCK) [13], which has broken the WPA2 secure-assumption. This has pushed the Wi-Fi Alliance to come up with a new security mechanism called WPA3, which was then announced in Summer 2018. Thus far, a 7-page specification document on WPA3 is available on the Wi-Fi Alliance website [14]. Device manufacturers are still implementing the protocol to commercialize Wi-Fi devices that are WPA3-certified. This has not prevented researchers from discovering a set of vulnerabilities, known as Dragonblood, in the WPA3 authentication protocol [15]. These vulnerabilities allow an attacker to perform different types of attacks, varying from denial of service to cracking the network password, using downgrading and side-channel attacks. Also, as part of our research, we have reported other vulnerabilities on WPA3 that can be exploited to generate denial of service attacks on WPA3 [16].

WPA3 applies SAE (Simultaneous Authentication of Equals), also known as Dragonfly [17], on top of the classical 4-way-handshake, for authentication and key establishment. The SAE key establishment protocol uses elliptic curve cryptography along with a Deffie-Hellman key exchange style and the shared network password, to allow two communication parties to establish a shared key. This key is known by PMK (Pairwise Master Key). It is employed further in the classical 4-way-handshake to derive other cryptographic keys, such as the encryption and message integrity keys. Thus, the hardness of this protocol relies on the difficulty of solving the ECDLP (Elliptic Curve Discrete Logarithm Problem)[1]. Also, WPA3 requires the use of MFP (Management Frame Protection)[2] mechanism to protect Wi-Fi users from being victims to denial of service attacks that are based on management frame spoofing, such as deauthentication attack [8].

In this paper, we present three potential connection deprivation attacks on WPA3. We start by presenting the WPA3-SAE authentication mechanism. Then,

---

[1] ECDLP is the problem of finding a scalar n given two elliptic points $P \in \xi(\mathbb{F}_p)$ and $Q \in \xi(\mathbb{F}_p)$ such that Q is the product of the scalar n by the point P ($Q = n.P$), where ξ is an elliptic curve defined over a finite field $\mathbb{F}_p$ and $p = q^m$ (q is prime) [18].

[2] MFP (Management Frame Protection) was introduced as part of the IEEE 802.11w amendment to add protection to management frames that are originally not authenticated and hence can be easily spoofed for denial of service attacks.

we analyze the mechanism and show the existence of specification flaws. An attacker can exploit these flaws to generate attacks on Wi-Fi availability and deprive legitimate Wi-Fi devices from connecting to WPA3 networks. We demonstrate the feasibility of these attacks and propose possible countermeasures to mitigate them.

The remainder of the paper is organized as follows: Sect. 2 presents WPA3 and its authentication mechanism. In Sect. 3, we present three possible attacks that abuse WPA3 authentication to deprive Wi-Fi users from connecting to WPA3 Wi-Fi networks. We show their practical feasibility and discuss possible countermeasures to mitigate them. Finally, Sect. 4 concludes the paper.

2   WPA3 Authentication Phases

WPA3 allows three possible operational modes. WPA3-SAE (Wi-Fi Protected Access-Simultaneous Authentication of Equals) is used when Wi-Fi devices only support WPA3. WPA3-SAE transition, also known as mixed mode, allows Wi-Fi devices that only support WPA2 to connect to a WPA3 network. WPA3-Enterprise 192-bit is used in sensitive enterprise environments, such as government and industrial networks. In the remaining part of this paper, we consider the WPA3-SAE and WPA3-SAE transition modes. In the following paragraphs, we present how authentication is performed in WPA3-SAE.

The WPA3 authentication consists of three phases: (1) The SAE (Simultaneous Authentication of Equals) handshake. (2) The association phase. (3) The 4-way handshake phase, as illustrated in the MSC[3] of Fig. 1. The first phase is also known as Dragonfly. It consists of four messages in which the supplicant[4] and the access point (authenticator) use the shared network password to derive the shared key PMK (Pairwise Master Key). This phase is illustrated with much details in the MSC(see footnote 3) of Fig. 2 and discussed in the next paragraph. The second phase consists of two messages, where the supplicant sends an association request and the access point replies back by an association response. During this phase, the supplicant indicates in the association request which security parameters (i.e., authentication, encryption, and authentication key management algorithms) it wishes to use. The access point confirms or rejects the parameters in the association response message. Finally, in the last phase, both parties use the previously derived PMK key to execute the classical 4-way handshake to derive and install the PTK (Pairwise Transient Key), which is the session key.

---

[3] MSC (Message Sequence Chart) is a graphical language for the description of the interaction between different components of a system. This language is standardized by the ITU (International Telecommunication Union).

[4] In 802.1X terminology, Wi-Fi users are called supplicants. They authenticate themselves to the access point, which is known by the authenticator. In the rest of the paper, we use the term Wi-Fi supplicant and Wi-Fi user interchangeably. We also use the term Wi-Fi access point and Wi-Fi authenticator interchangeably.

During the SAE-handshake phase shown in Fig. 2 (Phase 1 in Fig. 1), both parties, i.e., the supplicant and the access point, agree on a cryptographic domain, ECP (Elliptic Curve groups) or MODP (Modular Exponential groups). Depending on the cryptographic domain, they use the shared network password along with a hash-to curve or hash-to-group algorithm to transform the password into an elliptic curve point P (when ECP is used) or into a multiplicative group modulo a prime element (when MODP is used). In both cases, the output is denoted by PWE (PassWord Element). In the remaining part of this paper, we only consider the ECP domain for WPA3-SAE description and experimentation.

Considering the ECP domain, each party $i \in \{S, A\}$ generates two random values, $rand_i$ and $mask_i$. These two random values are used to compute two commit values, $scal_i = (rand_i + mask_i) [r]$ and $elem_i = Inv(mask_i \bullet PWE)$. The value $scal_i$ is a scalar, whereas $elem_i$ is an elliptic curve point which corresponds to the inverse (Inv) of the point that results from the elliptic point multiplication '$\bullet$' of the scalar $mask_i$ by the elliptic point PWE. Once computed, each party sends to the other one an authentication message with an authentication sequence number set to 0x0001[5]. This message is also known as the commit message and contains the tuple ($scal_i$, $elem_i$).

Upon receiving the tuple, each party verifies whether the values of $scal_i$ and $elem_i$ are within the curve definition domain or not, i.e., $scal_i \in [1, r[$ and $elem_i \in \xi(\mathbb{F}_p)$, where r is the prime order of the generator G of the finite cyclic group $\mathbb{G}$ that defines the addition operation in the elliptic curve ξ. The used elliptic curve ξ is defined over the prime finite filed $\mathbb{F}_p$ of order p (large prime number). Once verified, both parties compute a token tok. This token is the result of applying a HMAC (Keyed-Hash Message Authentication Code) over five concatenated elements (the concatenation is denoted by '$|$' in Fig. 2). For $i, j \in \{S, A\}$ and $i \neq j$, the first element is $F(rand_i \bullet (scal_j \bullet PWE \diamond elem_j))$, where F is a hash function and '$\diamond$' the elliptic curve point addition operator. The second element is $F(elem_i)$, the third is the scalar $scal_i \in [1, r[$, the fourth is $F(elem_j)$, and the fifth is the scalar $scal_j \in [1, r[$. Each party $i \in \{S, A\}$ sends its token tok_i to the other party in an authentication message with an authentication sequence number set to 0x0002(see footnote 5). This message is also known as the commit message. Each party verifies the correct derivation of the token by the other party. A token constitutes a proof of knowledge of the password for a given party. If both tokens are validated, the SAE-handshake succeeds and both parties use the value $F(rand_i \bullet (scal_j \bullet PWE \diamond elem_j))$ as the shared PMK, which is used as a seed in the last phase to perform the 4-way-handshake.

---

[5] In the IEEE 802.11 standard, the authentication sequence number indicates the type of the authentication frame: 0x0001 is used to indicate an authentication request frame, whereas 0x0002 is used to indicate an authentication response frame.

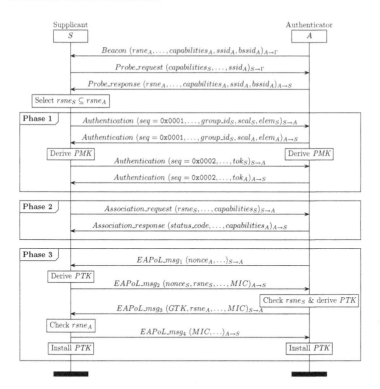

Fig. 1. WPA3-SAE authentication mechanism, where **Phase 1** is the SAE-handshake phase, **Phase 2** is the association phase, and **Phase 3** is the WPA2-4-way-handshake phase. The notation $M_{x \to y}$ indicates a message M sent from x to y. Also, E_x indicates an element E that is generated by $x \in \{S, A\}$. For $y = \Gamma$, the destination is set to the broadcast MAC address (i.e., FF:FF:FF:FF:FF:FF).

3   Connection Deprivation Attacks on WPA3-SAE

In the following subsections, we present three connection deprivation attacks on WPA3: (1) Attack on the 4-way-handshake downgrade protection. (2) Attack on SAE-handshake commit values. (3) Attack on the group/curve negotiation. The three attacks exploit specification flaws in the WPA3-SAE handshake to deprive Wi-Fi supplicants from connecting and joining WPA3 networks. We describe each attack individually, show its practical implementation, and provide countermeasures as well. As the same countermeasure can be applied to mitigate the three attacks, we discuss the countermeasure in Subsect. 3.5. First, we describe the environment used to generate all three attacks as follows.

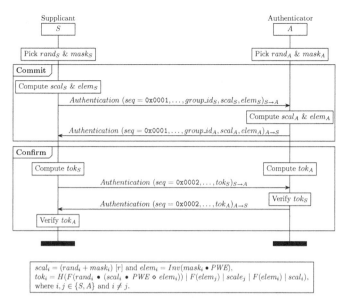

Fig. 2. Simultaneous Authentication of Equals Handshake, also known as Dragonfly. The notation $M_{x \to y}$ indicates a message M sent from x to y. Also, E_x indicates an element E that is generated by $x \in \{S, A\}$.

3.1 Attack Environment

To put the previous attacks into practice, we have used two Raspberry Pis B3+ and one laptop. The first Raspberry Pi runs *hostapd-2.7*[6] Linux utility (on Raspbian OS) to emulate a WPA3-SAE access point. The second Raspberry Pi runs *wpa_supplicant-2.7*[7] Linux utility (on Ubuntu MATE) to emulate a WPA3-SAE supplicant. The access point is configured to use WPA3 with SAE key management algorithm and AES-CCMP for encryption. It operates on channel 6 with an SSID set to QRST_WPA3. We have also augmented the two Raspberry Pis with a Wi-Fi interface (ODROID Wi-Fi Module 4) as the built in Wi-Fi network card does not support the WPA3-SAE as well as the monitor mode. We have also configured the supplicant with the correct network settings to be able to connect to the access point. We have run the access point and then run the supplicant which successfully got authenticated and associated to the access point. As the Wi-Fi network interfaces that were in our possession do not support MFP (Management Frame Protection), we have not enabled this option. Although MFP is mandatory in WPA3, enabling or disabling it does not affect

---

[6] *hostapd-2.7* is an open source package that allows to emulate access points on a computer. The version 2.7 supports the use of WPA3-PSK authentication protocol. It can be downloaded from https://w1.fi/releases/hostapd-2.7.tar.gz.

[7] *wpa_supplicant-2.7* is an open source package that allows to implement Wi-Fi supplicant on a computer. The version 2.7 supports the use of WPA3-PSK. It can be downloaded from https://w1.fi/releases/wpa_supplicant-2.7.tar.gz.

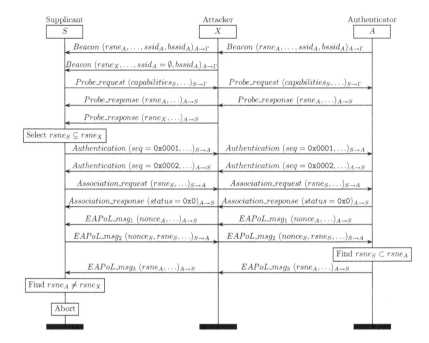

Fig. 3. Man-in-the-middle attack on WPA3-SAE downgrade protection. The notation $M_{x \to y}$ indicates a message M sent from x to y. Also, E_x indicates an element E that is generated by $x \in \{S, A\}$. For $y = \Gamma$, the destination is set to the broadcast MAC address (i.e., `FF:FF:FF:FF:FF:FF`).

the discussed attacks. In fact, it is infeasible to protect the management frames that are sent before the 4-way handshake (those are sent prior key establishment) and hence the discussed attacks are still feasible. Finally, the attacker uses the laptop (HP Probook 6560b) that runs *hostapd-2.7* on Linux (Ubuntu 16.04 LTS) to emulate an evil twin of the legitimate access point. We have set the attacker's security mechanism to be WPA2-PSK or WPA3-SAE depending on the attack scenario and set its SSID to be `QRST_WPA3` and hidden. This allows the attacker to be as passive as possible. In fact, only one SSID=`QRST_WPA3` will appear on the supplicant's device screen when scanning for Wi-Fi networks.

3.2   Attack on the 4-Way Handshake Downgrade Protection

Observation. In a Wi-Fi network that adopts the infrastructure mode, the access point periodically broadcasts management frames called beacons. These beacons reveal information about the network settings, such as synchronization information, BSSID (Basic Service Set IDentifier), SSID (Service Set IDentifier), and security information. The security information are revealed in an elementary structure called RSNE (Robust Security Network Element), which informs Wi-Fi supplicants that are interested in connecting to the network, about the supported security mechanisms (in a cipher-suite). The cipher-suite indicates which authentication, encryption, and authentication key management algorithms are supported by the access point. Wi-Fi supplicants can then choose the highest security mechanism that they can support from the received cipher-suite.

In the WPA3 authentication, the supplicant and the access point go through three phases as illustrated in the MSC(see footnote 3) of Fig. 1. Specifically, during the 4-way-handshake, both the supplicant and access point verify whether the RSNE that the other party wishes to use is still the same and has not been modified by a third party. The access point checks whether the $rsne_S$ of the supplicant is supported. The supplicant however, checks whether the indicated RSNE in the beacon frames and probe responses (i.e., $rsne_A$) is still the same. If the supplicant detects an RSNE mismatch, it passively aborts the handshake. In case of the access point, the latter sends a rejection message that could be a deauthentication frame. In a nutshell, this prevents an attacker from spoofing beacon or probe response frames and announcing weaker RSNE to trick supplicants into choosing a weaker cipher-suite rather than a more secure one [11].

Attack Generation. An attacker exploits this abortion behavior and sets up a MITM (Man In The Middle) attack as illustrated in the MSC(see footnote 3) of Fig. 3. By spoofing the legitimate access point and broadcasting beacon frames that announce weaker cipher-suite, such as WPA2-PSK ($rsne_X$ in Fig. 3) instead of WPA3-SAE ($rsne_A$ in Fig. 3). The supplicant may choose WPA2-PSK over WPA3-SAE and start the authentication with the legitimate access point. At this point, the attacker stays idle and watches the scene. The supplicant will detect that the access point is actually supporting WPA3 in addition to WPA2 when it receives the third message of the 4-way handshake (viz., last message in Fig. 3). The supplicant detects a mismatch and aborts the connection. The attacker repeats this scenario again and again to deprive the supplicant from connecting to the Wi-Fi network. The attacker just has to send beacon frames at a higher rate[8] and rapidly reply to supplicant's probe requests.

To experiment the attack on the 4-way-handshake downgrade protection, we have configured the WPA3 supplicant in a way so that it can connect to WPA2-PSK or WPA3-SAE access points. We have configured the attacker access point to behave as an evil twin of the legitimate access point but using WPA2-PSK instead of WPA3-SAE. We have started both access points and then executed the supplicant. We have observed (using *Wireshark*) that the supplicant has chosen to operate the WPA2-PSK instead of WPA3-SAE. In fact, after receiving probe responses from both access points (indicating the supported cipher-suite in the RSNE), the supplicant has replied back by sending an authentication frame (seq=0x0001) indicating the authentication algorithm 0x0, i.e., Open System, to be used. Interestingly, both access points have replied with an authentication frame (seq=0x0002). The supplicant has proceeded by sending an association request in which it has indicated the selected RSNE (i.e., WPA-PSK-CCMP). The legitimate access point replied first by sending an association response indicating a rejection message with a status code 0x002b. This code carries the

---

[8] Typically, beacons are sent every 100 time units (beacon interval), where a time unit is 1.024 ms. The attacker can change the beacon interval to be 15 instead of 100.

message "Invalid AKMP", which indicates invalid authentication key manage-ment protocol. The supplicant has also received the association response from the attacker (with success massage 0x0000), but it was ignored as the supplicant has already aborted the authentication right after the rejection. We can see that an attacker can easily trick a supplicant into choosing WPA2-PSK instead of WPA3-SAE, which is the first goal in this attack. We were able to repeat this attack scenario and deprive the legitimate supplicant from connecting to the right access point. Even if the legitimate access point was configured to adver-tise the capability of operating both WPA2-PSK and WPA3-SAE (which is not possible in *hostapd-2.7*), the authentication would have happened through the Open System authentication. Then, during the 4-way-handshake, in particular, after receiving the third EAPoL[9] message, the supplicant would have aborted the authentication due to RSNE mismatch and have had restarted the authen-tication again.

3.3   Attack on WPA3-SAE's Commit Values

Observation. As described in Sect. 2, the WPA3-SAE handshake runs through two subphases (viz., Fig. 2): commit and confirm. Specifically, during the first subphase both the supplicant and the authenticator generate a tuple ($scal_i$, $elem_i$) and send it to the other party using a commit message (an authentication message with seq=0x0001). Each party $i \in \{S, A\}$ verifies whether the tuple ($scal_{j\neq i}$, $elem_{j\neq i}$) contains values that are within a predefined range. If one of the parties finds out that the received tuple is out of the predefined range, i.e., $scal_{j\neq i} \notin [1, r[$ or $elem_{j\neq i} \notin \xi(\mathbb{F}_p)$, the handshake is aborted.

Attack Generation. An attacker exploits this value-range checking operation to cause a denial of service on the supplicant. When the supplicant sends its first commit message (containing commit values $scal_S$ and $elem_S$), the attacker in a race condition with the legitimate authenticator, replies with a rejection message as if the generated commit values ($scal_S$ and $elem_S$) were out of the range. The attacker just has to spoof the authenticator and reply first to the supplicant with a crafted commit message that carries an "out of range" error information. The supplicant receives the latter message and aborts the handshake as illustrated in the MSC(see footnote 3) of Fig. 4 (consider $m_2 = m_4$ and $error\_code_1$ to be "Invalid commit values"). The attacker performs this injection repeatedly, at specific instants of time, and prevents legitimate supplicants from connecting to the network.

To implement this attack, we have modified the source code of *hostapd-2.7*[10] in such as way so that the attacker's access point replies to the supplicant's commit message with a commit message that contains the rejection status code 0x0001 (stating "Unspecified failure"). Next, we have run the two access points followed by the supplicant. We have observed that the supplicant has sent its

---

[9] EAPoL (Extensible Authentication Protocol over LAN) is a network protocol used in 802.1X for authentication. It uses EAP protocol over Ethernet.

[10] We have modified the code located in `/hostapd-2.7/src/ap/ieee802_11.c`.

commit message and then received a first commit message from the attacker access point. As the message contained the rejection message, the supplicant has straightforwardly aborted the authentication. Although it has received the second commit message from the legitimate access point, the latter message got ignored. The legitimate access point has re-transmitted the commit message many times before aborting the authentication process.

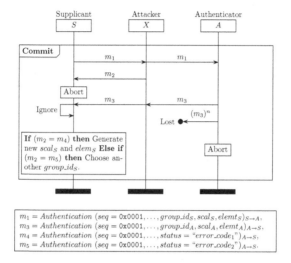

Fig. 4. Man-in-the-middle attack on WPA3-SAE commit subphase: in the case where $m_2 = m_4$, this MSC depicts the commit values attack. Otherwise, when $m_2 = m_5$ this MSC depicts the group/curve negotiation attack. The notation $M_{x \to y}$ indicates a message M sent from x to y. Also, E_x indicates an element E that is generated by $x \in \{S, A\}$ and $(m_{v \in \mathbb{N}})^n$ a message $m_{v \in \mathbb{N}}$ sent $n \in \mathbb{N}$ times.

3.4   Attack on WPA3-SAE's Group/Curve Negotiation

Observation. During the SAE handshake, the supplicant sends to the authenticator a commit message indicating which elliptic curve or multiplicative group (denoted by $group\_id_S$) it wishes to use along with the tuple $(scal_S, elem_S)$. If the authenticator does not support the desired elliptic curve or multiplicative group, it sends a commit message to the supplicant to inform it that the access point does not support the desired multiplicative group or elliptic curve group.

Attack Generation. The attacker exploits this protocol behavior and sets up a MITM attack between the supplicant and the authenticator. It waits for a supplicant to send a commit message and quickly replies with a forged commit message informing the supplicant that the authenticator does not support the desired $group\_id_S$ before the supplicant receives the commit message from the

legitimate authenticator. The attacker repeats this attack each time the supplicant proposes whatever cryptographic option and prevents the supplicant from
connecting to the network as illustrated in the MSC(see footnote 3) of Fig. 4 (consider $m_2 = m_5$ and $error\_code_2$ to be "Unsupported Deffie-Hellman-group").

To implement this attack, we have modified the same file (i.e., `ieee802_11.c`)
in such a way so that the attacker's access point replies to commit messages with
a rejection message that contains the status code `0x004d` (stating "Authentication is rejected because the offered finite cyclic group is not supported"). We
have run the attack and have observed that each time the supplicant tried to
initiate the authentication, it receives the rejection message from the attacker's
access point first. We have run this attack during 30 min and have observed that
the supplicant has performed 23 authentication attempts and all of them failed.
The supplicant has tried to authenticate using the ECP finite cyclic groups 19,
20, 21, 25, and 26 (then repeating from 19) and have failed in each of them due to
the attack. In this way, we have successfully managed to deprive the supplicant
from getting connected to the right access point.

3.5   Countermeasure

The three attacks discussed in Subsects. 3.2, 3.3 and 3.4 have a common vulnerability nature, which consists of foolishly replying back to messages upon
their reception. In the attack on the 4-way-handshake downgrade protection
(discussed in Subsect. 3.2), the supplicant has received a probe response from
the attacker and then has taken a straight decision to apply the security mechanism that the attacker proposes based on the information contained inside the
received message (i.e., RSNE in probe response) and the supplicant's local network configurations. In the case of the attack on the commit values (discussed in
Subsect. 3.3) and the attack on the group/curve negotiation (discussed in Subsect. 3.4), the supplicant has taken the decision to abort the handshake upon
the reception of the first "rejection" message. Overall, the behavior taken by the
supplicant is coherent with the specification. However, we believe that future
supplicants should be smarter. Instead of taking a decision based on one message, supplicants should take a decision based on a group of quasi-similar messages. Therefore, to mitigate the previous three attacks, the supplicants should
be implemented in such a way so that they do not take a decision and reply
upon the reception of the first probe, authentication, or association response.
The supplicant would take a longer time than usual but with a guarantee of not
being fooled. In this way, we can prevent these attacks from occurring in future
Wi-Fi networks that will be supporting WPA3.

4   Conclusion

The WPA3 has been recently announced as the next generation of Wi-Fi security. This new security standard promises higher security and aims to completely
replace the WPA2 mechanism. In April 2019, WPA3 has been shown to contain

some vulnerabilities that could affect the availability of the Wi-Fi network and the security of the whole network by cracking the network password. In this paper, we have analyzed the WPA3-SAE authentication protocol and presented three possible attacks. These attacks aim to affect Wi-Fi network availability by depriving legitimate users from connecting to the network. We have shown the practical feasibility of these attacks and proposed countermeasures to mitigate the attacks. We claim that if the next generation access points (i.e., those implementing WPA3) do not apply the countermeasures and follow the recommendations, the presented attacks will still be possible.

Acknowledgment. This work is partially supported by the Natural Sciences and Engineering Research Council of Canada (NSERC) and the Canada Research Chairs (CRC).

References

1. Tews, E., Beck, M.: Practical attacks against WEP and WPA. In: Proceedings of the Second ACM Conference on Wireless Network Security, pp. 79–86 (2009)
2. AlFardan, N., Bernstein, D.J., Paterson, K.G., Poettering, B., Schuldt, J.C.N.: On the security of RC4 in TLS. In: Presented as part of the 22nd USENIX Security Symposium, pp. 305–320. USENIX (2013)
3. Stubblefield, A., Ioannidis, J., Rubin, A.D.: Using the Fluhrer, Mantin, and Shamir attack to break WEP. In: Proceedings of the Network and Distributed System Security Symposium (2002)
4. Fluhrer, S., Mantin, I., Shamir, A.: Weaknesses in the key scheduling algorithm of RC4. In: Vaudenay, S., Youssef, A.M. (eds.) SAC 2001. LNCS, vol. 2259, pp. 1–24. Springer, Heidelberg (2001). https://doi.org/10.1007/3-540-45537-X_1
5. Borisov, N., Goldberg, I., Wagner, D.: Intercepting mobile communications: the insecurity of 802.11. In: Proceedings of the 7th Annual International Conference on Mobile Computing and Networking, pp. 180–189. ACM (2001)
6. IEEE: "IEEE STD 802.11i" amendment 6: medium access control security enhancement (2004)
7. Paterson, K.G., Poettering, B., Schuldt, J.C.N.: Plaintext recovery attacks against WPA/TKIP. In: Cid, C., Rechberger, C. (eds.) FSE 2014. LNCS, vol. 8540, pp. 325–349. Springer, Heidelberg (2015). https://doi.org/10.1007/978-3-662-46706-0_17
8. Bellardo, J., Savage, S.: 802.11 denial-of-service attacks: real vulnerabilities and practical solutions. In: Proceedings of the 12th Conference on USENIX Security Symposium, vol. 12, pp. 15–27. USENIX Association (2003)
9. Alabdulatif, A., Ma, X., Nolle, L.: Analysing and attacking the 4-way handshake of IEEE 802.11i Standard. In: The IEEE 8th International Conference for Internet Technology and Secured Transactions, pp. 382–387 (2013)
10. Singh, R., Sharma, T.P.: On the IEEE 802.11i security: denial-of-service perspective. In: Security and Communication Networks, pp. 1378–1407 (2014)
11. Vanhoef, M., Piessens, F.: Denial-of-service attacks against the 4-way Wi-Fi handshake (2017). https://papers.mathyvanhoef.com/ncs2017.pdf
12. Bai, Z., Bai, Y.: 4-way handshake solutions to avoid denial of service attack in ultra wideband networks. In: The 3rd International Symposium on Intelligent Information Technology Application, vol. 3, pp. 232–235 (2009)

13. Vanhoef, M., Piessens, F.: Key reinstallation attacks: forcing nonce reuse in WPA2. In: The Proceedings of the ACM Conference on Computer and Communications Security, pp. 1313–1328 (2017)
14. Wi-Fi-Alliance. WPA3 specification version 1.0 (2018). https://www.wi-fi.org/
15. Vanhoef, M., Ronen, E.: Dragonblood: a security analysis of WPA3's SAE handshake, April 2019. https://papers.mathyvanhoef.com/dragonblood.pdf
16. Lounis, K., Zulkernine, M.: Bad-token: a denial of service attack on WPA3. In: Proceedings of the 12th International Conference on Security of Information and Networks, Sochi, Russia, 12–15 September 2019
17. Harkins, D.: Simultaneous authentication of equals: a secure, password-based key exchange for mesh networks. In: Second International Conference on Sensor Technologies and Applications, pp. 839–844 (2008)
18. Hankerson, D., Menezes, A., Vanstone, S.: Guide to Elliptic Curve Cryptography. Springer, New York (2004). https://doi.org/10.1007/b97644

An Approach for Thwarting Malicious Secret Channel: The Case of IP Record Route Option Header-Based Covert Channels

Firas Saidi[1]([⊠]), Zouheir Trabelsi[2], and Henda Ben Ghézela[1]

[1] National School of Computer Sciences, Manouba, Tunisia
Firas.saidi@ensi.rnu.tn,
henda.benghezala@riadi.rnu.tn
[2] College of Information Technology, UAE University, Abu Dhabi,
United Arab Emirates
Trabelsi@uaeu.ac.ae

Abstract. The Internet constitutes actually one of the main communication platforms for cybercriminals and terrorists to exchange secret messages and hidden information. The use of clear or non-encrypted network traffic to communicate over the Internet allows steganalysis process and surveillance agencies to easily identify the presence of secret messages and hidden information, and classify the involved entities as potential cyber criminals or terrorists. However, covert channels can be an efficient and remedial communication solution for cybercriminals and terrorists to exchanged secret messages and hidden information. In fact, most covert channels attempt to send clear and non- encrypted messages embedded in the fields of network packets in order to offer robust communication channels against steganalysis. Nevertheless, covert channels are an immense cause of security concern and are classified as a serious threat because they can be used to pass malicious messages. This explains why detection and elimination of covert channels are considered a big issue that faces security systems and needs to be addressed. In this paper, a novel approach for detecting a particular type of covert channels is discussed. The covert channel uses the IP Record route option header in network IP packets to send secret messages and hidden information. The paper demonstrates that this type of covert channels is not robust enough against steganalysis. The proposed detection approach is based on the IP Loose source route option header. Conducted experiments show that the proposed approach is simple and straightforward to implement and can contribute to identifying malicious online activities of cyber criminals and terrorists.

Keywords: Cyber terrorism · Covert channel · IP header option ·
Steganalysis · Covert channel detection

1 Introduction

The emergence and proliferation of the Internet served criminals and terrorists not only to polarize new members but also to flourish their malicious cyber activities in the virtual space. In fact, the rapid development of computer networks has led cyber

S. Kallel et al. (Eds.): CRiSIS 2019, LNCS 12026, pp. 177–192, 2020.
https://doi.org/10.1007/978-3-030-41568-6_12

criminals and terrorists to find new ways to leak or steal confidential information, and exchange secret messages without being detected. A covert channel is a possible and good opportunity to do this. A covert channel is a communication channel that permits the transfer of hidden information and the exchange of secret messages between entities on the Internet in an undetectable manner [1].

Nowadays, network covert channels in which covert information can be encoded into network protocols are the most popular covert channel types [2]. In fact, covert channels in network protocols look similar to steganography techniques. Both use a carrier to send a covert message, although the nature of the carrier is different. In the case of steganography techniques, information is hidden in a carrier such as an image, video, text, sound, etc., known as an unstructured carrier. In the network covert channel, a network protocol is used as a carrier; this is known as a structured carrier [3, 4].

Covert channels are an immense cause of security concern because they can be used to pass malicious messages [5]. The messages could be in the form of computer viruses, spy programs, terrorist messages, etc. A covert channel is classified as a serious threat when combined with such malicious activities. This explains why detection and elimination of covert channels are considered a big issue that faces security systems, and need to be addressed [6]. Commonly, it is known that covert channels cannot be fully eliminated [7, 8]. But there is a possibility that they could be reduced through careful analysis and design [5].

As covert techniques are still new, further work and research need to be done regarding detection, prevention, and elimination. Barroso and Santos [9] discussed the art of covert techniques in network protocol packets. They addressed the fact that new protocols continue to burst, so new covert techniques will continue to grow accordingly. Therefore, data confidentiality may be at risk. Moreover, Barroso and Santos pointed out the importance of developing security techniques that are capable of analyzing network traffic and presenting effective mechanisms to fight against unauthorized data transmissions [9].

The TCP/IP suite is widely used by most Internet applications. It represents the biggest communication channel for overt communications. Numerous methods were developed for covert transmission using TCP/IP headers, and, accordingly, many detection methods have been developed to detect such threats [10]. This paper proposes a novel mechanism to detect a particular type of network covert channels that uses the IP Record route option header in network packets. The proposed mechanism is based on the IP Loose source routing option header. The paper demonstrates clearly that covert channels that use the IP Record route option header are not robust enough against steganalysis. Conducted experiments show that the proposed mechanism is simple and straightforward to implement. The mechanism can be used by surveillance and intelligence agents to identifying cybercriminals and terrorists, that are exchanging malicious messages using IP Record route option header-based covert channels.

The paper is organized as follows: Sect. 2 presents a brief background about the IP Record route option and the IP Loose source route option headers in IP packets, in order to introduce the terms used in this paper and lay the groundwork for what follows. Section 3 discusses related works on covert channels countermeasures. Section 4 presents the principle of IP Record route option header-based covert channel. Section 5 discusses the proposed mechanism for detecting IP Record route option header-based covert channel. Section 6 describes the conducted experiments regarding the implementation of the proposed mechanism. Section 7 concludes the paper.

2   Background

In order to introduce the terms used in this paper and lay the groundwork for what follows, we will briefly explore the main fields and options in the IP protocol header [11]. The IP protocol is the most commonly used protocol in the network layer today, and is used for almost all traffic moving across the Internet. Upon receiving a TCP, UDP or ICMP packet, the IP protocol generates an IP header, which includes the fields shown in Fig. 1. Then, the IP header is added to the front of the TCP, UDP or ICMP packet to create the resulting IP packet, which will be used to carry the entire packet's contents (IP header, TCP/UDP/ICMP header, and application-level data) across the network.

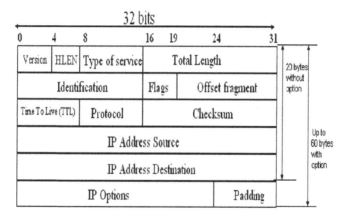

Fig. 1. The IP header structure

An IP header without the *Option* field has a length of 20 bytes. However, an IP header with the *Option* filed may have a length of up to 60 bytes. It is important to indicate that most IP packets do not use the *Option* field. Therefore, in most cases, a covert channel can use the unused 40 bytes of the *Option* field in an IP header to insert hidden information and secret messages.

2.1   The Fields of the IP Header Option

The IP *Option* field is not required in every IP datagram. Options are included primarily for network testing or debugging. Figure 2 shows the structure of the IP header option. The field *Code* indicates the type of the option in the IP header. The field *Length* indicates the size of the field *Option*. The *Pointer* field plays a particular function, depending on the type of the option. The four most used IP header options are:

- *Record routing*: used to trace a route.
- *Loose source routing*: used to route a datagram along a partial specific path.
- *Strict source routing*: used to route a datagram along a strict specified path.
- *Internet timestamp*: used to record timestamps along a route.

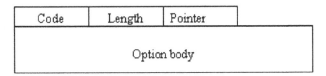

Fig. 2. The IP header option structure

For the proposed covert channel in this paper, we are only interested with the IP Record route and IP Loose source route options.

2.2   The IP Record Route Option Header

The IP Record *route* option header allows the source host to create an empty list of IP addresses and arrange for each router that handles the datagram to add its IP address to the list. Figure 3 shows the format of the IP *Record route* option. The *Code* field is set to the value 7. The *Length* field specifies the total length of the IP R*ecord route* option, including the first three bytes. The *Pointer* field specifies the offset within the IP *Record route* option of the next available slot. That is, it specifies the position in the *IP Record route* option where the next gateway can insert its IP address.

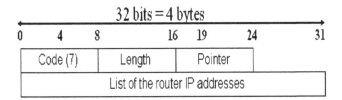

Fig. 3. The format of the IP *Record route* option header

Whenever a router handles an IP datagram that has the IP Record route option set, the router adds its IP address to the record route list. It is clear that enough space must be allocated in the IP Record route option by the original source host to hold all the IP addresses of the routers. To add its IP address to the list, a router first compares the values in the *Pointer* and *Length* fields. If the value in the *Pointer* field is greater than the value in the *Length* field, this means that the list is full, the router then forwards the IP datagram without inserting its IP address. If the list is not full, the router inserts its 4-bytes IP address at the position specified by the *Pointer* field, then increments the *Pointer* by four. When the IP datagram reaches its destination, the destination host extracts and processes the record route list of IP addresses.

2.3   The IP Loose Source Route Option Header

The IP Loose source route option allows one to partially specify a collection of routers that the packet must traverse before reaching the destination. That is, IP Loose source routing option partially specifies the route the packet takes through the network. Hence, IP Loose source route option provides a means for the source of an IP datagram to supply routing information to be used by the routers in forwarding the datagram to the destination.

Figure 4 shows the format of the IP Loose source route option. The *Code* field is set to the value 3. The *Length* field specifies the total length of the IP Loose source route option, including the first three bytes. The *Pointer* field specifies the offset within the IP Loose source route option of the next router's IP address. That is, it specifies the position in the IP Loose source route option where the next destination router's IP address can be extracted to route the IP datagram. Hence, IP Loose source route option field contains a pointer field and a list of IP addresses indicating the routers' IP addresses to be used for transit. Practically, the destination IP address in an IP datagram is replaced by the next router's IP address in the IP Loose source routing list. Also, the Pointer field is updated to the next router's IP address.

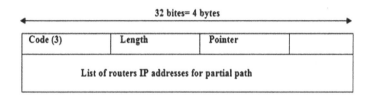

Fig. 4. The format of the IP *Loose source route* option header in an IP datagram

3   Related Work on Covert Channel Countermeasures

In [4], Zander et al. provided a comprehensive survey on countermeasures against common covert channels. Countermeasures include mainly methods for detecting, eliminating, and limiting the capacity of covert channels [4]. Other research works proposed countermeasures for specific types of covert channels [6, 12–18].

To apply countermeasures, Zander et al. [4] proposed first identifying the covert channel that is being used and then applying a specific countermeasure. This indicates that a particular countermeasure can be applied after the identification of a potential covert channel. In fact, there are two causes of covert channels [4]: design oversights and weaknesses inherent in the system design. While covert channels caused by oversights may be corrected once discovered, those intrinsic to the system can never be removed without redesigning the system. Therefore, ideally covert channels should be identified and removed during the design phase.

If a covert channel was not removed in the design phase, the next best option is to eliminate its possible use. However, covert channels cannot all be completely eliminated as indicated in [4]. If a channel cannot be eliminated, its capacity should be reduced. Limiting the channel capacity is often problematic, because it means slowing down system mechanisms or introducing noise, which both limit the performance of the system. Any covert channels that cannot be removed should be audited. Auditing acts as deterrence to possible users of the channel. Covert channels with capacities too low to be significant or that cannot be audited should at least be documented (e.g., in the protocol specification) so that everybody is aware of their existence and potential threat.

In summary, the countermeasures can be grouped into four categories [4]:

(a) Eliminating the covert channel (i.e. normalizing protocol headers)
(b) Limiting the covert channel bandwidth (i.e. random traffic padding technique)
(c) Auditing the covert channel (requires reliable passive warden as a detector)
(d) Documenting the covert channel.

Most of the proposed detection approaches depend on the recognition of non-standard or abnormal behavior [4, 6, 12–18]. Typically, the warden knows the normal traffic behavior in a certain network, so it can easily detect the abnormal behavior that is caused by covert communication. However, if the normal traffic includes considerable variations, then these approaches will fail to detect covert traffic. Moreover, any covert traffic that looks similar to normal traffic will be hard to detect. The depth of knowledge about covert channel techniques is a key to developing countermeasures. Due to the rapid development of computer network communication technology, and its complex nature, it is illogical to look for full elimination of all potential covert channels or to prove their nonexistence. Instead some methods have been developed to detect or eliminate different types of covert channels [6, 12–18]. Other methods attempted to lower or degrade the bandwidth of potential covert channels [4]. But, in those cases, a balance should be maintained to keep the overt channel intact and effective while trying to degrade the covert bandwidth. Some common methods for bandwidth reduction or capacity reduction are: introducing noise, setting a fixed size for network packet length, limiting the host to host connections and inserting dummy packets [9].

In [6, 12–18], recent and relevant work on covert channels detection and mitigation techniques along with their achievements and limitations are surveyed and discussed. In addition, the focus is on covert channel capacity reduction as one of the common mitigation techniques. Among all proposed countermeasures in the literature, there are research works that proposed countermeasures against IP Record route option header-based covert channels [19].

4   The Principle of IP Record Route Option Header-Based Covert Channel

Many network protocols support extension of the standard header [11]. Usually there are some predefined header extensions that allow transport of non- mandatory information on demand, but many network protocols also allow header extensions to carry data not foreseen in the original specification, thus extending the capabilities of the protocols. Covert information can be encoded in existing or new header extensions. For example, covert data can be masked as IP addresses in IP route record option headers [4, 19]. Another approach is to use the presence or absence of optional header fields as a covert channel.

In [19], the proposed covert channel's objective is to allow a source host to use the available bytes in the IP record route option header to insert secret message, and at the same time prevent any router (along the path to the destination host) from inserting its IP address to keep the secret message intact. Figure 5 shows the structure of an IP packet without, and with, the IP record route option [11]. When the IP header option designates a record route, the *Code* and *Pointer* fields should be set to the standard values 7 and 4, respectively. Also, the maximum value in the *Length* field should be 39 (Table 1). On its way to its destination, any packet with such an IP header option would ask each router to insert its IP address in the 4-bytes field pointed by the *Pointer* field (Fig. 6). Then, the value of the *Pointer* field in the IP header option is increased by 4. So, the next router would write its IP address in the next 4-bytes field in the IP header option. However, if the value of the *Pointer* field becomes greater than the value of the *Length* field, then no more routers can insert their IP addresses. Therefore, we may establish a covert channel for sending secret messages if the initial value of the *Pointer* field is greater than the value of the *Length* field (Fig. 7(a)), or just greater than the length of the secret message (Fig. 7(b)).

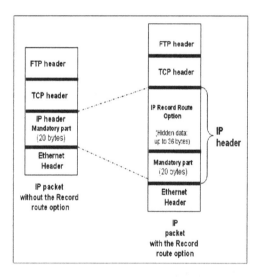

Fig. 5. Structure of an example IP packet without and with the IP record route option header

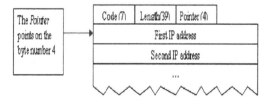

Fig. 6. A standard IP *record route* option header

Table 1. The standards values of the fields of the IP Record route header

Fields	Value
Code	7
Maximum length	39
Pointer	4

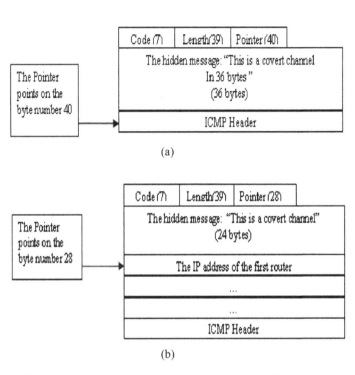

(a)

(b)

Fig. 7. Examples of possible values of the *Pointer* field used for a covert channel

If we set the initial value of the *Pointer* field greater than the value of the *Length* field, then no router can insert its IP address. In this case, we can use all the 36 bytes of the IP Record route option header to insert secret messages (Fig. 7(a)). However, if we set the initial value of the *Pointer* field just greater than the length of the secret message, then a number of routers can insert their IP addresses in the remaining bytes of the IP Record route option header (Fig. 7(b)). In [19], this type of covert channels is discussed in details.

4.1 Examples of ICMP Packets with IP Record Route Option Header

As an example of an ICMP ping packet carrying a secret message, the packet generator of CommView sniffer tool [20] is used to build and send the packet with IP record route option header. Figure 8 shows that the IP addresses of the source and destination hosts are 172.16.16.3 and 172.16.16.20, respectively. In addition, the secret message inserted in the *Option* field is: "*This is a covert channel*", whose length is 24 bytes. Therefore, the value of the L*ength* field is 39 bytes. The value of the *Pointer* field is set to 28, in order to force any router to add its IP address in the 4-bytes field following just the secret message. Using CommView sniffer, the contents of the two IP record route option headers in the packet sent to the destination host and in the packet received from the source host are decoded. Figure 8 illustrates this and shows that the first router (which is the destination host in our case) added its IP address just after the secret message. This demonstrates that the manipulation of the value of the fields in the IP record route option header, allows us to propose a covert channel.

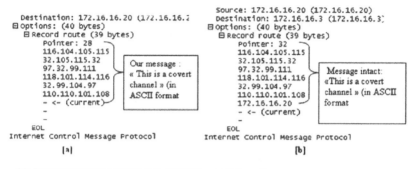

[a] : Request packet that carries the message "this is a covert channel"
[b] : Replay packet : the first hope write its IP address just after the hidden message

Fig. 8. ICMP packets with IP record route option header captured by *Ethereal* sniffer

5 Detection Approach Based on the IP Loose Source Route Option Header

IP header record route option header-based covert channels allow malicious hosts to insert secret messages instead of inserting valid router's IP addresses. When using this type of covert channel, most network traffic analyzers would assume that the IP record route option header contains a valid list of router's IP addresses. However, an advanced steganalysis process may be able to notice that these router's IP addresses are not valid and consequently the involved hosts may have exchanged secret messages.

To identify whether or not the list of router's IP addresses in the IP record route option header is valid, the following sub-section discusses a detection mechanism based on the use of the IP Loose source route option header.

5.1 Detection Technique's Steps and Algorithm

We assume that an IP packet that is carrying a secret message and belonging to an IP record route option header-based covert channel has been exchanged between two cyber terrorist hosts (*Terrorist Host 1* and *Terrorist Host 2*), as shown in Fig. 9. We also assume that the IP packet traversed 4 routers (R1, R2, R3 and R4) with IP addresses (IP_R1, IP_R2, IP_R3 and IP_R4), while in its route to the final destination, as shown in Fig. 9.

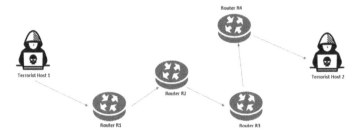

Fig. 9. Router path between Host 1 and Host 2

The proposed technique consists into verifying if the collected path of routers (R1, R2, R3 and R4) between the two hosts is valid or not. If it is valid, then the IP packet is mostly not carrying secret messages and does not belong to a covert channel that is using the IP record route option header to exchange secret messages. If it is not a valid path, then the IP packet is most probably carrying secret messages in the IP record route option header. The following algorithm depicts the proposed technique's steps to detect the validity of a given path of routers found in an IP record route option header.

5.1.1   Router Path Validity Process's Steps
The proposed technique uses two testing hosts (T1 and T2), with IP addresses T1_IP and T2_IP, respectively. The testing hosts will be used for conducting the aforementioned described router path validity process.

Step #1
- First, the testing host T1 generates an ICMP packet (Type = 8 and Code = 0) to attempt to ping host T2. The ping packet has the IP Loose source route option header set, as shown in Fig. 10. That is, the IP Loose source route option header includes the IP addresses of the first couple of routers (R1 and R2) found in the collected path of routers, as shown in Fig. 10. This specifies the partial route (i.e., R1 and R2) that the ping packet should take to reach its destination.

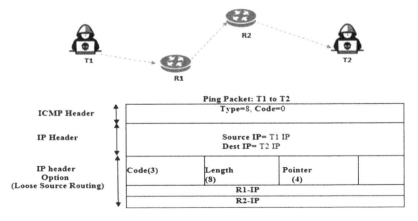

Fig. 10. Ping packet with the partial path (R1_IP and R2_IP) in the IP Loose source record option header

- After sending the ping packet, if the testing host T1 receives an ICMP reply message (Type = 0 and Code = 0) from the testing host T2, then we can conclude that the path between the two routers R1 and R2 is a valid path. Otherwise, this path is invalid, and consequently a packet sent by the testing host T1 cannot traverse firstly router R1 and then router R2 to reach the testing host T2. Hence, the collected packet is most probably belonging to an IP record route option header-based covert channel.

Step #2

- In case the first path (R1 and R2) is a valid path, the testing host T1 will generate a new ICMP ping packet with IP loose route option header set with the next couple of routers (i.e., R2 and R3) found in the collected list of routers. The same above path validation process is applied, Fig. 11. This process stops if an invalid path is detected, or all routers of the collected list were used. Hence, in the example shown in Fig. 9, if the path of routers found in the IP record route option header is valid, then the validation process is called three times using three couples of router IP addresses, namely (R1, R2), (R2, R3) and (R3, R4).

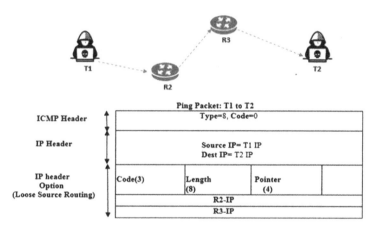

Fig. 11. Ping packet with the partial path (R2_IP and R3_IP) in the IP Loose source record option header

It is important to mention that this router path validity process may use different types of packets, such as UDP and TCP packets, since the ping traffic may be denied by security devices, such as firewalls, routers and intrusion prevention systems (IPS).

5.1.2   Router Path Validity Process's Algorithm

The pseudocode of the proposed router path validity process is illustrated as follows:

Alog. 1: Validation of the router path found in the IP Record route option header

Input: Path /* A list containing the router's IP addresses found in the IP Record route option header */

Var path_empty = false; /* A Boolean variable indicating if the list Path is empty or not */
Var IP_R1, IP_R2; /* Two variables containing the first two IP addresses found in the list Path*/

Var valid_path = true;/* A Boolean variable indicating if the list Path is valid or not */

Function extract_path(IP_R1, IP_R2, Path) /* A function that extracts the first two IP addresses found in the list Path, and return them as IP_R1 and IP_R2 */

Function validation_process(IP_R1, IP_R2) /* A function that return true if the path (IP1, IP2) is valid */

Function length_of_path(path) /* A function that returns the number of IP addresses in the list Path */

While (valid_path == true)
{
  o   **If** (path_empty == true)
  o   **Then:**
      ▪   exit;
  o   **Else:**
      ▪   Extract_path(IP_R1, IP_R2, Path);
      ▪   **If** (validation_process (IP_R1, IP_R2) == True)
      ▪   **Then:**
          •   Remove the first IP address (IP_R1) from the list Path;
          •   **If** (length_of_path (Path) == 1)
              o   **Then:**
                  ▪   path_empty == true;
                  ▪   exit;
      ▪   **Else:**
          •   valid_path = false;
} **While End**

Output:
If (valid_path == true)
• **Then:**
    o   Display message: "*Most probably, there is no IP Record route option header-based covert channel.*"
• **Else:**
    o   Display message: "*Most probably, there is an IP Record route option header-based covert channel.*"
----

6 Experiments

Experimentations conducted shows that the proposed mechanism is simple and straightforward to implement and can be used by investigators and intelligence agents to identify the presence of IP Record route option header-based covert channels. The first experiment demonstrates the process of sending an example secret message to a destination host using IP header Record routing option header-based covert channel. The second experiment shows the detection process of this type of covert channel using the proposed mechanism.

Figure 12 shows the network's architecture used in the experiments. The network has three routers (Cisco 2600 series) connected via serial interfaces, and a source host (IP address: 1.1.1.2) and a destination host (IP address: 4.4.4.2).

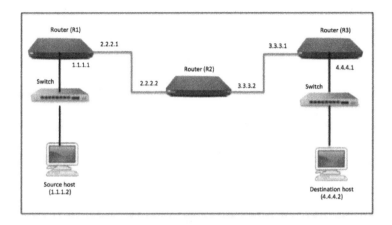

Fig. 12. Network architecture

Experiment #1: Covert Channel Packet Generation

Step *1*: At the source host (1.1.1.2), using a CommView tool as a packet generator, an IP packet is built (e.g., an ICMP ping packet) and the IP address of the destination host (4.4.4.2) is added. Moreover, the secret message (*'Meet you in the Mall'*) is inserted in the IP record route option header of the packet, as shown in Fig. 13. The Code, Length and Pointer fields of the IP Record route option header are set to 7, 28 and 28, respectively (Fig. 13). Once the destination host receives the ping packet, the secret message is easily extracted from the IP Record route option header.

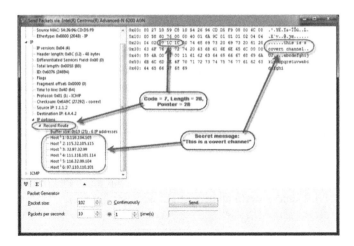

Fig. 13. Generation of an IP packet carrying the secret message "*This is a covert channel*"

Experiment #2: Router Path Validation Process

Step 2: We assume that the above exchanged ping packet has been captured by a surveillance host. The exchanged packet includes in its IP record route option header a list of IP addresses representing the routers traversed by the packet before reaching its destination. To valid the list of router's IP addresses extracted from the ping packet's IP record route option header, the surveillance host calls the above proposed path validation algorithm. The algorithm will attempt to valid the first partial path found in the list of router IP addresses. The first partial path is made of the first couple of router IP addresses represented by the 8 bytes: "*this is*". These two router IP addresses are inserted in the IP Loose source route option header of a ping packet, as shown in Fig. 14. Once this ping packet is sent, and since the partial path is not valid, the destination host will not be able to receive the packet and consequently the path is invalid. This allows concluding that the exchanged packet belongs most probably to an IP Route record option header-based covert channel.

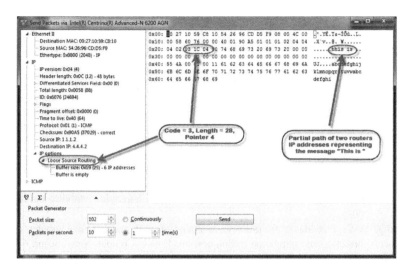

Fig. 14. IP packet with Loose source routing option header to valid the first partial path

7 Conclusion

Covert channels can be key communication channels for cyber criminals and terrorists to exchange secret and malicious messages. There are many possibilities of creating covert channels in computer network protocols, and the complete elimination of all these channels seems quite challenging for security professionals. In fact, with the evolution of network protocols technology and communication technology, it is difficult to maintain security policies or deterrence systems that could limit the rapid growth of network covert channels and techniques. Also, it is illogical to look for full elimination of all potential covert channels or to prove their nonexistence. Hence, the need for detection and mitigation mechanisms will remain important to assist intelligence and surveillance agencies to identify and eliminated covert channels. Moreover, deep knowledge of covert channel techniques is a key to developing covert channels countermeasures.

This paper demonstrated that IP Record route option header-based covert channels are not robust enough against steganalysis. Practically, the paper described a mechanism based on the IP Loose source route option header to detect IP Record route option header-based covert channels. Conducted experimentations showed that the proposed mechanism is simple and straightforward to implement and can be used by investigators and intelligence agents to identify this type of covert channels. Future research could focus on developing a security framework that takes into consideration all or most of the aforementioned observations in order to come up with sufficient security solutions to enhance covert channels detectability, elimination and prevention.

References

1. Yuwen, Q., Huaju, S., Chao, S., Xi, W., Linjie, L.: Network covert channel detection with cluster based on hierarchy and density. Procedia Eng. **29**, 4175–4180 (2012)
2. Wendzel, S., Zander, S., Fechner, B., Herdin, C.: Pattern-based survey and categorization of network covert channel techniques. ACM Comput. Surv. (CSUR) **47**, 50 (2015)
3. Craver, S.: On public-key steganography in the presence of an active warden. In: Aucsmith, D. (ed.) IH 1998. LNCS, vol. 1525, pp. 355–368. Springer, Heidelberg (1998). https://doi.org/10.1007/3-540-49380-8_25
4. Zander, S., Armitage, G., Branch, P.: A survey of covert channels and countermeasures in computer network protocols. IEEE Commun. Surv. Tutor. **9**, 44–57 (2007)
5. Hammouda, S., Maalej, L., Trabelsi, Z.: Towards optimized TCP/IP covert channels detection, IDS and firewall integration. In: 2008 New Technologies, Mobility and Security, pp. 1–5 (2008)
6. Elsadig, M.A., Fadlalla, Y.A.: Survey on covert storage channel in computer network protocols: detection and mitigation techniques. Int. J. Adv. Comput. Netw. Secur. **6**(3), 11–17 (2016)
7. Lampson, B.W.: A note on the confinement problem. Commun. ACM **16**, 613–615 (1973)
8. Rowland, C.H.: Covert channels in the TCP/IP protocol suite. First Monday **2** (1997)
9. Barroso, L., Santos, M.: A review on covert techniques
10. Dakhane, D.M., Deshmukh, P.R.: Active warden for TCP sequence number base covert channel. In: 2015 International Conference on Pervasive Computing (ICPC), pp. 1–5 (2015)
11. Fall, K.R., Stevens, W.R.: TCP/IP Illustrated, Volume 1: The Protocols, 2nd edn. Addison-Wesley Professional, Boston (2011)
12. Luo, X., Chan, E.W.W., Chang, R.K.C.: TCP covert timing channels: design and detection. In: International Conference on Dependable Systems & Networks, USA (2008)
13. Cai, Z., Zhang, Y.: Integrated covert channel countermeasure model in MLS networks. In: International Conference on Information Engineering and Computer Science, China (2009)
14. Kaur, J., Wendzel, S., Meier, M.: Countermeasures for covert channel-internal control protocols. In: 10th International Conference on Availability, Reliability and Security (ARES), France, pp. 422–428 (2015)
15. Elsadig, M.A., Fadlalla, Y.A.: A balanced approach to eliminate packet length-based covert channels. In: Proceedings of the 4th IEEE International Conference on Engineering Technologies and Applied Sciences (ICETAS), Bahrain (2017)
16. Elsadig, M.A., Fadlalla, Y.A.: Network protocol covert channels: countermeasures techniques. In: Proceedings of the 9th IEEE-GCC Conference and Exhibition (GCCCE) (2017)
17. Elsadig, M.A., Fadlalla, Y.A.: Packet length covert channel: a detection scheme. In: The 1st International Conference on Computer Applications & Information Security (ICCAIS), Saudi Arabia (2018)
18. Epishkina, A., Kogos, K.: A random traffic padding to limit packet size covert channels. In: 2015 Federated Conference on Computer Science and Information Systems (FedCSIS), pp. 1107–1111 (2015)
19. Trabelsi, Z., El-Sayed, H., Frikha, L., Rabie, T.: Traceroute based IP channel for sending hidden short messages. In: Yoshiura, H., Sakurai, K., Rannenberg, K., Murayama, Y., Kawamura, S. (eds.) IWSEC 2006. LNCS, vol. 4266, pp. 421–436. Springer, Heidelberg (2006). https://doi.org/10.1007/11908739_30
20. CommView tool. www.tamos.com

Toward Ciphertext Policy Attribute Based Encryption Model: A Revocable Access Control Solution in Cloud Computing

Mariem Bouchaala$^{(\boxtimes)}$, Cherif Ghazel, and Leila Azouz Saidane

CRISTAL Laboratory, ENSI, University of Manouba, Manouba, Tunisia
`bouchaala.mariem@gmail.com`

Abstract. Cloud Computing is the most promising paradigm in recent times. It offers on-demand services to individuals and industries. However, outsourcing sensitive data to entrusted Cloud servers impedes the adoption of Cloud concept. Security presents the most important issue. Consequently, Cloud service provider should implement fine grained access control models. Ciphertext Policy Attribute Based Encryption (CPABE) is considered as one of the most appropriate approach in Cloud Computing environment. However, it suffers from revocation, data owner overhead and computational cost limitations. In this work, we propose a Revocable algorithm (R-CPABE). The main idea of this work is to divide the original data after publishing in cloud server. In case of user revocation, one single slice is affected. Data owner need to retrieve, re-encrypt and re-publish it. To confirm the safety of our solution, we provide a security analysis. To evaluate its efficiency, a performance evaluation is performed.

Keywords: Cloud Computing · Access control · CPABE · Revocation · Splitting

1 Introduction

Storage as a service is one of the most popular Cloud Computing services. It offers on demand logical storage area accessible through Internet using multiple devices and heterogeneous platforms. Despite its effectiveness, the use of cloud storage is obstructed by many security issues such as network attack, untrusted cloud provider, information leakage, loss of control over outsourced data... For these reason, Cloud users want to encrypt and enforce self-authorization in their private data before outsourcing it to cloud storage server through internet. As far as the security is essentially a responsability of the Cloud provider, he is concerned with improving data access. For this reason, the choice of access control model remains a heavy and critical task. It represents one of the most important layer in Cloud security architecture [1].

© Springer Nature Switzerland AG 2020
S. Kallel et al. (Eds.): CRiSIS 2019, LNCS 12026, pp. 193–207, 2020.
https://doi.org/10.1007/978-3-030-41568-6_13

The concept of Attribute Based Encryption (ABE) [2] is studied to fulfill these requirements. ABE model presents one to many encryption access control scheme. It introduces the concept of access structure and descriptive attributes among users private key and ciphertext. We can distinguish between two variants Ciphertext Policy Attribute Based Encryption (CPABE) and Key Policy Attribute Based Encryption (KPABE). In CPABE access structure is embedded into ciphertext during encryption and private keys are labeled with descriptive attributes. In KPABE, ciphertexts are branded by data owner with a set of attributes while user's private key is delivered based on access structure. KP-ABE schemes are suitable for structured organizations with rules where authorized user's attributes are predefined. For these reason, it's not obvious in case of large-scale environment. In our work, we will use CPABE flavor defined in 2007 by Bethencourt et al. [3]. It protects not only the privacy of user's data but also the access policy. It ensures scalability, flexibility, collusion resistance and fine grained access. Yet, this method suffer from some limitations namely dual revocation(user and attribute revocation), Data Owner overhead (due to frequent update of public parameter) and computational complexity. In literature, many outstanding contributions have been found to resolve those challenges separately. Therefore, it is still an open challenge to design an efficient, secure and fine-grained access control overcoming these issues.

In this paper, we propose a revocable access control scheme adapted to Cloud Computing Environment. Contributions can be summarized as follows:

1. After publishing data, Data Owner (DO) splits the original file based on splitting algorithm and (n, n)threshold scheme. These slices are regrouped into static and dynamic data. One single slice will be selected randomly to perform revocation. It is considered as dynamic data. Remaining slices will construct together the static data.
2. Dynamic data is encrypted with 256-AES and the key K will be encrypted with CPABE algorithm.
3. When a revocation occurs, DO retrieves the dynamic data and choose a new random key. It performs re-encryption only in the selected slice. Static data will not be affected.

The remainder of this paper is organized as follows. Section 2 provides an overview of related schemes. Section 3 exposes the cryptographic used tools and algorithms. In Sect. 4, we describe the proposed access control solution R-CPABE. We defines scheme architecture, design goal and construction. Security analysis is exposed in Sect. 5. We provide performance evaluation in Sect. 6. We conclude the paper and discuss future work in Sect. 7.

2   Related Work

Ciphertext-Policy Attribute Based Encryption (CPABE) represents one to many public key encryption in which data owners embed their policies into the access structure [4].

This scheme suffers from a high Data Owner computational overhead. He should perform setup, key generation, encryption and revocation. In order to resolve this problem, many solutions are proposed. In [5], authors use a trusted root authority responsible of top-level domain authorities functioning. Using a hierarchical model improve the DO overhead but suffer from key-collusion attacks and require trust authorities. Eliminate a global coordinator presents the proposed approach in [6]. It decentralizes key generation process and makes it collusion resistant. These approaches increase remarkably data owner overhead. Thereupon, we focus in our solution to alleviate the data owner overhead by delegating heavy operations to Cloud server instead of using multi-attribute authorities. When it comes to security features, they suffer from revocation limitation.

Revocation presents the act of eliminating officially an agreement. This problem is one of the major brake of CPABE implementation in Cloud Computing. Work in [7] present the first attempt to resolve revocation. It introduce expiration time-frame for each attribute. As consequence, the date of encryption should be less than the expiration date of an attribute. Nevertheless, the time-based approach does not ensure forward secrecy and degrade the security of CPABE. Flexible ciphertext-policy attribute-based proxy re-encryption (PRE) based on two secret key was introduced in [8]. This concept use a semi-trusted server to re-encrypt data. The limit of this approach lies in the fact that the PRE discipline can be guessed based on launching different combination by supercomputer. Proxy can represent a security breach. In [9] attribute revocation method consist of re-encrypting both the key based on an update key in order to ensure forward and backward secrecy. In [10], the length of a encryption key is fixed. Authors assume that limiting and fixing the key length improve the system performance. When it comes to large attribute encryption system, this solution suffer from scalbility limitations (Table 1).

Table 1. Taxonomy of related works

Schemes	Authority	Attribute universe	Revocation type	Revocation level	Forward secrecy	Backward secrecy
[6]	Single	Small	Lazy	Attribute	x	$\checkmark$
[7]	Single	Large	Complete	Attribute	x	$\checkmark$
[8]	Single	Small	Lazy	Attribute	$\checkmark$	$\checkmark$
[9]	Single	Small	Lazy	User	x	$\checkmark$
Our	Single	Large	Complete	Dual	$\checkmark$	$\checkmark$

After studying different related works, some of them deals with the problem of attribute revocation (update of user attribute) others work in user revocation (definitive withdrawal of a user). Revocation can be performed directly or indirectly. In Direct revocation, DO need to issue an update key for non-revoked user periodically based on a revocation list. In indirect revocation, data owner embed revocation list in the ciphertext during encryption. Complete revocation improves security of the overall system (backward and forward secrecy) but requires a little more computation cost. Indirect revocation enhances performance but ensures only forward secrecy. We plan to propose an approach that enforce immediately revocation operation under the constraint of consuming only a little extra bandwidth and a few extra computing resources. To fill these gaps, we use splitting algorithm and involve Cloud computing server in access control. Experimentation results in Sect. 6 will improve that both computational and data owner overhead will be improved.

3   Preliminaries

3.1   Cryptographic Background

We review the access structure, bilinear pairing technique, as well as Bilinear Diffie Hellman. Then, we provide a definition of Ciphertext Policy Attribute Based Encryption (CP-ABE) scheme and its security assumption.

Bilinear Pairing. Suppose G_1 and G_2 two cyclic groups of same prime order q. Note that G_1 is an additive group and G_2 is a multiplicative group. Let P and Q be the two generators of G_1. We consider $\hat{e} : G_1 * G_1 \longrightarrow G_2$ a computable bilinear map if it verifies the following proprieties:

– Bilinear: $\forall P, Q \in G_1$ and $\alpha, \beta \in Z_q^*, \hat{e}(P^\alpha, Q^\beta) = \hat{e}(P, Q)^{\alpha\beta}$
– Non-degenerate $\hat{e}(P, Q) \neq 1$
– Computable: $\forall P, Q \in G_1$, there is an efficient algorithm to compute $\hat{e}(P, Q)$

Bilinear Diffie-Hellman (BDH) Assumption. Given g a generator of G_1 of prime order q and $g^\alpha, g^\beta, g^\gamma\, with\, \alpha, \beta, \gamma \in Z_q^*$. The BDH problem is to find a probabilistic polynomial time algorithm (PPT) solving $<q, G_1, G_2, e, g>$ with a negligible adversary such that the $Adv(A) = Pr(A(g, g^\alpha, g^\beta, g^\gamma) = e(g, g)^{\alpha\beta\gamma} \geqslant \epsilon$.

– Decisional Bilinear Diffie-Hellman (DBDH) assumption: Given $\theta \in Z_q^*$ no PPT algorithm cam distinguish the tuple $\left[(g, g^\alpha, g^\beta, g^\gamma), \hat{e}(g, g)^{\alpha\beta\gamma}\right]$ from $\left[(g, g^\alpha, g^\beta, g^\gamma), \hat{e}(g, g)^\theta\right]$ with non negligible advantage.
– Decisonal Linear (DL) assumption: Given $\theta\, and\, \lambda \in Z_q^*$ no PPT algorithm cam distinguish the tuple $\left[g, g^\alpha, g^\beta, g^{\alpha\gamma}, g^{\beta\lambda}, g^{\gamma+\lambda}\right]$ from $\left[g, g^\alpha, g^\beta, g^{\alpha\gamma}, g^{(\beta\lambda)}, g^\theta\right]$ with non negligible advantage.

3.2 Information Dispersal Algorithm

Information Dispersal Algorithm (IDA) [11] is developed by Rabin in 1989 in order to split a file into n slices. These sliced can be stored in multitude storage nodes. IDA algorithm use essentially matrix-vector product. The user data $\mathbf{D}$ is broken into n slices with equal length. The (n, n) generator matrix Ω is multiplied by the n-element vector $\mathbf{D}$ to generate an n-element vector of slices. To reconstruct the original data the inverted matrix Ω^{-1} is used. This algorithm is suitable for Cloud Computing context on the ground that it aims to propose a high level of data security. For legal users, Cloud Provider can offer rapid reconstruction service by virtue of huge bandwidth and storage capability.

3.3 All-Or-Nothing Transform (AONT)

All-Or-Nothing Transform is proposed in 1997 by Rivest [12]. It is considered as $(n+1, n+1)$ threshold scheme. AONT encodes a data with n shares into n+1 shares to ensure integrity. The aim of this scheme is to ensure that a user can not decrypt the entire ciphertext only if succeeds to retrieve all message block. The complexity of AONT is in order of $O(n)$. Consequently, it's considered as the best and faster scheme in data secrecy.

3.4 Access Policy

An access control policy T in CPABE scheme is modeled as a non empty subsets of a collection. The descriptive attributes values are embedded in the leaf nodes and internal nodes are used to mark out relation. We distinguish AND, OR and threshold(n,m)) gates.

For a given access policy $T = [T_1, T_2, ..., T_n]$ and attribute set $\Lambda = [\lambda 1, \lambda 2, ..., \lambda_n]$, Λ satisfies T $(\Lambda \vDash T)$ if it return true for all λ_i in Λ and T_i in T. Otherwise, Λ does not match T $(\Lambda \nvDash T)$.

In our work, we will use monotonic access structure. We consider a collection T monotonic if for all T_1 and $T_2 : T_1 \in$ T and $T_2 \subset T_1$ then $T_2 \in$ T.

3.5 Review of the Boneh-Franklin's Encryption Scheme

An Ciphertext Policy Attribute Based Encryption (CPABE) algorithm [5] consists of Four fundamental algorithms:

1. Setup (k): This randomized algorithm generates Master Secret Key (MSK) and a Public Key(PK) from the implicit security parameter k.
2. Encrypt(PK, T, M): This algorithm takes as input Public Key (PK), access structure T and a message M to generate a ciphertext CT. Data Owner (DO) construct the access policy T by selecting a polynomial q_x for each node in T in top-down manner, set a degree for each polynomial such that it should be one less than threshold value. For the root node, it chooses a random $s \in Z_p$ and sets $q_R(0) = s$. For any other node x, it sets $q_{x(0)} = q_{parent(x)}((index(x))$. By this procedure, DO will assume that CT implicitly contains the set of attributes for authorized users.

3. KeyGen(MSK, Λ, υ): This algorithm take as inputs a Master Secret Key (MSK), subset of attribute Λ and a subset of user υ to generate for each user i a descriptive private key SK_{u_i}.
4. Decryption Decrypt(CT,SK_{u_i}): this algorithm takes as input the public key (PK), the ciphertext(CT) and the secret key (SK) and outputs the message M only if the attributes set in SK_{u_i} matches with the access structure T embedded in the ciphertext. Do this, a recursive algorithm Decryptnode(CT, SK, x) is executed in each node x in T starting by the root node to attempt the leaf node associated with the attribute value.

4   Proposed Revocable-Sliced CPABE (R-CPABE)

4.1   R-CPABE Model

The aim of R-CPABE scheme is to ensure a fine-grained access control model in Cloud Computing environment. It remedies the previously discussed limits.

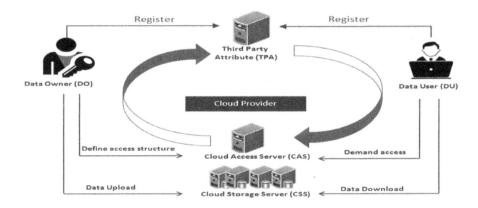

Fig. 1. R-CPABE model

The system model proposed in Fig. 1 includes four main entities:

− Data Owner (DO) is responsible of data publication and access structure definition. It enforces an access structure policy on the appropriate data and control as consequence all authorized/unauthorized access to it.
− Third Party Authority (TPA) presents an honest authority. It correctly performs the different requests and provides honest results. It's a fundamental party in setup and secret key generation.
− Cloud Provider (CP) is composed by the following interactive entities:
  • Cloud Access Server (CAS) is a dedicated server for access control. Its principal role is to guarantee a high level of security and to optimize the use of resources. To do this, it split the file into n shares and execute re-encryption on one random selected slice. It execute XOR operation and

compute hash of different slices in order to ensure data integrity. Finally, it sends to Cloud server the encrypted data, the re-encrypted slice and receive as a response the corresponding URL.

- Cloud Storage Server (CSS) represents the hardware device in which data will be stored.
- Data user (DU): entities that request to execute some operations in a specific file such as read or write. These privileges are predefined by the DO based on user's attributes. Each DU is registered in a specific directory and described with a set of attributes. He/she intend to access the encrypted data stored in the Cloud. DU can decrypt this file if and only if he/she their attributes match with the predefined attribute list in the access structure associated with the solicited file.

4.2 R-CPABE Construction

In our work, we will resolve the revocation problem by dividing the data into static and dynamic. In order to improve computational cost, we will perform revocation only in dynamic data. We add also that we will use symmetric encryption in large data size and asymmetric encryption in small key size. Table 2 reveals the way we have followed to resolve these problems.

Table 2. Resume of R-CPABE

Limits	Proposed solution
Revocation	Splitting encrypted data and re-encrypting one single slice
DO overhead and computational cost	Outsourcing heavy operation to Cloud server
Encryption cost	Hybrid encryption (symmetric and assymetric)

To do so, we develop six phases: Setup, Key generation, encryption, re-encryption, reconstruction and decryption. Revocation is simplicity involved on these six algorithm.

We consider G_0 a bilinear group of prime order p and g a generator of G_0. We denote with e: $G_0 * G_0 \longrightarrow G_1$ a bilinear map. Let k the size of the group used as a security parameter. Let $H : \{0,1\}^* \longrightarrow G_0$ a hash function which map any binary string attribute to a random group element. We will model H as a random oracle. Let Γ an access structure, $\upsilon = u_1, u_2...u_n$ be the universe of Cloud users and $\Lambda = \lambda_1, \lambda_2...\lambda_n$ the universe of attributes.

CP-ABE Basic Algorithms. In this section, we will detail CPABE setup and key generation algorithms. R-CPABE setup algorithm is executed by Third Party Attribute(TPA) to generate the public key and the secret master key as illustrated in Algorithm 1. A Cloud user (CU) construct the decryption secret key based on Algorithm 2. Each leaf node of user descriptive attribute present a partial key component.

Algorithm 1. Third Party Attribute Setup

Input   : Bilinear group G0, prime order p , generator g and two random exponents α
              ,$\beta \in Z_p$
Output: Public Key PK and Master Secret Key MSK
1: PK = $(g, g^{\beta}, g^{1/\beta}, \hat{e}(g,g)^{\alpha})$
2: MSK = (β, g^{α})

Algorithm 2. Secret key generation

Input   : MSK, set of attribute S, user u
Output: sk_u
1: Choose a random $r \in Z_p$
2: Select randomly r_j for each attribute $j \in S$
3: Compute and return $sk_u = (D = g^{(\alpha+r)/\beta}, \forall j \in S : D_j = g^r . H(j)^{r_j}, D\prime_j = g^{r_j}$

Splitting and Reconstruction. Before splitting the original data m, the server performs AONT scheme. After that, m will be split into n shares with (n, n) IDA algorithm. Algorithm 3 presents AONT and IDA implementation. The reconstruction of this data is easy from $s_1...s_n$ and the key k. Algorithm 4 illustrates different steps.

Algorithm 3. Data splitting

Input   : Original data m, the number of slice
Output: key k_1, the shares $s_1...s_n$
1: Execute (n,n) RABIN IDA Algorithm to split file m and generate t slices $m_1...m_t$
2: Compute m_{t+1}= hash($m_1...m_t$) to check the integrity of the reconstructed data
3: Choose a random temporary key for encryption algorithm
4: Compute the shares $c_1....c_{t+1}$ by letting $c_i = m_i \oplus E_k(c_i)$.
5: Compute $K_1 = k \oplus h_1 \oplus h_2 \oplus .... \oplus h_{t+1}$ where $h_i = hash(c_i)$
6: package $c_1, c_2...., c_t, ct + 1$ together as input to (n,n) IDA.
7: run (n,n) IDA and generate n shares $s_1, ...s_n$

Algorithm 4. Data reconstruction

Input   : key k_1, the shares $s_1...s_n$
Output: Original message $m_1...m_t$
1: Execute (n,n) RABIN IDA algorithm to reconstruct the package data m
2: Unpackage the IDA output to obtain t+1 worlds $c_1...c_t, c_{t+1}$.
3: Compute the key $K = K_1 \oplus h_1 \oplus h_2 \oplus .... \oplus h_{t+1}$
4: Compute $m_1...mt + 1$ where $m_i = c_i \oplus E_k(i)$
5: Compute $m\prime_{t+1}$= hash($m_1...m_t$)
6: Compare $m\prime_{t+1}$ and m_{t+1} to check the integrity of the reconstructed message

---

Publishing and Retrieving. After splitting the original data to n slices, encryption will be performed in the random slice and encryption key. Since the published data have already been encrypted, the URL will be generated in turn. It will be no longer sensitive to internet attacks. Consequently, it can be sent via unsafe channels. Any Cloud user can retrieve the encrypted data but only authorized users will success to decrypt it. Algorithms 5 and 6 illustrate respectively publication and retrieve process.

Algorithm 5. Data publishing

Input   : Original message $m_1.....m_t$, the number of slice n
Output: data URL
1: rum algorithm 1 to split the original message to n slices and obtain K_1
2: Choose a random slice s_i
3: Choose a random key k_2 and compute $E_{k_2}(s_i)$
4: Compute $E\prime_T(K_1 + K_2)$ where $E\prime$ is a CPABE algorithm and T is the access structure.
5: Publish and return the URL of $E\prime_T(K_1 + K_2)$, $E_{K_2}(s_i)$ and $s_1...s_n$ to cloud server

---

Algorithm 6. Data retrieving

Input   : private key sk, URL
Output: Original data $m_1...m_t$
1: Obtain $E\prime_T(K_1 + K_2)$, $E_{k_2}(s_i)$ and $s_1...s_n$ by URL
2: **if** S does not satisfy T **then**
3:     failure and abort
4: **end if**
5: Decrypt $E\prime_T(K_1 + K_2)$ to obtain K_1 and K_2
6: Decrypt $E_{K_2}(s_i)$ to obtain s_i
7: input $K_1, s_1...s_n$ to execute algorithm 4

Revocation. In order to perform revocation, we will update the encryption key. First of all, DO will retrieve $E\prime_T(K_1 + K_2)$, $E_{k_2}(s_i)$. Second, he will choose randomly a new key and perform re-encryption based on the new access and the new key.

Algorithm 7. Revocation

Input   : New access structure $T\prime$, URL
1: Retrieve by URL $E\prime_T(K_1 + K_2)$, $E_{k_2}(s_i)$
2: Decrypt $E\prime_T(K_1 + K_2)$ to extract $K_1 and K_2$
3: Decrypt $E_{k_2}(s_i)$ to obtain s_i
4: Select a random key $K\prime_2$
5: Set $K_2 = K\prime_2$
6: Compute $E\prime_{T\prime}(K_1 + K_2)$ and $E_{k_2}(s_i)$
7: Outsource $E\prime_{T\prime}(K_1 + K_2)$ and $E_{k_2}(s_i)$ to Cloud server to replace old values of $E\prime_T(K_1 + K_2)$ and $E_{k_2}(s_i)$

---

5   Security Evaluation

To highlight the strength of R-CPABE, we present a discussion based on security attacks and issues. This evaluation confirms that our solution is robust and ensures most of the required security direction in a Cloud Computing environment.

– Data confidentiality and privacy: In 2011, Green et al. proved that the Attribute Based Encryption model is secure against Replayable Chosen Ciphertext Attacks (RCCA-secure) and choosen-plaintext attacks (CPA) [2]. We assume the basic algorithm of CPABE. For these reason, we admit that our proposed scheme is Indistinguishability against selective ciphertext-policy and chosen-plaintext attacks secure (IND-sCP-CPA-secure) like all CPABE based access control solution. We assume also that the symmetric encryption key based on AES is secure.
– Eavesdropping and matching attacks: To decrypt a message, an attacker need to compute $e(g, g)^{\alpha s}$ but it is blinded by $e(g, g)^r s$ where r is a randomized blinding value. For this reason, our solution resist also eavesdropping and matching attacks.
– Network security: the combination of symmetric and asymmetric encryption methods enforces protection against network attacks. The aim of the use of an hybrid cryptosystem is to ensure data integrity and secure exchange between different participants. It ensures also data authentication and non repudiation. Only the appropriate receiver can decrypt the content of data.
– Collusion resistance: In our model, we propose to encrypt the symmetric key with CP-ABE encryption algorithm. Given that authors in [13] have proved that CP-ABE model resist collusion attacks. For this reason, our model is collusion resistance. In other words, it is hard to find two inputs that hash to the same output.
– Forward security: is the process of blocking access in future published data to revoked users. In CPABE scheme, DO should re-encrypt all the affected data in order to realize this directive. For these reason, most of works ignore this constraint because it requires a huge DO overhead. In our R-CPABE, we delegate this heavy operation to Cloud server. We assume that a user can not decrypt all data only if success to decrypt one slice based to session key. The decryption request will be rejected as the user claimed is not in the authorized list of CAS server.
– Integrity: The use of Secure Hash Algorithm (SHA) in encryption and splitting process ensures the provenance of a file and its integrity.

6   Performance Evaluation

In this section, we provide a theoretical analysis of required computing times for different algorithms. We expose also an evaluation of some performance metrics resulting from the simulation.

6.1 Theoretical Analysis

In this section, we will expose required computational time of different algorithm. Let $T_{split}, T_{reconstruct}, T_{publish}, T_{retreive}$ and T_{revoke} are respectively the time required to split, reconstruct, publish, retrieve ans revoke data. Table 3 shows the description of different symbol used in performance evaluation.

$$T_{split} = \frac{N_w}{E_{hash}} + \frac{(N+1)w}{E_{aes}} + \frac{2(N+1)w}{E_{xor}} + \frac{(N+1)w}{E_{hash}} + \frac{(N+1)w}{E_{ida}}$$

$$T_{reconstruct} = \frac{(N+1)}{D_{ida}} + \frac{(N+1)w}{E_{hash}} + \frac{N_w}{E_{hash}} + \frac{(N+1)w}{E_{aes}} + \frac{2(N+1)w}{E_{xor}}$$

$$T_{publish} = T_{split} + \frac{(N+1)w}{nE_{aes}} + \frac{2w_k}{E_{cpabe}} + \frac{(N+1)w+2w_k}{B}$$

$$T_{retreive} = T_{reconstruct} + \frac{(N+1)w}{nD_{aes}} + \frac{2w_k}{D_{cpabe}} + \frac{(N+1)w+2w_k}{B}$$

$$T_{revoke} = \frac{(N+1)w/n+2w_k}{B} + \frac{2w_k}{D_{cpabe}} + \frac{(N+1)w}{nD_{aes}} + \frac{2w_k}{E_{cpabe}} + \frac{1}{n}\left[\frac{(n+1)w}{nE_{aes}} + \frac{(N+1)w/n+2w_k}{B}\right] + \frac{n-1}{n}\left[\frac{(n+1)w}{nB} + \frac{(n+1)w}{nE_{aes}} + \frac{2(n+1)w/n+2w_k}{B}\right]$$

Table 3. Symbols used in simulation

Symbol	Description
n	Number of slices
w	Number of worlds
N	Size of original data
E_x	Encryption and encoding rate with x can be hash, ida, aes, cpabe and xor
D_x	Decryption rate with x can be cpabe, ida, aes
B	Bandwidth

6.2 Simulation Results

We simulate R-CPABE based on CP-ABE toolkit and Java Pairing-Based Cryptography library [14]. To do so, we implement our proposal with java programming language. The experiments are performed using a machine with an Intel Core i7 processor 8th generation and 16 GB total memory. We also simulate at the same conditions basic CP-ABE and solutions proposed in [8] and [9]. In this section, we compare storage overhead, computation and energy with two different solutions for dual revocation.

We consider G_0 a bilinear group. We denote with e: $G_0 * G_0 \longrightarrow G_1$ a bilinear map. We assume that pairing and multiplications are executed in the group G_0 and exponentiation in the group G_1. Let $H : \{0,1\}^* \longrightarrow G_0$ a hash function(H). We model H as a SHA-512. All the simulation results are the mean of 100 trials.

Table 4. R-CPABE computational time

Number of attributes	Encryption (s)	Decryption (s)	Revocation time (s)		Total (s)
			E_{s_i}	D_{s_i}	
3	0.18	0.030	0.02	0.01	0.240
5	0.20	0.037	0.02	0.01	0.267
7	0.24	0.048	0.02	0.01	0.318
10	0.26	0.057	0.02	0.01	0.347

Note: In all simulation results, we treat only the case of revoked user. Normal scenario give the best results in encryption and decryption process.

Storage Overhead. We apply 256-AES symmetric encryption in data and CP-ABE asymmetric encryption in key. We assume that applying CPABE in key encryption dramatically improves storage space. We notice that splitting algorithm requires a little more space to store the dynamic data. Since we use a typical access tree with hundred of lead nodes, keys lengths encryption can achieve some KB. We admit that a Cloud file is in the order of a MB or GB. When compared to data and key size, a re-encrypted slice storage overhead can be ignored.

Computation Time. In our simulation, Computation time is considered as encryption, decryption and revocation time. Encryption time is non other than the encryption time required to encrypt both dynamic data, static data and keys. Decryption is the opposite process. Revocation contains the required time to retrieve the keys and dynamic data, update encryption key and re-encrypt. Based on Table 4, we deduce that both encryption and decryption algorithms are linear to the number of attributes. The more number of attributes increases, the more number of access structure leaf nodes are involved and the more the computation time is high. Revocation process is not influenced by the number of attributes which represents a strength for our scheme. it depends only on the key length and the bandwidth.

The simulation scenario in Fig. 2 include encryption and decryption time based on different number of attributes. We define discussions bellow:

- Encryption: We deduce that the performances in R-CPABE are better than basic-CPABE, [8] and [9]. This come down to the fact that our solution applies symmetric encryption in large data size and asymmetric encryption in constant key size. This process saves about $[0.01s; 0.04s]$ compared to related works.
- Decryption: R-CPABE do not show the best decryption time. This is expalined by the fact that a user need to perform a match then decrypt phase before decrypting the original date. It's required in order to verify that the

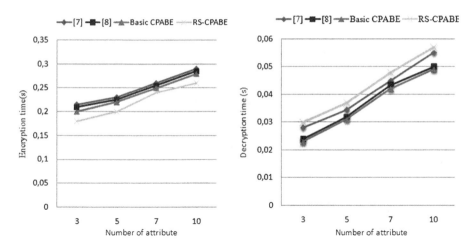

Fig. 2. Computational time

Table 5. Comparison of R-CPABE and related schemes computational time

Operation	[7]	[8]	Basic CPABE	R-CPABE
Encryption (s)	0.24	0.25	0.23	0.22
Decryption (s)	0.040	0.037	0.036	0.042
Revocation (s)	0.05	0.07	--	0.03
Total (s)	0.33	0.035	0.26	0.29

user is not revoked. It have 0.002 ms more than [8], 0.005 ms more than [9] and 0.006 ms more than basic scheme. This variation is of the order of 10^{-6} s. This seems very acceptable since we have remarkably improved the security of the overall system.

The aim of our scheme is to improve revocation process without degrading performances. Table 5 compares R-CPABE to related works. We compute the average values for all schemes in order to elaborate a comparison. We deduce that R-CPABE presents best computational time in encryption and revocation. Despite that it increases decryption time, it offers best total time.

Energy Consumption. Figure 3 shows consumed energie in [8,9] and R-CPABE in encryption, decryption and revocation algorithms. We deduce that energies reflects computational time. R-CPABE presents the least energy in encryption and revocation and the highest energy in decryption compared to [8] and [9]. However, these values are not very satisfactory since users still trying to use their mobile devices that have a significant energy constraint. When it comes to mobile computing, this level of energy is important in decryption process.

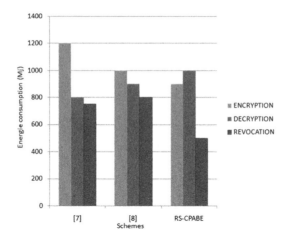

Fig. 3. Energy

Table 6. Energy cost

Solution	Cryptographic operations	Energy	Total
R-CPABE	DO: publication and Encryption of original data slices and keys	300 Mj	1150 MJ
	Data user: Decryption of static, dynamic data and encryption keys	200 MJ	
	Attribute authority: Setup + KeyGen	250 MJ	
	Cloud access server: Splitting, reconstruction, retrieve and revoke algorithms	400 Mj	
R-CPABE for non revoked user	Encryption+ decryption+ keygen+ setup	$- - -$	900 Mj
Basic CPABE	Encryption+ decrytpion+ keygen+ setup	$- - -$	1000 Mj

Table 6 illustrates that revocation add only 150 Mj to be performed. We can assume that this level shared between user side and Cloud provider side is acceptable since security is highly improved. We notice that without revocation, our model offers best energy compared with basic CPABE scheme.

7   Conclusion and Perspectives

Access control in the Cloud Computing presents one of the most important research field. In this paper, we exposed a revocable sliced Ciphertext-Policy Attribute Based Encryption. We used splitting algorithm and re-encryption in revocation process. We delegated heavy computational operations to Cloud servers in order to improve performance. When it comes to security analysis, our scheme is robust to various attacks. It is secure under BDH assumption. The simulation results illustrate that our scheme improves total execution time. We are strongly confident that R-CPABE offers fine grained access control and can applied in Cloud Computing context. Yet, our scheme have some limitations. It consume an important level of energy. When applied to mobile Cloud, this inconvenient can represent a brake in R-CPABE implementation. We add also that it suffer from key escrow. In future work, we will propose a multi-authorities solution resolving this issue.

References

1. Bouchaala, M., Ghazel, C., Saidane, L.A.: End to end cloud computing architecture based on a novel classification of security issues. In: IEEE on International Conference on Computer Systems and Applications (AICCSA), March 2018
2. Matthew, G., Susan, H., Brent, W.: Outsourcing the decryption of ABE ciphertexts. In: Proceeding SEC 11 Proceedings of the 20th USENIX Conference on Security, pp. 34–34, August 2011
3. John, B., Amit, S., Brent, W.: Ciphertext-policy attribute-based encryption. In: Proceedings of the 2007 IEEE on Symposium on Security and Privacy, SP 2007, pp. 321–334, May 2007
4. Bouchaala, M., Ghazel, C., Saidane, L.A.: Revocable sliced ciphertext policy attribute based encryption scheme in cloud computing. In: 15th International Wireless Communications Mobile Computing Conference (IWCMC), June 2019
5. Zhiguo, W., June, L., Robert, H.D.: HASBE: a hierarchical attribute-based solution for flexible and scalable access control in cloud computing. IEEE Trans. Inf. Forensics Secur. $7(2)$, 743–754 (2012)
6. Lewko, A., Waters, B.: Decentralizing attribute-based encryption. In: Paterson, K.G. (ed.) EUROCRYPT 2011. LNCS, vol. 6632, pp. 568–588. Springer, Heidelberg (2011). https://doi.org/10.1007/978-3-642-20465-4_31
7. Matthew, P., Patrick, T., Patrick, M., Brent, W.: Secure attribute-based systems. J. Comput. Secur. 18, 799–837 (2010)
8. Kawai, Y.: Outsourcing the re-encryption key generation: flexible ciphertext-policy attribute-based proxy re-encryption. In: Lopez, J., Wu, Y. (eds.) ISPEC 2015. LNCS, vol. 9065, pp. 301–315. Springer, Cham (2015). https://doi.org/10.1007/978-3-319-17533-1_21
9. Kan, Y., Xiaohua, J.: Expressive, efficient, and revocable data access control for multi-authority cloud storage. IEEE Trans. Parallel Distrib. Syst. $25(7)$, 1735–1744 (2014)
10. Zhou, Z., Huang, D., Wang, Z.: Efficient privacy-preserving ciphertext-policy attribute based-encryption and broadcast encryption. IEEE Trans. Comput. $64(1)$, 126–138 (2015)
11. Rabin, M.O.: Efficient dispersal of information for security, load balancing, and fault tolerance. J. ACM $36(2)$, 335–348 (1989)
12. Canda, V., Van Trung, T.: A new mode of using all-or-nothing transforms. In: Proceedings IEEE International Symposium on Information Theory, July 2002
13. Su, J.-S., Cao, D., Wang, X.-F.: Attribute-based encryption schemes. J. Softw. 22, 1299–1315 (2011)
14. Angelo, D.C., Vincenzo, I.: jPBC: Java pairing based cryptography. In: IEEE Symposium on Computers and Communications (ISCC), June 2011

Information Security Policy

A Framework for GDPR Compliance
in Big Data Systems

Mouna Rhahla[1,2](✉), Sahar Allegue[1,2](✉), and Takoua Abdellatif[1](✉)

[1] Polytechnic School of Tunisia, SERCOM, University of Carthage, Tunis, Tunisia
Takoua.Abdellatif@ept.rnu.tn
[2] Proxym-Lab, Proxym-IT, Sousse, Tunisia
{Mouna.rhahla,Sahar.allegue}@proxym-it.com
http://www.proxym-group.com

Abstract. The verification and implementation of the GDPR regulation that aims at protecting European citizens' privacy, is still a real challenge. In particular, in Big Data systems where data is of huge volume and heterogeneous, it is hard to track data evolution through its complex life cycle ranging from collection, ingestion, storage and analytics. In this context, from 2016 to 2019 research has been conducted and security tools designed. However, they are either specific to special applications or address only partially the regulation articles. In order to identify the covered parts, the missed ones and the necessary metrics for comparing different works, we propose a framework for GDPR compliance that identifies the main components for the regulation implementation. Based on this framework, we compare the main GDPR solutions in Big Data domain and we propose a guideline for GDPR verification and implementation in Big Data systems.

Keywords: The general data protection regulation · Big data analytics · Security · Privacy

1   Introduction

GDPR [1] sets new standards on security through 99 articles and 173 recitals and aims to protect the rights and freedoms of natural persons. Every organization that deals with data has to comply with GDPR, to protect these rights and to be accountable while improving business models [2]. Accountability aims at demonstrating how controllers comply with data protection principles. Each organization must answer the following questions: what information is processed? why? how and where is data stored? who can access it and why? is it up-to-date and accurate? how long will you keep it for? how will it be safeguarded and how do you reach accountability?

This project is carried out under the MOBIDOC scheme, funded by the EU through the EMORI program and managed by the ANPR.

S. Kallel et al. (Eds.): CRiSIS 2019, LNCS 12026, pp. 211–226, 2020.
https://doi.org/10.1007/978-3-030-41568-6_14

Answering all these questions guides system designers and developers to verify and implement GDPR compliance. It involves several tasks, namely the reading of the regulation articles, the knowledge extraction and the characterization of the regulation concepts following the system specification. Mapping the regulation articles and concepts to software can be a tedious and confusing task. Consequently, a model is needed to describe the concepts captured from different GDPR documentations, to extract GDPR principles, actors and dependencies. The model should identify the main building blocks to be implemented for GDPR compliance verification and implementation. To reach this goal, our work promotes an improved understanding of the legal, organizational and technical concepts present in GDPR documentation and classifying, the different related works in a clear manner.

In the last few years, topics about GDPR have been widely discussed across a range of academic publications and industry papers from different theoretical and practical perspectives, including numerous implementations and design concepts for GDPR compliance [35]. These works are still in their infancy and mature and formal tools that implement GDPR articles are still missing especially in the area of big data analytics. The term big data analytics alludes to the entire data management life cycle from ingestion and storage to analysis of high volumes of data with heterogeneous format from different sources. As presented in Fig. 1, the reference architecture of big data systems covers 4 main layers: data sources, ingestion, processing, storage and services. At service and processing layers, sophisticated algorithms are being developed to analyze such large amount of data to gain valuable insights for accurate decision-making, detecting unprecedented opportunities such as finding meaningful patterns, presuming situations, predicting and inferring behaviors. Due to the large data volume and the complexity of processing, tracking data dependencies and privacy verification are challenging. For this purpose, data security and governance layer is a cross-layer generally used for data security and management. It represents a key part of the system in implementing GDPR principles. However, accurate metrics are needed to evaluate the GDPR coverage of this management layer.

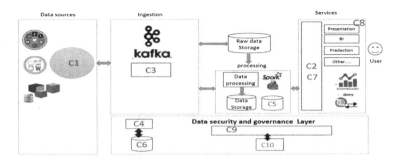

Fig. 1. A classical Big Data system following a reference architecture

Recent academic and industrial tools [14] implement privacy by design translating automatically the privacy policies to software and providing accountability. However, these works address only partially GDPR principals such as purpose limitation, data minimisation, storage limitation, transparency or security [11,12]. Other works concentrate on particular articles of the regulation and do not cover all of them [10] like the right to data portability, the right to be forgotten, the access right or the right to be informed [21,22]. Also, these works generally address one particular type of data source (logs, IoT sensors or classical SQL data bases). It is not clear how to apply proposed solutions that consider uniform data, to big data architectures with multi-channel data sources, different purposes and intensive processing. Consequently, we still lack guidelines to verify GDPR compliance and to implement the regulation in a Big Data context. As a starting point, in order to address this issue, a comprehensive overview of the regulation and a common understanding of its key concepts are necessary. Later, the study of recent works on privacy and GDPR allows the identification of the main building blocks for GDPR compliance verification. Thanks to both theoretical and the implementation analysis of the regulation, we propose a framework with well-defined components to implement the regulation. According to these components, we situate the different works carried out on GDPR in the domain of Big Data. Furthermore, we provide an overview of how to use the framework to assist Big Data engineers and system administrators to build GDPR-compliant systems and applications. As a use case, we consider the example of Big Data client segmentation application and we propose an implementation of the framework components to have the application GDPR-compliant. This paper's contributions can be summarized into the following points:

- A framework for GDPR compliance in Big Data systems.
- A classification of the state of the art conducted on GDPR solutions implemented between 2016 and 2019 in both academic and industrial areas.
- A guideline for GDPR-compliance in Big Data applications based on the framework components.

This paper is structured as follows. Section 2 is an overview of GDPR principles and its main actors. In Sect. 3, we describe a framework for GDPR in Big data systems. In Sect. 4, we present the framework used to classify GDPR-related works in Big Data. Section 5 describes the framework usage to implement GDPR compliance in a Big Data application. Finally, Sect. 6 gives a summary of the main findings of this paper and highlights new opportunities for future work.

2 Analysis of GDPR Principles and Actors

The GDPR regulation aims at delivering a harmonized, consistent and high-level data protection across Europe. It has 99 articles grouped into 11 chapters. In those chapters, it addresses a set of principles, actors and obligations.

2.1 GDPR Principles

GDPR regulation sets out seven key principles for the processing of personal data stipulated in Article 5 [13]. They can be summarized into the following points:

- **Lawfulness, fairness and transparency:** "Personal data shall be processed lawfully, fairly and in a transparent manner in relation to the data subject." Art.5(1)(a). More detailed provisions on lawfulness are set out in Articles 6 to 10 and detailed transparency obligations set out in Articles 13 and 14. Lawfulness, fairness and transparency may overlap, but all three must be satisfied in a system. In fact, it is not enough to show your processing is lawful if it is basically unfair to or hidden from the data subject concerned.
- **Purpose limitation:** "Personal data shall be collected for specified, explicit and legitimate purposes and not further processed in a manner that is incompatible with those purposes." Art.5(1)(b). This principle aims to make sure that you are clear and open about your reasons for collecting personal data and that what you do with the data is in line with the reasonable expectations of the data subject concerned. Specifying your purposes from the beginning helps you to be responsible and accountable for your processing.
- **Data minimisation:** "Personal data shall be adequate, relevant and limited to what is necessary in relation to the purposes for which they are processed." Art.5(1)(c). The minimum amount of personal data is revealed to satisfy the application purpose. The accountability principle means that you need to be able to prove that you have appropriate processes to make sure that you only collect and hold the personal data you need.
- **Accuracy:** "Personal data shall be accurate and, where necessary, kept up to date; every reasonable step must be taken to ensure that personal data that are inaccurate, having regard to the purposes for which they are processed, are erased or rectified without delay." (Art 5(1)(d)). Here we find clear links to the right to rectification, which gives data subjects the right to have incorrect personal data corrected.
- **Storage limitation:** "kept in a form which permits identification of data subjects for no longer than is necessary for the purposes for which the personal data are processed; personal data may be stored for longer periods insofar as the personal data will be processed solely for archiving purposes in the public interest, scientific or historical research purposes or statistical purposes in accordance with Article 89(1) subject to implementation of the appropriate technical and organizational measures required by this Regulation in order to safeguard the rights and freedoms of the data subject." Art.5(1)(e). So, even if you collect and use personal data fairly and lawfully, you cannot keep it for longer than you actually need it. GDPR does not set specific time limits for different types of data. This is up to you, and it will depend on how long you need the data for your specified purposes. Once information is no longer needed, personal data must be securely deleted.
- **Integrity and confidentiality:** "processed in a manner that ensures appropriate security of the personal data, including protection against unauthorized

or unlawful processing and against accidental loss, destruction or damage, using appropriate technical or organizational measures." Art.5(1)(f).

– **Accountability:** "The controller shall be responsible for, and be able to demonstrate compliance with Art 5(1)." Art.5(2). The accountability principle requires you to take responsibility for what you do with personal data and how you comply with the other principles. You must have appropriate measures and records in place to be able to prove your compliance.

2.2 GDPR Actors and Their Dependencies

There are five main actors in the regulation [13]:

– **Data Subject:** "an identified or identifiable natural person, directly or indirectly, by means reasonably likely to be used by the controller or by any other natural or legal person".

– **Controller:** "a natural or legal person, public authority, agency or any other body which alone or jointly with others determines the purposes, conditions and means of the processing of personal data". It ensures compliance with GDPR principles related to the processing of the personal data (Accountability), implements data protection policies and data security measures, carries out data protection impact assessment (DPIA) for high risk processing, informs data subjects on their rights, in case of personal data breach, notifies the supervisory authority within 72 h and transfers personal data to third country or international organization, per specific safeguarding provisions.

– **Processor:** (a person or a legal entity) processes personal data on behalf of the Data Controller, specifically: collects personal data online through registration, contact forms, email or digital payments and invoicing, stores, uses, records, organizes, retrieves, discloses, deletes the collected personal data on behalf of and under the instructions of the Data Controller and creates inventories for all above mentioned data processing categories.

– **Data Protection Officer (DPO):** (a person or a legal entity) manages and supervises all data protection activities, specifically: monitors compliance to GDPR's personal data protection and security provisions and cooperates with the supervisory authority.

– **Supervisory Authority (SA):** Article 46 states that supervisory authorities are responsible for monitoring the application of this Regulation and for contributing to its consistent application. The independent public authority is responsible for monitoring regulated entity compliance with GDPR.

Figure 2 shows the main actors and their relations following the regulation articles. For example in Fig. 2, the data subject can declare his consent to the controller (Art.4). He can also request data from the controller (Art.12). On the other hand, the controller provides information to data subjects (Art.12) and communicates data breaches to them Art.34).

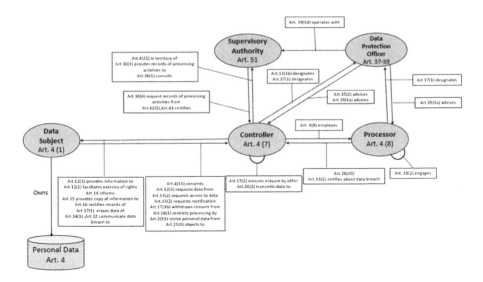

Fig. 2. GDPR main actors and their relations following GDPR articles

3   A GDPR Framework for Big Data Systems

In order to satisfy GDPR principles, data has to be tracked during all its life cycle and the processing stages. Furthermore, a governance layer is required for the controller.

For a GDPR framework definition, two complementary approaches are followed:

- A top-down approach. We start from GDPR documentation to define a model serving as a language for describing GDPR obligations and requirements in terms of principles, actors and actions. This is what we have presented in previous sections.
- A bottom-up approach. It is used for complementing the previous model by providing a more fine-grained set of components, based on the analysis of relevant related works that will be presented in the next sections.

Figure 3 represents the overall architecture of our proposed framework. For each GDPR actor, we define its main components.

We have set up 10 components (from C1 to C10). Each Ci respects a set of properties as follows:

- **C1:** Data Subject (DS) that represents the data sources. A DS puts restrictions on the use of its collected and exploited data. In the context of Big Data, three Vs are defined as component properties: Volume, Velocity and Variety.
- **C2:** DS API. It provides a tracking dashboard and notifications management interface to the DS. A view of the security control and sensitive data is provided. Furthermore, this API translates the consent and restrictions of the

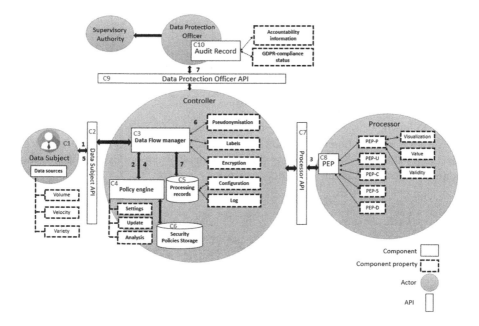

Fig. 3. The GDPR framework architecture

DS from human language to machine language. These restrictions can provide purpose limitation, storage limitation, data minimisation and access control.

- **C3:** Data Flow manager. It allows the DS to define or modify his security policies and his data. It is also used to receive and send data and/or notifications to different components. The Data Flow manager component provides a set of properties: pseudonymisation for data minimisation, labels for data tagging and tracking, and encryption for integrity and confidentiality. Two types of data can be returned to the processor: either pseudonymous data or encrypted data for the processing which have to keep the DS identity secret.
- **C4:** Policy engine. It receives queries from users and as a result, a decision is returned to give the user access to collect data or not. It provides three properties: policy settings, update and analysis.
- **C5:** Processing records. It is a component where all operations applied to data are stored to satisfy transparency principal. Two types of records are stored: logs and configurations.
- **C6:** Security Policies Storage. This component interacts with C4. Indeed, policies defined or updated by C4 are stored in C6.
- **C7:** Processor API. It allows the controller to interact with the processor and more specifically the PEPs (Policy Enforcement Points).
- **C8:** Policy Enforcement Point. It is the point where the processor executes a specific purpose. PEP tasks or properties are: Processing (P), Collection (C), Usage (U), Storage (S) or Distribution (D). Every PEP must take into

account Big Data Vs constraints such as: Visualization, Value and Validity for PEP-P (PEP-Processing).

- **C9:** Data Protection Officer API. It helps the controller interact with the Data Protection Officer to demonstrate compliance and accountability.
- **C10:** Audit Record. It records information and data to provide accountability and to track GDPR-compliance status.

In the following table, we present the matching of GDPR principles against the framework components. It shows that the framework covers all principles. Also, this table can guide systems designers and developers in identifying the components to implement for a given purpose.

GDPR principles	The framework components
Lawfulness, fairness and transparency	C2, C3, C5 and C9
Purpose limitation	C3, C4 and C6
Data minimisation	C3, C4 and C6
Accuracy	C4 and C6
Storage limitation	C4 and C6
Integrity and confidentiality	C3, C4 and C6
Accountability	C10

4 GDPR-Oriented Solutions in Big Data Systems

As the GDPR regulation was initiated in 2016 and came into effect on the 25th of May 2018 as a new privacy regulation for the European Union (EU), related work on GDPR compliance is limited. The proposed works have been investigated from either the perspective of jurisdiction or information system implementation. In our study we collected 6 major refereed academic databases (Education Resources Information Center (ERIC), JSTOR, Google Scholar, ACM publication, IEEEXplorer, Wiley Online Library and SpringerLink) in the field of Computer science indexed by Journal Citation Reports using the search terms "EU GDPR" and "EU General Data Protection Regulation". This resulted in 170 papers to be included in our study. After an analysis of the papers title and abstract, the number was reduced to 62 papers.

We applied a set of selection criteria as follows:

1. Papers on GDPR for organization or focusing on personal data protection.
2. Papers providing experimental or empirical studies from actual observations and case studies with private data.
3. Papers presenting a new design for GDPR compliance.

The selections resulted in 62 peer-reviewed publications that fit the criteria above. A high number is reached in 2018 and the number of works still increasing in 2019.

These related works are divided into 4 main categories: (1) Jurisdictional analysis of GDPR, (2) Academic solutions, (3) Industrial tools and (4) Apache Big data technologies and tools. The next sections summarize these four categories.

4.1   Jurisdictional Analysis of GDPR

Several authors and organizations have analyzed GDPR and privacy by design [35]. However, they only provided documentation and support for the law without providing any framework or guidelines to apply this law in company's projects or products [13,25–27]. Other research papers focus on specific sectors such as healthcare [3,4] or specific purposes like storage compliance with GDPR [5]. Although interesting for better understanding of GDPR, they do not come up with tools or implementations of GDPR articles. They rather analyze and discuss the impact of GDPR on the considered specific fields and sectors [6,9,41] or discuss the feasibility of the privacy by design principle [42].

4.2   Academic GDPR Solutions

In the past three years, many authors have worked to provide privacy tools for GDPR. These tools partially cover partially GDPR principles. In [21] a privacy tool is developed for DNS applications. Indeed, some DNS data may reveal personal data (resolver IP addresses and domain names looked up by users). A thorough and transparent approach to privacy protection in this field is considered vital to the Dutch economy and society. This work targets DNS data and only the GDPR transparency principle is treated.

Authors in [10] propose privacyTracker, a GDPR-compliant tool that covers data tractability and transparency. They implement some GDPR rights such as data portability and right to erasure. For GDPR accountability in IoT systems, an IoT Databox model is proposed providing the mechanisms to build trust relations IoT [22]. In a previous work [23], we proposed a GDPR Controller for IoT systems where security, transparency and purpose limitation are implemented. In A4Cloud project [14], a tool-set is composed of eleven tools implementing transparency, privacy, trust and technology for tracking and controlling data [12,31,32] as well as for policy management [33].

In [24] authors present TagUBig - Taming Your Big Data, a tool to control and improve transparency, privacy, availability and usability when users interact with applications. For IoT system, ADvoCATE [11] allows data subjects to easily control consents regarding access to their personal data. The proposed solution is based on Blockchain technology. Juan Camilo proposed another Blockchain-based solution to implement consent in GDPR [8]. This work provides the data subjects a tool to assert their rights and get control over their consents and personal data. In [43], authors discussed how static program analysis can be applied to detect privacy violation in programs. The solution is based on classical information flow control techniques, tainting and backward slicing. Although important, the solution addresses a limited part of data control requirements in GDPR.

4.3 Industrial GDPR Tools

In addition to academic papers, many industrial security tools have been proposed. We identify some of them in this section:

- **The Absolute Platform:** This tool provides visibility and control. It addresses GDPR prerequisites by observing and verifying PII (Personally identifiable information), avoiding data breaches and automating remediation [15].
- **Alien Vault USM:** This tool helps to detect data breaches and monitor data security. The unified platform centralizes essential capabilities like asset discovery, vulnerability scanning, intrusion detection, behavioral monitoring, log management and threat intelligence updates [16].
- **BigId:** This tool assures data minimisation through duplication discovery and correlation. It satisfies customer data portability, supports and enables right-to-be-forgotten. In addition, it reveals enforcement of customer consent for personal data collection, data residency flows and risk profiling with breach notification windows [17].
- **BWise GDPR Compliance solution:** this tool helps to build data views, data control and compliance [18].
- **Consentua:** It is a consent choice and control tool that enables users to choose and control over their personal data. It empowers an increasingly trusted and straightforward relationship between the client and the service provider [19].
- **PrivacyPerfect:** This work is composed of a set of tools such as assessment, processing and dashboard tools specially designed for chief privacy officers, reports, legal processing grounds and graphical overviews [20].

4.4 Apache Solutions

Apache has developed a set of tools to provide security to Big data systems architectures. These technologies can be used to address parts of GDPR requirements. Here are some popular solutions:

- **Apache Eagle:** Apache Eagle is an open-source solution for identifying security and performance issues instantly on big data platforms like Apache Hadoop and Apache Spark. It analyzes data activities and daemon logs. It provides state of the art alert engine to identify a security breach, performance issues and shows insights [28].
- **Apache Atlas:** Apache Atlas is an open-source solution used for data tagging. It provides open metadata management and governance capacities for

organizations to make a catalog of their data assets, classify and govern these assets and provide collaboration capabilities around these data assets for data scientists, analysts and the data governance team [29].

- **Apache Ranger:** Apache Ranger is an open solution that helps developers to enable, monitor and manage the entire data security across the Hadoop platform. The vision with Ranger is to provide a framework for central administration of security policies and user access monitoring [30].
- **Apache Knox:** Knox Gateway provides a single access point for all REST and HTTP connections with Apache Hadoop clusters. Knox API Gateway is structured as a turn around intermediary with thought for pluggability in the areas of policy enforcement, through providers and the back-end services for which it proxies requests [34].

4.5   A Comparative Study

The comparison of the studied works and tools is tedious work since they come from different communities and target different objectives and variant application contexts. Nevertheless, it is important to situate these works to measure their compliance with GDPR and also for reuse purpose. Indeed, instead of reinventing the wheel, some ideas and implementations can be reused for designed big data systems, even though the work context can be different. Consequently, a global picture of these solutions and their implemented parts of the regulation can be very helpful to big data system designers. Using the defined framework, we can set up the comparative table below. We adopt the following notations:

- ✓: indicates that the component is implemented by the referenced work.
- ∼: indicates that the component is partially addressed by the referenced work and some of its properties are not implemented.
- ×: indicates that the component is not implemented by the referenced work.

In Table 1, the framework components defined in Fig. 3 are partially implemented in each solution. There are no works that implement all components. More precisely, we can clearly see that the components that are most covered are C2, C4 and C6. They mainly focus on security policy definition and management. This can be explained by the fact that involving people in the definition of their security constraints and the tracking of their data is the focus of many research works even before GDPR was voted. Indeed, providing practical and intuitive API for users, not necessarily experts in security, was considered, for many years, a priority in privacy-sensitive systems like e-health and other IoT systems. On the other hand, C3 addressing data tagging is less implemented compared to other components. Indeed, with data heterogeneity and the multi-sources of Big data, data tagging becomes necessary for tracking and controlling data flows. This technique is less required in small systems with uniform data format and source. Also, C9 and C10 are two components not really dealt with except in recent few efforts. A new need comes in with GDPR consists in interfacing with the data protection officer and the supervisory authority. More generally, a GDPR audit tool is required bridging the gap between regulation texts and implementations. The challenge consists in creating robust tools that analyse software systems and check automatically that they respect the regulation text. In the opposite direction, translating regulation constraints expressed in human languages to a code respecting regulation constraints is also an interesting axis of research that needs to be developed.

Table 1. Comparative table

Related works by Category		Our framework Components									
		C1	C2	C3	C4	C5	C6	C7	C8	C9	C10
Jurisdictional analysis of GDPR	GDPR for healthcare [3]	×	×	×	×	×	×	×	×	×	×
	GDPR in Health Clinics [4]	×	×	×	×	×	×	×	×	×	×
	Storage system for GDPR [5]	×	×	✓	~	✓	~	×	×	×	×
	GDPR investigation [6]	×	×	~	~	×	~	×	×	×	×
Academic GDPR solutions	Tool for DNS big data [21]	~	×	×	~	~	×	×	✓	×	×
	PrivacyTracker [10]	~	✓	×	~	✓	✓	~	×	×	×
	IoT Databox [22]	~	✓	~	×	×	~	✓	~	×	×
	GDPR Controller [23]	~	✓	~	✓	×	✓	×	~	×	×
	TagUBig [24]	~	~	×	✓	~	✓	×	~	×	×
	ADvoCATE [11]	~	~	~	✓	×	✓	×	~	×	×
	Consent management [8]	~	×	~	✓	✓	✓	×	~	×	~
	The A4Cloud project [14]	~	✓	~	✓	~	✓	~	~	×	×
	Trust and Tracking [12,31,32]	~	✓	~	✓	~	✓	×	×	×	×
	Policy management [33]	~	✓	×	✓	×	✓	×	~	×	×
Industrial GDPR tools	The Absolute Platform [15]	×	✓	~	✓	✓	~	×	×	×	~
	Alien Vault USM [16]	×	✓	~	×	~	×	×	×	×	×
	BigId [17]	×	✓	~	×	×	×	×	×	×	×
	BWise GDPR solution [18]	×	✓	~	✓	✓	✓	×	×	~	~
	Consentua [19]	×	✓	~	~	×	×	×	~	×	×
	PrivacyPerfect [20]	×	✓	~	×	~	×	×	×	×	~
Apache solutions	Apache Eagle [28]	×	✓	~	~	~	~	✓	✓	×	×
	Apache Atlas [29]	×	~	~	×	~	×	×	×	×	×
	Apache Ranger [30]	×	~	~	✓	×	✓	×	×	×	~
	Apache Knox [34]	×	×	~	~	×	~	×	×	×	~

5   Using the Framework for GDPR-compliance Implementation in a Big Data Application

In this section, we consider a classical Big Data application: a customer segmentation [36]. Segmentation enables marketers to better customize and maximize sales to diverse audience subcategories. Customer segmentation may be based on demographic, geographic, behavioral or psycho-graphic criteria and, therefore, generally processes private customer data. As for GDPR actors, the customer represents the data subject, services using data for collection, storage, visualization and analysis represent processors and the controller is represented by the governance layer of the Big Data ecosystem. Classically two kinds of processes are used, RFM and clustering [36]. We can consider them as black-boxes with user data as input and customer classification information as output in the processing layer of Fig. 1. Customers are grouped based on common characteristics that can be private.

The first step allows the DS to define his restrictions about data access. In our context, this means that he precises via a user interface the persons allowed to access his data, the period of time data will be stored (Storage limitation), the purposes his data will be processed for (purpose limitation) and other access conditions. Component C1 collects and aggregates different types of data about customer transactions. It is deployed at the data source layer and it is connected to C2 so that collected data is aggregated and displayed through the user interface. Indeed, a dashboard is provided by C2 to the customer in order to track his data, to check his timeline and processing records and to check if restrictions adjusted in his configuration settings are respected. For this objective, the solution of [12] can be adopted. Also, C2 can translate defined policies from a human language to security policies as machine language. For that, a tool such as [33] can be integrated.

As a second step, security policies set by the DS are stored into C6 component by component C4. The DS can define, update or delete his consent and/or his data. For that, Apache Ranger [30] is a good candidate for C4 and C6 because it allows different security policies to set up automatically. Furthermore, thanks to its open architecture, Apache Ranger can be extended for specific policy formats and contexts and for third party implementation of policies more specifically, Ranger adopts Attribute Based Access Control (ABAC) [37]. We can add other types of attributes in the PIP (Policy Information Point) so that we can manage the semantics of the policy and even combine different policies to provide new rules. Many works are proposed on ABAC architecture [23,37] that can be integrated into the Apache Ranger. But work is still needed to evaluate this cryptography overhead on processing time. At regular periods, the application sends a segmentation query that crosses components C3 to C7. The query is evaluated at C4 to check if the application processors are allowed to use the DS data for the segmentation purpose. More precisely, the security policy is evaluated: purposes limitation, storage limitation with the fixed period by the DS, data minimisation and access control restrictions. Then, according to policies, data is filtered at C3 that takes place in the ingestion layer of Fig. 1. Kafka [39] is classically used as a pipeline for Big Data. Furthermore, Kafka can be a good hub between the different framework components. Thanks to the publish/subscribe architecture, components are notified about new data, new security policies or for other data management purposes. For example, we can choose a topic for notification management, another topic for policy management and a topic per data source [23]. Before reaching the processing step, C3 provides a set of possible features to implement the GDPR "Data minimisation" principle. Data may go through labeling, encrypting or pseudonymisation process depending on the DS restriction. The goal is to communicate data only relevant, adequate and limited to what is necessary. Tokenization is an interesting technique to distinguish private data from public [38]. It can be enforced by encryption property using the crypto-engine component [23] so that only processors involved in the segmentation application can have access to data. C5 archives the different processing logs in NoSQL or SQL databases [40] for visualization and for accountability. Indeed, accountability information is displayed to the data Protection Officer thanks to C10.

Although some implementations of GDPR principles are available, integrating them together in a single solution is still an open issue. Interoperability between security solutions and performance overhead have to be measured and evaluated especially in a Big Data context.

6   Conclusion and Future Work

This paper presents a framework that details the main components for GDPR compliance verification and implementation. The framework allows classifying and comparing different works related to GDPR, particularly for Big Data systems. Furthermore, this framework can be used as a guideline for implementing solutions and products respecting GDPR. Few works address new requirements related to the heterogeneity and multi-source data of Big Data systems like tagging techniques. Also, a lot of work still be needed to address specific interfaces introduced by the regulation like audit tools for the data protection officer and the supervisory authority. The example of a segmentation application illustrates how to use the framework to assist developers and system designers to implement privacy by design and by default and highlight missing work in the state of the art.

As future work, we plan to implement the framework components in a real segmentation big data application. The goal is to demonstrate its GDPR-compliance and to evaluate the overhead of GDPR-compliance implementation mainly on the system performances. As a second step, we are very interested in developing audit tools for GDPR in Big Data systems.

References

1. Regulation (EU) 2016/679 of the European Parliament and of the Council of 27 April 2016 on the protection of natural persons with regard to the processing of personal data and on the free movement of such data, and repealing Directive 95/46/EC (General Data Protection Regulation). Off. J. Eur. Union **L119**, 1–88 (2016)
2. Pham, P.L.: The applicability of the GDPR to the Internet of Things. J. Data Prot. Priv. **2**(3), 254–263 (2019)
3. Yuan, B., Jiannan, L.: The policy effect of the General Data Protection Regulation (GDPR) on the digital public health sector in the European Union: an empirical investigation. Int. J. Environ. Res. Public Health **16**(6), 1070 (2019)

4. Lopes, I.M., Guarda, T., Oliveira, P.: Improvement of the applicability of the general data protection regulation in health clinics. In: Rocha, Á., Adeli, H., Reis, L.P., Costanzo, S. (eds.) WorldCIST 2019. AISC, vol. 930, pp. 155–165. Springer, Cham (2019). https://doi.org/10.1007/978-3-030-16181-1_15

5. Shah, A., Banakar, V., Shastri, S., Wasserman, M., Chidambaram, V.: Analyzing the impact of GDPR on storage systems. In: 11th USENIX Workshop on Hot Topics in Storage and File Systems (HotStorage 2019) (2019)

6. Gonçalves, A., Correia, A., Cavique, L.: An approach to GDPR based on object role modeling. In: Rocha, Á., Adeli, H., Reis, L.P., Costanzo, S. (eds.) WorldCIST'19 2019. AISC, vol. 930, pp. 595–602. Springer, Cham (2019). https://doi.org/10. 1007/978-3-030-16181-1_56

7. Kotsios, A., Magnani, M., Rossi, L., Shklovski, I., Vega, D.: An analysis of the consequences of the general data protection regulation (GDPR) on social network research. arXiv preprint arXiv:1903.03196 (2019)

8. Camilo, J.: Blockchain-based consent manager for GDPR compliance. Open Identity Summit 2019 (2019)

9. Krempel, E., Jürgen, B.: The EU general data protection regulation and its effects on designing assistive environments. In: Proceedings of the 11th PErvasive Technologies Related to Assistive Environments Conference. ACM (2018)

10. Gjermundrød, H., Dionysiou, I., Costa, K.: privacyTracker: a privacy-by-design GDPR-compliant framework with verifiable data traceability controls. In: Casteleyn, S., Dolog, P., Pautasso, C. (eds.) ICWE 2016. LNCS, vol. 9881, pp. 3–15. Springer, Cham (2016). https://doi.org/10.1007/978-3-319-46963-8_1

11. Rantos, K., Drosatos, G., Demertzis, K., Ilioudis, C., Papanikolaou, A., Kritsas, A.: ADvoCATE: a consent management platform for personal data processing in the IoT using blockchain technology. In: Lanet, J.-L., Toma, C. (eds.) SECITC 2018. LNCS, vol. 11359, pp. 300–313. Springer, Cham (2019). https://doi.org/10. 1007/978-3-030-12942-2_23

12. Fischer-Hübner, S., Angulo, J., Karegar, F., Pulls, T.: Transparency, privacy and trust – technology for tracking and controlling my data disclosures: does this work? In: Habib, S.M.M., Vassileva, J., Mauw, S., Mühlhäuser, M. (eds.) IFIPTM 2016. IAICT, vol. 473, pp. 3–14. Springer, Cham (2016). https://doi.org/10.1007/978-3-319-41354-9_1

13. General Data Protection Regulation. https://gdpr-info.eu. Accessed 20 June 2019

14. Fernandez-Gago, C., et al.: Tools for cloud accountability: A4Cloud tutorial. In: Camenisch, J., Fischer-Hübner, S., Hansen, M. (eds.) Privacy and Identity 2014. IAICT, vol. 457, pp. 219–236. Springer, Cham (2015). https://doi.org/10.1007/978-3-319-18621-4_15

15. The Absolute Platform. www.absolute.com. Accessed 20 June 2019

16. Alien Vault USM. www.alienvault.com. Accessed 20 June 2019

17. BigId. https://bigid.com/eu-gdpr/. Accessed 20 June 2019

18. BWise GDPR Compliance solution. www.bwise.com/solutions/regulatory-compliance-management/global-data-protection-regulation-gdpr. Accessed 20 June 2019

19. Consentua. https://consentua.com. Accessed 20 June 2019

20. PrivacyPerfect. https://www.privacyperfect.com/fr. Accessed 20 June 2019

21. Hesselman, C., Jansen, J., Wullink, M., Vink, K., Simon, M.: A privacy framework for DNS big data applications. Technical report (2014)

22. Crabtree, A., et al.: Building accountability into the Internet of Things: the IoT Databox model. J. Reliab. Intell. Environ. 4(1), 39–55 (2018)

23. Rhahla, M., Abdellatif, T, Attia, R., Berrayana, W.: A GDPR controller for IoT systems: application to e-health. In: WETICE (2019)
24. Ferreira, A., Joana, M.: TagUBig-Taming your Big Data. In: 2018 International Carnahan Conference on Security Technology (ICCST). IEEE (2018)
25. Data protection by design and default. https://ico.org.uk/for-organisations/guide-to-data-protection/guide-to-the-general-data-protection-regulation-gdpr/accountability-and-governance/data-protection-by-design-and-default/?q=necessary. Accessed 20 June 2019
26. Cavoukian, A.: Privacy by design: the 7 foundational principles. Information and Privacy Commissioner of Ontario, Canada 5 (2009)
27. Danezis, G., et al.: Privacy and data protection by design-from policy to engineering. arXiv preprint arXiv:1501.03726 (2015)
28. Apache Eagle. https://eagle.apache.org/. Accessed 20 June 2019
29. Apache Atlas. https://atlas.apache.org/. Accessed 20 June 2019
30. Apache Ranger. https://ranger.apache.org/. Accessed 20 June 2019
31. Fischer-Hübner, S., Hedbom, H., Wästlund, E.: Trust and assurance HCI. In: Camenisch, J., Fischer-Hübner, S., Rannenberg, K. (eds.) Privacy and Identity Management for Life, pp. 245–260. Springer, Heidelberg (2011). https://doi.org/10.1007/978-3-642-20317-6_13
32. Angulo, J., Fischer-Hübner, S., Pulls, T., Wstlund, E.: Usable transparency with the data track: a tool for visualizing data disclosures. In: Proceedings of the 33rd Annual ACM Conference Extended Abstracts on Human Factors in Computing Systems. ACM (2015)
33. Benghabrit, W., et al.: A cloud accountability policy representation framework. In: Closer (2014)
34. Apache Knox. https://knox.apache.org/. Accessed 20 June 2019
35. D'Acquisto, G., Domingo-Ferrer, J., Kikiras, P., Torra, V., de Montjoye, Y. A., Bourka, A.: Privacy by design in big data: an overview of privacy enhancing technologies in the era of big data analytics. arXiv preprint arXiv:1512.06000 (2015)
36. Wu, J., Zheng, L.: Research on customer segmentation model by clustering. In: Proceedings of the 7th International Conference on Electronic Commerce. ACM (2005)
37. Cavoukian, A., Chibba, M., Williamson, G., Ferguson, A.: The importance of ABAC: attribute-based access control to big data: privacy and context. Ryerson University, Toronto, Canada, Privacy and Big Data Institute (2015)
38. Tokenization. https://www.pcidss.com/listing-category/pci-dss-tokenization/. Accessed 20 June 2019
39. Apache Kafka. https://kafka.apache.org/. Accessed 20 June 2019
40. Cattell, R.: Scalable SQL and NoSQL data stores. Acm Sigmod Rec. **39**(4), 12–27 (2011)
41. Yod-Samuel, M., Kung, A.: Methods and tools for GDPR compliance through privacy and data protection engineering. In: IEEE European Symposium on Security and Privacy Workshops (EuroSPW), IEEE 2018, pp. 108–111 (2018)
42. Schneider, G.: Is privacy by construction possible? In: Margaria, T., Steffen, B. (eds.) ISoLA 2018. LNCS, vol. 11244, pp. 471–485. Springer, Cham (2018). https://doi.org/10.1007/978-3-030-03418-4_28
43. Ferrara, P., Fausto, S.: Static analysis for GDPR compliance. In: ITASEC (2018)

"I do it because they do it": Social-Neutralisation in Information Security Practices of Saudi Medical Interns

Saad Altamimi[1]($\boxtimes$), Karen Renaud[2,3]($\boxtimes$), and Timothy Storer[1]($\boxtimes$)

[1] School of Computing Science, University of Glasgow, Glasgow, UK
s.altamimi.1@research.gla.ac.uk, Timothy.Storer@glasgow.ac.uk
[2] School of Design and Informatics, University of Abertay, Dundee, UK
k.renaud@abertay.ac.uk
[3] University of South Africa, Pretoria, South Africa

Abstract. Successful implementation of information security policies (ISP) and IT controls play an important role in safeguarding patient privacy in healthcare organizations. Our study investigates the factors that lead to healthcare practitioners' neutralisation of ISPs, leading to non-compliance. The study adopted a qualitative approach and conducted a series of semi-structured interviews with medical interns and hospital IT department managers and staff in an academic hospital in Saudi Arabia. The study's findings revealed that the MIs imitate their peers' actions and employ similar justifications when violating ISP dictates. Moreover, MI team superiors' (seniors) ISP non-compliance influences MI's tendency to invoke neutralisation techniques. We found that trust between medical team members is an essential social facilitator that motivates MI's to invoke neutralisation techniques to justify violating ISP policies and controls. These findings add new insights that help us to understand the relationship between the social context and neutralisation theory in triggering ISP non-compliance.

Keywords: Neutralisation theory · Health care · Information security policies · Privacy · Medical Interns

1 Introduction

Many healthcare organisations have encountered security and privacy challenges due to the wide adoption of Healthcare Information Systems (HIS). Electronic Medical Records (EMR) or Electronic Health Records (EHR) are both instances of HISs. In this context, a privacy breach is "*a situation where personally identifiable information is processed in violation of one or more relevant privacy safeguarding requirements*" [18]. Reports from information security agencies state

---

The original version of this chapter was revised: The spelling of the second author's name was corrected. The correction to this chapter is available at https://doi.org/10. 1007/978-3-030-41568-6_25

© Springer Nature Switzerland AG 2020, corrected publication 2020
S. Kallel et al. (Eds.): CRiSIS 2019, LNCS 12026, pp. 227–243, 2020.
https://doi.org/10.1007/978-3-030-41568-6_15

that healthcare organisations are susceptible to internal and external security threats, which can jeopardise the information security controls and policies of healthcare organisations and increase risks for EMRs. According to the Verizon 2019 Data Breach Investigation Report (DBIR) [35], there were 41,686 security incidents, of which 2,013 were data breaches. In the healthcare industry, a total of 304 confirmed data breaches occurred, with 179 of these associated with employees. To reduce privacy breaches,several countries have developed strict information security and privacy regulations to force adherence by healthcare organisations in terms of collecting, processing and exchanging patient information to ensure the privacy and confidentiality of patient data. These regulations, for instance, include the Health Insurance Accountability Act 1996 (HIPPA) in the US and General Data Protection Regulation (GDPR) in Europe in 2018.

Security and privacy breaches are costly for individuals and organisations. The accidental or intentional disclosure of patient information can have consequences, such as employment termination, personal embarrassment, identity theft and loss of the health insurance [37]. Likewise, any breach within healthcare organisations could lead to legal liabilities, which could imply severe loss of trust and reputational damage, as well as financial penalties and pecuniary compensations [36].

In the information security literature, scholars have postulated that technology controls alone can not ensure integrity, availability and confidentiality of information held by an organisation without encouraging employees to meet the organisation's information security goals [31,38]. They call for more studies to explore the motivations behind individuals' intentions to violate or comply with ISPs. Instead of focusing on the effects or the consequences of the individual's ISP violations or compliance with organisational ISPs, there is the need take a step backwards to understand the factors that contribute to their intention to comply.

This study extend previously published compliance-related research [3,31, 34], which found that individuals would adopt cognitive justifications or embrace neutralisation techniques to overcome feelings of shame or guilt when they commit, or intend to commit, any particular violation.

However, this study distinguishes of the previous work by investigating the impact of the social factors on Medical Interns (MI) motivations to free themselves from the obligation to comply with the hospital's ISPs. We argue that the MIs' ISP violations can originate from social aspects that influence them to employ neutralisation techniques and to behave insecurely. Here, we make a distinction between *malicious* and *non-malicious* violations of ISPs. A malicious violation involves an individual intentionally committing an act to harm the organisation's IT assets. This study, on the other hand, focuses on non-malicious behaviour, i.e. when an individual violates an ISP without intention to harm the hospital IT assets. In particular, they are likely to employ neutralisation techniques to justify their deviant behaviours [4]. Consequently, we sought to answer the following research questions:

RQ1: *What are the common neutralisation techniques that medical interns invoke to justify ISP violations?*

RQ2: *What are the social factor(s) that trigger invocation of such neutralisation techniques?*

To answer the questions, we conducted semi-structured interviews with MIs (n = 21) and IT specialists (n = 8) in a Saudi hospital. This study revealed that both peers and superiors influence MIs' misconduct and ISP breaches and that neutralisation techniques were used to justify their non-compliance. This paper is organised as follows: Sect. 2 provides theoretical foundations for neutralisation theory, specifically individuals' deviant behaviour related to ISP non compliance; Sect. 3 details the study's methodology, data collection, and analysis; Sect. 4 reports on the study's findings; and Sect. 5 presents the study's conclusion and suggests directions for future work.

2 Theoretical Background

2.1 Information Security Policy Compliance and Privacy Protection

According to Parks *et al.* [25], privacy safeguards refer to the organisation's efforts to ensure personal information protection by implementing various types of security solutions, both technical and non-technical. Despite these efforts to safeguard healthcare organisations' IT assets and information, security and privacy breaches by healthcare organisations keep occurring. For instance, in 2018, several healthcare organisations in the USA registered a new record of paying around 28 million dollars in fines and settlements due to HIPPA rule violations. This was 22% more than the fines paid in 2016 [19]. In response to the severe consequences of HIPAA non-compliance, healthcare organisations invested massively in strengthening technical controls to repel hacking attempts [28]. They adopted many IT and security "best practices", and developed a wide range of information security policies (ISPs) to assign responsibilities to employees and delineate their role in protecting organisations' information and technology resources [7]. Chan *et al.* [9] detail ISP compliance as *"core information security activities that need to be carried out by individuals to maintain information security as defined by ISP."* Thus, an internal security threat exists when an employee with legitimate access to the organisation's IT assets fails to comply with the organisation's ISPs [29]. In an effort to improve individual compliance and reduce undesirable behaviours, information security scholars have published a large number of studies that incorporate theories from sociology, criminology, psychology, and other disciplines to achieve a deeper understanding of the antecedents of ISP non-compliance triggers [12,13].

2.2 Neutralisation Theory

Sykes and Matza [33] introduced neutralisation theory to explain the deviant behaviour of juveniles. Deviant behaviour is any action that conflicts with the shared values of a social group; the group members consider the behaviour unacceptable. Rogers and Buffalo [27] defined neutralisation techniques as "*a method whereby an individual renders behavioural norms inoperative, thereby freeing himself to engage in behaviour which would otherwise be considered deviant.*" These neutralisation techniques help the offender to balance and negate the impact of the inner feelings of shame or guilt and make it possible for an offender to commit the non-compliant behaviour without self-blaming. Sykes and Matza [33] list five neutralisation techniques: (1) denial of responsibility, (2) denial of injury, (3) the appeal of higher loyalty, (4) denial of victim, and (5) condemnation of condemners.

Further applications of Sykes' original work have identified additional neutralisation techniques that support the effort to explain different types of crimes and deviant behaviours. For instance, Klockars [20] added the "*metaphor of the ledger*", while Minor [24] mentions the "*defence of necessity*". Others are "*claim of normalcy*" introduced by [10], the "emphclaim of individuality", the "*claim of relative acceptability*", the "*claim of entitlement*" [17], "*justification by postponement*" and "*justification by comparison*" [14]. Neutralisation theory was the basis for various criminological studies of criminal behaviours, such as hate crime [8], car theft [11], and drug addiction [26].

2.3   Neutralisation Theory in the IT and IS Contexts

Given the theoretical explanation of neutralisation theory in terms of investigating deviant behaviours, several scholars propose the application of this theory as a suitable lens to understand computer abuse [16], cyber-loafing [21], and digital piracy [30]. Willison and Warkentin [38] stated that it was worth applying neutralisation theory to explore employees' deviant security behaviours within organizations. They argue that the employee might use neutralisation to offset feelings of guilt or shame when they intend to break organisational rules. In the IS context, ISPs are a set of essential roles and responsibilities that are encoded in ISPs to guide employee security behaviours in the workplace. Siponen and Vance's [31] study revealed that the organisations' deterrence measures were not effective in the face of neutralisation techniques. They concluded that neutralisation techniques were correlated with employee intentions to commit ISP violations regardless of the presence or absence of formal or informal organisational sanctions. Moreover, other empirical studies [2,34] found that neutralisation theory is a significant predictor of individuals' intention to breach information security and privacy policies.

2.4   Medical Interns in Saudi Arabia

In Saudi Arabia, medical schools have designed their medical curricula to include a year of compulsory clinical training after the medical students complete their mandatory medical courses. During the internship year, MIs work in teams under close supervision of seniors, such as medical consultants and residents. This arrangement improves the MI's clinical and practical experience as they gain continuous feedback during involvement with patients' treatment. Every month, each intern works in a different clinic in the hospital and engages with different medical teams. The aim is to help MIs improve their learning and ability to identify their preferred future medical specialty. Although these monthly shifts between clinics allow the MIs to enhance their clinical training, it also expands other non-medical or professional competencies, such as improving communication skills. This year enhances their professional attitudes and ethics with respect to patient care and safety [1].

3   Methodology

The study conducted a series of semi-structured interviews to collect data and applied a thematic analysis approach based on [6] to obtain answers to the research questions. The research environment was a Saudi Arabian hospital that is considered one of the biggest academic hospitals. It has more than 1400 beds in various specialties and several medical research centres around the country. Every year, the hospital admits more than 30,000 patients and provides health care services to more than 250,000 registered patients. In the hospital, MIs have access to the hospital's IT systems. The MI's privileges include accessing the hospital health care systems (HIS), which allows them to enter, view, and edit patients' medical records. Over the last few years, the hospital has been impacted by several security incidents from internal sources. Medical employees' non-compliance with the hospital's ISP was the primary cause of internal security incidents, such as unauthorised access to the hospitals' HISs and the use of infected USB devices. We sought to investigate whether neutralisation techniques were used by MIs to justify their ISP violations and the motivations behind their justifications.

3.1   Data Collection

The interview protocol had three main parts. During the *first* part, the authors explained the purpose of the study and asked the interviewee to sign the consent form. The *second* part commenced with general questions, collecting demographics, job descriptions and information security backgrounds. The *last* part of the interview explored the information security environment in the hospital in five major areas: (1) ISP development, (2) implementation, (3) enforcement, (4) awareness & training, and (5) incident reporting. Specifically, we investigated the impact of the existing security policies on the health practitioners' daily practices and activities. The initial questions were revised after the first interview to include more probing questions, which were used to explore the reactions of MIs to ISPs. We also explored the drivers of neutralisation technique adoption. In total, we interviewed twenty-nine participants, including MIs and eight IT staff members. Each interview lasted between 45 and 60 min. All interviews were conducted face-to-face in the hospital and were carried out by the first author between Sep 2018 and Nov 2019.

3.2 Participants

IT Participants: We wanted to interview IT managers and staff who directly interacted with health practitioners in meetings or discussions. Specifically, we dealt with those IT department employees responsible for developing, implementing and enforcing ISPs and controls to protect the hospital's IT infrastructure and patient record privacy. The Associate Executive Director of the IT department distributed interview invitations to the department staff via email. A total of eight participants from the IT department volunteered to be interviewed (six IT managers and two IT employees). The study aimed to explore their perceptions about current ISP violations, and the IT department's efforts to ease the conflict between IT security needs and the impact of those policies on healthcare practitioners' duties. The IT department's awareness of the medical employees' justifications (neutralisation techniques) for ISP violations were explored, as well as their mitigation solutions.

Medical Interns: The study recruited twenty-one MIs (10 Female, 11 Male) via snowball sampling [5], which allowed us to reach this group more efficiently. Each of the MIs was asked to refer the interview invitation to other colleagues. Our aim was to gain insights into the interactions between MIs, as a group, and the ISPs, during daily activities. Another aim was to investigate the social factors that influenced MIs to violate ISPs, i.e. what prompts them to justify such non-compliance by invoking neutralisation techniques. We continued to collect data until we reached saturation i.e. no new themes emerged [22].

3.3 Data Analysis

The interviews' audio files and transcripts were analysed as advised by Braun and Clarke [6] (Fig. 1). Thematic analysis is a method that searches for common patterns within a qualitative data set and systematically underlines repeated themes. This encourages a better understanding of the context and ensures greater organisation of the dataset. We identified all the relative passages in the responses that revealed security policy violations and the corresponding neutralisation technique(s) used to justify such violations. Also, the study focused on the possible reasons that led MIs to invoke such techniques. The data relating to neutralisation techniques and ISP violations was then analysed thematically using an inductive approach to code any relevant information in the text excerpt. Afterward, all the codes that reflected a similar concept were grouped to create meaningful themes. Qualitative software QSR NVivo Version 12, was used to conduct the thematic analysis and facilitate the management of the audio files and transcripts.

4 Findings: Social Factors and Neutralisation Techniques

Using thematic analysis, the study identified a number of social factors that motivated MIs to justify their violations of the hospital ISPs. According to [23]

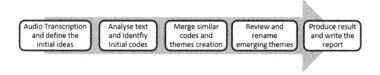

Fig. 1. Thematic analysis processes by Braun and Clarke [6]

several neutralisation techniques might overlap, which may lead to inconsistent findings during technique identification. Thus, we used Fritsche's [15] typology as a guideline to improve our understanding of how to identify and select the neutralisation techniques, which improved our ability to reduce arbitrariness and inconsistent or overlapping techniques. We found that the social meta-categories influencing the invocation of neutralisation techniques include:(1) peer influence, and (2) superior influence.

4.1 Peer Influence

Sutherland [32] stated that: *"An individual learns not only the techniques of committing the crime, no matter how complex or simple, but he/she learns specific motives, drives, rationalisations and attitude"* [p. 75].

The MIs are a subgroup of health care members who work to improve their practical healthcare skills. These interns share many individual characteristics such as age, medical experience, and educational background, which make their relationship and behaviours stronger and help them to solve work issues in similar ways. They are at an important stage of their medical education and perform medical duties within healthcare teams during their clinical rotation. They get most of their training benefits from interacting with other peers and practitioners, such as medical residents, consultants, and nurses. Interns work hard to prove their medical competence and by so doing hope to gain a residency position after their internship year. This passion motivates their tendencies to focus on medical training practices and duties more than anything else.

Several MIs indicated that accomplishing their medical responsibilities is prioritised over complying with ISPs. MI4: *"We take things based on priorities, and we don't consider information security a priority for us, and unfortunately, it might be considered the lowest of the priorities between our colleagues"*. Other MIs stated the importance of their medical duties compared to the hospital's concerns about compliance with ISPs: MI13: *"To be honest, we don't focus on this topic; we focus onpatient treatment management. For us, as MIs, we focus more on the medical skills and how to make a diagnosis or read its result, and so on. But information security topics are not a priority for us."*

Many MIs indicated that the healthcare team norms impacted their behaviour as they imitated their colleagues non-compliance actions. Thus, they inherit and commit the same security policies violations and tend to evoke the same justifications. MI11: *"To be honest, I have not read a security policy document, but I have heard that from my colleagues about what I can do or not, all of my knowledge is bits of advice that come from people in the practices"*; MI16: *"you see what people around you are doing, and you will do the same. Even though a person is supposed to know the wrong or right by himself"*.

MIs indicated that they and other peers heavily rely on each other to overcome their daily practices issues, especially issues related to security controls, such as limited internet access. MI20: *"When I face a situation, I read about it or inquire from someone knows such as my colleagues. For instance, I need to print files in the hospital, so I ask my colleagues how to do that. Therefore, each one of them gives me his experience to solve my issue with controls here because we have limited internet access and we cannot open Gmail, Hotmail, etc. So, I get benefits from their feedback and experiences"*.

Therefore, the social impact of the peers' behaviour can form their perception as they followed and imitated each other's actions and used the same justifications for their non-compliant behaviour with the hospital ISPs. We identified four neutralisation techniques that the MIs use to justify their non compliance behaviour under the influence of their peers: (1) defence of necessity, (2) appeal to higher loyalty, (3) everybody else is doing it, and (4) denial of injury.

Defence of Necessity: The majority of the MIs ($N = 16$), indicated that they used this technique to justify their behaviour when they share their passwords or healthcare system account with peers. The common belief among the participants who illustrated evidence of this technique was that complying with the ISP was not a matter of urgency to them. Thus, they focused their attention on their primary mission of providing treatment to patients and dealing with the clinical workload. Some of the MIs argued that they shared their password with a colleague when it was necessary. Therefore, being a part of a medical team required them to tightly collaborate with other peers and force them to perform some acts regardless of compliance with the ISPs.

They stated that if an MI in the team found it difficult to access his/her account, then this would impact team performance. The argument, in this situation, was the necessity to improve work performance, which made it justifiable to share their HIS password or account. As respondents reported: MI16: *"…. at the end, you have to see the big picture, there are patient interests might be disrupted or delayed because one of the medical team members does not have access"*; MI09: *"if someone refuses to give you the password of his account, this would delay work because I would wait until he comes and opens his account to complete the order. It would delay the work performance."*

Appeal to Higher Loyalty: Participants who used this technique tend to *"legitimise deviant behaviour when a non-conventional social bond creates more immediate and pressing demands than one consistent with conventional society"*. [14]. This technique is considered the second most common neutralisation technique that reported by the MIs with ($n = 15$). The primary ISP violation that evoked *"appeal of higher loyalty"* was sharing passwords or the HIS accounts between MIs, who started their internship without an active account to access the hospital health care system. It was not surprising, given the close relationships between MIs who were working together to serve clinical requirements and their practical goals. The MIs who indicated support for this technique felt that they were doing the right thing, in providing professional help to peers to accomplish team duties without disruption. Here, some of the participants argued that they were sharing their passwords or HIS account and neutralising their behaviour by referring to the greater good. For instance, some MIs justified their password sharing behaviour as support and help, especially during the internship period, in which any disruption of performance can impact MI training and evaluation. MI17: *"I think it is a kind of attitude that we need to get the work done. It is professional support."*; MI23: *"To be honest, here we have this kind of behaviour that we like to help people sometimes more than what is supposed to be. So, this is considered "help" in our culture."*

Everybody Else Is Doing It: This technique refers to the impression that the damaging behaviour is common to the group, so there was no need to feel guilty or ashamed. Six MIs ($N = 6$) justified their behaviour by saying *"everyone of my peers is doing it"*, especially when they left their PCs without logging out, shared a password or account with others, or used an external Internet router to bypass Internet access restrictions. The participants argued that their behaviour was normal because other team members were commonly doing the same thing: MI09: *"I mean, the behaviours of others because the majority are doing this thing; we will do the same, even if it is wrong."*

Also, they argued their behaviour was acceptable and referred to the fact that a large number of their colleagues commonly shared passwords, left their PCs unlocked, or utilised their own Internet routers: MI14: *"I see the majority share their passwords, for example, and leave their account open without Logging out. Sometimes, I leave my account open to let my colleague work on the same note."*; MI27: *"I have to use my mobile Internet router, which I bring with me. Actually, a lot of my colleagues do the same, not only me."*

Also, they stated that no one got caught or punished for performing such actions, which implied that the IT department had not considered these acts to be information security breaches. They referred to the existence or absence of ISP violation sanctions to evaluate which of the typical behaviours in their peer groups was considered a breach of the hospital's ISPs or not. The MIs evoked this technique based on their observation of the social context that influenced their decision-making processes to decide which behaviour was acceptable: MI27: *"Also, as I have mentioned everybody is doing it, from the physicians to the nurses and residents. Everyone leaves their account open and there is no specific punishment."*

Denial of Injury: The offender who uses this technique claims that the outcomes of his/her deviant behaviour are harmless, and he/she does not show any concern about the expected consequences of non-compliant behaviour [33]. More than half of the MIs ($N = 13$) referred to this neutralisation technique when they revealed some of their daily practices. One MI who adopted this technique refused to acknowledge the fact that, by sending photos from patients' medical records via a social media application (e.g Whatsapp) or sharing the password or the HIS account with a colleague, they could cause any harm to patient privacy or the hospital.

There were three main arguments behind these non-compliant actions; the first was that the MIs' HIS accounts had limited privileges, as they could only access the patient records to write patients' diagnoses. They did not have any authority to issue medical orders, such as prescribing medicines or conducting lab tests. The MI's judgment was concentrated on the physical harm that could impact the patients' health due to incorrect medical orders. Thus, they failed to pay attention to the information security risks that could originate from sharing passwords. They reported that: MI10: *"Technically speaking, my account is limited as a medical intern, and we only can write notes. So, she is going to write notes like me, and she cannot do something major. There is no security breach in my perspective because we both know what the limit is"*; MI7: *"We are not allowed, as medical interns, to make medical orders, so I'm not worried that the person who I share my account will do something that can harm me or the patient in the future."*

Some of the MIs conducted a type of risk comparison as a way to decrease the injury that could occur from sharing their HIS account password. Denial of injury via reducing the impact and magnitude of the risk originated when they compared it to other team members in a higher position of authority, such as consultants. So, they thought that sharing passwords would have a small negative impact on the hospital's security. This thought affected the MIs' reporting of any observed violations of ISPs. An MI explained: MI15: *".....what I'm saying is I know there is something that is important, but what interns think themselves is that they are only interns !! So, whatever threats come from us, no one is going to consider. Threats coming from MIs are less impactful than threats coming from CIOs or the heads of department. This is because they have more responsibilities. So, their email is strong,because if a CIO sent an email to a department, then it will be read and followed. But If I sent an email to a department no one is going to do anything. This is my belief."*

The last argument was that several MIs habitually took pictures and shared these with peers via mobile social media applications. They believed that the recipient of the medical record photos was trusted, and would use these for medical purposes and keep them confidential. Some MIs confirmed that they had sent or received an image of a patient's records, including lab results or x-rays, where the patients' information was clear. Others revealed that they had taken precautions to protect patient confidentiality by hiding the patient's identifiable information, such as the patient's name or Medical Record Number (MRN). This action was explained by different MIs, as follows: MI5: *"Today, one of my colleagues took a picture of a screen and all the information was there except the patient MRN. However, there were some cases where the MRN and the patient name have appeared."*; MI11: *"I have seen a lot of my colleagues not pay attention to cover the MRN before they take a picture of the system screen, specifically the X-ray picture, for instance, where the patient information always appears in X-ray corner. They directly take a picture of the X-ray without considering covering the patient information located in the corner. They usually say we share it with our colleagues,so they don't hide such information"*; MI16: *"Yes, I have sent some pictures for discussion with my medical team but without the name or MRN of the patient."*

4.2   Superior Influence

The central role of the MIs during their monthly rotation was to learn from their superiors, including consultants or residents and to work closely with them to provide healthcare services. During the internship, the interaction between the MIs and their superiors is considered an essential part of the learning process for the MI. The consultant has the power to offer a residency position to any intern who successfully meets the practical training criteria. Thus, the superiors' decisions were a significant part of the evaluation process in subsequently gaining a residency position in the hospital.

The majority of the MIs explained that their superiors influenced their behaviours both directly and indirectly in several situations related to the ISPs. Therefore, this influenced their tendencies to invoke several neutralisation techniques as part of the decision-making processes to deal with their superiors' requests. These orders could conceivably lead to an ISP violation.

In addition, the MIs provided evidence of several neutralisation techniques to justify their ISP violations and showed how the influence of their superiors had motivated them directly, and indirectly, to justify their abuse of passwords and the HIS access policies. Thus, four main neutralisation techniques were identified and invoked due to the influence of the superiors: (1) *Denial of responsibility*, (2) *Denial of injury*, (3) *Defence of necessity*, and (4) *Defence of Convenience*.

Denial of Responsibility: Many MIs cited their superiors' or seniors' authority as an essential factor that helps them to accomplish their aims, do their duties, and gain better practical experience in the field. This close relationship might extend to informing ISP-related perceptions, as an MI indicated: M12: *"I observe what my seniors are doing regarding the information security and I do whatever they do."*

The MIs revealed that accountability towards the hospital's ISP was influenced by the orders issued by their seniors, such as consultants or residents. Therefore, they shifted the responsibility of any potential harm of the ISP violations to their superiors. MI26: *"It is coming from the attending consultant, so usually people obey the person in authority even if it is the wrong action, they will follow it."*

Furthermore, they explained that their work environment was complex and required full collaboration from the entire medical team to deliver health care services to patients. So, being a trainee in a medical team made it difficult for any MI to deny carrying out an order from a consultant, even if the request could lead to an ISP violation or privacy breach. For instance, an MI explained his fear of the consequences of a refusal on his application for a residency position when a consultant asked him to share his account with another intern: MI4: *"for seeking approval or recommendation from the supervisors. They might see you as part of the team, which increases your chance of acceptance as a resident. I will lose if I refuse to do it. If I say NO because I want to follow the rules, they might abuse you and isolate you from the team."*

Besides, few MIs felt that their seniors used their authority to violate the ISPs by delegating more responsibilities to the MIs than expected by hospital management. For instance, some of the consultants shared their HIS accounts with MIs to allow them to perform extra work duties, such as issuing medical orders. Thus, the MIs were forced to exceed their designated privileges to use the healthcare information system, which is considered a violation of the hospital's HIS access control policy: MI27: *"some physicians abuse the medical interns by letting them do more duties, so if medical interns said that his/her account privileges are limited in order to conduct the requested order, the physician simply respons by saying that's ok, take my account or password and conduct the order."*

Denial of Injury: Several MIs reported evidence of using this neutralisation technique to justify their superiors' impact on the hospital's ISP non-compliance. For example, some of the MIs justified their use of the consultant's HIS account if the medical orders included only simple and routine procedures. In this case, the expected consequences of any wrong order on patient health were minor, regardless of the fact that the behaviour itself was a violation of any ISPs: MI5: *"It depends on the case. If the MI will use the consultant's account for minor orders or routine medical procedures like ordering Paracetamol, X-rays, or blood tests, the harm of these procedures, such as increasing the dose or asking for the X-ray,is trivial."*

Two of the IT managers acknowledged the occurrence of this violation and described the consultants' perceptions as harmless when sharing their HIS account credentials with others: ITE1: *"They say nobody will be harmed if I share my password, and I will simply change the password if there is a risk"*; ITD1: *"Also, the fact is that the consultant and the resident don't see sharing their password as an issue for the email and [the health care system] and they think it is ok"*.

Other MIs invoked this technique to justify their behaviour of sending a photo of the HIS screen to their seniors. They referred to this as a practical way of getting things done, enhancing convenience, and not wasting the seniors' time. They sometimes received a request from a physician to send a photo of a patient record, and sometimes they sent the picture to the physician's mobile seeking treatment advice. In fact, the MIs blamed the IT department's technical restrictions such as the lack of remote access (VPN), as being responsible for this type of security violation. Therefore, instead of verbally reading the patient information over the phone or asking the consultant to come to the clinic to read the patient's diagnoses or lab results, they took photos of the patients' records and sent them to the consultants' mobiles. They argued that they sent the photo to the consultants' phone directly, as requested, and only two people had the images. This reduced the chances that these pictures would be leaked: MI17:

"I understand there is a risk, but what is the probability of it happening? Your example has a very minimal chance of occurring if any"; M11: *"most of the people in the medical field are looking for practicality rather than professionalism. They prefer practicality, so instead of asking the physician to come to the hospital, they take a picture and send him the findings and the lab results to let him give his diagnoses or treatment plan. So, they think it is more practical and it is better to get the job done."*

MIs stated that their seniors had sent photos containing patients' records to their mobiles, where the identifiable patient information was clearly shown. The seniors took these pictures for some of the patients' unique case records and shared them with many MIs in the team, as part of the learning process: MI9: *"It is the wrong behaviour, but they do it a lot. Also, the seniors might take a picture of the patient information that includes the name and the MRN and share it with others; they don't care about hiding this information that much. They do that for many reasons, such as teaching or discussion. That frequently occurs, even it is a wrong action."*

Defence of Necessity: Several MIs reported that they had no choice for performing their work efficiently than to share their password. Some of the MIs related situations where their seniors shared their HIS accounts with them temporarily. For instance, some had started their internship program without an active HIS account, which conflicted with their training objectives to gain practical experience. A significant part of the training consisted of writing patients' medical documentation. Thus, the consultant or the resident had to share their HIS account credentials until the IT department activated the intern's HIS account. MI09: *"The problem is that many medical interns don't receive their healthcare system account from the IT department before they start the program. If the resident realised that the medical intern does not have an account, in this case, the resident usually shares his/her health care system account with the medical intern and logs out when he/she finished writing the notes."*

Another group of MIs reported a situation where a large number of patients in some clinics created a significant burden on the physicians, which forced them to seek help from the team to provide healthcare services and reduce treatment time. If the physician spent most of his/her time handling routine duties such as writing medical notes rather than examining patients, treatment time would increase. M18: *"If the doctor strictly complies with security policies and does not share his account, I think that may impact his work performance. In the end, when the doctor stops dealing with the patient in order to do some simple tasks, that can impact the doctor's performance in the clinic."*

An IT security employee confirmed a previous justification from a consultant to share their HIS account password: ITE1: *"The doctor's justification for such behaviour, which I have heard that from them, here I will quote the doctor's speech: 'I'm here in the clinic for patient treatment and I have many patients to look after, so I don't have time to access the system each time to make medical orders or procedures, such as lab orders or pharmacy orders and so on. Thus, this is part of the nurse's duties as she is an assistant of the doctors, therefore, I give her my password to conduct such orders, while I'm doing my primary work to meet and examine the patients'. End of quote."*

Also, several MIs justified the impact of their seniors' behaviours on them, which could lead to their violating the password policy. They indicated the importance of sharing passwords, especially when the consultant was too busy and tired dealing with patients all day or dealing with many urgent cases, which increased the risk of making mistakes in HIS orders. Their argument was that the consultant benefits from sharing their HIS account credentials in this situation, and this offsets the ISP violation behaviour. M12: *"Sometimes when a person is tired, he is more likely to make mistakes because he maybe does the medical orders quickly to finish the work. So, I think it is justifiable in this situation if the doctor gives others colleagues, a trusted person, his account to overcome the tiredness risk."*; M18: *"Regarding sharing passwords, the doctors share their passwords because there is a need for doing that. ...in the emergency clinic, several doctors have shared their passwords with me, so I can order anything for the patient and it comes directly without delay."*

Defence of Convenience: This justification emerged from several MIs as a new neutralisation technique. They claimed that that the violation of the information security policy met the violator's needs. They considered ISP compliance a subjective matter based on their judgment and evaluation in the current situation. The MIs who engaged in this delinquent behaviour seemed in an intermediate position between a denial of injury and a defence of necessity. So, MIs who used this justification moved back and forth between ISP compliance and non-compliance to gain more personal and work benefits. They argued that they could use better ways to make their work more convenient or more efficient, while, in reality, they wanted to accumulate personal credits with work benefits. Some MIs reported that the consultants shared their password because they wanted to stay home and made the interns perform their tasks. Some MIs stated that consultants were simply too lazy to do their duties: MI19: *"Because it is more convenient for the consultant to stay home and ask his juniors to complete a specific task."*

5   Limitation and Conclusion

Like all research, this study has its own limitation relates to the sample chosen for the interviews. Here, all the collected data was limited to a single academic hospital in Saudi Arabia. Thus, it is suggested being cautious when generalising the study findings in other contexts. Another limitation is the Social Desirability Response Bias (SDRB) during face to face interviews, where the participants answer the interviewer's questions in favour to preserve their self-image. Therefore, we attempted to overcome this research issue by asking indirectly the participants to report their colleagues' behaviour to violate ISPs and related justifications instead of their own behaviour.

In conclusion, employees' adherence to ISPs cannot be taken for granted. They sometimes drift to non-compliance and adopt neutralization techniques to slave their conscience when they decide not to comply with ISP dictates. On the other hand, sometimes the environment and social norms explicitly encourage non-compliance: people follow the descriptive norms (what others are doing) rather than injunctive norms (what the ISPs tell them to do). We carried out a study that revealed a number of motivations that encourage MIs to invoke behavioural justifications when not complying with ISPs: neutralization techniques that helped them to feel better about not complying. For future work, we plan to consider amelioration strategies that could reduce the likelihood that medical interns will use neutralization techniques instead of complying with hospital ISPs.

References

1. Al-Moamary, M.S., Mamede, S., Schmidt, H.G.: Innovations in medical internship: benchmarking and application within the King Saud bin Abdulaziz University for Health Sciences. Educ. Health (Abingdon Engl.) **23**(1), 367 (2010)
2. Altamimi, S., Storer, T., Alzahrani, A.: The role of neutralisation techniques in violating hospitals privacy policies in Saudi Arabia. In: 2018 4th International Conference on Information Management (ICIM), pp. 133–140. IEEE (2018)
3. Barlow, J.B., Warkentin, M., Ormond, D., Dennis, A.R.: Don't make excuses! discouraging neutralization to reduce IT policy violation. Comput. Secur. **39**, 145–159 (2013)
4. Bauer, S., Bernroider, E.W.N.: An analysis of the combined influences of neutralization and planned behavior on desirable information security behavior. In: 13th Annual Security Conference, Las Vegas, USA (2014)
5. Biernacki, P., Waldorf, D.: Snowball sampling: problems and techniques of chain referral sampling. Sociol. Methods Res. **10**(2), 141–163 (1981)
6. Braun, V., Clarke, V.: Using thematic analysis in psychology. Qual. Res. Psychol. **3**(2), 77–101 (2006)
7. Bulgurcu, B., Cavusoglu, H., Benbasat, I.: Information security policy compliance: an empirical study of rationality-based beliefs and information security awareness. MIS Q. **34**(3), 523–548 (2010)
8. Byers, B., Crider, B.W., Biggers, G.K.: Bias crime motivation: a study of hate crime and offender neutralization techniques used against the Amish. J. Contemp. Crim. Justice **15**(1), 78–96 (1999)
9. Chan, M., Woon, I., Kankanhalli, A.: Perceptions of information security in the workplace: linking information security climate to compliant behavior. J. Inf. Priv. Secur. **1**(3), 18–41 (2005)
10. Coleman, J.W.: The Criminal Elite: The Sociology of White Collar Crime. Macmillan (2001)
11. Copes, H.: Streetlife and the rewards of auto theft. Deviant Behav. **24**(4), 309–332 (2003)
12. Cram, W.A., D'Arcy, J., Proudfoot, J.G.: Seeing the forest and the trees: a meta-analysis of the antecedents to information security policy compliance. MIS Q. **34**(2), 525–554 (2019)
13. Cram, W.A., Proudfoot, J.G., D'Arcy, J., Alec, W.: Organizational information security policies: a review and research framework. Eur. J. Inf. Syst. **26**(6), 605–641 (2017)

14. Cromwell, P., Thurman, Q.: The devil made me do it: use of neutralizations by shoplifters. Deviant Behav. **24**(6), 535–550 (2003)
15. Fritsche, I.: Account strategies for the violation of social norms: integration and extension of sociological and social psychological typologies. J. Theory Soc. Behav. **32**(4) (2002)
16. Harrington, S.J.: The effect of codes of ethics and personal denial of responsibility on computer abuse judgments and intentions. MIS Q. **20**(3), 257–278 (1996)
17. Henry, S., Eaton, R.: Degrees of Deviance: Student Accounts of Their Deviant Behavior. Avebury (1989)
18. ISO/IEC29100. ISO/IEC 29100:2011(en): Information technology—Security techniques—Privacy framework
19. HIPAA Journal. Healthcare data breach statistics (2018). https://www.hipaajournal.com/healthcare-data-breach-statistics/
20. Klockars, C.B.J.: The Professional Fence. Tavistock Pubns (1975)
21. Lim, V.K.G.: The it way of loafing on the job: cyberloafing, neutralizing and organizational justice. J. Organ. Behav.: Int. J. Ind. Occup. Organ. Psychol. Behav. **23**(5), 675–694 (2002)
22. Marshall, M.N.: Sampling for qualitative research. Fam. Pract. **13**(6), 522–526 (1996)
23. Maruna, S., Copes, H.: What have we learned from five decades of neutralization research? Crime Justice **32**, 221–320 (2005)
24. Minor, W.W.: Techniques of neutralization: a reconceptualization and empirical examination. J. Res. Crime Delinq. **18**(2), 295–318 (1981)
25. Parks, R., Xu, H., Chu, C.-H., Lowry, P.B.: Examining the intended and unintended consequences of organisational privacy safeguards. Eur. J. Inf. Syst. **26**(1), 37–65 (2017)
26. Piquero, N.L., Tibbetts, S.G., Blankenship, M.B.: Examining the role of differential association and techniques of neutralization in explaining corporate crime. Deviant Behav. **26**(2), 159–188 (2005)
27. Rogers, J.W., Buffalo, M.D.: Neutralization techniques: toward a simplified measurement scale. Pac. Sociol. Rev. **17**(3), 313–331 (1974)
28. Narayana Samy, G., Ahmad, R., Ismail, Z.: Security threats categories in healthcare information systems. Health Inform. J. **16**(3), 201–209 (2010)
29. Silic, M., Barlow, J.B., Back, A.: A new perspective on neutralization and deterrence: predicting shadow it usage. Inf. Manag. **54**(8), 1023–1037 (2017)
30. Siponen, M., Vance, A., Willison, R.: New insights into the problem of software piracy: the effects of neutralization, shame, and moral beliefs. Inf. Manag. **49**(7), 334–341 (2012)
31. Siponen, M.T., Vance, A.: Neutralization: new insights into the problem of employee information systems security policy violations. MIS Q.: Manag. Inf. Syst. **34**(SPEC. ISSUE 3), 487–502 (2010)
32. Sutherland, E.H., Cressey, D.R., Luckenbill, D.F.: Principles of Criminology. Altamira Press (1992)
33. Sykes, G.M., Matza, D.: Techniques of neutralization: a theory of delinquency. Am. Sociol. Rev. **22**(6), 664–670 (1957)
34. Teh, P.-L., Ahmed, P.K., D'Arcy, J.: What drives information security policy violations among banking employees? Insights from neutralization and social exchange theory. J. Glob. Inf. Manag. **23**(1), 44–64 (2015)
35. Verizon: Data breach investigations report. Verizon Bus. J. 1–77 (2019)

36. Wall, J., Lowry, P.B., Barlow, J.B.: Organizational violations of externally governed privacy and security rules: explaining and predicting selective violations under conditions of strain and excess. J. Assoc. Inf. Syst. **17**(1), 39–76 (2015)
37. Wartenberg, D., Thompson, W.D.: Privacy versus public health: the impact of current confidentiality rules. Am. J. Public Health **100**(3), 407–412 (2010)
38. Willison, R., Warkentin, M.: Beyond deterrence: an expanded view of employee computer abuse. MIS Q. **37**(1), 1–20 (2013)

Data Protection and Machine Learning for Security

Unsupervised Machine Learning for Card Payment Fraud Detection

Mario Parreno-Centeno$^{(\boxtimes)}$, Mohammed Aamir Ali, Yu Guan, and Aad van Moorsel

Newcastle University, Newcastle upon Tyne, UK
{m.parreno-centeno1,m.a.ali2,yu.guan,aad.vanmoorsel}@ncl.ac.uk

Abstract. Credit card fraud is one of the most common cybercrimes experienced by consumers today. Machine learning approaches are increasingly used to improve the accuracy of fraud detection systems. However, most of the approaches proposed so far have been based on supervised models, i.e., models trained with labelled historical fraudulent transactions, thus limiting the ability of the approach to recognise unknown fraud patterns. In this paper, we propose an unsupervised fraud detection system for card payments transactions. The unsupervised approach learns the characteristics of normal transactions and then identify anomalies as potential frauds. We introduce the challenges on modelling card payment transactions and discuss how to select the best features. Our approach can reduce the equal error rate (EER) significantly over previous approaches (from 11.2% to 8.55%ERR), for a real-world transaction dataset.

Keywords: Card payments · Fraud detection · Machine learning · Deep learning · Card Not Present · Unsupervised learning

1 Introduction

The value of global non-cash transactions is growing every year and it is estimated to reach beyond 720 billion of dollars in 2020 [8]. Figure 1 breaks down the total transactions value by global growth regions, i.e., North America, Europe, Mature Asia-Pacific (APAC), Emerging Asia, Central Europe Middle East and Africa (CEMEA), and Latin America (LATAM), between 2012 and 2021 (note that values between 2019 and 2021 are estimated). There is a clear increasing trending which is significantly stronger in emerging Asia and CEMEA. In these regions, where the card network development is relatively immature, the proliferation of card use is mainly due to the increase in mobile payments and wallets. On the other hand, in mature markets such as North America, Europe and mature APAC, the adoption of Near Field Communication (NFC)/contactless technology has powered the increment of the card operations.

With the growth of the value of global card payments transactions, fraud activities and losses related to them have increased as well. During the last few

© Springer Nature Switzerland AG 2020
S. Kallel et al. (Eds.): CRiSIS 2019, LNCS 12026, pp. 247–262, 2020.
https://doi.org/10.1007/978-3-030-41568-6_16

years, most of the losses are related to Card Not Present interfaces [32], which refers to online, telephone and mail transactions, in which the card is not physically present at the merchant. The most recent report on card payments fraud of the European Central Bank specified that Card Not Present fraud increased 66% over a period of five years with an approximate 1000 EUR millions of losses in 2016 in Europe [13].

Fighting fraud is a difficult task, and merchants are very sensitive to the fact that overhead associated with security measures (such as PINs) may degrade the customer experience. Moreover, security procedures against online fraud that require extensive personal information can also turn in another source of vulnerability. For example, this information may be exposed after a data breach, and once stolen, it can be used in fraudulent activities.

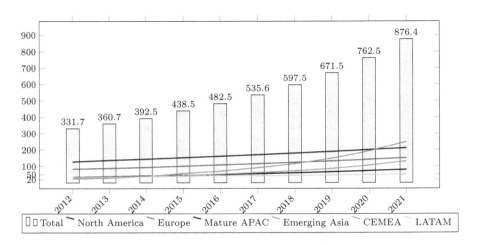

Fig. 1. Estimated value of world wide non-cash transactions from 2012 to 2021 [38].

The first Fraud Detection Systems (FDSs) for Card Not Present (CNP) transactions were based in rules, i.e., a set of thresholds established by experts trigger the alarm. However, card payments ecosystem is fast-changing and rules used in establishing fraudulent activity are likely to become ineffective or obsolete as time passes. More recently, machine learning techniques (ML) have been used to improve detection dynamically [27]. The ML approach learns fraudulent and/or normal patterns from past transactions to inform its fraud detection.

Most of the ML approaches for card payment fraud detection proposed so far are based on *supervised* learning techniques, i.e., the model is trained to find previously known fraud patterns. Thus, the model will not be able to identify *unknown* fraudulent patterns. Furthermore, transactional datasets used to train supervised fraud detection models are often highly skewed toward the number of samples of normal transactions compared to fraudulent ones. Usually, the percentage of fraudulent transactions is between 0.1% and 0.5% [7]. In this scenario, misclassification arises because of the difficulty of the FDS to learn fraud patterns.

In this paper, we propose an unsupervised approach which learns the patterns of normal transactions to detect potentially fraudulent transactions. Thus, it can detect previously undiscovered types of fraud and it does not rely on labeling fraudulent transactions within the data set. We study several Machine Learning and Deep Learning models: an autoencoder, a Multivariate Gaussian distribution and a One Class Support Vector Machine (OC-SVM, proposed already in the literature [17]). We conduct the experiments using a real-world transaction dataset from a European acquirer (the organisation that processes credit card transactions for its merchants). Furthermore, we study the importance of the transactional attributes and show their effect on the detection performance.

In summary, the contributions of this paper are as follows:

- a survey of the state of the art card payment fraud detection systems proposed so far.
- an exhaustive description of the challenges of applying machine learning approaches to detect card payment fraud.
- an evaluation of different unsupervised approaches on real-world card payment transactions dataset.
- an assessment of the effectiveness of feature selection approaches.

This paper is organized as follows. Section 2 introduces a set of well-established performance metrics and Sect. 3 discusses the traditional fraud detection systems and those based on machine learning techniques proposed so far. Section 5 describes the feature selection process and discuss the importance of the transaction's attribute. Section 4 introduces the dataset used to evaluate our approach. Section 6 discusses the performance of the unsupervised approach proposed based on three different algorithms and the trade-off number of attributes-performance. Section 7 concludes the paper.

2   Evaluation Metrics

In this section we introduce a set of well-established performance metrics which will be used throughout this work to evaluate the proposed FDS, and to compare its performance in terms of:

- The false acceptance rate, or FAR, is the measure of the likelihood that the fraud detection system will incorrectly accept a payment (incorrect since it is fraudulent). A system FAR is stated as the ratio of the number of false acceptances divided by the number of transactions considered.
- The false rejection rate, or FRR, is the measure of the likelihood that the fraud detection system will incorrectly reject a legal transaction. A system FRR is stated as the ratio of the number of false recognitions divided by the total number of transactions.

- Equal Error Rate (ERR) is the percentage value when FAR and FRR are equal. The ERR identifies under which parameter settings the proportion of false acceptances is equal to the proportion of false rejections. The lower the equal error rate value, the better the fraud detection system.
- Receiver Operating Characteristic curve (ROC curve), is a graphical plot that illustrates the diagnostic ability of a binary classifier system as its discrimination threshold varies. The ROC curve is created by plotting the true positive rate (TPR) against the false positive rate (FPR) at various threshold settings. The true-positive rate is also known as sensitivity or recall. Furthermore, it can be calculated a 1-FRR. A diagonal (the line with intercept one and slope minus one) can be introduced to divide the ROC space. Points above the diagonal represent good classification results (better than random), points below the line represent poor results (worse than random). The intersection between the curve with the diagonal indicates the ERR.

3 Machine Learning Approaches for Card Fraud Detection

In this section, we discuss some of the machine learning approaches proposed so far. We classify them in supervised and unsupervised systems. The distinction of the group is done based on whether the specific target value to predict is known for the available samples and in the manner that the algorithm is trained.

Table 1. Card payment fraud detection approaches based in unsupervised machine learning techniques

Authors	Year	Techniques	Dataset	Quantitative results
Aleskerov et al. [1]	1997	Auto-associative NN	Synthetic	Yes
Quah et al. [26]	2008	Self Organized Maps	Collected	No
Srivastava et al. [30]	2008	Hidden Markov model	Synthetic	Yes
Bhusari et al. [6]	2011	Hidden Markov model	Synthetic	Yes
KhanT et al. [22]	2011	Hidden Markov model	Synthetic	Yes
Iyer et al. [19]	2011	Hidden Markov model	Synthetic	Yes
Hejazi et al. [17]	2013	One-class SVM	Collected	Yes
Bansal et al. [2]	2014	Self Organized Maps	Collected	Yes
Tech et al. [31]	2014	K-Menas	Synthetic	No

3.1 Supervised Learning

The emphasis on card payments fraud detection systems is on supervised classification methods. It is a discriminative technique trained to find previously known fraud patterns. In classification problems, the system scores the input transaction based in similarities with the attributes of the previously seen fraudulent patterns. Depending on whether the score exceeds a predefined threshold, the transaction will be classified such as legitimate or fraudulent.

Neural Networks (NNs) were one of the first ML techniques use to develop FDS more than 20 years ago and they have become very popular since then. In 1994, [16] developed a fraud detection system based on a 3-layers P-RCE feedforward network. They used a dataset of transactions processed by Mellon Bank during six months of 1991. The original training dataset was sampled to include 3.33% of fraudulent accounts and a feature selection process was applied to the original group of attributes. The results showed that when the system flagged 50 accounts as fraudulent per day, 40% of fraudulent transactions were detected. That meant an improvement of the previous operative FDS based on rules. In [7] an FDS was proposed combining a NN with a rule-based approach. Both modules were combined in a unique sequential system improving the FRR but decreasing the TPR. Reference [24] compared the accuracy of an Artificial Neural Network (ANN) with a Bayesian Belief network. BBN performed better. Reference [15] compared the performance of an FDS based in a NN with four other systems based in an Artificial Immune Systems (AIS), a Naive Bayes (NB), a Bayesian Network (BN) and a Decision Tree (DT) algorithms. The NN and the AIS methods obtained the best accuracy results. [3] compared the performance of FDSs based in two different NNs, a Committed Neural Network and a Clustered Committed Neural Network. The Clustered Committed network architecture showed better detection results. More recently, [14] compared the performance of a NN with a Convolutional Neural Network (CNN), a Random Forest (RF) and a Support Vector Machine (SVM). CNN, RF, and SVM obtained better accuracy results than the approach based on a NN.

In [20] an FDS based on the cardholders profiles was proposed using Recurrent Neural Networks (RNNs). They conclude that a base model based on an RF performed similarly to the proposed deep learning model.

[34] proposed a game-theoretic approach. They model the interaction between an attacker and an FDS such as a multi-stage game between two players both trying to maximize financial gain.

In 2010 [5] compare the accuracy of SVM, RF and Logistic Regression (LR). RF obtained the highest accuracy with a 78% F-score, followed by LR with 70% and SVM with 62%.

In [28] the authors compared the effectiveness of two FDSs based in an SVM and DT algorithms. The dataset was the same used in [5]. DT obtained the best accuracy rate with approximately 95% while SVM 93%.

[37] conducted a study to show whether transaction aggregation may improve the fraud detection rate. The analysis showed that RF, LR, SVM, KNN and Quadratic Discriminant (QDA) improve their accuracy with aggregation. However, DT (CART) did not. They showed the result in two independent datasets from two banks. In both analyses, QDA obtained the highest detection accuracy.

Machine Learning (ML) techniques have demonstrated to be useful to detect fraudulent payments transactions, but keeping a low FAR with a high detection rate is a difficult task. We have seen that FDS has a high FAR when keeping a high detection rate, [4]. FAR has a high impact on the effectiveness of the system. It has associated a cost and customer relations are directly affected.

On the other hand, one characteristic present on all the real card fraud transactional datasets used to train the model is that they are very imbalanced. Percentage of fraudulent transactions is extremely lower than that for legitimate transactions. Usually, the percentage of fraudulent transactions is just between 0.1% and 0.5% [7]. In this scenario, misclassification arises because of the difficulty of the FDS to learn the fraud patterns.

3.2 Unsupervised Learning

One of the main advantages of using unsupervised techniques in card fraud detection system is the possibility of found undiscovered fraudulent patterns. However, approaches for card fraud detection systems based on unsupervised techniques are less common.

In 1997, an FDS based in an auto-associative NN was proposed in [1]. Differently from the FDSs based in Supervised Neural Networks proposed in [16] and [7], this model was trained only with legitimate transactions (300 samples). They test the approach in a synthetic dataset generated with a Gaussian model. Each transaction consists of four attributes and the rate of normal samples was 5:1. The results of the test showed that the system classified correctly all the legitimate transactions and misclassified 15.09% of the fraudulent transactions. The limitation of this system is that they used one network per customer and they tested the approach only in synthetic data simulated from a Gaussian distribution.

In 2008, an FDS based on a Hidden Markov Model (HMM) was proposed in [30]. Same that in [1], this FDS created a spending habit model for each cardholder. The category of items purchased was represented as the underlying finite Markov chain. The transactions were observed through the stochastic process that produces the sequence of the amount of money spent on each transaction. The observation symbols were defined clustering the purchase values of the historical transactions of each cardholder. They were clustered in three price ranges low, medium and high. They tested the system in a synthetic dataset. The test results showed the best result of 80% of accuracy.

In 2014, [2] compared two approaches based on SOM and ID3 algorithms. The approaches clustered the data in four groups low, high, risky and highly risky. Both methods were tested in four datasets including 500, 100, 1500 and 2000 transactions (not more information was specified about the data). SOM had slightly better FPR (23.52% and 28% respectively) and 20% better TPR than ID3 (92.5% and 72.5%). Furthermore, the authors conclude that using the longest dataset, FPR improved 50% and TPR 20%.

In the same year, an unsupervised FDS based on a K-Means algorithm was suggested in [31]. The system was tested in a synthetic dataset. Some of the attributes of the dataset were transaction ID, transaction amount, transaction country, transaction date, credit card number, merchant category id, cluster id and indicative of fraud. The classification classes were the same four groups of the previous approach [2] i.e. low, high, risky and high risky. The authors did not show quantitatively the results.

Table 1 synthesizes the main aspects i.e. authors, technique, type of dataset and analysis of quantitative results for each of the unsupervised approaches reviewed in this section. We can see that only two of the approaches [2,17] were tested in real-world data while showing quantitative results. Between these two approaches, the one based on the OC-SVM model [17] achieved a higher accuracy result i.e. 93%.

4   Dataset

A card transnational payments dataset is a vector of m transactions $\mathbf{t}$:

$$\mathbf{T} = (\mathbf{t}_1, ..., \mathbf{t}_m) \tag{1}$$

Each transaction can be seen as a data tuple of d attributes a:

$$\mathbf{t}_i = (a_1, ..., a_d) \tag{2}$$

In the unsupervised card fraud detection literature, only a few publications use real card payments transactional datasets [15]. It is complicated access to transactional datasets because:

- Anonymity and security reasons [36] i.e. financial institutions usually do not make public the private information of their customers.
- Companies are not in the position to share sensitive information with their competitors.
- Usually, reveal information concerned to fraud detection systems is declared to violate vital security interests.

To show the effectiveness of our approach, we use an anonymised publicly available dataset realized for a leader in electronic transactions [25]. The datasets contain transactions made by credit cards by European cardholders. Each transaction consists of 30 features. To preserve the confidentiality of the customers most of the variables are the principal components transformation of the original values and features name are not specified for most of the attributes. Only features 'Time' and 'Amount' preserve the original value and authors describe the attribute. 'Time' is the seconds elapsed between each transaction and the first transaction in the dataset. The feature 'Amount' is the economic transaction amount. No more extra background information has been given for the rest of the features.

Furthermore, each transaction has associated a label which indicates whether the transaction is either legitimate or fraudulent i.e. equal to 1 if the transaction is fraudulent and equal to 0 otherwise.

However, the authors of the dataset have not specified how they have flagged the fraudulent transaction and they have not given a proof that 100% of fraudulent transactions are detected.

The dataset includes transactions that occurred over two days, where 492 out of 284,807 are fraudulent transactions. Note that the dataset is highly unbalanced, the positive class (frauds) account for 0.172% of all transactions.

We normalize the feature Time and Amount with the max-min technique. Furthermore, we transform the feature Time to indicate the hour of the day which the transaction in the following manner:

$$f(t) = \left[\frac{t}{60 * 60} \% 24 \right].$$

To show the performance of each of the proposed approaches in Sect. 6, we have split the original dataset in a Training dataset including 75% of the legitimate transactions and a testing dataset including the 25% of the legitimate transactions and all the fraudulent transactions and we use 10 folder cross-validation (for the normal samples).

5   Feature Selection

Most of the FDS in the literature use a feature selection process because: - Improve training time: some models are computationally intensive when building the models. If they compute lower-dimensional data, the time to train the model will be lower. - Improve the response of real-time systems: FDS is expected to detect fraudulent transactions in real-time. Detection can be faster if the number of attributes of each transaction is lower. Some authors reduce the number of attributes of the system significantly, for example in [15] the number of attributes was reduced from 33 to 17.

Some of the techniques to reduce the feature dimensional space are GA and PCA [33].

To compare the accuracy between different approaches is common training the system in several datasets, each with a different number of attributes. In [16], the authors compared the performance of an FDS when using two different groups of attributes. One of the groups included payment-related information. The results showed that the model trained without payment-related information increased accuracy.

We have used an extra-Trees algorithm to calculate the importance of the features of the dataset such as in [23]. We use the depth of the node assigned to each of the features to calculate the relative importance of that feature. Features on the top of the tree contribute to a higher rate to the final prediction of the model. To reduce the variance of the estimation, we used the average between several randomized trees.

Figure 2 shows the relevance importance of the features obtained. We can observe that features 'V17' and 'V14' are relatively much more informative than other features. Later, we will test the accuracy of the different approaches taking into account different groups of features.

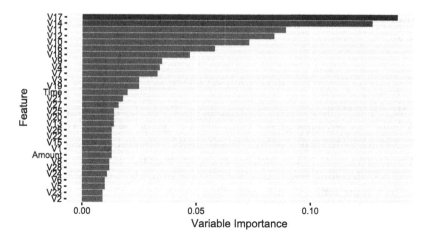

Fig. 2. Feature importance.

6   Proposed Approaches for Card Payments FDS

We propose an unsupervised FDS for card payments transactions. We compare the performance of three systems based on a deep learning technique (autoencoder) and two ML models i.e. multivariate Gaussian distribution model and OC-SVM (the last one previously used in [17] to detect fraudulent payment transactions obtaining the highest accuracy of the all unsupervised approaches reviewed in Sect. 3).

In our system, transactions are collected and recorded i.e. for two days. After that, during a window of time, fraudulent transactions will be flagged manually i.e. after a customer complaint, the same as in previous work showed in Sect. 3. At this point, we will use only normal transactions to train the model. Thus, the approach learns the characteristics of the normal samples. Once the model has been trained, each new transaction is classified as normal or fraudulent depending on how similar they are to the learned patterns according to the ML technique employed what we discuss next.

Deep Learning Autoencoders. Deep Learning is a popular method in image [12,29] and speech recognition [11,18] because of the superior classification performance obtained. It is a class of feature-learning methods, where the input data is transformed into an abstract representation, which has been widely used in pattern recognition and classification. Different levels of abstraction can be achieved by iterating layers.

We use a particular deep learning method called an autoencoder, which consists of an input layer, an output layer of equal size, and one or more hidden layers connecting them. In our model, the number of input units is equal to the number of selected attributes of the transaction. Autoencoders have been used for data representation [39] and more recently for authentication [9].

In this context, the input is the transaction vector $\mathbf{t}_i = (a_1, ..., a_d)$ and the output is:

$$\mathbf{u}(\mathbf{t}) = h_u(\mathbf{W}_u \mathbf{t} + \mathbf{b}_u), \tag{3}$$

where $\mathbf{W}_u \in \mathbb{R}^{d \times s}$ is a weight matrix, $\mathbf{b}_u \in \mathbb{R}^s$ is the bias vector, $a_1, a_2, ..., a_d \in \mathbb{R}^d$ are the attribute of the transaction i and h_u is called the activation function, which in this approach we define such the hyperbolic tangent function [21]. The process of the classification approach is performed in two stages: the encoding and decoding steps. In the encoding step, the input a is mapped to the abstract representation $\mathbf{u}(\mathbf{t})$ according to Eq. 3, and in the decoding step, the transformation is reconstructed to the output representation $\hat{\mathbf{t}}$, which is an approximation of the input transaction, according to the decoder function:

$$\hat{\mathbf{t}} = h_d[\mathbf{W}_d\{\mathbf{u}(\mathbf{t})\} + \mathbf{b}_d],$$

where $\mathbf{W}_d \in \mathbb{R}^{s \times d}$ is the weights decoding matrix, $\mathbf{b}_d \in \mathbb{R}^s$ is the decoding bias vectors, and h_d the decoding activation function. We restrict the degrees of freedom using a tied architecture, where the encoding matrix is the transpose of the decoding matrix, i.e. $\mathbf{W}_d = \mathbf{W}_u^t$ [35].

More than one hidden layer can be applied to achieve higher flexibility (and abstraction) in the model. In a multiple layers architecture, encoders and decoders are stacked symmetrically, where the output from the kth encoder, is the input of the $k + 1^{th}$ encoder.

Once the model has been training using backpropagation, we compute the mean squared error (MSE) between the original transaction t and its representation $\hat{t}$ on the output of the autoencoder, obtaining a validation match score. Here, we classify the instance such as normal or fraudulent based on a decision threshold.

Multivariate Gaussian Distribution. Given the card payments transnational dataset $\mathbf{T} = (\mathbf{t}_1, ..., \mathbf{t}_m)$ we will take into account only those transactions labeled as a normal. We assume that each attribute is normally distributed and we calculate the Gaussian parameters i.e. the mean μ_i and variance σ^2 for each of the features as follow:

$$\mu_i = \frac{1}{m}\Sigma_{j=1}^m a_i^{(j)} \tag{4}$$

$$\sigma_i^2 = \frac{1}{m}\Sigma_{j=1}^m (a_i^{(j)} - \mu_i)^2 \tag{5}$$

where $i \in \{1, 2, ..., d\}$ and d equal to the number of features.

Given a new transaction, we will calculate the probability to belong to the distribution as follow:

$$P(\mathbf{t}) = P(a_1; \mu_1, \sigma_1^2)P(a_2; \mu_2, \sigma_2^2)...P(a_d; \mu_d, \sigma_d^2) =$$

$$= \prod_{j=1}^{d} P(\mathbf{a}_j; \mu_j, \sigma_j^2) = \prod_{j=1}^{d} \frac{1}{\sigma_j \sqrt{2\pi}} e^{-(a_j - \mu_j)^2 / 2\sigma_j^2} \qquad (6)$$

And we will consider the transaction as fraudulent if $P(\mathbf{t}) < \epsilon$ where ϵ is the probability threshold.

6.1 Comparison of Unsupervised Approaches for Card Payment Fraud Detection

In this section, we compare the performance of the two proposed approaches i.e. autoencoder and multivariate Gaussian model, with an approach proposed in [17] which was based on an OC-SVM model. So, we compare the performance of these approaches:

- an autoencoder with one hidden layer and 15 hidden units.
- a multivariate Gaussian model.
- a one-class SVM.

And we will consider the transaction as fraudulent if $P(\mathbf{t}) < \epsilon$ where ϵ is the probability threshold.

Table 2 shows the EER obtained by each model. We can see that the autoencoder and Gaussian models get the best EER values, 9.8% and 9.7% respectively. On the other hand, OC-SVM obtains the worst EER value (11.2%).

Figure 3 shows the ROC curve of the three different models. The ROC curve of the autoencoder and Gaussian models are very similar. On the other hand, although the OC-SVM is the model with the highest EER, it keeps a higher True Acceptance Rate ($TAR = 1 - FRR$), when the FAR is very small i.e. approximately $0, 1\%$.

Table 2. ERR of three different unsupervised models on the dataset shown previously.

Models	ERR
Autoencoder	9.8%
Gaussian	9.7%
OC-SVM	11.2%

6.2 Feature Importance Experiments

We have seen that autoencoder and Gaussian models obtained very similar accuracy results. However, while deep learning models can manage adequately high dimensional inputs [10], Gaussian models work better on low dimensional space

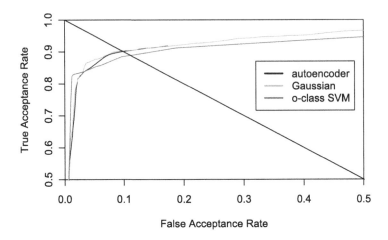

Fig. 3. ROC curves of the three unsupervised approaches i.e autoencoder, Gaussian and oc-svm used to model normal card payment transactions.

problems. Thus, we are going to reduce the number of features of the transactions from 30 to 7 using a five layers autoencoder i.e. the embedded representation of the middle layer of the autoencoder is used as the input of the Gaussian model. Figure 4 shows the ROC curve of the approach and the ROC curve of the Gaussian model for comparison. We can see that EER does not improve.

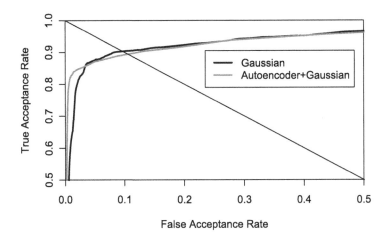

Fig. 4. ROC curve of the model autoencoder+GMM train end to end.

On the other hand, we are going to test the Gaussian model when changing the input vector to take into account different number of attributes. We group the attributes according to the importance calculated in Sect. 5. Figure 5 show the ROC curve of the results. We can observe that the model taking into account the two more informative features has the lowest EER (8.55%) and the model only taken into account the most informative feature has the highest (12.5%).

When the model includes features one by one (by incremental importance), the EER increase constantly until including 8 features, after that the EER increase but not improving the accuracy of the model taking into account four or fewer features (except the model taking into account one feature).

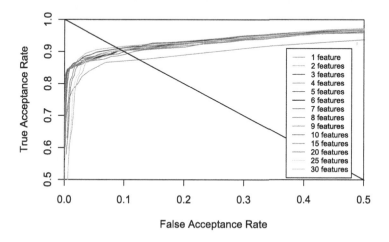

Fig. 5. ROC curves of Gaussian models taking into account different groups of features by importance.

7 Conclusion

In this paper, we proposed two unsupervised ML approaches to model card payments transactions and detect fraudulent activity. The approaches are based on a deep learning technique i.e. an autoencoder and in an ML technique i.e. a Gaussian model. Both systems improve the detection accuracy over a previously proposed approach based on a One-class SVM which was the model with the highest accuracy in the literature and tested on real-world data.

We also have shown that in this case, deep learning feature extraction does not help to improve the accuracy of the Gaussian model. However, taking into account only the two most important attributes selected by a tree model, EER of the Gaussian model improves from 9.7% to 8.5% ERR.

References

1. Aleskerov, E., et al.: CARDWATCH: a neural network based database mining system for credit card fraud detection. In: Proceedings of the IEEE/IAFE 1997 Computational Intelligence for Financial Engineering, pp. 220–226 (1997)

2. Bansal, M.: Credit card fraud detection using self organised map. Int. J. Inf. Comput. Technol. **4**, 1343–1348 (2014)

3. Bekirev, A.S., Klimov, V.V., Kuzin, M.V., Shchukin, B.A.: Payment card fraud detection using neural network committee and clustering. Opt. Mem. Neural Netw. **24**(3), 193–200 (2015). https://doi.org/10.3103/S1060992X15030030

4. Benson Edwin Raj, S., et al.: Analysis on credit card fraud detection methods. In: 2011 International Conference on Computer, Communication and Electrical Technology, pp. 152–156, March 2011

5. Bhattacharyya, S., Jha, S., Tharakunnel, K., Westland, J.C.: Data mining for credit card fraud: a comparative study. Decis. Support Syst. **50**(3), 602–613 (2011). https://doi.org/10.1016/j.dss.2010.08.008, http://www.sciencedirect.com/science/article/pii/S0167923610001326, on quantitative methods for detection of financial fraud

6. Bhusari, V., Patil, S.: Application of hidden Markov model in credit card fraud detection. Int. J. Distrib. Parallel Syst. **2**, 203 (2011)

7. Brause, R., et al.: Neural data mining for credit card fraud detection. In: Proceedings 11th International Conference on Tools with Artificial Intelligence, pp. 103–106 (1999)

8. Capgemini; BNP Paribas: World payments report 2017. Technical report (2017)

9. Centeno, M.P., et al.: Smartphone continuous authentication using deep learning autoencoders. In: 2017 15th Annual Conference on Privacy, Security and Trust (PST), pp. 147–1478, August 2017. https://doi.org/10.1109/PST.2017.00026

10. Centeno, M.P., et al.: Mobile based continuous authentication using deep features. In: Proceedings of the 2nd International Workshop on Embedded and Mobile Deep Learning, EMDL 2018, pp. 19–24 (2018)

11. Deng, L., et al.: New types of deep neural network learning for speech recognition and related applications: an overview. In: 2013 IEEE International Conference on Acoustics, Speech and Signal Processing, pp. 8599–8603, May 2013

12. Dong, C., Loy, C.C., He, K., Tang, X.: Learning a deep convolutional network for image super-resolution. In: Fleet, D., Pajdla, T., Schiele, B., Tuytelaars, T. (eds.) ECCV 2014. LNCS, vol. 8692, pp. 184–199. Springer, Cham (2014). https://doi.org/10.1007/978-3-319-10593-2_13

13. European Central Bank: Fifth report on card fraud. Technical report (2018)

14. Fu, K., Cheng, D., Tu, Y., Zhang, L.: Credit card fraud detection using convolutional neural networks. In: Hirose, A., Ozawa, S., Doya, K., Ikeda, K., Lee, M., Liu, D. (eds.) ICONIP 2016. LNCS, vol. 9949, pp. 483–490. Springer, Cham (2016). https://doi.org/10.1007/978-3-319-46675-0_53

15. Gadi, M.F.A., Wang, X., do Lago, A.P.: Credit card fraud detection with artificial immune system. In: Bentley, P.J., Lee, D., Jung, S. (eds.) ICARIS 2008. LNCS, vol. 5132, pp. 119–131. Springer, Heidelberg (2008). https://doi.org/10.1007/978-3-540-85072-4_11

16. Ghosh, S., Reilly, D.L.: Credit card fraud detection with a neural-network. In: 1994 Proceedings of Twenty-Seventh Hawaii International Conference on System Science, pp. 621–630 (1994). https://doi.org/10.1109/HICSS.1994.323314

17. Hejazi, M., et al.: One-class support vector machines approach to anomaly detection. Appl. Artif. Intell. **27**, 351–366 (2013)

18. Hinton, G., et al.: Deep neural networks for acoustic modeling in speech recognition: the shared views of four research groups. IEEE Sig. Process. Mag. **6**, 82–97 (2012)

19. Iyer, D., et al.: Credit card fraud detection using Hidden Markov Model. In: 2011 World Congress on Information and Communication Technologies, pp. 1062–1066, December 2011

20. Jurgovsky, J., et al.: Sequence classification for credit-card fraud detection. Exp. Syst. Appl. **100**, 234–245 (2018). https://doi.org/10.1016/j.eswa.2018.01.037

21. Karlik, B., Olgac, A.: Performance analysis of various activation functions in generalized MLP architectures of neural networks. Int. J. Artif. Intell. Exp. Syst. (IJAE) **1**(4), 111–122 (2010)

22. KhanT, A., et al.: Credit card fraud detection using hidden Markov model **2**, 1062–1066 (2011)

23. Louppe, G.: Understanding random forests: from theory to practice. Ph.D. thesis, October 2014

24. Maes, S., Tuyls, K., Vanschoenwinkel, B., Manderick, B.: Credit card fraud detection using Bayesian and neural networks. In: Maciunas, R.J. (ed.) Interactive Image-Guided Neurosurgery. American Association Neurological Surgeons, pp. 261–270 (1993)

25. Pozzolo, A.D., Caelen, O., Johnson, R.A., Bontempi, G.: Calibrating probability with undersampling for unbalanced classification. In: Proceedings of - 2015 IEEE Symposium Series on Computational Intelligence, SSCI 2015, pp. 159–166 (2015). https://doi.org/10.1109/SSCI.2015.33

26. Quah, J.T., et al.: Real-time credit card fraud detection using computational intelligence. Exp. Syst. Appl. **35**(4), 1721–1732 (2008)

27. Ryman-Tubb, N.F., Krause, P., Garn, W.: How artificial intelligence and machine learning research impacts payment card fraud detection: a survey and industry benchmark. Eng. Appl. Artif. Intell. **76**, 130–157 (2018). https://doi.org/10.1016/j.engappai.2018.07.008, http://www.sciencedirect.com/science/article/pii/S0952197618301520

28. Sahin, Y., Duman, E.: Detecting credit card fraud by decision trees and support vector machines. In: International Multi Conference of Engineers and Computer Scientists, IMECS 2011, vol. 1, pp. 442–447, March 2011

29. Socher, R., et al.: Convolutional-recursive deep learning for 3D object classification. In: Proceedings of the 25th International Conference on Neural Information Processing Systems, NIPS 2012, vol. 1, pp. 656–664 (2012)

30. Srivastava, A., et al.: Credit card fraud detection using hidden Markov model. IEEE Trans. Dependable Secure Comput. **5**, 37–38 (2008)

31. Tech, V.M.: Fraud detection in credit card by clustering approach. Int. J. Comput. Appl. **98**(3), 975–8887 (2014)

32. Bryan, T., et al.: Card-Not-Present Fraud around the World. U.S. Payments Forum 1, March 2017. https://www.uspaymentsforum.org/wp-content/uploads/2017/03/CNP-Fraud-Around-the-World-WP-FINAL-Mar-2017.pdf

33. Ush, A., Khan, S., Akhtar, N., Qureshi, M.N.: Real-time credit-card fraud detection using artificial neural network tuned by simulated annealing algorithm

34. Vatsa, V., Sural, S., Majumdar, A.K.: A game-theoretic approach to credit card fraud detection. In: Jajodia, S., Mazumdar, C. (eds.) ICISS 2005. LNCS, vol. 3803, pp. 263–276. Springer, Heidelberg (2005). https://doi.org/10.1007/11593980_20

35. Vincent, P., et al.: Extracting and composing robust features with denoising autoencoders. In: Proceedings of the 25th International Conference on Machine Learning, ICML 2008, pp. 1096–1103 (2008). https://doi.org/10.1145/1390156.1390294

36. Wang, S.: A comprehensive survey of data mining-based accounting-fraud detection research. In: 2010 International Conference on Intelligent Computation Technology and Automation, vol. 1, pp. 50–53, May 2010. https://doi.org/10.1109/ICICTA.2010.831
37. Whitrow, C., Hand, D.J., Juszczak, P., Weston, D., Adams, N.M.: Transaction aggregation as a strategy for credit card fraud detection. Data Min. Knowl. Discov. **18**(1), 30–55 (2009). https://doi.org/10.1007/s10618-008-0116-z
38. WorldPay: The art and science of global payments a definitive report from Worldpay Global Payments Report, November 2018
39. Yaginuma, Y., et al.: Multi-sensor fusion model for constructing internal representation using autoencoder neural networks. In: Proceedings of International Conference on Neural Networks (ICNN 1996), vol. 3, pp. 1646–1651, June 1996

Intrusion Detection Study and Enhancement Using Machine Learning

Hela Mliki[1,2(✉)], Abir Hadj Kaceam[1,3], and Lamia Chaari[1,3]

[1] Laboratory of Technology and Smart Systems (LT2S),
Digital Research Center of Sfax (CRNS), University of Sfax, Sfax, Tunisia
`mliki.hela@gmail.com`, `hadjkaceamabir3@gmail.com`, `lamia.chaari@enis.rnu.tn`
[2] Science Faculty of Gabes, University of Gabes, Gabes, Tunisia
[3] Higher Institute of Computer Science and Multimedia of Sfax, University of Sfax,
Sfax, Tunisia

Abstract. IoT is an emerging technology, which represents a complex and heterogeneous environment. Thus, security in IoT could be an issue of concern, in particular detecting and identifying malicious events. Malicious events are triggered when anomalous traffic attempts to threaten and abuse the IoT network. Machine learning approaches provide interesting tools to detect new attacks and prevent unauthorized access. Therefore, the aim of this paper is to investigate and compare the performances of the classical machine learning methods: Support Vector Machine (SVM), K-Nearest Neighbor (KNN), and K-means. The performance metrics considered in this study are Accuracy, Detection Rate, False Alarm Rate, Recall, Precision, F1- Score, Time Training and Time Assigned Label. Then, a proposed solution for enhancement is elaborated by leveraging the multi-level tweak. The proposed solution shows the best performance results compared to classical machine learning methods for intrusion detection.

Keywords: Internet of Things (IoT) · Machine Learning (ML) · Intrusion Detection (ID).

1 Introduction

IoT extends the original Internet set and allows the connection of various smart objects via Internet, which produces massive data traffic in the network. Protecting the IoT network against intrusion attacks is a hot topic of research, since it is a heterogeneous environment and many of its protocols were conceived without security background [11,16]. Intrusion Detection System (IDS) is a solution for controlling and monitoring events in a network to mitigate intrusion and identify malicious activities such as Denial of Service (DoS), sinkhole, and probe attacks. IDS could be classified into three categories according to the detection method used: misuse detection, anomaly detection, and hybrid detection. Indeed, misuse detection is able to detect known attacks based on

© Springer Nature Switzerland AG 2020
S. Kallel et al. (Eds.): CRiSIS 2019, LNCS 12026, pp. 263–278, 2020.
https://doi.org/10.1007/978-3-030-41568-6_17

a rules dataset; yet, new attacks that are not considered in the rules dataset are unable to be detected via this method. Anomaly detection method builds a model that could distinguish between normal and anomalous traffic thanks to a building profile of normal behavior. Thus, new attacks that deviate from normal behavior could be detected and identified. Hybrid detection method leverages the misuse and anomaly detection method and builds two detection modules: one for new attacks detection, and another for known attacks detection [7,29]. Machine learning is the artificial intelligence subfield and allows the provision of predictive and classification analysis from data thanks to a variety of algorithms deployed for such a purpose. Hence, machine learning algorithms could be classified mainly into two categories as follows:

- Supervised algorithms, which generate a model by learning from labeled training data. The labeled data define the desired results.
- Unsupervised algorithms, which generate a model by learning from unlabeled training data and clustering the input data according to their statistical properties [5,10,20].

This paper investigates anomaly based IDS using machine learning approaches. It studies and analyzes classical recommended supervised and unsupervised algorithms in the literature (i.e., Support Vector Machine (SVM), K-nearest neighbors (KNN), and K-means) for intrusion detection. Then, we proposed a new approach as an enhancement to boost the performance of these classical machine learning algorithms. Therefore, we leveraged the multi-level tweak, which is a statistical model of parameters that vary at more than one level in the detection phases. The proposed approach has three methods to boost intrusion detection by deploying supervised, unsupervised and hybrid methods. In the first proposition for enhancement called SVM^2, we recommend the use of binary SVM at the first level of detection; then, the multi-class SVM at the second level of detection. Thus, SVM^2 is a supervised machine learning proposition. The second proposition called $k - means^2$, uses k-means++ as first level for detection; then, reuses k-means++ as a second level for detection. Thus, $k - means^2$ is an unsupervised machine learning proposition for enhancement. The third proposition called SVM+K, uses the binary SVM at the first level of detection and the K-means++ at the second level of detection. Thus, SVM+K is an hybrid proposition that combines supervised and unsupervised methods at different detection level.

The remainder of this paper is organized as follows: In Sect. 2, we present related works that study recent research works in the field of intrusion detection based machine learning for IoT network. In Sect. 3, we explore the NSL-KDD dataset, which is the widely used dataset for intrusion detection study. In Sect. 4, we consider and analyze the classical machine learning methods for intrusion detection: SVM, KNN and K-means. In Sect. 5, we develop and discuss our proposed approach for intrusion detection. Finally, the paper is concluded in Sect. 6.

2   Related Works

Recently, there are different research works that study anomaly based intrusion detection system. In this section we review some of them.

The research work in [33] proposed an intrusion detection framework that combines SVM with feature augmentation. The feature augmentation method aims to improve the quality of training data, which boost the SVM detection capability and reduces training time. The performance of the proposed solution was evaluated in terms of accuracy, detection rate, and false alarm rate.

Authors in [13] proposed an anomaly model for intrusion detection. The solution uses Information Gain as a feature selection method and improves the SVM detection method by a modified version of the Bat algorithm, where the randomization was enhanced with Lévy flights. The model was tested for the NSL-KDD dataset and the accuracy, detection rate and false alarms metrics were considered to evaluate the performance of the proposed solution.

In [12], authors study the distributed denial of service (DDoS) detection in IoT network traffic with different machine learning algorithms (i.e., K-nearest neighbors, random forests, decision trees, support vector machines, and deep neural networks). To build the dataset for training and testing the detection models, the normal traffic was collected from three IoT devices for 10 min. However, the DoS attack traffic was simulated. Then, the normal traffic, the Dos attack traffic, and spoofing source IP addresses, MAC addresses, and packet send times were combined to created the IoT traffic that has malicious events. The authors study the precision, Recall, False alarm, and accuracy performance metrics to evaluate the IoT traffic classification algorithms.

Authors in [1] investigate the performance of intrusion detection model based on SVM, random forest, and Extreme Learning Machine (ELM) machine learning techniques. Authors show that ELM outperforms other techniques in terms of accuracy, precision and recall performance metrics when it is about to analyze a huge data amount.

In [31], authors propose an adaptive collaboration intrusion detection solution to improve anomaly detection in a network. The authors propose a combination of SVM, DecisionTree (DT) and adaptive scheduling mechanisms as a solution to create an efficient distributed detection model. Performance was evaluated using KDDCUP99 dataset and the accuracy performance metric.

Research work in [2] proposes a multi-level hybrid intrusion detection solution. This solution combines Support Vector Machine (SVM) with Extreme Learning Machine (ELM) to improve anomaly detection. The studied performance metrics for evaluation are: accuracy, detection rate and False alarm.

Research works in [26,27] overview the features and performances of different widely used dataset in studying the intrusion detection system in a network (i.e., KDDCup 99, NSLKDD, and kyoto2006+). Indeed, the NSL-KDD dataset is an enhancement of the KDDCup99, which remove redundant and duplicate records from training and test sets. The KDDCup99 and NSLKDD datasets traffic are generated by simulation over a virtual computer network, whereas kyoto2006+ is generated on real three year-network traffic data from Honeypots of the Kyoto

University. Nevertheless, the kyoto2006+ dataset has a lack of information on particular attacks and ignore features with redundant records.

3 NSL-KDD Dataset Exploration

In order to fix issues of the KDD Cup 99 dataset, NSL-KDD dataset was proposed [27]. NSL-KDD [25] has been developed to resolve the weak spots of KDD Cup 99 dataset by removing redundant and duplicated records on the training and testing dataset [26,27]. Many researches have exploit this dataset to carry out their study such as feature selection, data stream, machine learning and intrusion detection [19,27,34]. Therefore, this dataset used to build our study.

3.1 Description of NSL-KDD

The dataset is split into two subset: 20% for testing and 80% for training [1]. The dataset consists of 41 features and each record is labeled as normal or anomalous. Table 1 shows observation on the training and testing dataset of the NSL-KDD, by providing information about the number of instances and time reading for training and testing datasets for subset. Table 2 shows the result of training dataset and the testing dataset in NSL-KDD dataset. NSL-KDD includes features categorized as Numeric, Nominal, and Binary as described in [22]. The anomalous records in the dataset are classified into one of four categories: Denial of service (DoS), Probing (Prob), Root2Local (R2L), and User2Root (U2R) [1,27]. Their description are as follows:

Table 1. Characteristics of the dataset.

Characteristic	Dataset	
	Training-dataset	Testing-dataset
Instances	125973	22544
Time of reading (sec)	6.874	0.778

Table 2. Occurrences number of normal and attack traffic.

Class	Samples in training-dataset	Samples in testing-dataset
Normal	67343	9711
Attack	58630	12833

– Denial of service attack (DoS): the intruder aims to block or restrict legitimate users access to computing resources or overloads them so that requests cannot be processed in real time [24,27].

- Users-to-root attack (U2R): the attacker explores vulnerabilities in order to win unauthorized access to privileges of local superuser (root access to the system). It is an attack type, through it the attacker connect into a victim system as the normal user account and exploit vulnerabilities in order to gain administrator privileges [24, 27].
- Remote-to-local attack (R2L): the attacker does not have access account to the victim machine, hence it tries to intrude into the remote machine system without having the account and to gain local access of the victim machine [24, 27].
- Probing attack (PROBE): the intruder aims to collect information by scanning the system or computer network in order to find vulnerabilities, which will be used later to launch attacks [24, 27].

Table 3 shows the sample amount of different types of attacks in training dataset and in the testing NSL-KDD dataset.

Table 3. Occurrence number of different types of attacks in training and testing dataset.

Attacks type	Number of samples in training-dataset	Number of samples in testing-dataset
DoS	45927	7458
Probe	11656	2421
R2L	995	2754
U2R	52	200

3.2 Data Pre-processing

The data pre-processing phase allows the noise decrease strained on the dataset. Indeed, this phase aims only to store noteworthy data. Moreover, it seeks to simplify subsequent treatments by using common strategies such as correction and normalization [3, 17]. In order to establish standard features values, this phase converts all non numerical values into numerical ones.

3.3 Preparing Dataset

Preparing Dataset phase focuses on evaluating and analyzing the features to be selected from the dataset. Features selection process by selecting a subset of relevant features from the original dataset features for use in model construct. Indeed, features selection is an important method in intrusion detection because it simplifies the model for interpretation, shortens the training times, and, increases the classifier's efficiency. Features selection are based on the following two common techniques for feature reduction:

- The wrapper technique, which generates relevant features subsets from a feature vector based on the learning algorithm performance [3,23].
- The filter technique, which generates relevant features subsets from a feature vector regardless of the learning algorithm performance. It evaluates features relevance according to heuristics based on general data characteristics [23].

The wrapper technique is considered to provide better selection of relevant features subsets than the filter technique. However, it has a significant computation time when the features number is large; and could increase over-fitting risk when the number of instances is insufficient [3,8,22].

In this work we used the Attribute Ratio (AR) method, which is a filter technique for features selection. It was proposed in [8,28], and can give better accuracy than the CFS (Correlation-based Feature Selection), IG (Information Gain) and GR (Gain Ratio) features selection methods. The AR feature selection formula is as follows:

$$AR(i) = MAX(CR(y)) \tag{1}$$

Here, CR represents the class ratio.

For numeric attributes, the CR is calculated as follows:

$$CR(y) = \frac{AVG(C(y))}{AVG(total)} \tag{2}$$

For binary attributes, the CR is calculated as follows:

$$CR(y) = \frac{Frequency(1)}{Frequency(0)} \tag{3}$$

3.4 Normalization

Normalization phase or features scaling is a method used to standardize the range of different data features values. The min-max normalization is a normalization method that consists in rescaling the features range to scale the range in $[0, 1]$ [3,21]. The min-max normalization general formula is as follows:

$$x' = \frac{(x - min(x))}{(max(x) - min(x))} \tag{4}$$

Here, x is an original value and x' is the normalized value. Figure 1(a) illustrates the different phases in classical solutions for intrusion detection.

4 Experiments and Results

In this section we will present the different performance metrics used to evaluate the mechanisms for intrusion detection. In addition, it draws a comparison between the different existed intrusion detection schema.

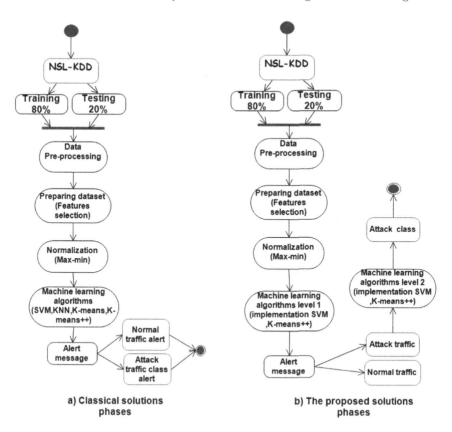

Fig. 1. Classical and proposed solutions phases for traffic classification.

4.1 Performance Metrics

The performance metrics for intrusion detection schema evaluation that we studied are: Accuracy, Detection Rate, False Alarm Rate, Recall, Precision, F1-Score, Time Training and Time Assigned Label.

Confusion Matrix. Called also an error matrix, it is a method for establishing a relationship between the current results and the predicted one. It is used to evaluate the Accuracy of a machine learning classifier [17,23,34]. The results of the confusion matrix are as follows:

- True Positive (TP): represents the normal traffics correctly classified by the generated model.
- True Negative (TN): represents the anomalous traffics correctly classified by the generated model.
- False Positive (FP): represents the normal traffics incorrectly classified by the generated model.

– False Negative(FN): represents the anomalous traffics incorrectly classified by the generated model.

Table 4 shows the confusion matrix for a machine learning classifier.

Table 4. Confusion matrix.

Actual	Predict	
	Normal	Attack
Normal	True Positive (TP)	False Positive (FP)
Attack	False Negative (FN)	True Negative (TN)

Accuracy. It is the ratio of the total number of true positive and true negative that are properly determined and divided by the total amount of the dataset positive and negative detection amount. The best Accuracy result is equal to 1.0 [22]. It is calculated by the following formula:

$$Accuracy = \frac{TP + TN}{TP + TN + FP + FN} \tag{5}$$

Detection Rate (DR). It is also called False Positive rate. It represents the correctly detected anomalous traffic instances. The Detection Rate best result is equal to 0.0, while the worst one is equal to 1.0 [1,22,23]. The Detection Rate formula is as follow:

$$DetectionRate = \frac{TP}{TP + FP} \tag{6}$$

False Alarm Rate (FAR). It is also known as the False Positive rate. It is about the incorrectly classified anomalous instances [6]. Its formula is defined as follow:

$$FalseAlarm = \frac{FP}{FP + TN} \tag{7}$$

Recall. It represents the amount of relevant instances detected. It represents the ratio of positive prediction to the total number of positive positive prediction [9,22,23]. It is defined as follows:

$$Recall = \frac{TP}{TP + FN} \tag{8}$$

Precision. It is the amount of relevant instances among the detected instances [1, 22, 23]. The precision formula is defined as follows:

$$Precision = \frac{TF}{TP + FP} \qquad (9)$$

Score. It combines Recall and Precision and it is used to evaluate the correctness of an experience [4]. Its formula is as follows:

$$F_1 \rightarrow Score = \frac{2 * precision * DetectionRate}{precision + DetectionRate} \qquad (10)$$

Time Training represents the time required for learning in the algorithms.

Time Assigned Label represents the time to assign label for the data to be classified.

4.2 Machine Learning Algorithms

There are three categories of machine learning algorithms: supervised, unsupervised and hybrid algorithms. The existing algorithms that we studied and evaluated are the SVM, KNN and K-means algorithms [2, 9, 17, 30]. Indeed, SVM and KNN are defined as the best algorithms for supervised machine learning mechanisms; whereas, the k-means is decided as the best unsupervised algorithm [1, 9, 14, 15]. These algorithms are implemented and evaluated within the NSL-KDD dataset. We draw a parallel between them using the following metrics: Accuracy, Detection Rate, False Alarm Rate, Recall, Precision, and Score.

SVM Mechanism. The SVM is a supervised algorithm that divides the space into planes and creates separating hyperplanes between them in order to classify data. Then, a new unseen data point is classified based on which side of the hyperplane it dives. There are many possible hyperplanes that could be selected to separate two data points' classes. The aim is, then, to find a plane that has the maximum distance between data points of both classes. This distance is defined as the margin. Maximizing the margin help future data points to be classified with confidence [32]. In our implementation we used SVM with linear kernel. In addition, we used the multiclass SVM, which is based on one-versus-all (called also "one-vs-the-rest") approach. In this approach a binary model is learned for each class that tries to separate that class from all of the other classes, resulting in as many binary models as there are classes. From our experiments for SVM we find that: Accuracy is equal to 92.8% of the total samples, the Detection Rate is equal to 0.918% of the total samples, the False Alarm is equal to 0.205% of the total samples, the Time Training is 3.753 s and the Time Assigned labels is 2038 s. Table 6 shows the evaluation results of SVM for attack and normal traffics for Precision, Recall and F1-score metrics.

KNN Mechanism. The KNN algorithm is a supervised algorithm used for the effective classifying objects. It builds the model by sorting the training dataset. To make a prediction for a new unseen data point, it finds the closest data points in the training dataset, which is considered as the nearest neighbors. Indeed, using a defined constant k, the algorithm assigns the unseen data point with the label that is the most frequent among the k training samples nearest to that unseen data point [35]. The Accuracy of the KNN algorithm depends on the k parameter, which represents the number of neighbors. We note from empirical experiments that $k = 2$ gives the best Accuracy (i.e., 92.62% of the total samples). We evaluated the KNN performance with $k = 2$ for precision, recall, F1 score, Accuracy, Detection Rate, False Alarm Rate, Time Training and the Time Assigned labels performance metrics. From our experiments we find that: Accuracy is equal to 92.6% of the total samples, the Detection Rate is equal to 0.687% of the total samples, the False Alarm is equal to 0.246% of the total samples, the Time Training is 495.395 s and the Time Assigned labels is 3106.4 s. Table 6 shows the evaluation results of KNN for attack and normal traffics for Precision, Recall and F1-score metrics.

K-means Mechanism. K-means is an unsupervised algorithm used to find patterns in an unlabeled dataset with n dimensions. This algorithm aims to generate k clusters from a given dataset by iteratively allocating each data point according to the existing features to one of the k clusters. Indeed, k refers to the number of centroids, which defines the cluster center needed for the dataset. After defining the k parameter, the algorithm allocates the unseen data point to the nearest cluster using the Euclidean distance [36]. We noted from empirical experiments that $k = 58$ gives the best Accuracy (i.e., 93% of the total samples). We evaluated the K-means performance with $k = 58$ for precision, recall, F1 score, Accuracy, Detection Rate, False Alarm Rate, Time Training and the Time Assigned labels performance metrics. From our experiments we find that: Accuracy is equal to 93.2%, of the total samples, the Detection Rate is equal to 0.856%, of the total samples, the False Alarm is equal to 0.13%, of the total samples, the Time Training is 144.909 s and the Time Assigned labels is 0.443 s. Table 6 shows the evaluation results of K-means for attack and normal traffics for Precision, Recall and F1-score metrics.

4.3   K-means++ Mechanism

K-means ++ algorithm is an enhancement of K-means, which aims to select the best initial random k parameter. Thus, it enhances the time efficiency and reduces the computational process of the K-means [18]. From our experiments we find that: Accuracy is equal to 93.2%, of the total samples, the Detection Rate is equal to 0.856%, of the total samples, the False Alarm is equal to 0.13%, of the total samples, the Time Training is 144.909 s and the Time Assigned labels is 0.443 s. Table 6 shows the evaluation results of K-means++ for attack and normal traffics for Precision, Recall and F1-score performance metrics.

4.4   Discussion and Comparison

We have established a thorough contrast between SVM, KNN, K-means and K-means++ performances metric and come out with the following results. Table 5 illustrates the comparison according to Accuracy, Detection Rate, False Alarm, Time Training and Time Assigned labels performance metrics. However, Table 6 illustrates the comparison according to Precision, recall and F1-measure metrics. From experiments results we conclude that SVM is the best one as a supervised mechanism, whereas k-means++ has the best performance metrics as an unsupervised mechanism. We highlight that SVM is better than K-means++ for Detection Rate, and Time Training performance metric. However, Accuracy, False Alarm and Time Assigned labels performance metrics have the best results under the K-means++ algorithm.

Table 5. Algorithms Comparison.

Algorithm	Accuracy (%)	Detection rate (%)	False alarm (%)	Time training (Sec)	Time assigned label (Sec)
SVM	92.8	0.918	0.205	3.753	2.038
KNN	92.6	0.687	0.246	495.395	3106.4
K-means	93.2	0.856	0.13	144.909	0.443
K-means++	93.2	0.856	0.13	144.909	0.443

Table 6. Performance measures for different algorithms (SVM, KNN, K-means, K-means++).

Algorithms	Traffic types	Precision	Recall	F1-score
SVM	Attack	0.91	0.97	0.91
	Normal	0.95	0.92	0.91
KNN	Attack	1.00	0.91	0.87
	Normal	0.92	0.95	0.87
K-means	Attack	0.90	0.99	0.94
	Normal	0.95	0.52	0.67
K-means++	Attack	0.93	0.99	0.96
	Normal	0.95	0.69	0.80

5 Proposed Approach

The aim of our proposed approach is to enhance the existed classical methods for intrusion detection using machine learning. For this end, we exploit a multi-level tweak. The multi-level tweak is also known as mixed models, which is a statistical model of parameters that vary at more than on level in the detection phases. We proposed three methods to boost intrusion detection: supervised, unsupervised and hybrid methods. Our contribution consists in suggesting a better solution to detect the different kind of anomalous data traffic. In the first proposition for enhancement, we recommend the use of binary SVM as a first level for detection; then, the multi-class SVM as a second level for detection. Therefore, we called this method SVM^2. This proposition is, then, a supervised mechanism, which assumes that the dataset is labeled. In the second proposition, we assumed that the dataset is unlabeled. Thus, this proposition is an enhancement for the unsupervised method. Indeed, our proposition is to use k-means++ as a first level for detection; then, we reuse k-means++ as a second level for detection. Therefore, we called this method $K - means^2$. The third proposition is a hybrid method that combines supervised and unsupervised techniques using multi-level tweak. It is, then, named SVM+k. Furthermore, we assume that the traffic in the dataset is labeled as normal or anomalous without defining the different kind of attacks. With the SVM+K proposed method, we used the binary SVM in the first level of detection. Then, in the second level we used the k-means++. Figure 1(b) describes the different level of our proposed approach.

5.1 SVM^2 Mechanism

To enhance the multi class SVM algorithm, we proposed the SVM^2 mechanism. This mechanism uses a multi-level tweak. It classifies the traffic using binary SVM, in the first level, as normal or anomalous. Then, in the second level, we apply the multi-class SVM on the anomalous detected traffic to classify the different attacks types. Table 7 highlights the evaluation results of our first proposition SVM^2 by studying precision, recall, and F1-score metrics. Our generated model has yielded the following metric performance results: the Accuracy is equal to 97.9% of the total samples, the Detection Rate is equal to 0.963% of the total samples, the False Alarm is equal to 0.006% of the total samples, the Time Training is equal to 3.288 s and, the Time Assigned label is equal to 1.231 s. It is clear that this proposition has far better performance results than the multi-class SVM method.

5.2 $k - means^2$ Mechanism

To enhance the K-means++ algorithm, we proposed the $k - means^2$ mechanism. This mechanism uses a multi-level tweak. It classifies the traffic using k-means++, in the first level, as normal or anomalous. Then, in the second level, we applied the k-means++ on the anomalous detected traffic to classify the different attacks types. Table 7 highlights the evaluation results of our first proposition $k-means^2$ by studying precision, recall, and F1-score metrics. Our generated model has yielded the following metric performance results: the Accuracy is equal to 97.2% of the total samples, the Detection Rate is equal to 0.982% of the total samples, the False Alarm is equal to 0.008% of the total samples, the Time Training is equal to 70.32 s and, the Time assigned label is equal to 0.305 s. It is clear that this proposition has far better performance results than the k-means++ method.

5.3   SVM+k Mechanism

To enhance the multi class SVM and k-means++ algorithm, we proposed the SVM+K mechanism. This mechanism uses a multi-level tweak. It classifies the traffic using binary SVM, in the first level, as normal or anomalous. Then, in the second level, we applied the K-means++ on the anomalous detected traffic to classify the different attacks types. Table 7 highlights the evaluation results of our first proposition SVM+K by studying precision, recall, and F1-score metrics. Our generated model has yielded the following metric performance results: the Accuracy is equal to 93.9% of the total samples, the Detection Rate is equal to 0.968% of the total samples, the False Alarm is equal to 0.087% of the total samples, the Time Training is equal to 1.532 s and, the Time assigned label is equal to 0.305 s.

5.4   Discussion and Comparison

We deem that our proposed approach, which consists of three methods (i.e., SVM^2,$k-means^2$, SVM+k) has better performance results than the classical existing methods (i.e., SVM, KNN, K-means++). Our approach gives better time trained results than KNN and the K-mean++ methods. Nevertheless, we noticed that the SVM^2 proposed method has the best time trained results. Table 7 illustrates the comparison according to Precision, recall and F1-measure metrics. Our approach gives better results than the classical existing algorithms (i.e., SVM, KNN, and K-means). Finally, we can conclude that our approach has better performances metric results than the classical existing methods. However, by comparing between our three proposed methods SVM^2, $k-means^2$ and the SVM+k we noticed that: SVM^2 has better performance results than the $k-means^2$ and SVM+k methods for the Accuracy, False Alarm, Time Training performance metrics. In the other hand, $K-means^2$ has better performance results than the SVM^2 and SVM+k methods when considering the Detection Rate metrics.

Table 7. Performances measures of different algorithms.

Algorithms	Traffic type	Precision	Recall	F1-score
SVM	Attack	0.91	0.97	0.91
	Normal	0.95	0.92	0.91
KNN	Attack	1.00	0.91	0.87
	Normal	0.92	0.95	0.87
K-means	Attack	0.93	0.99	0.96
	Normal	0.95	0.69	0.80
K-means++	Attack	0.93	0.99	0.96
	Normal	0.95	0.69	0.80
SVM^2	Attack	0.97	0.99	0.98
	Normal	0.99	0.96	0.98
$k-means^2$	Attack	0.92	0.94	0.96
	Normal	0.99	0.97	0.96
SVM+k	Attack	0.95	0.98	0.96
	Normal	0.98	0.94	0.96

6   Conclusion

Many mechanisms are used to mitigate intrusion in the IoT security system. However, there is a constant need to enhance the existing solutions and to implement more efficient one able to detect new or former intrusions. In this work, we studied the implementation of four classical existing methods for intrusion detection: SVM, KNN, K-means, and K-means++. We found that the SVM and K-means has the best performance results. Nevertheless, the SVM method is better than the k-means method for Detection Rate, and Time Training metrics performance, while the K-means is better than the SVM in terms of Accuracy, False Alarm, and Time Training metrics. Thereafter, we proposed an enhancement approach for the existing methods (i.e., SVM, KNN, and K-means). This approach involves three methods: SVM^2, $K-means^2$ and SVM+K. These methods leverage the multi-level tweak to boost the intrusion detection. From the different performance metrics studied (i.e., Accuracy, Detection Rate, False Alarm, Time Training, Time Assigned Label, Precision, Recall and the F1- score) we can conclude that our approach has far better results than the classical existing one.

References

1. Ahmad, I., Basheri, M., Iqbal, M., Raheem, A.: Performance comparison of support vector machine, random forest, and extreme learning machine for intrusion detection. IEEE Access **6**, 33789–33795 (2018)

2. Al-Yaseen, W.L., Othman, Z.A., Nazri, M.Z.A.: Multi-level hybrid support vector machine and extreme learning machine based on modified k-means for intrusion detection system. Exp. Syst. Appl. **67**, 296–303 (2017)
3. Aljawarneh, S., Aldwairi, M., Yassein, M.B.: Anomaly-based intrusion detection system through feature selection analysis and building hybrid efficient model. J. Comput. Sci. **25**, 152–160 (2018)
4. Ashraf, N., Ahmad, W., Ashraf, R.: A comparative study of data mining algorithms for high detection rate in intrusion detection system (2018)
5. Boutaba, R., et al.: A comprehensive survey on machine learning for networking: evolution, applications and research opportunities. J. Internet Serv. Appl. **9**(1), 16 (2018)
6. Buczak, A.L., Guven, E.: A survey of data mining and machine learning methods for cyber security intrusion detection. IEEE Commun. Surv. Tutorials **18**(2), 1153–1176 (2016)
7. Chaabouni, N., Mosbah, M., Zemmari, A., Sauvignac, C., Faruki, P.: Network intrusion detection for IoT security based on learning techniques. IEEE Commun. Surv. Tutorials **21**, 2671–2701 (2019)
8. Chae, H.S., Choi, S.: Feature selection for efficient intrusion detection using attribute ratio. Int. J. Comput. Commun. **8**, 1–6 (2014)
9. Chand, N., Mishra, P., Krishna, C.R., Pilli, E.S., Govil, M.C.: A comparative analysis of SVM and its stacking with other classification algorithm for intrusion detection. In: International Conference on Advances in Computing, Communication, & Automation (ICACCA) (Spring), pp. 1–6. IEEE (2016)
10. da Costa, K.A., Papa, J.P., Lisboa, C.O., Munoz, R., de Albuquerque, V.H.C.: Internet of Things: a survey on machine learning-based intrusion detection approaches. Comput. Netw. **151**, 147–157 (2019)
11. Deep, S., Zheng, X., Hamey, L.: A survey of security and privacy issues in the Internet of Things from the layered context. arXiv preprint arXiv:1903.00846 (2019)
12. Doshi, R., Apthorpe, N., Feamster, N.: Machine learning DDoS detection for consumer Internet of Things devices. arXiv preprint arXiv:1804.04159 (2018)
13. Enache, A.C., Sgârciu, V.: Anomaly intrusions detection based on support vector machines with an improved bat algorithm. In: 2015 20th International Conference on Control Systems and Computer Science (CSCS), pp. 317–321. IEEE (2015)
14. Faria, M.M., Monteiro, A.M.: Intrusion detection in computer networks based on KNN, K-Means++ and J48. In: Arai, K., Kapoor, S., Bhatia, R. (eds.) IntelliSys 2018. AISC, vol. 868, pp. 256–271. Springer, Cham (2019). https://doi.org/10. 1007/978-3-030-01054-6_19
15. Haq, N.F., Onik, A.R., Hridoy, M.A.K., Rafni, M., Shah, F.M., Farid, D.M.: Application of machine learning approaches in intrusion detection system: a survey. IJARAI-Int. J. Adv. Res. Artif. Intell. **4**(3), 9–18 (2015)
16. Kaur, K.: A survey on Internet of Things-architecture, applications, and future trends. In: 2018 First International Conference on Secure Cyber Computing and Communication (ICSCCC), pp. 581–583. IEEE (2018)
17. Kumar, B.N., Raju, M.S.S.B., Vardhan, B.V.: Enhancing the performance of an intrusion detection system through multi-linear dimensionality reduction and multi-class SVM. Int. J. Intell. Eng. Syst. **11**(1), 181–190 (2018)
18. Li, Y.: Generalization of k-means related algorithms. arXiv preprint arXiv:1903.10025 (2019)
19. Miller, N.J.: Benchmarks for evaluating anomaly-based intrusion detection solutions. Ph.D. thesis, California State University, Long Beach (2018)

20. Mishra, P., Varadharajan, V., Tupakula, U., Pilli, E.S.: A detailed investigation and analysis of using machine learning techniques for intrusion detection. IEEE Commun. Surv. Tutorials **21**(1), 686–728 (2018)

21. Mohamad Tahir, H., et al.: Hybrid machine learning technique for intrusion detection system (2015)

22. Mohamed, H., Hefny, H., Alsawy, A.: Intrusion detection system using machine learning approaches. Egypt. Comput. Sci. J. **42**(3), 1–13 (2018)

23. Nisioti, A., Mylonas, A., Yoo, P.D., Katos, V.: From intrusion detection to attacker attribution: a comprehensive survey of unsupervised methods. IEEE Commun. Surv. Tutorials **20**, 3369–3388 (2018)

24. Nkiama, H., Said, S.Z.M., Saidu, M.: A subset feature elimination mechanism for intrusion detection system. Int. J. Adv. Comput. Sci. Appl. **7**(4), 148–157 (2016)

25. NSL-KDD: NSL-KDD data set for network-based intrusion detection systems. http://nsl.cs.unb.ca/NSL-KDD/

26. Özgür, A., Erdem, H.: A review of kdd99 dataset usage in intrusion detection and machine learning between 2010 and 2015. PeerJ PrePrints **4**, e1954v1 (2016)

27. Protić, D.D.: Review of kdd cup'99, nsl-kdd and kyoto 2006+ datasets. Vojnotehnički glasnik **66**(3), 580–596 (2018)

28. Roman, R., Zhou, J., Lopez, J.: On the features and challenges of security and privacy in distributed Internet of Things. Comput. Netw. **57**(10), 2266–2279 (2013)

29. Santos, L., Rabadao, C., Gonçalves, R.: Intrusion detection systems in Internet of Things: a literature review. In: 2018 13th Iberian Conference on Information Systems and Technologies (CISTI), pp. 1–7. IEEE (2018)

30. Sree, S.B.: Kernel based intrusion detection using data mining techniques (2018)

31. Teng, S., Wu, N., Zhu, H., Teng, L., Zhang, W.: SVM-DT-based adaptive and collaborative intrusion detection. IEEE/CAA J. Automatica Sinica **5**(1), 108–118 (2018)

32. Tharwat, A.: Parameter investigation of support vector machine classifier with kernel functions. Knowl. Inf. Syst. **61**, 1–34 (2019)

33. Wang, H., Gu, J., Wang, S.: An effective intrusion detection framework based on SVM with feature augmentation. Knowl.-Based Syst. **136**, 130–139 (2017)

34. Xin, Y., et al.: Machine learning and deep learning methods for cybersecurity. IEEE Access **6**, 35365–35381 (2018)

35. Zhang, S., Cheng, D., Deng, Z., Zong, M., Deng, X.: A novel KNN algorithm with data-driven k parameter computation. Pattern Recogn. Lett. **109**, 44–54 (2018)

36. Zhao, W.L., Deng, C.H., Ngo, C.W.: K-means: a revisit. Neurocomputing **291**, 195–206 (2018)

Watch Out! Doxware on the Way...

Routa Moussaileb[1,2(✉)], Charles Berti[1], Guillaume Deboisdeffre[1],
Nora Cuppens[1], and Jean-Louis Lanet[2]

[1] IMT Atlantique, Rennes, France
{routa.moussaileb,nora.cuppens}@imt-atlantique.fr,
{charles.berti,guillaume.deboisdeffre}@imt-atlantique.net
[2] LHS-PEC, Inria, Rennes, France
ruta.moussaileb@irisa.fr, jean-louis.lanet@inria.fr

Abstract. From spyware to ransomware to leakware, the world is on
the verge of getting struck by a myriad of advanced attacks. Security researchers' main objective is protecting the assets that a per-
son/company possesses. They are in a constant battle in this cyber war
facing attackers' malicious intents. To compete in this arm race against
security breaches, we propose an insight into plausible attacks especially
Doxware (called also leakware). We present a quantification model that
explores Windows file system in search of valuable data. It is based on
some solutions provided in the literature for natural language processing
such as term frequency-inverse document frequency (TF-IDF). The best
top 15 file "contestants" will be then exfiltrated over the Internet to the
attacker's server. Our approach delivers an observation of the evolution
of malware throughout the last years. It enables users to prevent their
sensitive information being exposed to potential risks.

Keywords: Doxware · Asset · Exfiltration · Content analysis ·
TF-IDF · NLP

1 Introduction

A Pact with the Devil is always made when a virus executes its payload on the
victim's computer as Bond *et al.* state: "The arms race between propagation and
defence will continue ad infinitum" [8].

Putting computer security on sounder footing, researchers seek to decrease
attacks on companies and end users. Startling news are conveyed in Symantec's
latest report published in 2019 [2]. Even though cryptojacking is down, but not
out, targeted attacks blossomed by 78% in 2018. Cloud security and formjacking
remain a concern for companies.

Cyber Security kill chain model consists of the attack's structure progressing
through several phases. It begins with a reconnaissance and, once the control
over the victim's machine is acquired, the payload is executed. This payload
marks the objectives of cyber criminals.

© Springer Nature Switzerland AG 2020
S. Kallel et al. (Eds.): CRiSIS 2019, LNCS 12026, pp. 279–292, 2020.
https://doi.org/10.1007/978-3-030-41568-6_18

To respond to those cyber-attacks, several strategies exist. A well-known malware is ransomware, a type of software that encrypts users documents asking for a ransom in exchange of the key used for encryption. One countermeasure is the calculation of Shannon's entropy of user's files [14,15,22]. In fact, if they are encrypted their value fluctuates around 8. However, this is a reactive solution. Our goal is to be a step ahead of the attacker to prevent security breaches. Thus, it will give us a better understanding of the possible intrusions.

Analysts also joined the uphill battle against cyber-attacks. In fact, it is not affecting end users only, governmental concern is on the rise since it compromises the security and serenity of a country. The ultimate goal of any company is protecting its resources: the data. Data is the most valuable asset a person could acquire. Indeed, it has and is being used for many purposes by the attacker: lucrative opportunities enabling them a monetary gain. For example, blackmailing victims in displaying their private pictures to the public. Company wise, it could be selling the information gathered to a concurrent one, which will lead to millions of dollars in term of losses.

Risk evaluation is a necessity in all the cases. Companies should take into account the potential danger of disgruntled employees that can jeopardize their supreme interests. Initial leakware threat emerged in the late 2015 with Chimera's ransomware [3]. However, no evidence prove the exfiltration of any personal information. To the best of our knowledge, no previous research was made on a plausible doxware attack and its feasibility. For all the aforementioned reasons, we endeavor presenting Doxware techniques that could be used for victim assets' extortion.

Outline. The paper is structured as follows. The context and language processing are presented in Sect. 2. The state of the art of is described in Sect. 3. Our proof of concept (POC) is developed in Sect. 4. Protection mechanisms are provided in Sect. 5. Finally, the conclusion is drawn in Sect. 6.

2   Context

2.1   From Ransomware to Doxware

Ransomware is a specific type of malware that encrypts victims' files [19]. A second type is ransom-locker that blocks the access to the desktop without encryption's process. Data's retrieval can be possible if the ransom required by the attacker is paid. Our main concern in this paper is crypto ransomware since they present a higher threat than locker ransomware.

Figure 1 presents ransomware and doxware workflow. Three main stages appear in both malware (phase 1, 2 and 3). The only difference resides in "valuable files hunting" followed by an exfiltration of the acquired data (phase 2D and 3D). To the best of our knowledge, no previous studies were made on this specific type of malware and it was only mentioned by researches as an advanced threat [10,18,20,23].

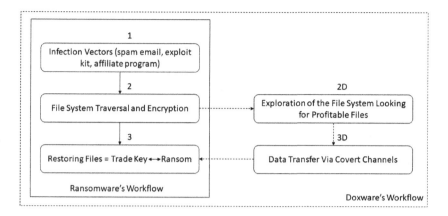

Fig. 1. Ransomware Vs Doxware.

Our proposed approach focuses on the file evaluation for score computation. The exfiltration phase will be presented in our future work. Doxware samples were not found on public repositories (VirusShare, MalwareDB, ...) or blogs, therefore, dynamic and static analysis were not carried out.

2.2 Data Formats Choice

Different data formats exist nowadays that are stored in a computer. They can be classified into three main categories:

1. Textual Documents: They represent files that contain mostly data in the form of a sequence of words or alphabetic characters. For example, contracts, agreements, company's balance sheet, medical records...
2. Pictures: Designs or representations made by various means (such as painting, drawing, or photography). For instance, a Magnetic Resonance Imaging (MRI), gradient descent convergence, trip pictures.
3. Videos: A recording of a motion picture or television program for playing through a television set (movies, video clip, news). These have to be personal in order to blackmail the victim in paying the ransom.

Nearly all processing methods in the literature for face recognition or body detection are based on machine learning algorithms [7,25]. Some additional information are mandatory to be able to recognize bodies, clothes, poses...

Many drawbacks reside in these approaches such as their weight: complex algorithms requiring considerable computation power. This means many false positives cannot be tolerated. Sending 50 Mb video that does not encompass sensitive information represents a huge loss for the attacker. For example, many packets will be transmitted over the network and cannot go unnoticed. Therefore, a compromise between efficiency and stealthiness is needed. Moreover, pictures of people represent often a red line since you are affecting their privacy that means they will feel threatened. For all the reasons cited above, our proof of concept developed in this paper is based on textual documents analysis, specifically contracts.

2.3 Natural Language Processing (NLP)

– Bag-Of-Words (BOW): It is a simple technique that is part of NLP. The idea relies on regrouping words by their occurrences.
   "Mankind must put an end to war before war puts an end to mankind."
   The result will be: ("mankind" : 2), ("must": 1), ("put": 1), ("an": 2), ("end": 2), ("to": 2), ("war": 2), ("before": 1), ("puts": 1). Nevertheless, this technique has some well-known flaws. Some words, existent in any kind of documents ("the", "an", "is", "are"...) called stop words, are not representative of the document itself compared to others. Their frequency will steal the light, as a consequence, non-relevant words will identify these documents. Hence, this technique will be backed up by the TF-IDF transformation addressing the problem encountered in BOW [26, 31].
– TF-IDF This process has the Bag Of Words as a basis but with an improved layer. To begin with, a corpus is needed, because the process compares documents one to another. The bigger the corpus, better specificities of the documents can be extracted.
   IDF: for a word i, a corpus of documents d_j (with j the index of the target document), and $|D|$ the total number of documents in the corpus, we define:

$$idf_{i,j} = \log(\frac{|D|}{|d_j : t_i \in d_j|})$$

For a given word i, its personal score is the logarithm of the number of documents divided by the number of documents that contain this word i. When the number of times a word is present in a document is significant, the value obtained in the logarithm is very close to 1, so idf_i will be close to 0. For a document d_j and a word, the score of this word in this particular document has a value of:

$$tfidf_{i,j} = tf_{i,j} * idf_i$$

having $tf_{i,j}$ the number of occurrences of the word i in the document d_j. The idf_i coefficient highlights rare words found only in few documents, even though not frequent enough, they carry some meaning and should be visible [21, 27].
– Latent Dirichlet Allocation LDA: In layman's terms, each document can be described by a distribution of topics and each topic can be described by a distribution of words. From a corpus we create the topics, so that with a single document we can link it with the appropriate topic. Considering a corpus of documents, the algorithm tries to build the topics from the content of this corpus. In the end of the execution, for each document, you get the list of the

probabilities for this document to belong to the various topics [1...k]. It uses Bayesian variables to determine those probabilities. However, the number of topics are given as in input. It was not used in our current POC.

3   State of the Art

3.1   Data Value

Google Scholar provides more than 5 million research papers regarding sensitive data. It is not limited to a particular field but represents a common concern for a myriad of sectors (healthcare, telecom, automotive, energy, ..). For example, mental health care is a delicate subject that could ruin a person's reputation under malicious manipulation. Netherlands data breach came mostly from the medical sector (29%) [1].

Sensitive information depends on the equipment being used. For instance, Yang *et al.* considered that the following items represent significant data on Android OS: Unique Device ID, Location, Phone number, Contact book, SMS messages and Calendar [30]. These elements carry a huge advantage. In fact, each cell phone possesses this data and any application could access it via simple API calls. Another method would be taint analysis that detects flows upcoming from known sources (IMEI of a cellphone) to untrusted sinks like the Internet. Tracking data is therefore a straightforward process in Android Devices. A similar tool developed by Sun *et al.* enables a multilevel information flow tracking by utilizing registers for taint storage, having only a 15% overhead on the CPU [24]. It presents an enhancement of TaintDroid developed by in terms of taint storage and resource consumption [9]. Considerable research is being conducted in this field as in [6, 11, 13, 28, 29].

On Android OS, attackers know what they are looking and where to find it, like extracting the GPS location of the victim. Yet, these sensitive elements cannot be predefined on a computer level. Indeed, sensitive data is only relevant to a particular end user (could be a project for a student or a painting for an artist). It exists in a variety of formats and is stored in different locations for each user.

Data's value is translated by the measure taken by a company to protect it. For instance, Zhu *et al.* provided TaintEraser a new tool that tracks sensitive user data as it flows through applications [32]. They are one of the pioneers in developing data protection from leakage on Windows OS. Their taint propagation was based on instruction and function level. They evaluated their solution on Notepad, Yahoo! Messenger and the Internet Explorer where they presented accurate results based on taint propagation. However, TaintEraser can be bypassed via data transfer in shared memory. Loginova *et al.* suggested to use cryptographic software to carry out on-the-fly encryption [17]. They stated that it represents the most effective approach to overcome data leakage and to protect the information.

3.2   Data Exfiltration

Data exfiltration is a security breach where this information is disclosed and can be published via the attacker's will. Researchers have long been interested in this domain since it can threaten a company or individual's wellbeing. Giani *et al.* revealed that the bandwidth constraints depends not only on the amount of data exchanged but also on the media being used [12]. Indeed, since 2006 little has changed. Leakage methods remain the same (FTP, SSH, email, ...).

Al-Bataineh *et al.* presented the detection of malicious data exfiltration in web traffic [5]. Their solution is based on analyzing initially the content of an HTTP POST request (using Shannon entropy) to check whether it is encrypted or not. Additional features were extracted to perform machine learning on the data gathered for malware classification.

Ahmed *et al.* tuned and trained a machine learning algorithm to detect anomalies in DNS queries [4]. Numerous elements are considered like Total count of characters in Fully Qualified Domain Name (FQDN), count of uppercase characters, count of characters in sub-domains, entropy,... Less than 5% of false positive rate is achieved in their work. Another example is based on Liu *et al.* work, where they were able to detect data theft by analyzing the content of the data being sent to generate a signature [16]. They extracted the information from videos via wavelets enabling them to identify covert communication using Hausdorff Distance.

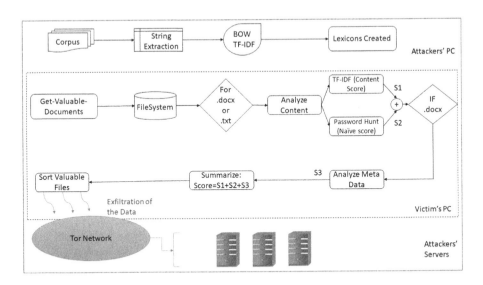

Fig. 2. Procedure's workflow.

4 Proposed Methodology

Procedure's Workflow is presented in Fig. 2. It will be thoroughly explained in the following sections.

4.1 Usable Corpus

Leakware or doxware subject is very broad and can be interpreted in many ways, whether it infects a personal or a professional machine, an individual user or a company. Our preference from among choices is the evaluation of professional documents (that can be found on both machines). Since a variety of extensions exist for textual analysis (.txt, .docx, .pdf, .rtf , .wpd, .odt...) we decided at first to restrain the study domain on .txt, .docx and .pdf files.

The content of a textual document bears its ultimate value. Therefore, the sequence of characters should be extracted for further analysis. PDF revealed later on to be quite a challenge: in fact, it could be a scanned document. Therefore, existent tools for words extraction will not be adequate. A possible solution is treating it as an image, extracting its content with the help of an Optical Character Recognition (OCR) and Tesseract (an open source OCR engine). However, many problems occurred regarding PDF files that led to discard them in our Proof of Concept. De facto, each page of the PDF document is converted into a .png image. The ratio of PDF to image can be 1/30, a memory consuming process. The program gets importantly less stealthy. In addition to that, another noticeable problem emerged: longer processing time compared to .txt.

Concerning the Textual Documents, a usable corpus is created of various extensions (.txt, .docx) to implement the different solutions mentioned in the State of The Art. They are downloaded from *onecle.com* and *contractsfinder.service.gov.uk*. Additional noise files are gathered from Google Scholar, online courses and our own documents. This database of files can be extended in the future by adding different topics.

4.2 Evaluation Algorithm

The evaluation algorithm built depends on some parameters of the document that the program is analyzing. It is divided in two parts: one related to the attacker, as in generating intelligent lexicons in order to focus on the subjects/topics she wants to exfiltrate, and another on the victim side, evaluating the documents of the victim to send them over the network.

To accomplish these tasks four elements are required in the analysis program: Lexical Generation, Document Content Evaluation, Password files Evaluation and Meta Data Evaluation.

Lexical Generation. On the attacker's machine, a pre-processing is made for lexicons generation of any desired subject. To fulfill this task, a corpus of various documents based on the specific subject (.docx or .txt) is required. This topic represents the files that the attacker will be searching for on the victim's machine once infected.

Initially, TF-IDF transformation is applied on the union of documents in the corpus. The TOP -n (n an integer of your choice) results represent the words having the best score for each document, yet not all of them are equally important. For example, some acronyms like "rdc" will not be valuable on the victim's pc. Since the transformation made has as an objective finding representative words for each document, then an acronym cannot be generalized to define a topic. Indeed, it is not relevant for the whole Lexicon as it must represent all documents of a specific subject.

The next step relies on creating a function that associates each word in the lexicon to an importance "score".

Let w_i be a word that represents the target subject. Let n be the number of words taken into consideration by a document (TOP n words with highest TF-IDF score). The word w_i has a $p_{i,j}$ position in the document j. Its value is built as following:

$$Sc(w_i, j) = \frac{n - p_{i,j}}{n}$$

As a result, the total score Sci will be:

$$Sc_i = \sum_{j=1}^{n} Sc(w_i, j) = \sum_{j=1}^{n} \frac{n - p_{i,j}}{n}$$

Sc_i is divided by n for normalization purposes so that any word can have a maximum score of 1. In the example of lexicon that will follow, the word "1look" arose and represents an important element in the subject corpus we acquired. Indeed, it has an important score for its own document but globally it is not representative of contract documents. A part of a lexicon produced and used on the victims machine is presented below: (1look,0.090) (company,0.6) (agreement,0.690) (section, 0.272) (purchaser, 0.181) (shares, 0.199) (shall, 0.736) (closing, 0.090) (material, 0.018) (date, 0.009) (buyer, 0.181) (acquisition, 0.045).

Document Content Evaluation. On the victim's side, the lexicons are already hidden in the malware source code and they will used to process a content score which will be merged with a meta data score for a final evaluation score. A modified bag of words is implemented. At first, a dictionary containing every word of the document with it's number of occurrences is extracted. The initial value of the content score is 0.

Let CS be this content score, L_i the score of the word i of the lexicon being studied, n the number of words in the lexicon and occ_i the number of occurrences of the word i in the document analyzed.

$$CS = \sum_{i=1}^{n} L_i * occ_i$$

Password Evaluation. Two methods are used for password evaluation:

1. A comparison of the words existing in a document is made with the 25 most common passwords (gathered from to Symantec). For each occurrence, the naive score is increased by one.
2. Hunting for password common patterns: for instance, if a word contains more than 8 characters including uppercase, lowercase, numbers, special characters and so on.
   - length : length of the word, caped between 6 and 16.
   - presence of more than two uppercase and more than one lowercase: +3.
   - presence of uppercase, lowercase and number: +3.
   - presence of a special character: +8.
   - presence of a known business (such as "facebook", "netflix" and so on): +5

   Then we sum them all before dividing by 10.

Meta Data Evaluation. Fifteen meta data can be accessed and extracted from a Word Document. Those are: author, category, comments, content status, created, identifier, keywords, language, last modified by, last printed, modified, revision, subject, title and version. However, most of the meta data are not filled in (the content is null), therefore, the only ones kept are the most relevant which are the number of revision, created, modified, last printed.

The algorithm Valuable File Hunting (VFHA) summarizes the steps developed in our paper.

4.3   Solution's Design

1. Initially: Lexicon Generation of Contract Topic (line 2 in VFHA).
2. Then: parsing the target file system looking for .txt and .docx extensions (line18 in VFHA).
3. File Score
   (a) .txt: Its content is extracted and vocabulary analyzed. Each word is compared with a lexicon previously created that contains recurrent and relevant words in a contract based document. An additional comparison is made to spot if there is any noun that appeared similar to a construction of a password. Either a common one ("passwd" for instance) or since it includes special characters, uppercase, lowercase and numbers in a string. For every method called, a score between 0 and 5 is returned. In the end, those scores are summed in order to have a total that represents the value of the file taken into consideration. If the score is not null, it means that the document may yield value. Therefore, we add the file to a dictionary of potentially valuable ones linked to its score (line 3 in VFHA)..
   (b) .docx: The same procedure is done for the .docx files. However, an additional step is made for the meta data analysis. The significant metadata are the number of revision, creation date, modification date and the date when it was last printed. They will be added to the total sum representing the value of a document (line 3 and 9 in VFHA).

4. "Summarize" step: Each document has a total score that has been assigned, so the list of tuple (path, score) is sorted according to the value obtained, where the attacker chooses which ones he/she wants to extract. For instance the first 50 files (line 23 and 24 in VFHA).

Algorithm. Valuable File Hunting VFH

1: **procedure** ALGORITHM 1
2:     $Topic\_Lexicon \leftarrow \{$ lexicon_generator (Corpus of same Topic: Contract) $\}$
3:     def analyse_content(File f):
4:     **for** word $\in$ **f do**
5:         **if** word $\in$ Topic_Lexicon **then**
6:             $f\_score+ = score(word) * number\_occurrences$
7:     return f_score/len(f)
8:
9:     def analyse_metadata(File f):
10:     **if** f.core_properties.revision > 1 **then**
11:         $f\_metadata\_score+ = 5$
12:     **else if** f.created $==$ "2019" **then**
13:         $f\_metadata\_score+ = 1$
14:     **else if** ... **then**
15:         ...
16:     return Sum(f_metadata_score)
17:
18:      Parse the File System
19:     **if** FileExtension $\in$ .txt or .docx **then**
20:         $FileList \leftarrow \{$Analyse MetaData and Content$\}$
21:     **else**
22:         $Continue;$
23:     Sort FileList by highest_Score
24:     Send n first valuable files to the attacker's server (future work)

4.4 Lexicon Generation

The chart presented in Fig. 3 shows the most common words in a contract document are: "shall", "partnership", "agreement" and also "section". Indeed, the corpus gathered is previously identified as a contract type document, which is an advantage allowing us to perform relatively simple algorithm to determine whether a document belongs to this category or not. Although, law documents acquire also an important score and may be also as valuable as a contract.

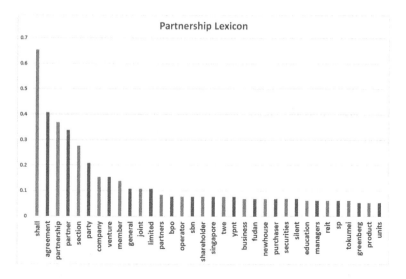

Fig. 3. An example of Lexicon with the associated scores.

4.5   Valuable Files Chase

Personal Computer. Two versions of the algorithm are tested. The first one, heavier program since it uses scikit learn library, outputs the valuable documents in 126 s. During the execution, 3578 readable documents were found that had a non null score.

   The second version is lighter because the scikit learn library is substituted by functions we created. Since it is not optimized, 242 s are required to perform a full disk analysis. Yet, the program is lighter than the initial version.

Virtual Machine. A Windows 7 Virtual Machine is created for the proof of concept. It holds 50 noise documents and 25 important files. After running the algorithm, 15 files are recovered. Among those there were six false positives, and 5 were Windows configuration files. To gain better results, specific Windows file system path can be removed from the file system traversal, in addition to Read-Me related documents. The time the victim suspects something the exfiltration process would be to an end, and the list of documents are being or sent to the attacker.

5   Security Recommendations

Protection against malware attacks, specially zero days, is a challenge for all researchers. Residual risk remains: de facto, despite various countermeasures employed by a party, an attacker can always find a way to penetrate the system (he/she still risks to be detected). If committed, anyone can reach their malicious intents. However, our goal is to complicate the intrusion task, detect it if possible, rather than handling it to the attackers on a golden plate. Users should know the existent vulnerabilities to see what patches can be used to circumvent malevolent attacks. Some countermeasure can be deployed by users to protect their data from being exfiltrated:

1. Honeypot Folders: They can be created in any environment, regardless the operating system used. Since doxware will traverse the whole file system looking for assets, any process or thread that will pass through this lure folder can be immediately flagged then stopped. A drawback would be malware's multi-threading techniques, it can still be exposed but after a certain epsilon time.
2. Data Tainting: Sensitive data in a computer is extremely private and depends on the end users, unlike Android OS (IMEI, GPS location, ... existent on all mobiles). Therefore, a general protection model is impossible to develop in real life. Yet, each individual can add a layer, a taint, on his preferred/sensitive information. Thus, each exfiltration attempt over the network will be detected. Nonetheless, a person can have an explosion of tainted data that may slow down the system.
3. Data Encryption: It remains a robust way adopted by the global community. Indeed, brute-forcing the encryption key can take decades. Even though an attacker acquired the encrypted files, he/she cannot menace the victims or blackmail them since no access to the decrypted data is possible.

6   Conclusion

We have discussed in this paper the potential danger of sensitive data localization and quantification that can be carried out by a Doxware malware. Windows OS is the target system throughout the experiments. A proof of concept is developed based on contract topic and passwords hunt. To accomplish this tasks, state of the art methods were used such as TF-IDF and Bag of Words in addition to a document's meta data. The associated score of each document is calculated then normalized. To identify new target topics, few samples of files regarding the same topic are needed. Even if the victim finds out he/she got hacked, the person will not have the means to reach the attacker or react to this intrusion. New options can be added as building bricks such as PDF and Images analysis which will strengthen the offensive invasion in attacker's point of view. Reducing false positive rate can be done by eliminating Windows system path and choosing randomly N last visited files in Windows' Quick Access. 40% of important files can be collected, by relying on a straightforward mechanism, and ready for exfiltration. Threats arising from this cyberwarfare are exponential. Therefore, end users should be aware of the possible attacks especially attack vectors in order to avoid and circumvent them protecting their assets.

References

1. Data Protection and Privacy across sectors and borders. https://bit.ly/2D2r77M
2. Internet Security Threat Report by Symantec. https://www.symantec.com/content/dam/symantec/docs/reports/istr-24-executive-summary-en.pdf
3. New ransomware program threatens to publish user files. https://www.computerworld.com/article/3002120/new-ransomware-program-threatens-to-publish-user-files.html
4. Ahmed, J., Gharakheili, H.H., Russell, C., Sivaraman, V.: Real-time detection of DNS exfiltration and tunneling from enterprise networks. In: Proceedings of IFIP/IEEE IM, Washington DC, USA (2019)
5. Al-Bataineh, A., White, G.: Analysis and detection of malicious data exfiltration in web traffic. In: 2012 7th International Conference on Malicious and Unwanted Software, pp. 26–31. IEEE (2012)
6. Arzt, S., et al.: FlowDroid: precise context, flow, field, object-sensitive and lifecycle-aware taint analysis for android apps. In: ACM SIGPLAN Notices, vol. 49, no. 6, pp. 259–269 (2014)
7. Bartlett, M.S., Littlewort, G., Frank, M., Lainscsek, C., Fasel, I., Movellan, J.: Recognizing facial expression: machine learning and application to spontaneous behavior. In: 2005 IEEE Computer Society Conference on Computer Vision and Pattern Recognition (CVPR 2005), vol. 2, pp. 568–573. IEEE (2005)
8. Bond, M., Danezis, G.: A pact with the devil. In: Proceedings of the 2006 Workshop on New Security Paradigms, pp. 77–82. ACM (2006)
9. Enck, W., et al.: TaintDroid: an information-flow tracking system for realtime privacy monitoring on smartphones. ACM Trans. Comput. Syst. (TOCS) **32**(2), 5 (2014)
10. Ensey, C.: Ransomware has evolved, and its name is doxware. DARKReading. InformationWeek Business Technology Network (2017)
11. Feng, Y., Anand, S., Dillig, I., Aiken, A.: Apposcopy: semantics-based detection of android malware through static analysis. In: Proceedings of the 22nd ACM SIGSOFT International Symposium on Foundations of Software Engineering, pp. 576–587. ACM (2014)
12. Giani, A., Berk, V.H., Cybenko, G.V.: Data exfiltration and covert channels. In: Sensors, and Command, Control, Communications, and Intelligence (C3I) Technologies for Homeland Security and Homeland Defense V, vol. 6201, p. 620103. International Society for Optics and Photonics (2006)
13. Graa, M., Cuppens-Boulahia, N., Cuppens, F., Lanet, J.-L., Moussaileb, R.: Detection of side channel attacks based on data tainting in android systems. In: De Capitani di Vimercati, S., Martinelli, F. (eds.) SEC 2017. IAICT, vol. 502, pp. 205–218. Springer, Cham (2017). https://doi.org/10.1007/978-3-319-58469-0_14
14. Kharaz, A., Arshad, S., Mulliner, C., Robertson, W., Kirda, E.: {UNVEIL}: a large-scale, automated approach to detecting ransomware. In: 25th {USENIX} Security Symposium ({USENIX} Security 16), pp. 757–772 (2016)
15. Kharraz, A., Robertson, W., Balzarotti, D., Bilge, L., Kirda, E.: Cutting the gordian knot: a look under the hood of ransomware attacks. In: Almgren, M., Gulisano, V., Maggi, F. (eds.) DIMVA 2015. LNCS, vol. 9148, pp. 3–24. Springer, Cham (2015). https://doi.org/10.1007/978-3-319-20550-2_1

16. Liu, Y., Corbett, C., Chiang, K., Archibald, R., Mukherjee, B., Ghosal, D.: Detecting sensitive data exfiltration by an insider attack. In: Proceedings of the 4th Annual Workshop on Cyber Security and Information Intelligence Research: Developing Strategies to Meet the Cyber Security and Information Intelligence Challenges Ahead, CSIIRW 2008, pp. 16:1–16:3. ACM, New York (2008). https://doi.org/10.1145/1413140.1413159

17. Loginova, N., Trofimenko, E., Zadereyko, O., Chanyshev, R.: Program-technical aspects of encryption protection of users' data. In: 2016 13th International Conference on Modern Problems of Radio Engineering, Telecommunications and Computer Science (TCSET), pp. 443–445. IEEE (2016)

18. Lueders, S., et al.: Computer security: enter the next level: Doxware (2017)

19. Luo, X., Liao, Q.: Awareness education as the key to ransomware prevention. Inf. Syst. Secur. **16**(4), 195–202 (2007)

20. Nadir, I., Bakhshi, T.: Contemporary cybercrime: a taxonomy of ransomware threats & mitigation techniques. In: 2018 International Conference on Computing, Mathematics and Engineering Technologies (iCoMET), pp. 1–7. IEEE (2018)

21. Ramos, J., et al.: Using TF-IDF to determine word relevance in document queries. In: Proceedings of the First Instructional Conference on Machine Learning, Piscataway, NJ, vol. 242, pp. 133–142 (2003)

22. Scaife, N., Carter, H., Traynor, P., Butler, K.R.: Cryptolock (and drop it): stopping ransomware attacks on user data. In: 2016 IEEE 36th International Conference on Distributed Computing Systems (ICDCS), pp. 303–312. IEEE (2016)

23. Sherer, J.A., McLellan, M.L., Fedeles, E.R., Sterling, N.L.: Ransonware-practical and legal considerations for confronting the new economic engine of the dark web. Rich. JL Tech. **23**, 1 (2016)

24. Sun, M., Wei, T., Lui, J.: TaintART: a practical multi-level information-flow tracking system for android runtime. In: Proceedings of the 2016 ACM SIGSAC Conference on Computer and Communications Security, pp. 331–342. ACM (2016)

25. Sun, X., Wu, P., Hoi, S.C.: Face detection using deep learning: an improved faster rcnn approach. Neurocomputing **299**, 42–50 (2018)

26. Wallach, H.M.: Topic modeling: beyond bag-of-words. In: Proceedings of the 23rd International Conference on Machine Learning, pp. 977–984. ACM (2006)

27. Wu, H.C., Luk, R.W.P., Wong, K.F., Kwok, K.L.: Interpreting TF-IDF term weights as making relevance decisions. ACM Trans. Inf. Syst. (TOIS) **26**(3), 13 (2008)

28. Xue, L., et al.: NDroid: toward tracking information flows across multiple android contexts. IEEE Trans. Inf. Forensics Secur. **14**(3), 814–828 (2019)

29. Yan, L.K., Yin, H.: DroidScope: seamlessly reconstructing the {OS} and Dalvik semantic views for dynamic android malware analysis. In: Presented as part of the 21st {USENIX} Security Symposium ({USENIX} Security 12), pp. 569–584 (2012)

30. Yang, Z., Yang, M.: LeakMiner: detect information leakage on android with static taint analysis. In: 2012 Third World Congress on Software Engineering, pp. 101–104. IEEE (2012)

31. Zhang, Y., Jin, R., Zhou, Z.H.: Understanding bag-of-words model: a statistical framework. Int. J. Mach. Learn. Cybern. **1**(1–4), 43–52 (2010)

32. Zhu, D.Y., Jung, J., Song, D., Kohno, T., Wetherall, D.: TaintEraser: protecting sensitive data leaks using application-level taint tracking. ACM SIGOPS Oper. Syst. Rev. **45**(1), 142–154 (2011)

CDISS-BEMOS: A New Color Document Image Steganography System Based on Beta Elliptic Modeling of the Online Signature

Anissa Zenati$^{(\boxtimes)}$, Wael Ouarda, and Adel M. Alimi

REGIM-Lab.: REsearch Groups in Intelligent Machines,
National Engineering School of Sfax (ENIS), University of Sfax,
BP 1173, 3038 Sfax, Tunisia
{anissa.zenati,wael.ouarda,adel.alimi}@ieee.org

Abstract. Based on the Beta elliptic Modeling, a new signature steganography color document image system is proposed in this paper. This system uses the Binary Robust Invariant Scalable Keypoint (BRISK) detector to obtain the potential feature points used for constructing the embedding regions. The Beta elliptic signature is transformed into a secret message bits representation using the Huffman Coding (HC) to increase the performance of our system. Then, the secret message bits are divided into three sub message bits m_R, m_G, and m_B, using the weights α_R, α_G, and α_B, respectively. Finally, each sequence bits is embedded into the corresponding channel, red (R), green (G), and blue (B) by modifying the first Least Significant Bit (LSB) of the embedding regions pixels. The robustness evaluation, quantitative and qualitative experimental results on multiple datasets: L3iDocCopies, LRDE Document Binarization Dataset, and on standard test images, demonstrates that the proposed color document images steganography system in the spatial domain maintains a better visual quality measured by Peak Signal to Noise Ratio (PSNR), Structural Similarity Index Matrix (SSIM), and Human Visual System (HSV) metrics, with relatively less computational complexity, which approves its effectiveness as compared to existing systems.

Keywords: Color document image steganography · Beta elliptic Modeling · Least Significant Bit · Information security

1 Introduction

With the advancement of technology and internet, security and application of data copyrights, authentication, and copy control, etc, have become a major problem in the "digital world". To resolve this issue, researchers proposed several solutions as soft biometrics recognition systems [14,15,24], face recognition

© Springer Nature Switzerland AG 2020
S. Kallel et al. (Eds.): CRiSIS 2019, LNCS 12026, pp. 293–307, 2020.
https://doi.org/10.1007/978-3-030-41568-6_19

systems [13,23], lie detection systems [21], and malicious document detection systems [22].

Even with the increasing digitization in several fields of our world, such as digitization academic and administrative systems, the digit document (or document image) as well as scanned documents [5], cheques bank [10], official documents [9], and e-government documents [3], modified by illegal persons, using powerful image processing tools, is becoming a significant issue. Thus securing this digit document becomes all the more necessary. Steganography is a successful method to insert secret data in the host document image in order to provide the authenticity of the documents as they are transmitted to their destinations. It is used in several applications, such as the secret communication between two communicating stations [1,31], the secure circulation of secret information on intelligence and military agencies [28], improving the security of mobile banking [10], and the security of online voting [19].

Steganography is a Greek origin word meaning protected writing. It is a special branch of information hiding and is considered as an art of science for invisible communication, aiming an imperceptible hiding of a secret message inside an image whose existence is known to the sender and receiver only. The image selected for this purpose is called the host-image and the image obtained after steganography is called the stego-image. The basic elements of steganography include a host image, a secret message, an embedding mechanism, an extraction mechanism, and a stego key for better security.

To deal with the document image security problems, we propose in this paper a new steganography system for color document image based on the Beta elliptic modeling. Firstly, the host color document image is converted to three color channels R, G, and B. The embedding regions is extracted from the host color document image using the Binary Robust Invariant Scalable Keypoints (BRISK) detector. Then the Beta elliptic signature is embedded as three sub-message bits m_R, m_G, and m_B, into the embedding regions in each one of the three color components, using the Least Significant Bits (LSB) substitution technique. The remainder of this paper is structured as follows. Section 2 introduces the relevant works of color image steganogaphy. The proposed steganography system and its detailed description are presented in Sect. 3. Empirical tests, qualitative and quantitative evaluations are described in Sect. 4. Finally, Sect. 5 concludes this paper.

2   Related Works

Steganography is used usually for copyright protection and to resist falsification, which embeds secret data imperceptibly in the host image. Many researchers have conducted deep research in image steganography. There are several different color spaces can be chosen for color image steganography, such as RGB, YCbCr, CMYK, YUV, Lab, etc. Sejpal and Shah [29] presented a comparative performance study of color image watermarking method on the basis of Lifting Wavelet Transform (LWT) and the Discrete Wavelet Transform (SVD) domain to embed an image in grayscale in YCbCr, YUV, and YIQ color spaces of the color cover image. The authors examined the different channels in terms of robustness and visual quality. The higher PSNR result is obtained for V channel in YUV color space with 90.6039 (db) bypassed the results in YCbCr and YIQ color spaces.

Patvardhan et al. [26] proposed an image watermarking scheme to hide the pertinent data into color images in the YCbCr color space. The proposed scheme embeds the Quick Response (QR) as watermark using wavelets transforms and Singular Value Decomposition (SVD). The experimental results demonstrate that embedding QR code is better than the other watermarks in terms of robustness and inaudibility. In the same color space, Pandey *et al.* [25] proposed a nonblind image watermarking method based on Arnold scrambling. The watermark is embedded as singular values in the Y channel of the host image by the usage of the variable scaling factor. The authors include the number of iterations in Arnold transform as a key in order to enhance security. The experimental results proved the effectiveness of the proposed color image watermarking method.

In present work, Su and Chen [30] present a watermarking algorithm that embeds the watermark into the blue channel. In the embedding process, the pixel values of the cover image are directly modified using the distribution features and the generative principle of direct current (DC) coefficient. Then, the watermark is subdivided into four sub-watermarks, and embedded, for four times, into the different areas of the cover image, respectively. The experiments illustrate that the proposed algorithm attains improved invisibility of the watermark and robust against various attacks. Abdulrahman and Ozturk introduces in [1] a new image watermarking scheme robust to the linear and nonlinear attacks. The proposed scheme uses both the Discrete Wavelet Transform (DWT) and Discrete Cosine Transform (DCT) to embed the watermark into the host color image. The watermark is a grayscale image scrambled using Arnold transform and subdivided into smaller parts. After that, the DCT coefficients of every equal part are hidden into four DWT bands of the R, G, and B, components of the host image.

A color image steganography based on stego key-directed adaptive least significant bit (CISSKA-LSB) is proposed by Muhammad *et al.* [19]. The stego key and secret data are ciphered via two-level encryption algorithm (TLEA) and multi-level encryption algorithm (MLEA), respectively. Then, the ciphered secret data is hidden in the cover image by the use of the LSB technique, based on the ciphered secret key and red component. The experimental results designate that the CISSKA-LSB system retains a great image quality and enhance the security aspect. In [17] a new color image watermarking system based on Schur decomposition and quaternion Hadamard transforms (QHT) is proposed. The watermark is hidden in the cover color image by changing the Q matrix using Schur decomposition. Experimental results show that the new system is stronger robustness against common attacks, especially for geometric distortions and color attacks.

Another axis of steganographic methods based on potential feature points, proposed ordinarily in the frequency domain. These methods demonstrated that they have the capacity to achieve better results in terms of robustness. Particularly, the authors in [27] introduce a watermarking system that exploits the scale-invariant feature transform (SIFT). The potential feature points extracted by SIFT, are used to correspond objects in combination with Discrete Cosine Transform (DCT). Then, the secret information is hidden into the selected points by changing the DCT coefficients. The embedded images are capable to resist common attacks and geometric distortion.

Actually, Loc *et al.* [5] proposed a new document image steganography scheme in spatial domain, based on Local Binary Pattern (LBP) and Local Ternary Pattern (LTP) techniques. Firstly, the Speed Up Robust Features (SURF) extract the potential feature points used to identify the embedding regions. Then, LBP is used to realize the embedding patterns in every embedding region. Finally, the secret bits are embedded inside embedding pattern via the LTP. The proposed scheme enables to detect the embedded secret bits without any references and resist to various image distortions. More recently, Munib and Khan [20] present a secure watermarking approach that embeds the secret data utilizing local Zernike moments and the robust image feature points. First, the host image is divided into diverse triangular segments using Delaunay tessellation. Then, for every selected triangular segment, Zernike moments are computed. Using dither modulation, the watermark is hidden in the magnitude of Zernike. The experimental results of the proposed approach to illustrate that they can extract the watermark even in the existence of geometric distortion.

The Beta-elliptic theory is widely employed in several fields of research for online handwriting, such as the regeneration of handwriting [4,18], Optical Character Recognition as and in copyright protection, like writer identification from Online Handwriting [8,11]. However, it has never been used in document image protection. Our idea consist in investing the Beta-Elliptic Modeling [6,6] in document image steganography by embedding the features extracted from an online signature in the embedding positions of the corresponding color channel of the color document image.

3   Proposed CDISS-BEMOS System

We propose a novel, yet the innovative steganographic system, since it is based on Beta elliptic modeling of online signature. However, most of the previous steganographic researchers focus their studies on the standard images and neglect the security aspect of the document image. The schematic representation of the CDISS-BEMOS system is illustrated in Fig. 1.

The CDISS-BEMOS system comprises of a set of sub-process as follows: (1) Detection of Potential Feature Points using the BRISK detector; (2) Beta elliptic signature acquisition and modeling; (3) Signature Preprocessing that transform the Beta elliptic signature to Huffman Code as a secret data; (4) Weighted Secret Data Repartition which subdivides the secret data to three

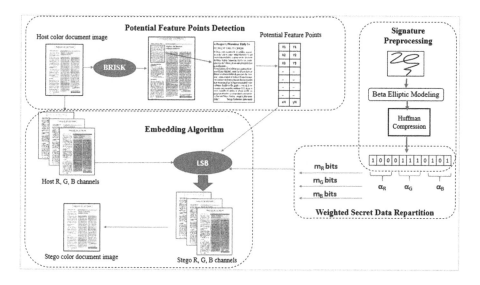

Fig. 1. CDISS-BEMOS architecture

repetitions m_R, m_G, and m_B; (5) the Embedding Process of modifying the LSB of the Potential Feature Points pixels in the R, G, and B channels; Finally, (6) Extracting Process where the secret data would be extracted from the three components R, G, and B of the document image. These processes are briefly described in the subsequent sections.

3.1 Potential Feature Points Detection

The Binary Robust Invariant Scalable Keypoint (BRISK) detector [16] is used to identify the potential feature points in order to construct the embedding regions in the document image. The Feature Points (FP) extracted from a document image D are then stored in a list Fp. The process is mathematically represented by: $Fp = \{p_i(x_i, y_i) \, i = 1...m\}$, where m represents the number of feature points.

3.2 Beta Elliptic Signature

The goal of our CDISS-BEMOS system is to exploit the Beta-elliptic model that models competently on real-time writing movements, in the color document image security. Here, the Beta elliptic signature represents the secret data that would be embedded in the host document image. The online signature is taken from a tablet similar devise [7] as a trajectory (x (t), y (t)). The Beta elliptic modeling extracts the features of this trajectory and generates the Beta elliptic signature. It involves its both profile units: the static profile (elliptic arc model segmented trajectory) and the dynamic profile (overlapped Beta signal model the velocity). Each trajectory stroke corresponds in the velocity domain to the generation of one Beta signal presented in Eq. 1:

$$pulse\beta(K,t,q,p,t_0,t_1) = \begin{cases} K.(\frac{t-t_0}{t_c-t_0})^p.(\frac{t_1-t}{t_1-t_c}) & if \; t \in [t_0,t_1] \\ 0 & elsewhere \end{cases} \qquad (1)$$

with: t_0 and t_1 are the initial and final Beta function time, respectively. The reals p and q are the intermediate parameters. K denotes the Beta impulse amplitude, and t_c presents the instant when the Beta function attains its extreme value K. A vector of 10 features composed in Table 1 models, each Beta stroke in the trajectory of the online signature.

Table 1. The 10 Features extracted by the Beta-Elliptic Modeling

Feature section	Parameter and formula	Signification
Dynamic profile model	$\Delta_t = t_1 - t_0$	Beta impulse duration
	$RapT_c = \frac{t_c-t_0}{\Delta_t}$	Rapport of Beta impulse asymmetry or culminating time
	p	Beta shape parameters
	k	Beta impulse amplitude
	$\frac{k_i}{k_{i+1}}$	Rapport of successive Beta impulse amplitude
Static profile model	a	Ellipse major axis half length
	b	Ellipse small axis half length
	ϑ	Ellipse major axis inclination angle
	ϑ_p	Angle of inclination of the tangents at the stroke endpoint M2
	POSITION STROKE	Position of stroke

3.3   Signature Preprocessing

The resulting Beta elliptic signature is in a complicated form, we use the Huffman Compression (HC) to simplify it, and to increase the performance of our system by reducing the size of secret data to be embedded. The Huffman compression algorithm relies on the frequency of the occurrence of a symbol in the file to be compressed [12]. Figure 2 illustrates how the Huffman code works in a text example. After the compression of the text ABEACADABEA, the obtained code is presented as 23 bits, while the resulting ASCII code is presented as 88 bits (11 characters 8 bits). Thus, the Huffman code saves more than 26% in the size of the message.

3.4   Weighted Secret Data Repartition

To embed the Beta Elliptic Signature, transformed by the Huffman Coding (BES-HC), into the color document image, we subdivide it into three sub-messages m_R, m_G, and m_B in order to embed it into the corresponding R, G, and B color channels. We associate to each color channel a weight α_R, α_G, and

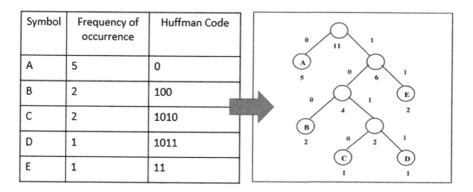

Symbol	Frequency of occurrence	Huffman Code
A	5	0
B	2	100
C	2	1010
D	1	1011
E	1	11

Fig. 2. Huffman compression algorithm

α_B, that represents the number of bits embedded into the selected channel. The weights are calculated as follows:

$$\alpha_C = P_C \times L, \text{ and } \sum \alpha_C = L, \text{ with } C = \{R, G, B\} \tag{2}$$

$$P_C = \frac{PSNR(C)}{PSNR(R) + PSNR(G) + PSNR(B)} \text{ and } \sum P_C = 1, \text{ with } C = \{R, G, B\} \tag{3}$$

where L denotes the length of BES-HC and PSNR is the Peak Signal to Noise Ratio defined while embedding the BES into the red, green, or blue channel separately. Finally, P_C represents the number of bits ratio embedded into each color channel C. Equation (3) represents the mathematical formula to obtain the number of bits ratio.

Since the BES is subdivided into three parts according to the values of α_R, α_G, and α_B, subsequently. The first range of the BES bits is fed to m_R which would be embedded into the red channel. The same process is done in the second range of the BES bits, representing the green sub-message (m_G) and same for the last range of bits (m_B). Equation 4 explains the message bit selection.

$$\begin{cases} m_R = BESHC(i), & 1 \leq i \leq \alpha_R \\ m_G = BESHC(i), & \alpha_R < i \leq \alpha_R + \alpha_G \\ m_R = BESHC(i), & \alpha_R + \alpha_G < i \leq L \end{cases} \tag{4}$$

3.5   CDISS-BEMOS Embedding Algorithm

The sub-message bits m_R, m_G, and m_B are sequentially embedded into the red, green, blue channels, in the embedding regions by replacing the 1-LSB of the concerned channel with the ith element of the associated weight. The embedding algorithm is mathematically stated as:

$$S(C) = LSB(C(Fp(i))), C = \{R, G, B\} \tag{5}$$

$$LSB(C(Fp(i))) = \begin{cases} m_R(i) \ if \ C = R, & 1 \leq i \leq \alpha_R \\ m_G(i) \ if \ C = G, \ \alpha_R < i \leq \alpha_R + \alpha_G \\ m_B(i) \ if \ C = B, \ \alpha_R + \alpha_G < i \leq L \end{cases} \tag{6}$$

where S is the stego color document image, and C is the host color channel R, G, or B, Fp(i) is the ith Feature points. Finally, combine the three stego channels S(R), S(G), and S(B) to obtain the stego color document image:

$$SDCI = S(R) + S(G) + S(B). \tag{7}$$

3.6   CDISS-BEMOS Extracting Algorithm

During the transmission, the color document images may be suffering from various distortions. To verify that the document was not altered, the extraction algorithm is used to extract the embedding Beta elliptic signature from the stego document image. The extracted sub-message bits m'_R, m'_G, and m'_B are retrieved by:

$$ExBES = \{m'_R + m'_G + m'_B\} \tag{8}$$

$$\begin{cases} m'_R(i) = LSB(S(R(Fp')_i)), & 1 \leq i \leq \alpha_R \\ m'_G(i) = LSB(S(G(Fp')_i)), \ \alpha_R < i \leq \alpha_R + \alpha_G \\ m'_B(i) = LSB(S(B(Fp')_i)), \ \alpha_R + \alpha_G < i \leq L \end{cases} \tag{9}$$

where $m_R'(i)$, $m_G'(i)$, and $m_B'(i)$ are the ith elements extracted from S(R), S(G), and S(B), respectively, Fp' is the feature points list identified from the stego color document image, and ExBES is the extracted Beta elliptic signature.

4   Experimental Results and Discussion

4.1   Setting and Parameters

Table 2 presents the parameters used in our study for Beta elliptic modeling and BRISK detector.

Table 2. Beta elliptic and BRISK parameters

Method	Parameters	Designations	Values
Beta Elliptic Model	(x(t), y(t))	Coordinates of the handwriting (signature) trajectory with pen points	–
	h	Height of handwriting (signature)	h = 128
	fcut	Cut-off frequency of Chebyshev type II filter	fcut = 12 Hz
BRISK	n	Number of octaves used in scale-space pyramid layers	n = 4
	AGAST	Detection process algorithm	–
	ρ	Side length of the square box mean filter	ρ = 2.6 · σ

4.2   Benchmarks

The CDISS-BEMOS system is tested on three benchmarks: L3iDocCopies, LRDE DBD, and standard test images. Since we did not find studies based on specialized databases for color image document steganography, except L3iDocCopies, we chose to test our system on the LRDE DBD database. Table 3 presents the benchmark details.

Table 3. Benchmarks used to evaluate the CDISS-BEMOS system

Benchmarks	Name	Number of documents used	Size
Type1	[a]L3iDocCopies	20	4.2 GB
Type2	[b]LRDE DBD	20	583 MB
Type3	[c]Standard Test Image	10	12.4 MB

[a]http://l3i-share.univ-lr.fr/datasets/DocCopiesWebsite/DocCopiesDataset.html
[b]http://www.iapr-tc11.org/mediawiki/index.php/LRDE_Document_Binarization_Dataset
[c]http://sipi.usc.edu/database/database

4.3   Evaluation Metrics

To evaluate the robustness of the CIDSS-BEMOS system, the common evaluation metrics of image distortion are used, like Peak Signal to Noise Ratio (PSNR) and Structural Similarity Index Metrics (SSIM). They can be calculated via the Eqs. 10–12 as follows:

$$PSNR = 10.\log_{10}(255^2/MSE) \qquad (10)$$

$$MSE = \frac{1}{NM}\sum_{x=1}^{N}\sum_{y=1}^{M}(H(x,y) - (S(x,y))^2 \qquad (11)$$

PSNR is calculated using Means Squared Error (MSE), where MN is the size of the host image H and stego images S respectively.

$$SSIM = \frac{(2u_h u_s + c1)(2o_{hs} + c2)}{(u_h^2 + u_s^2 + c1)(o_h^2 + o_s^2 + c2)} \qquad (12)$$

where μ_h and μ_s are the average of H and S, and σ_h and σ_s denote the standard deviation of H and S respectively. Moreover, σ_{sh} is the covariance of H and S. c1 and c2are two variables to stabilize the division with weak denominator where $C1 = (k1 * L)^2$, $C2 = (k2 * L)^2$, L is the dynamic range of the pixel-values (typically this is 2 (bit per pixel) -1), k1 = 0.01 and k2 = 0.03 by default.

4.4   Quantitative Study

In this study we have used one signature to evaluate the performance of CDISS-BEMOS on three types of datasets. The signature image is shown in Fig. 3. The size of the Beta elliptic signature after the Huffman compression is $L = 127$ bits where we obtain the values of $P_R = 0.3341$, $P_G = 0.3321$, $P_B = 0.3338$. So the obtained weight values are $\alpha_R = 0.3341* L = 43$ bits, $\alpha_G = 0.3321* L = 42$ bits, and $\alpha_B = 0.3338* L = 42$ bits. However, the BES-HC is subdivided into three sub-message bits m_R, m_G, and m_B. The first 43 bits of the BES are fed to the m_R, the second 42 bits of the BES are fed to m_G and the last 42 bits are fed to the m_B. The results of applying the proposed system on three types of datasets are presented in Table 4.

Fig. 3. The image signature

In order to prove the performance of the proposed CDISS-BEMOS system, a quantitative evaluation is carried out on the three benchmarks. In addition, We have tested our system in the YCbCr color space by hiding the BES-HC into the Y component, in order to choose the best color space for color document image steganography, according to the achieved results.

Table 4 illustrates the resulting PSNR values of the CDISS-BEMOS system on 20 images of L3iDocCopies, LRDE DBD, and 10 images of Standard test images benchmarks, compared to the YCbCr-LSB-BRISK, Sejpal and Shah [29], Muhammad et al. [19], and Abraham and Paul [2] systems. It demonstrates that our system is more efficient compared with YCbCr-LSB-BRISK method and the related work in terms of distortion measurement.

Table 4. Comparison PSNR results of CDISS-BEMOS system and existing systems

Benchmarks	PSNR				
	CDISS-BEMOS	YCbCr-LSB-BRISK	[29]	[2]	[19]
L3iDocCopies	93,0712	37,0583	–	–	–
LRDE DBD	92,1843	44,5265	–	–	–
Standard test images	93,4291	56,4678	90.6093	53.5833	45.0309

Accordingly, the SSIM metric has been used to evaluate the performance of our CDISS-BEMOS and the existing systems. Table 5 shows the quantitative results based on SSIM and PSNR on 10 standard test images. Compared to previous researches, our proposed system realized better results, demonstrating its effectiveness in terms of SSIM and PSNR.

Table 5. Quantitative evaluation using PSNR & SSIM of CDISS-BEMOS and existing system

Images	CDISS-BEMOS		[19]		[2]	
	PSNR	SSIM	PSNR	SSIM	PSNR	SSIM
Lena	93.4232	0.9989	48.7445	–	53.6400	0.9927
Baboon	93.5656	0.9990	47.8747	0.9992	53.4600	0.9969
House	93.5656	0.9991	52.7303	0.9989	–	–
F16jet	92.9663	0.9989	53.1665	0.9985	–	–
Tree	93.2164	0.9986	49.7496	0.9970	–	–
Scene	93.1517	0.9979	46.8066	–	–	–
Flowers	93.8652	0.9985	42.3607	–	53.6500	0.9980
Building	93.4007	0.9979	56.8918	0.9973	–	–
Parrot	93.7128	0.9995	49.2153	–	–	–
Masjid	93.4232	0.9900	44.7425	0.9828	–	–
Average	**93.4291**	**0.9978**	**45.0309**	**0.9956**	**53.5833**	**0.9958**

The results comparison of the CDISS-BEMOS system based on PSNR with related works methods including Sejpal and Shah [29], Muhammed et al. [19], and Abraham and Paul [2] are presented in Fig. 4. It is clear from Fig. 4 that the performance of the CDISS-BEMOS system bypass those of Sejpal and Shah [29], Muhammed et al. [19], and Abraham and Paul [2]. However, Sejpal and Shah [29] predominate other systems except for the proposed system. Muhammed et al. [19], gives worse results in proportion to this experiment.

4.5 Qualitative Study

The qualitative evaluation of the CDISS-BEMOS can be measured using the Human Visual System (HVS) by analyzing the histograms variability of host and stego document images for three examples images of benchmarks, produced by our system. The HVS is examined as shown in Fig. 5. From HVS results, it could be deduced that the histograms of the host images are the same as the histograms of stego images generated via the CDISS-BEMOS system, thus confirming the validity of our system.

4.6 Robustness Evaluation of Extracted Secret Message

To further evaluate the robustness of the extracted Beta elliptic signature, we have used the accuracy ratio exploited in [5]. The method is computed using Eq. 13 as follows:

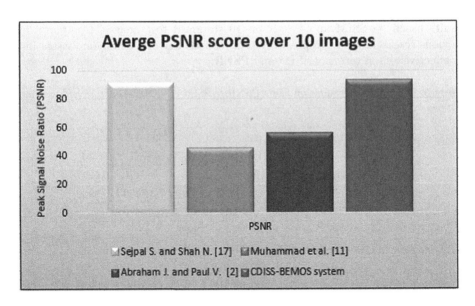

Fig. 4. PSNR based comparison of the CDISS-BEMOS system with state-of-the-art methods

$$AccR = \frac{\sum_{i=1}^{m} \neg(BES(i) \oplus ExBES(i)))}{m} \tag{13}$$

where:

- BES(i) is the ith bit in the original Beta elliptic signature,
- ExBES(i) is the ith bit in the extracted Beta elliptic signature,
- m is the length of Beta elliptic signature,
- $\neg$ denotes the NOT operator,
- and $\oplus$ depicts the exclusive-OR operator.

Table 6 illustrates that the embedded BES could be totally extracted with 100% accuracy ratio which demonstrate that the proposed steganography system in RGB color space is able to attain the extreme accuracy ratio under the context without noises.

Table 6. Accuracy ratio and quality of embedded documents

Benchmarks	Name	PSNR	SSIM	AccR
Type1	L3iDocCopies	93,0712	0.999	100%
Type2	LRDE DBD	92,1843	0.999	100%
Type3	Standard test image	93,4291	0.999	100%

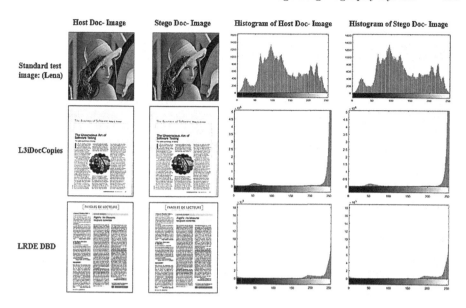

Fig. 5. Visual quality of stego images (Standard test image Lena, L3iDocCopies, LRDE DBD) produced by CDISS-BEMOS system

5   Conclusion

A new color document image steganography system based on the Beta elliptic modeling of online signature is presented in this paper, in order to provide the security of these documents when its transmission over the public network. The Beta elliptic signature is hidden into the three color channels R, G, and B, in the specific embedding regions identified by the BRISK detector. The embedding process is based on the LSB technique using the weighted secret data repartition step. Our CIDSS-BEMOS system retains a stronger document security, a better image quality, and less computational complexity. In the next works, we aspire to increase the scanned document security by combining both the steganography and cryptography approaches.

Acknowledgment. The research leading to these results has received funding from the Ministry of Higher Education and Scientific Research of Tunisia under the grant agreement number LR11ES48.

References

1. Abdulrahman, A.K., Ozturk, S.: A novel hybrid DCT and DWT based robust watermarking algorithm for color images. Multimed. Tools Appl. **78**, 17027–17049 (2019)
2. Abraham, J., Paul, V.: An imperceptible spatial domain color image watermarking scheme. J. King Saud Univ.-Comput. Inf. Sci. (2016)

3. Al-Haj, A., Barouqa, H.: Copyright protection of e-government document images using digital watermarking. In: 2017 3rd International Conference on Information Management (ICIM), pp. 441–446. IEEE (2017)
4. Bezine, H., Alimi, A.M., Derbel, N.: Handwriting trajectory movements controlled by a beta-elliptic model. In: Proceedings of the Seventh International Conference on Document Analysis and Recognition, p. 1228. IEEE (2003)
5. Burie, J.C., Ogier, J.M., Loc, C.V.: A spatial domain steganography for grayscale documents using pattern recognition techniques. In: 2017 14th IAPR International Conference on Document Analysis and Recognition (ICDAR), vol. 9, pp. 21–26. IEEE (2017)
6. Dhieb, T., Njah, S., Boubaker, H., Ouarda, W., Ayed, M.B., Alimi, A.M.: An online writer identification system based on beta-elliptic model and fuzzy elementary perceptual codes. arXiv preprint arXiv:1804.05661 (2018)
7. Dhieb, T., Ouarda, W., Boubaker, H., Alimi, A.M.: Beta-elliptic model forwriter identification from online arabic handwriting. J. Inf. Assur. Secur. **11**(5), 263–272 (2016)
8. Dhieb, T., Ouarda, W., Boubaker, H., Halima, M.B., Alimi, A.M.: Online Arabic writer identification based on beta-elliptic model. In: ISDA, pp. 74–79 (2015)
9. García-Soto, R., Hernández-Anaya, S., Nakano-Miyatake, M., Rosales-Roldan, L., Perez-Meana, H.: Sender verification system for official documents based on watermarking technique. In: 2013 10th International Conference on Electrical Engineering, Computing Science and Automatic Control (CCE), pp. 227–232. IEEE (2013)
10. Gonge, S.S., Ghatol, A.A.: Combined DWT-DCT digital watermarking technique software used for CTS of bank. In: 2014 International Conference on Issues and Challenges in Intelligent Computing Techniques (ICICT), pp. 776–783. IEEE (2014)
11. Hamdani, M., El Abed, H., Kherallah, M., Alimi, A.M.: Combining multiple HMMS using on-line and off-line features for off-line Arabic handwriting recognition. In: 10th International Conference on Document Analysis and Recognition (ICDAR 2009), pp. 201–205. IEEE (2009)
12. Huffman, D.A.: A method for the construction of minimum-redundancy codes. Proc. IRE **40**(9), 1098–1101 (1952)
13. Jarraya, I., Ouarda, W., Alimi, A.M.: Deep neural network features for horses identity recognition using multiview horses' face pattern. In: Ninth International Conference on Machine Vision (ICMV 2016), vol. 10341, p. 103410B. International Society for Optics and Photonics (2017)
14. Lazzez, O., Ouarda, W., Alimi, A.M.: Age, gender, race and smile prediction based on social textual and visual data analyzing. In: Madureira, A.M., Abraham, A., Gamboa, D., Novais, P. (eds.) ISDA 2016. AISC, vol. 557, pp. 206–215. Springer, Cham (2017). https://doi.org/10.1007/978-3-319-53480-0_21
15. Lazzez, O., Ouarda, W., Alimi, A.M.: Understand me if you can! Global soft biometrics recognition from social visual data. In: Abraham, A., Haqiq, A., Alimi, A.M., Mezzour, G., Rokbani, N., Muda, A.K. (eds.) HIS 2016. AISC, vol. 552, pp. 527–538. Springer, Cham (2017). https://doi.org/10.1007/978-3-319-52941-7_52
16. Leutenegger, S., Chli, M., Siegwart, R.Y.: BRISK: binary robust invariant scalable keypoints. IEEE (2011)
17. Li, J., Yu, C., Gupta, B., Ren, X.: Color image watermarking scheme based on quaternion Hadamard transform and Schur decomposition. Multimed. Tools Appl. **77**(4), 4545–4561 (2018)

18. Ltaief, M., Bezine, H., Alimi, A.M.: A neuro-beta-elliptic model for handwriting generation movements. In: 2012 International Conference on Frontiers in Handwriting Recognition (ICFHR 2012), pp. 803–808. IEEE (2012)

19. Muhammad, K., Ahmad, J., Rehman, N.U., Jan, Z., Sajjad, M.: CISSKA-LSB: color image steganography using stego key-directed adaptive LSB substitution method. Multimed. Tools Appl. **76**(6), 8597–8626 (2017)

20. Munib, S., Khan, A.: Robust image watermarking technique using triangular regions and Zernike moments for quantization based embedding. Multimed. Tools Appl. **76**(6), 8695–8710 (2017)

21. Nasri, H., Ouarda, W., Alimi, A.M.: ReLiDSS: novel lie detection system from speech signal. In: 2016 IEEE/ACS 13th International Conference of Computer Systems and Applications (AICCSA), pp. 1–8. IEEE (2016)

22. Nissim, N., Cohen, A., Elovici, Y.: ALDOCX: detection of unknown malicious microsoft office documents using designated active learning methods based on new structural feature extraction methodology. IEEE Trans. Inf. Forensics Secur. **12**(3), 631–646 (2016)

23. Ouarda, W., Trichili, H., Alimi, A.M., Solaiman, B.: Bag of face recognition systems based on holistic approaches. In: 2015 15th International Conference on Intelligent Systems Design and Applications (ISDA), pp. 201–206. IEEE (2015)

24. Ouarda, W., Trichili, H., Alimi, A.M., Solaiman, B.: Towards a novel biometric-system for smart riding club. J. Inf. Assur. Secur. **11**(4), 201–213 (2016)

25. Pandey, M.K., Parmar, G., Gupta, R., Sikander, A.: Non-blind Arnold scrambled hybrid image watermarking in YCbCr color space. Microsyst. Technol., 1–11 (2018)

26. Patvardhan, C., Kumar, P., Lakshmi, C.V.: Effective color image watermarking scheme using YCbCr color space and QR code. Multimed. Tools Appl., 1–23 (2018)

27. Pham, V.Q., Miyaki, T., Yamasaki, T., Aizawa, K.: Geometrically invariant object-based watermarking using SIFT feature. In: 2007 IEEE International Conference on Image Processing, vol. 5, pp. V–473. IEEE (2007)

28. Prasad, V., Dhavale, S.: H. 264/AVC video protection model based on private cloud for military organisation. In: 2016 International Conference on Circuit, Power and Computing Technologies (ICCPCT), pp. 1–9. IEEE (2016)

29. Sejpal, S., Shah, N.: Comparative performance analysis of secured LWT-SVD based color image watermarking technique in YUV, YIQ and YCbCr color spaces. Int. J. Comput. Appl. **147**(7), 34–40 (2016)

30. Su, Q., Chen, B.: Robust color image watermarking technique in the spatial domain. Soft. Comput. **22**(1), 91–106 (2018)

31. Wang, H.: Communication-resource-aware adaptive watermarking for multimedia authentication in wireless multimedia sensor networks. J. Supercomput. **64**(3), 883–897 (2013)

Distributed Detection System and Blockchain

A Graph Based Model for UAVs Group-Wide Collaboration Applied on an Anti-terrorism Scenario

Amal Gassara[1,2](✉) and Ismael Bouassida Rodriguez[1,2]

[1] ReDCAD Research laboratory, University of Sfax, B.P. 1173, 3038 Sfax, Tunisia
amal.gassara@redcad.org
[2] Digital Research Center of Sfax, B.P. 275, 3021 Sakiet Ezzit, Sfax, Tunisia

Abstract. Adaptation of collaboration is needed to maintain the connectivity and quality of communication in group-wide collaborative activities. This becomes quite a challenge to handle when mobile entities are part of a wireless environment. In this paper, these challenges are addressed within the context of the SUPERSENS project where Unmanned Aerial Vehicles (UAVs) have to collaborate either between themselves or with remote human actors during search-and-rescue missions. This paper presents our first results. The final goal is to propose new concepts, models and architectures that support cooperative adaptation which is aware of the mission being executed. Thus, the collaboration can be adequately adapted in response to the mission requirements and to the changes in the resource constraints.

Keywords: A graph based model · Unmanned Aerial Vehicles · Collaboration

1 Introduction

Drones or Unmanned Aerial Vehicles (UAVs) have become a subject of innovation in different fields and their use are expanded for several types of missions such as search-and-rescue missions, surveillance systems, military uses, delivery services, etc. They present a promising solution for the most dangerous missions or costly to be performed by humans.

With advances in the UAV technology and their availability in the market, research and development are more interested in collaborative UAV systems (a set of drones that are networked to achieve a mission). These systems are needed especially for missions that are dangerous or span a large geographical area where one drone is insufficient due to its limited energy and payload.

The design of an architectural model for UAVs collaboration in changing environments is among the main research directions of autonomic computing and communication. Providing such solutions for distributed software systems supporting group collaboration [1] requires managing evolving group membership.

ⓒ Springer Nature Switzerland AG 2020
S. Kallel et al. (Eds.): CRiSIS 2019, LNCS 12026, pp. 311–324, 2020.
https://doi.org/10.1007/978-3-030-41568-6_20

For a number of group communication-based applications, anticipate reconfiguration is important. In order to be applicable in different situations, one has also to ensure tractability of the elaborated solutions when the mission is changing or evolving. Providing generic and scalable solutions for reconfiguration in group collaboration support systems can be driven by rule-based architectural reconfiguration policies. This is the approach we adopt and we propose in this paper. We elaborate a structural model that may represent the different interactions dependencies from different mission points of view.

To be illustrated, our approach is applied on the SUPERSENS project where UAVs have to collaborate during search-and-rescue missions. The project provides a real-world case study that introduces a network of collaborative UAVs. The UAVs network is used for a surveillance system that aims to detect terrorists and follow them in closed military zones (i.e., vast, dangerous areas and difficult to be accessed).

In order to design the adaptation of collaboration, we provide a rule-based reconfiguration model consisting of a set of graph adaptation rules. These rules will be triggered according to defined events related to environment and resource changes in order to achieve the mission. To execute this model, we implemented the graph rules using GMTE [2], a graph matching and transformation engine. Then, we executed and applied them on graphs representing the UAV system giving then new graphs representing the new system architectures after adaptations.

The remainder of this paper is organized as follows. We present in Sect. 2 the SUPERSENS project and our case study of a drone collaborative system. Section 3 presents our approach for modeling the architecture and the dynamic aspect of an UAVs system. Then, we present in Sect. 4 the experimentation with GMTE tool and in Sect. 5 the related work. Finally, Sect. 6 concludes this paper and presents future work.

2   Context: The SUPERSENS project

Our work is part of the SUPERSENS project that provides a real-world case study presenting an anti-terrorism scenario. In the following, we give a brief description of this project and then we present the drone collaborative system and how it works with the use case scenario.

2.1   Description of the SUPERSENS project

In last years, terrorist threats are becoming more and more preoccupying for governments. Thus, the governments have classified as high-risk areas the borders, the desert, etc. The surveillance of these zones is an important task for the military and the police. The monitoring of these extensive areas -difficult to access- remains a complex task to be covered entirely by a human presence. Several digital technologies make possible to monitor (eg. high resolution remote sensing (HR), wireless sensor network), information processing (image and video processing, heterogeneous data analysis). We are interested in this paper to UAV technology: autonomous and cooperative. To ensure military/police needs, we propose to define a system to automate surveillance using autonomous and cooperative UAVs. These UAVs cooperate and adapt their behavior according to the environment of the mission.

2.2   Description of a Drone Collaborative System

A drone collaborative system can have a centralized or decentralized architecture. Within the centralized architecture, an entity on the ground collects information, makes decisions for drones, and updates the mission or tasks. However, within the decentralized architecture, the drones need to explicitly cooperate on different levels to achieve the system goals and exchange information to share tasks and make collective decisions [3].

For both architectures, the drones should, first, observe the environment. Then, they should evaluate their own observations and information received from other drones, and reason from them. Reasoning can be done at the centralized control entity or on board the drones. Finally, they act in an effective way.

2.3   Use Case of a Drone Collaborative System

In our work, we use a centralized drone collaborative system. All drones are connected to a supervision station that collects data from drones and make decisions to adapt the system in order to achieve the mission. This mission consists in the surveillance of a military area, the detection of terrorists and tracking them by drones.

To monitor an area, we propose a surveillance scenario by a drone patrol. This surveillance scenario involves sending a drone patrol regularly. Each drone monitors a specific area and follows a predefined trajectory.

The activity diagram in Fig. 1 presents the scenario. At the beginning, each drone (D_{area}) monitors its area following its trajectory and sends the data stream (video) to the supervision station supervised by an operator agent. This agent supervises the video in order to verify if there is an intruder. If an intruder is detected, he/she sends an order to the drone to track the intruder as well as he/she sends a new drone as enhancement. While tracking, if the D_{area} drone reaches the border of its area, it backs to its area for surveillance and the agent sends an order to its neighbor (D_{neighb}) to continue the tracking.

Moreover, while tracking, if a drone (D_{area}, D_{new} or D_{neighb}) has a low battery level, the agent sends a new drone to replace the drone and continue its mission (i.e., tracking or surveillance) and the latter drone returns to the supervision station.

Furthermore, if a drone (D_{area}, D_{new} or D_{neighb}) is tracking an intruder, and it detects a new intruder, the agent sends a new drone as an enhancement.

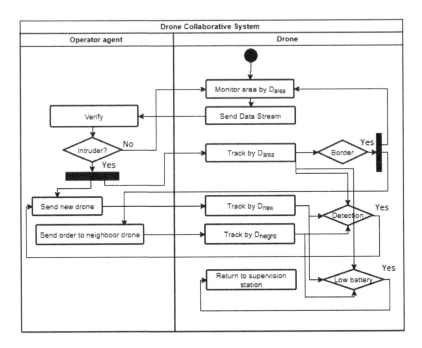

Fig. 1. Activity diagram of the surveillance scenario by a drone patrol

3   Modeling UAVs Systems

The solution we propose here is a Monitor-inference-results loop, as illustrated in Fig. 2. The first step in the loop is to capture the state of the world, that is to say the set of information that we want to represent. In our case, this state includes the drones presenting their position, battery levels, flows that send each other, etc. This capture is done by the code of the application, which then represents the captured state as an instance represented by a graph. Such instance is a set of drones that belongs at the mission and are represented to the graph. This graph is used by the application as a template representing the state of the mission at a given moment. The application can execute the rules associated with the mission and perform transformations done by a graph matching and transformation engine (i.e., we use GMTE) on the first graph. The result is a graph modified with the new state to the mission it evolved. Then, the application scans the new graph and performs the actions necessary to arrive at the desired state.

In this paper, we focus on the inference part of the loop that takes as inputs the graph representing the current system architecture and the graph rules representing the system reconfigurations. For this reason, we present in the following sections modeling the system architecture as well as modeling its dynamic aspect (reconfigurations).

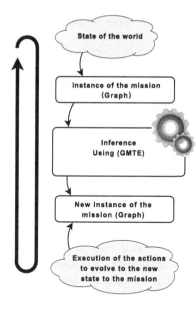

Fig. 2. Capture-inference-results loop

3.1   Modeling Language: Graphs

Graphs and graphs rewriting have been successfully applied for the description of software architectures and modeling communicating systems. Within graph-based approaches, a system configuration is represented by a graph and graph rewriting rules can express reconfigurations. Besides, as a generic model, graphs may be used to represent different structures and components types such as software components, hardware components, locations, physical entities, etc. This motivates us to adopt graphs as a modeling formalism of drone collaborative system.

A graph [4] is a graphical representation composed of a set of nodes and edges that connect some pairs of these nodes. Graph nodes represent system entities. Whereas, edges represent communications (connections) between them. In order to describe the dynamic of a system, reconfigurations are defined using graph rewriting rules. A rule is a pair of graphs (L, R) where L is the left-hand side and R is the right-hand side. Applying the rule means finding a match of L in the source graph and replacing it by R, leading to the target graph. These rules describe the topology changes of an architecture in terms of adding and/or removing components and/or connections.

3.2   Modeling the System Architecture

With graphs, a system configuration is modeled by a graph where the nodes represent the components of the system and the links represent the connections between them. Nodes are tagged with labels to represent information about system components.

We define the following nodes:

- D representing a Drone. It is tagged by the following labels: position, battery level, time stamp and state (which can be on the ground, exploration, detection, tracking or failed).
- SS representing the Supervision Station.
- AP representing the Analysis Platform.
- I representing an Intruder. It is tagged by position and time stamp labels.

In order to achieve the surveillance scenario by a drone patrol, it is first necessary to divide the military area in partitions. Each partition will be monitored by a drone. For a maximum coverage of the area, we propose to divide it into sectors of a circle as shown in Fig. 3(a). Also, we propose a trajectory for each drone as depicted in Fig. 3(b). Using this partitioning of the area and the trajectory of drones, we can calculate the number of drones participating in the patrol. In our case, we find that we need six drones for covering the studied area after calculations based also on the used drone characteristics.

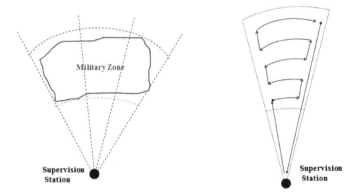

(a) The military area divided into circle sectors

(b) The drone trajectory in a partition

Fig. 3. The partitioning of the area

Using the node types, we model the initial configuration of the system, depicted in Fig. 4, where D_{zi} are the identifiers of the drones (For instance, D_{z1} is the drone that will monitor the first partition of the military zone). For sake of clearness, we present in the figure only the position and state labels. The SS node representing the supervision station is connected to an AP node that represents the analysis platform. This platform ensures the treatment and the analysis of data from different sources. It allows, for example, to verify if the detected intruder is a terrorist.

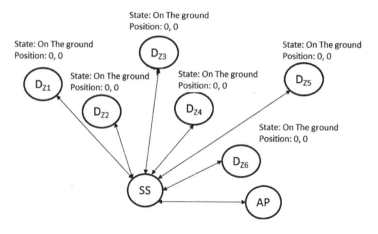

Fig. 4. The graph describing the first system architecture

3.3 Modeling the Dynamic Aspect of the System: Reconfigurations

The dynamic aspect is represented by reconfigurations. These reconfigurations are defined through graph rules. To do this, we define five rules.

- R1: Exploration rule: This rule allows to start the exploration mission of the collaborative drone system. It modifies each drone state from the on ground state to the exploration state. And then, the drone will fly on the air and follows its defined trajectory in order to reach its zone for surveillance.
- R2: Detection rule: This rule is triggered when a drone detects an intruder. First, it modifies the drone state to "tracking" state. Then, it connects the drone to a new node representing the intruder. Also, it adds a new drone node connected to the supervision station.
- R3: Border rule: This rule is triggered when a drone approaches to the border of its zone while is tracking an intruder. Hence, the rule modifies the drone state to "exploration" and disconnects it from the intruder node. Then, it modifies the sate of the neighbor drone to tracking and connects it to the intruder node.
- R4: Low battery rule: This rule allows to add new drone to the graph model when a drone having a low battery level in order to continue the tracking process.
- R5: Breakdown drone rule: This rule allows to add a new drone to the graph model when a drone is breakdown to continue the exploration or the tracking process.

These reconfiguration rules will be described with more details in the experimentation section.

4   Experimentation

To test our approach, we will deploy the control loop which is composed of three main software components: the monitoring component that is used to capture the state of drones; GMTE which executes reconfiguration graph rules and finally, the execution component which executes the necessary actions to apply reconfigurations by sending orders to drones and updating their states.

In the following, we focus on implementing the use case with GMTE.

4.1   Implementing the Uses Case with GMTE

GMTE is a tool for graph matching and transformation, for executing an encoded rule on an encoded graph. The GMTE rule graph is partitioned into three zones that determine the rule application and the changes that occur when a rule is applicable (Fig. 5(a)).

– The Inv zone: representing a fragment of the rule which must be identified in the graph;
– The Del zone: is under a fragment of the Inv zone that will be deleted on the application of the rule;
– The Add zone: is the fragment that will be added after the application of the rule.

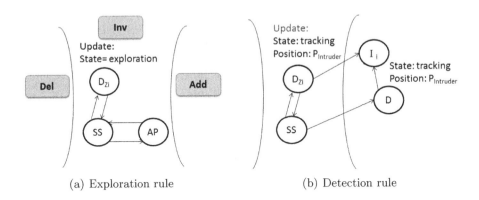

(a) Exploration rule   (b) Detection rule

Fig. 5. Reconfiguration rules

Using GMTE, we have implemented our defined reconfiguration rules. In the following, we present the first three rules with their graphical representation:

– R1: Exploration rule: As depicted in Fig. 5(a), this rule modifies a drone state to exploration state.

- R2: Detection rule: As depicted in Fig. 5(b), this rule modifies, first, the drone (D_{Zi}) state to tracking state. Then, it connects the drone to a new node representing the Intruder (I_i). Also, it adds a new node drone (D) connected to the supervision station (SS).
- R3: Border rule: This rule, as showed in Fig. 6, modifies the drone state (D_{zi}) to exploration and disconnects it from the intruder node (I_i). Then, it modifies the sate of the neighbor (D_{neigh}) drone to tracking and connects it to the intruder node.

After implementing the rules and the graph representing the initial system architecture, we can execute some rules according to our proposed algorithm.

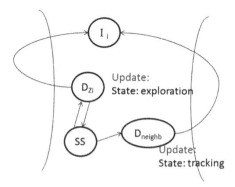

Fig. 6. Border rule

4.2   Proposed Algorithm

We proposed an algorithm that is used in the inference part of the control loop. It defines the reconfiguration rule to be executed when an event is triggered.

Listing 1.1. Reconfiguration Algorithm

```
1   Let A0: initial system architecture
2   Let Ei: an event from {E1: start exploration, E2: detection, E3: border,
3                          E4: low battery, E5: breakdown drone}
4   Let Ri: a graph reconfiguration rule from {R1: Exploration rule, R2: Detection
5           rule, R3: Border rule, R4: Low battery rule,  R5: Breakdown drone rule}
6   Let n=1
7   If Ei=E1 then A1 <- Apply as possible (A0, R1)
8   While (true)
9       If Ei= E2 (D_{Zi}, I_{i}) then
10              An+1 <- Apply (An, R2(D_{Zi}, I_{i})); n++
11          If Ei= E3 (D_{Zi}, I_{i}) then
12                  An+1 <- Apply (An, R3(D_{Zi}, I_{i}, D_{neigh})); n++
13          If Ei= E4 (D_{Zi}, I_{i}) then
14                  An+1 <- Apply (An, R4(D_{Zi}, I_{i})); n++
15          If Ei= E5 (D_{Zi}) then
16                  An+1 <- Apply (An, R5(D_{Zi})); n++
17  End while
```

At the beginning, the exploration event (E1) is triggered and then, the exploration rule (R1) will be executed on the first system architecture A0 (cf. line 7 of Listing 1.1). This rule is applied as possible that's means it is applied until all drones in the graph will have the exploration state. In other words, it is applied as times as the number of drones in the graph (e.g., in our case, it is six). The application of this rule gives a new graph representing a new system architecture A1.

After that, according to the triggered event, a rule will be applied. For example, if the event is a detection of an intruder I_1 by the drone D_{Z2}, the rule R2 with the parameters D_{Z2} and I_1 will be applied on the current system architecture to obtain a new system architecture (cf. lines 9 and 10 of Listing 1.1).

In order to implement this reconfiguration with GMTE, we should give as inputs the graph of the current system as an xml representation (Fig. 9) and also the xml representation of the graph rule (Fig. 7). In these xml files, the values of drone positions will be given by the application of the control loop. It allows to give the current location of each node in the network.

The application of the rule on the graph gives a new graph depicted in Fig. 8. For sake of clearness, we present in this graph only the state and position labels of nodes.

5   Related Work

In the literature, the essence of UAV systems is captured by a high level building blocks [3] consisting of the Sensing block, Communication and Networking block and the Coordination block. The Sensing block is responsible for observing the environment and analyzing the collected data from the environment and/or other vehicles, whereas Communication and Networking block enables dissemination of information between devices in the network. The decision- making (e.g., path planning and task sharing) is handled by Coordination block, which processes feedback and constraints from the remaining building blocks.

Many projects used the UAVs system for search and rescue applications. Each project focuses on the design of one or more of these blocks. For example, COMETS [5] is a research project that aims at designing and implementing a distributed control system for cooperative activities using heterogeneous UAVs. It addressed mission planning and cooperative imaging. Also, it focused on developing and implementing control algorithms. RESCUECELL [6] aims at developing a cost-effective, robust and lightweight UAV system, that can easily be transported to disaster struck areas. The system allows to spread the UAVs properly to cover the entire zone, and also to guide rescuers by giving precise indications of the location of injured people.

However, the SINUS project [7] aims at using an autonomous UAVs system for SAR missions by focusing on a complete system integration considering all the system modules coordination, communication and sensing. Closed to this project, the SUPERSENS project aims also at implementing a complete system. However, in this paper, we present our proposal for the coordination block.

```
<rule id="0">
    <zones>
        <zoneInv>
            <node id="n0">
                <data typedata="const">Dz5</data>
                <data typedata="const">Position:rD5,alphaD5</data>
                <data typedata="const">batteryLevel:80%</data>
                <data typedata="const">timeStamp:t1</data>
                <data typedata="const">state:exploration</data>
            </node>
            <node id="n1"><data typedata="const">SS</data></node>
            <node id="n2"><data typedata="const">AP</data></node>
        </zoneInv>
        <zoneAdd>
            <node id="n3">
                <data typedata="const">Dnew</data>
                <data typedata="const">Position:rI1,alphaI1</data>
                <data typedata="const">batteryLevel:95%</data>
                <data typedata="const">timeStamp:t2</data>
                <data typedata="const">state:tracking</data>
            </node>
            <node id="n4">
                <data typedata="const">I1</data>
                <data typedata="const">Position:rI1,alphaI1</data>
                <data typedata="const">timeStamp:t2</data>
            </node>
        </zoneAdd>
    </zones>
    <edges>
        <edge source="n0" target="n4"></edge>
        <edge source="n1" target="n3"></edge> ..
    </edges>
    <modifInstructions>
        <node id="n0">
            <data typedata="const">Dz5</data>
            <data typedata="const">Position:rI1,alphaI1</data>
            <data typedata="const">batteryLevel:80%</data>
            <data typedata="const">timeStamp:t2</data>
            <data typedata="const">state:tracking</data>
        </node>
    </modifInstructions>
</rule>
```

Fig. 7. The xml representation of detection rule

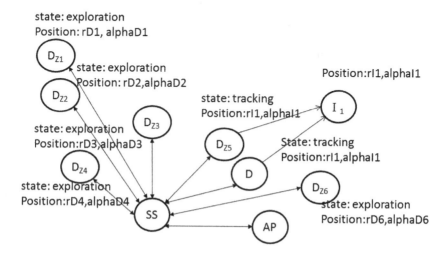

Fig. 8. The graph obtained after the execution of the detection rule

```
<graphml>
    <graph id="0">
        <node id="n1">
            <data>Dz1</data>
            <data>Position:rD1, alphaD1</data>
            <data>batteryLevel:80%</data>
            <data>timeStamp:t1</data>
            <data>state:exploration</data>
        </node>
        .
        .
        <node id="n5">
            <data>Dz5</data>
            <data>Position:rD5, alphaD5</data>
            <data>batteryLevel:80%</data>
            <data>timeStamp:t1</data>
            <data>state:exploration</data>
        </node>
        .
        .
        <node id="n7">
            <data>SS</data>
        </node>
        <node id="n8">
            <data>AP</data>
        </node>
        <edge source="n7" target="n1">
        <edge source="n7" target="n2">
        .
        .
    </graph>
</graphml>
```

Fig. 9. The xml representation of the graph before applying the detection rule

With the development of technology related to drones, several research activities studied the paradigm distributed aspects related to security [8] and UAVs. The Dynamicity Aware Graph Relabelling System [9], an extension of the local computation model, has been modified for UAVs functioning using proven algorithms [10]. Other research activities are based on the grammars of graph for dealing with emergency situations [11]. In addition, research activities has focused on autonomous flight training, the realization of multi-node missions (UAVs) with possible loss of one of the nodes [12].

The work of Xueping Zhu et al. [13] proposed a prototype application for UAV swarm control study by using agent technology and a way to model UAVs in principle of multi-agent system. The work presents a model of communication to achieve interaction purpose. A six-degree-of-freedom mathematic model was used in order to fully represent constraints and uncertainties of flying vehicles. It combines the traditional calculus based mathematical methods with computational techniques.

The work of Evsen Yanmaz et al. [3] describe a high-level architecture for the design of a collaborative aerial system that consists of UAVs with on-board sensors and embedded processing, sensing, coordination, and communication & networking capabilities. The paper presents a multi-UAV system consisting of quadrotors and demonstrates its potential in a disaster assistance scenario. The objective of the system is to monitor a certain area in a given time period and with a given update frequency to assist rescue personnel in a disaster situation.

It is designed to capture aerial images and provide an overview image of the monitored area in real time.

6 Conclusion and Future Work

In this paper, we addressed the design of architectural models for distributed systems supporting group collaboration applied on the SUPERSENS project where UAVs collaborate in the context of search-and-rescue missions. We proposed an approach that focuses on modeling the adaptation of collaboration in order to maintain the mission requirements and to satisfy the environment and resource constraints.

This approach provides a structural model using graphs. It represents the different interactions dependencies between UAV nodes from different mission points of view. Adaptation is driven by rule-based architectural reconfiguration policies. We defined a set of reconfiguration rules that will be triggered according to defined events related to environment and resource changes in order to meet the mission.

For experimentation, we implemented these graph rules using GMTE, a graph matching and transformation engine. Then, we executed them on graphs representing the UAV system.

As future work, we aim at enhancing our adaptation model and enabling drones to communicate together without the need to an actor that gives them orders.

Acknowledgements. This research was supported by the PRF Tunisian project SUPERSENS (**Super**vision **Sen**sitive des lieux Sensibles).

References

1. Bouassida Rodriguez, I., Van Wambeke, N., Drira, K., Chassot, C., Jmaiel, M.: Multi-layer coordinated adaptation based on graph refinement for cooperative activities. Commun. SWIN **4**, 163–167 (2008)
2. Hannachi, M.A., Bouassida Rodriguez, I., Drira, K., Pomares Hernandez, S.E.: *GMTE*: a tool for graph transformation and exact/inexact graph matching. In: Kropatsch, W.G., Artner, N.M., Haxhimusa, Y., Jiang, X. (eds.) GbRPR 2013. LNCS, vol. 7877, pp. 71–80. Springer, Heidelberg (2013). https://doi.org/10.1007/978-3-642-38221-5_8
3. Yanmaz, E., Quaritsch, M., Yahyanejad, S., Rinner, B., Hellwagner, H., Bettstetter, C.: Communication and coordination for drone networks. In: Zhou, Y., Kunz, T. (eds.) ADHOCNETS 2016. LNICST, vol. 184, pp. 79–91. Springer, Cham (2017). https://doi.org/10.1007/978-3-319-51204-4_7
4. Ehrig, H., Ehrig, K., Prange, U., Taentzer, G.: Fundamentals of Algebraic Graph Transformation. MTCSAES. Springer, Heidelberg (2006). https://doi.org/10.1007/3-540-31188-2
5. COMETS project. http://www.comets-uavs.org/
6. RESCUECELL project. http://www.rescuecell.eu/the-project/

7. Scherer, J., et al.: An autonomous multi-UAV system for search and rescue. In: Proceedings of the First Workshop on Micro Aerial Vehicle Networks, Systems, and Applications for Civilian Use (DroNet 2015), New York, NY, USA, pp. 33–38. ACM (2015)

8. Bouaziz, R., Kallel, S., Coulette, B.: An engineering process for security patterns application in component based models. In: Proceedings of the International Workshops on Enabling Technologies: Infrastructure for Collaborative Enterprises (WETICE), pp. 231–236. IEEE Computer Society (2013)

9. Casteigts, A., Chaumette, S.: Dynamicity aware graph relabeling systems (DA-GRS), a local computation based model to describe manet algorithms. In: IASTED PDCS (2005)

10. Casteigts, A., Chaumette, S., Ferreira, A.: Characterizing topological assumptions of distributed algorithms in dynamic networks. In: Kutten, S., Žerovnik, J. (eds.) SIROCCO 2009. LNCS, vol. 5869, pp. 126–140. Springer, Heidelberg (2010). https://doi.org/10.1007/978-3-642-11476-2_11

11. Bouassida Rodriguez, I., Drira, K., Chassot, C., Guennoun, K., Jmaiel, M.: A rule driven approach for architectural self adaptation in collaborative activities using graph grammars. Int. J. Auton. Comput. 1(3), 226–245 (2010)

12. Chaumette, S., Guinand, F.: Control of a remote swarm of drones/robots through a local (possibly model) swarm: qualitative and quantitative issues. In: Proceedings of the 14th ACM Symposium on Performance Evaluation of Wireless Ad Hoc, Sensor, and Ubiquitous Networks (PE-WASUN 2017), New York, NY, USA, pp. 41–45. ACM (2017)

13. Zhu, X., Liu, Z., Yang, J.: Model of collaborative UAV swarm toward coordination and control mechanisms study. Procedia Comput. Sci. 51, 493–502 (2015). International Conference On Computational Science (ICCS 2015)

Modelling and Executing Time-Aware Processes in Trustless Blockchain Environment

Amal Abid[1]($\boxtimes$), Saoussen Cheikhrouhou[1], and Mohamed Jmaiel[1,2]

[1] ReDCAD, University of Sfax, BP. 1173, 3038 Sfax, Tunisia
amal.abid05@gmail.com
[2] Digital Research Center of Sfax, BP. 275, Sakiet Ezzit, 3021 Sfax, Tunisia

Abstract. Blockchain is an emergent technology which enables the execution of collaborative business processes while ensuring trust by replacing central authority with cryptographic proof and distributed consensus. Thus, Blockchain technology can be used to find agreement between untrusted collaborating parties in business processes. However, temporal constraints of processes need more investigation. Indeed, Blockchain platforms do not offer means to represent nor to manage temporal constraints for business processes. Moreover, transaction completion time is not fixed, it can take from a few seconds to several minutes. In this paper, we include temporal constraints in smart contracts, which could mitigate the violation of time constraints, minimize the costly execution time, and avoiding thus financial penalties. To achieve this, we extend Caterpillar tool, which is the first open-source blockchain-based BPMN execution engine, to enable the automatic transformation of a large set of temporal constraints for business process model to smart contract code. We illustrate our approach with a use case, which we deploy in Ethereum Testnet.

Keywords: Blockchain · BPMN · Business process · Smart contract · Temporal constraints · Trust

1 Introduction

Business Process Management (BPM) aims to improve Business Processes (BPs) to reach better system performance including greater services, higher profit and faster response. With the evolution and integration of modern technologies such as Cloud Computing, Cyber-Physical Systems and Internet of Things in Industry 4.0, centralized BPM tools meet their limits in facing the inconsistent requirements and trade-off of security, trust, openness, scalability, and cost [1]. In particular, the crucial bottleneck to evolve BPM systems is to achieve mutual trust between inter-organizational processes, in other words ensuring the transformation of trustworthiness and digitized assets. Thus, modern BPM systems need to automate and digitize business processes while ensuring transparent interoperations of service providers.

© Springer Nature Switzerland AG 2020
S. Kallel et al. (Eds.): CRiSIS 2019, LNCS 12026, pp. 325–341, 2020.
https://doi.org/10.1007/978-3-030-41568-6_21

The described lack-of-trust problem can be assigned to the emergent Blockchain technology which has the potential to radically change how the inter-organizational processes operate. Thanks to its key properties of transparency, integrity and resilience, Blockchain technology has become an attractive choice to enterprises to revolutionize their business processes. In fact, Blockchain is a novel technology for decentralized and transactional data sharing over a peer-to-peer network of untrusted participants [2]. The goal of this technology is to eliminate any third party validation by replacing the trust of a central authority with cryptographic proof. So, Blockchain technology can be used to find agreement between collaborating parties in BP systems without trusting a central authority or any particular participant. In addition to the shared data property, some Blockchain offers a global computational infrastructure, that runs programs called smart contracts [3]. These smart contracts are executed across the Blockchain network and automatically enforce the conditions defined in the agreements to enable, for example, conditional secure payment. Different works [4–8] suggest deploying BPs over Blockchain using smart contracts to tap into their trust. Nevertheless, these latter works still at a very early stage since the first platform executing smart contracts, called Ethereum, dates from 2014 [3].

In line with these works, we denote the Caterpillar [9,10], which is the first open-source blockchain-based BPMN execution engine. It proposes an automated transformation of BPMN processes into a smart contract code written in Solidity. This work does not deal with temporal constraints on BPs. Consequently, the generated smart contract code could be undetermined, may temporal constraints be violated due to delays in executing BP tasks, or a lower affected bidding price, for example.

Considering BPs temporal constraints in Blockchain environment is of paramount importance since it is a way that would mitigate the violation of time constraints, minimize the execution time which is costly, and avoid thus financial penalties due to product delay delivery. At the best of our knowledge, there is no research attempts to consider BPs temporal constraints in Blockchain smart contract code, which constitutes our main contribution in this paper.

To achieve this, we extend the Caterpillar tool to enable the automatic transformation of a large set of temporal constraints for BPs into Solidity code. Considering temporal constraints in our approach is beneficial for BP execution since the notion of time misses precision in a Blockchain platform such as Ethereum. Indeed, the time is not fixed for a transaction completion, it can take from a few seconds to several minutes. Furthermore, generating smart contracts with temporal constraints from process models reduces the development time and liberates developers from using external services to verify time violation. Finally, we illustrate our approach with a use case deployed in Ethereum Testnet.

The remainder of this paper is organized as follows: Sect. 2 briefly introduces some concepts upon which our approach is built. Section 3 clarifies the basics of Caterpillar transformation rules. Section 4 details our approach. Section 5 illustrates our approach with a supply-chain use case. Section 6 summarizes related work. Section 7 concludes and suggests future directions.

2 Background

This section introduces the main concepts and definitions related to Blockchain, smart contracts and time-aware business process.

2.1 Blockchain and Smart Contracts

Introduced by an anonymous contributor under the pseudonym of Nakamoto over the last decade [2], the Blockchain technology has the potential to impact a variety of sectors including finance, government, manufacturing, health and research. Blockchain can be defined as a constantly growing distributed Ledger that holds a permanent record of all the transactions in a secure, chronological and immutable way over a peer-to-peer network. Founded on various well-known core technologies, such as cryptographic hash function, cryptographic signature and distributed consensus, it provides some key features including data persistence, anonymity, auditability, fault-tolerance, resilience, execution in a trustless environment.

More recently, the revelation of smart contract has enriched the Blockchain functionalities. The term of smart contract proposed in [3] refers to a Turing-complete program that checks and executes a set of rules over a Blockchain network. More specifically, it is a digital protocol which implements terms and promises predefined by parties who proceed to an agreement. The first platform enabling smart contracts execution is called Ethereum. It makes this possible through a computational language named Solidity that stores smart contract programs in the form of Ethereum Virtual Machine (EVM) bytecode, and it enables transactions as function calls into that code.

The integration of BPM and Blockchain technology leads to smarter business processes execution. Indeed, untrusted parties exploit smart contracts to encode and encapsulate the transaction rules and processes that hold transactions. When smart contracts are executed, they ensure automatically that contractual conditions are met and engagements are enforced. Furthermore, replacing middleman or third party by Blockchain reduces potentially costs for all parties.

2.2 Time-Aware Business Process

In [11], we propose the specification of BPs' temporal constraints that can be relative and/or absolute. Relative constraint measures the time that passes between 2 observable events. And, absolute constraint uses absolute time stamped with a global time clock, which is never reset [12].

Relative Temporal Constraints. We refer by *Relative temporal constraints* to requirements such as activity duration, temporal constraint over cardinality and temporal dependency.

First, we consider *duration* constraint, which is an *intra-task* temporal constraint. Let $s(t)$ (resp., $e(t)$) be the starting (resp., the ending time) of a task t.

Let d be a relative time value representing the duration of this task. The *Duration* constraint is defined as:

$$Duration(t, d) \stackrel{\text{def}}{=} e(t) - s(t) \leq d \tag{1}$$

Second, we consider the *temporal constraint over cardinality*, which is an *intra-task* temporal constraint. It sets the number N of times an activity can be executed during a certain time frame. Let N_{max} be the maximum of times that the activity can be executed and D_{max} be the maximum allowed time frame. *Cardinality* is defined as follows:

$$Cardinality(A, N_{max}, D_{max}) \stackrel{\text{def}}{=} e(A_N) - s(A_1) \leq D_{max} \text{ and } N \leq N_{max}$$

where at run-time, A_1 is the first execution of activity A and A_N is the last execution of A.

Afterwards, we consider *inter-task* temporal constraints of type execution *dependency* that could be:

- Start-to-Finish (SF): t_j can not finish until t_i has started within a given time interval.
- Start-to-Start (SS): t_j can not begin before t_i starts within a time interval.
- Finish-to-Finish (FF): t_j can not finish until t_i has finished within a time interval.
- Finish-to-Start (FS): t_j can not begin before t_i ends within a time interval. As per Eq. 2, t_j should start its execution no later than $MaxD$ time units and no earlier than $MinD$ time units after t_i ends.

$$TD(FS, t_i, t_j, MinD, MaxD) \stackrel{\text{def}}{=} MinD \leq s(t_j) - e(t_i) \leq MaxD \tag{2}$$

Absolute Temporal Constraints. We refer by *Absolute temporal constraints* to *intra-activity* temporal constraints focusing particularly on controlling the start and finish times of process activities. This is due to the fact that the Start/End temporal constraints use absolute time stamps. The succeeding listing summarizes the set of absolute temporal constraints that we consider in our verification approach.

- *Start As Soon As Possible (SASAP)/Finish As Soon As Possible (FASAP)*
- *Start As Late As Possible (SALAP)/*Finish As Late As Possible (FALAP)*
- *Must Start On (MSO)/Must Finish On (MFO)*
- *Start No Earlier Than (SNET)/Finish No Earlier Than (FNET)*
- *Start No Later Than (SNLT)/Finish No Later Than (FNLT)*.

3   Caterpillar BPMN-to-Solidity Compiler

Caterpillar compiler translates a BPMN process model into Solidity code. Only the basics will be clarified in order to use them in our approach afterwards. Thus, we refer the reader to [9, 10] for more details.

The dynamics of the control flow execution of a process is implemented in terms of a token-game as defined in the BPMN standard. A token is a theoretical object that facilitates the creation of a descriptive simulation of BPMN elements behaviors.

Once a process model instance is created, the start event generates a token which traverses the structure of the process until attaining the end event(s). When a token arrives at any incoming sequence flow of an activity, this latter become enabled. As the activity is executed, the token in the incoming sequence flow is consumed and a new token is generated for each outgoing sequence flow. Knowing that, at most one token is existing on a sequence flow at any time which is referred to 1-safeness in the literature. This property allows to represent the distribution of tokens in a given state of a process instance with a bit array as following: each sequence flow is corresponding to a slot in the array and the value of such slot is designated with the presence/absence of a token.

An illustration of the former idea is given by a simple process model in Fig. 1 and its corresponding Solidity code in Listing 1.1. This simple process example contains a start event, task A, task B and an end event. Since the flow of this process exploits the token-game concept, crossing each step will be as follows: Each node verifies if a token exists in it. After verification, the node will be executed and then the token will be passed to its successor.

To understand the code in listing 1.1, we explain the use of the *marking* variable, the *step* function, and the *bit-wise* operations.

Marking: Each smart contract has a variable that encodes the full state of a process instance, in other words the overall distribution of tokens across the sequence flows. This variable is designed as *marking* (Listing 1.1, line 2). The variable marking is a bit-array encoded as 256-bits unsigned integers, which is the default word size in the Ethereum Virtual Machine. Each sequence flow is combined with one bit in this variable: 1 if a token is present in the sequence flow, 0 otherwise. Note that, the initial marking will be programmed as 1 in the position 0 (i.e. 2^0) since tokens are 2^i (i is the rank of a sequence flow in the process model).

Step: *Step* is a function that is used to compute the new process state (Listing 1.1, lines 17–30). It allows to make steps during a whole business process execution. For security reasons, this function is internal, which means that external actors cannot call it directly. However, each time an external entity's function call updates to the process state, the function step is invoked. To handle these updates, the step function use bit-wise operations which is explained just afterwards.

Bit-Wise: The bit-wise operations are used to ensure all the queries/updates on the process state. To check if an element is started or enabled, the bit-wise AND is used to permit the testing of set inclusion. Besides, the bit-wise OR provides a method to encode the set union as an integer. Finally, the combination of OR and AND allows to replace the old token of the variable marking by a new one corresponding to the successor sequence flow.

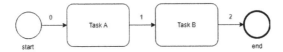

Fig. 1. Process model of the simple example

```
 1  contract MySimpleContract {
 2      uint marking = 1 ;
 3      function taskA() returns (bool) {
 4          uint localMarking = marking;
 5          if (localMarking & 2 != 2)
 6              return false;
 7          // doTaskA();
 8          step (localMarking & uint ( ~ 2) | 4) ;
 9          return true ; }
10      function taskB() returns (bool) {
11          uint localMarking = marking;
12          if (localMarking & 4 != 4)
13              return false ;
14          // doTaskB();
15          step (localMarking & uint (~4) | 8 ) ;
16          return true; }
17      function step(uint localMarking) internal {
18          bool done = false;
19          while (!done) {
20              if (localMarking & 2 == 2) {
21                  localMarking = localMarking & uint(~2);
22                  continue;
23              }
24              if (localMarking & 4 == 4) {
25                  localMarking = localMarking & uint(~4);
26                  continue;
27              }
28              done = true;
29          }
30          marking = localMarking; }
31  }
```

Listing 1.1. Solidity code of the simple example

Table 1. Transformation rule summary [5]

BPMN element	Scope	Solidity code summary
All patterns	All	On execution, deactivates itself and activates the subsequent element
Parallel-split	All	Executes on activation, activates all subsequent elements
Parallel-join	All	Executes on activation of all incoming edges
XOR-split	All	Executes on activation, conditionally activates all subsequent elements. If one of them is executed, it deactivates all others
XOR-join	All	Executes on activation of one incoming edge
Temporal constraints	Activity	On execution of an activity, verifies its conformance with its temporal constraint

For brevity, an overview of translation rules of the BPMN-to-Solidity transformation is given in Table 1. During the process model traversal, once the translator meets a BPMN element (left column), it inserts code corresponding to the right column into the smart contract code. The timed process model transformation to Solidity code will be explained in the next section.

4   Extended Caterpillar Compiler to Support the Temporal Constraints

This section presents our temporal extension to the Caterpillar compiler. Indeed, the majority of activities (task or sub-process) in BPs are constrained by hard timing requirements. Therefore, it is crucial to take into consideration the transformation of BPs' temporal constraints into smart contract code.

Before starting the transformation of business process models enriched with temporal constraints to Solidity code, we will provide an overview of the approach. Then, we will give the transformation corresponding to the following temporal constraints: duration, temporal constraint over cardinality, temporal dependency and start/end temporal constraints.

4.1   Approach Overview

This subsection details the transformation rules from timed process model to smart contract code in Solidity. To do so, we propose some execution constructs that will be subsequently instantiated (Subsects. 4.2 to 4.5) to transform a large set of BP temporal constraints.

- **Timer variable:** When a process model holds a timer event or an advanced temporal constraint, a corresponding variable will be generated at the creation of the contract. This variable will be initialized with the same name as the timer concatenated with the timer type (i.e. duration, cardinality, dependency). Besides, it will contain the value of a timestamp when the timer is invoked.
- **Timer function:** This function will be invoked by the activity to check its conformance with its temporal constraint. The generated timer function will be internal for security reasons.
- **Timer guard:** The generated code is a bit similar to the previous example without timer. The difference is not huge but it is major. Since a timer is added, the only guard of tokens will not suffice. Therefore, an extra timer guard will be generated to basically check timestamps and thus meet the timer requirements.

4.2   Duration

This subsection details the transformation of a process task enriched with duration constraint to Solidity code. For illustration, Fig. 2 exhibits a process model, in which task A has a minimum value MinTime and a maximum value Max-Time duration-constraint. This is transformed into the Solidity code in Listing 1.2. This code is obtained by following the transformation rules previously mentioned in Subsect. 4.1. It basically contains:

- The marking variable, the step function and the bit-wise operations as any process without a timer.
- The timer variable *"timerName_duration"* which comprises the duration of the activity (Listing 1.2, line 3).
- The timer function *"calculate_duration"* that performs the required calculations. In our example, if the duration is exceeded, the designer will be notified (Listing 1.2, lines 14–19).
- The *"minTime"* and the *"maxTime"* values, related to the duration constraint, are given as parameters to the function of the activity (a simple task in the example).

Note that, *"now"* is an alias of *"block.timestamp"*, which take the timestamp in UNIX time at the moment at which it is invoked within a smart contract.

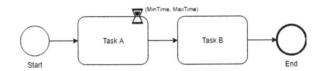

Fig. 2. Process model enriched with a duration temporal constraint

```
1  contract DurationContract {
2      uint marking = 1 ;
3      uint taskATimer_duration = 0 ;
4      function taskA(uint minTime, uint maxTime) returns (bool) {
5          uint localMarking = marking;
6          uint startTime = now;
7          if (localMarking & 2 != 2)
8              return false;
9          doTaskA();
10         uint endTime = now;
11         taskATimer_duration = calculate_duration(startTime, endTime,
    minTime, maxTime);
12         step(localMarking & uint (~2) | 4) ;
13         return true; }
14     function calculate_duration(uint startTime, uint endTime, uint
    minTime, uint maxTime) internal returns (uint) {
15         uint duration;
16         duration = endTime - startTime;
17         if (duration > minTime || duration < maxTime)
18             notifyDesigner(); //time exceeded
19         return duration; }
20     function step(uint localMarking) internal {
21         // The same code as the first example }
22 }
```

Listing 1.2. The generated Solidity code of the duration temporal constraint

4.3 Temporal Constraint over Cardinality

This subsection serves to ensure the transformation from a process model that contains a temporal constraint over cardinality to Solidity code. As mentioned in the background section, a temporal constraint over cardinality is a constraint in which a given activity can be executed successively at most N times within a time period T.

Let's consider the process model in Fig. 3, the corresponding generated Solidity code is shown in Listing 1.3. This code is obtained by following the transformation rules previously cited in Subsect. 4.1. It basically holds:

- The marking variable, the step function and the bit-wise operations as any process without a timer.
- The timer variable "*timerName_cardinality*" which holds the period time of the activity (Listing 1.3, line 3).
- The timer function "*calculate_cardinality*" that implements the required calculations. In our example, if the period or the maximum number of trials will be exceeded, the execution of the task will be interrupted and the token will be moved to the next sequence flow (Listing 1.3, lines 16–27).
- The "*period*" and the "*maxLoop*" values, related to the temporal constraints over cardinality, are given as parameters to the function of the activity (a simple task in the example).

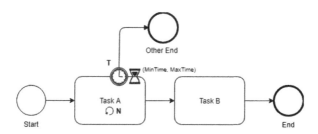

Fig. 3. Process model enriched with a temporal constraint over cardinality

```
 1  contract  TCardinalityContract {
 2      uint  marking = 1 ;
 3      uint  taskATime_cardinality=0;
 4      function  taskA (uint  period ,  uint  maxLoop)  returns  (bool) {
 5          uint  localMarking = marking;
 6          taskATime_cardinality = now + period ;
 7          if  (localTokens & 2 != 2)
 8              return  false ;
 9          bool  test = calculate_cardinality (taskATime_cardinality ,
        period ,  maxLoop ) ;
10          if  (test)
11              doTaskA () ;
12          else
13              notifyDesigner () ;  //time  or  maximumLoop  exceeded
14          step (localTokens & uint  (~ 2) | 4) ;
15          return  true ; }
16      function  calculate_cardinality (uint  taskATime_cardinality ,  uint
        period ,  uint  maxLoop)  internal  returns  (bool) {
17          bool  test = false ;
18          uint  i =0;
19          while  (i<maxLoop && now<taskATime_cardinality )
20          {
21              test = verifyTaskA () ;
22              if  (test) {
23                  break ;
24              }
25              i++;
26          }
27          return  test ; }
28      function  step (uint  localMarking)  internal  {
29          // The  same  code  as  the  first  example  }
30  }
```

Listing 1.3. The generated Solidity code of the temporal constraint over cardinality constraint

4.4   Temporal Dependency

This subsection presents the transformation from a process model that holds a temporal dependency temporal constraint to Solidity code. As mentioned in the background section, a temporal dependency is a relationship between two activities in which one activity depends on the start or finish of another activity in order to begin or end. Four temporal dependencies can be specified: Start-to-Finish (SF), Start-to-Start (SS), Finish-to-Start (FS) and Finish-To-Finish (FF). Since the transformation of these dependencies are similar, we choose to provide only the transformation corresponding to FS.

The generated code in Listing 1.4 is associated to the process model in Fig. 4. This code is obtained by following the transformation rules previously mentioned in Subsect. 4.1. It basically contains:

- The marking variable, the step function and the bit-wise operations as any process without a timer.
- The timer variable "*timerName_temporaldependency*" which holds the start time or the finish time of the activity depending on the case. In FS constraint, it holds the finish time (Listing 1.4, line 3).

– The timer function *"calculate_temporaldependency"* that implements the required calculations. In FS example, if the time is exceeded, the execution of the task will be interrupted and the token will be moved to the next sequence flow. In addition, the designer will be notified (Listing 1.4, lines 30–32).
– The *"fromValue"* and the *"toValue"* values, related to the temporal dependency constraints, are given as parameters to the function of the activity (a simple task in the example).

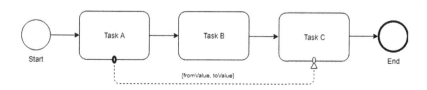

Fig. 4. Process model with a finish-to-start temporal dependency constraint

```
1  contract  TemporalDependencyFSContract {
2      uint  marking = 1;
3      uint  taskAFinishTime_FS = 0;
4      function  taskA () returns (bool) {
5          uint  localMarking = marking;
6          if (localMarking & 2 != 2)
7              return false;
8          doTaskA () ;
9          taskAFinishTime_FS = now;
10         step(localMarking & uint (~2) | 4) ;
11         return true ; }
12     function  taskB () returns (bool) {
13         uint  localMarking = marking;
14         if (localMarking & 4 != 4)
15             return false ;
16         doTaskB () ;
17         step (localMarking & uint (~4) | 8 ) ;
18         return true; }
19     function  taskC (uint  fromValue, uint  toValue) returns (bool) {
20         uint  localMarking = tokens;
21         if (localMarking & 8 != 8)
22             return false ;
23         bool  timeExeeded = calculate_temporaldependencyfs(
    taskAFinishTime_FS , fromValue, toValue);
24         if (timeExeeded)
25             notifyDesigner (); //time exceeded
26         else
27             doTaskC () ;
28         step (localMarking & uint (~8) | 16 ) ;
29         return true; }
30     function  calculate_temporaldependencyfs (uint  taskAFinishTime_FS ,
    uint fromValue, uint toValue) internal returns (bool) {
31         return (taskAFinishTime_FS < fromValue || taskAFinishTime_FS >
    toValue); }
32     function step (uint  localMarking) internal {
33         // The  same  code  as  the  first  example }
34  }
```

Listing 1.4. The generated Solidity code of the temporal dependency FS constraint

4.5   Start/End Temporal Constraint

This subsection serves to provide the transformation from a process model that contains a start/end temporal constraint to Solidity code. As mentioned in the background section, a start/end temporal constraint is a constraint using an absolute time. In this paper, we exhibit only the transformation associated to *Must Start ON* constraint.

The generated code in Listing 1.5 is corresponding to the process model in Fig. 5. This code is obtained by following the transformation rules previously cited in Subsect. 4.1. It basically holds:

- The marking variable, the step function and the bit-wise operations as any process without a timer.
- The timer variable *"timerName_mso"* which holds the point in time value of the activity (Listing 1.5, line 3).
- The timer function *"calculate_mso"* that implements the required calculations. In our example, if the start time of the activity does not correspond to the desired start time, the designer will be notified (Listing 1.5, lines 16–18).

Fig. 5. Process model enriched with a Must Start At temporal constraint

```
 1  import "DateTime.sol";
 2  contract MustStartOnContract {
 3      uint marking = 1 ;
 4      uint constant TASKA_MSO = toTimestamp(0, 0, 0, 8, 0, 0);
 5      function taskA() returns (bool) {
 6          uint localMarking = marking;
 7          uint startTime = now;
 8          if (localMarking & 2 != 2)
 9              return false;
10          if (calculate_mso)
11              doTaskA();
12          else
13              notifyDesigner();
14          step(localMarking & uint (~2) | 4) ;
15          return true ; }
16      function calculate_mso(uint startTime) internal returns (bool) {
17          return (startTime==TASKA_MSO); }
18      function step(uint localMarking) internal {
19          // The same code as the first example }
20  }
```

Listing 1.5. Must Start At temporal constraint transformation code

5 Use Case

In Fig. 6, the purchase order process of a manufacturing organisation is triggered when a manufacturer instantiates the contract in Ethereum Blockchain. Then a customer can submit a purchase order. The manufacturer checks whether the ordered articles are available or not, modified and even canceled or not. In case of order modification, the availability of the order is checked again. If the ordered articles are available in stock, the customer is asked for financial settlement and the goods are delivered. Otherwise, the process meets its end by the reception of an order cancellation. Within business processes, the temporal perspective is crucial since temporal constraints must be respected. For instance, we can mention the following constraints:

- Duration ❶: The activity availability check takes between 10 and 30 s to be achieved.
- Temporal constraint over cardinality ❷: During 15 min, a customer can only do 3 failed payment trials. This constraint enhances secure payments.
- Temporal dependency SF ❸: If an order cancellation exists, it should be finished before the settlement activity begins
- Temporal dependency FS ❹: The order modification is only allowed maximum 1 day after the making order activity finishes.
- Start/End temporal constraint ❺: Delivering goods must starts at 8 am.

The main difference when using Blockchain is the absence of middleman or third party, which potentially reduces costs for both suppliers and customers. Therefore, the system core is just a smart contract implementing an escrow-based transaction without the need of middleman. Moreover, payments are secure and use the Ether crypto-currency of the Ethereum platform. Finally, considering temporal constraints of business processes allows the business rules enforcement by activating or deactivating some branches of the sequence flow before or after a given amount of time.

Smart Contract Deployment. The generated smart contract of the supply chain example is successfully deployed in the Rinkeby network test of Ethereum (see Fig. 7). Note that, the smart contract is assigned to unique identifier, called its address, which is the hash of the contract's code (i.e. 0x56385e30a9c0cf097-c0131808f6dd7cb459087a1). Through this address, the smart contract is visible for everyone around the world in a secure and immutable way. In Ethereum, the deployment of a smart contract is designated as a transaction which is identified by its hash and costs some fees.

6 Related Work

The BPM community perceived Blockchain as a promising technology and published a seminal paper [4]. The community focuses mostly on the exploitation

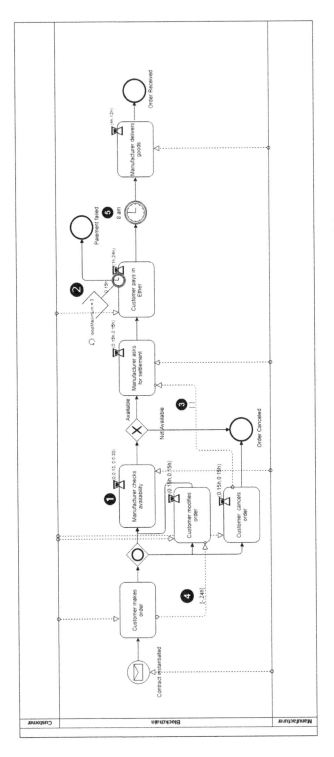

Fig. 6. The purchase order handling business process model

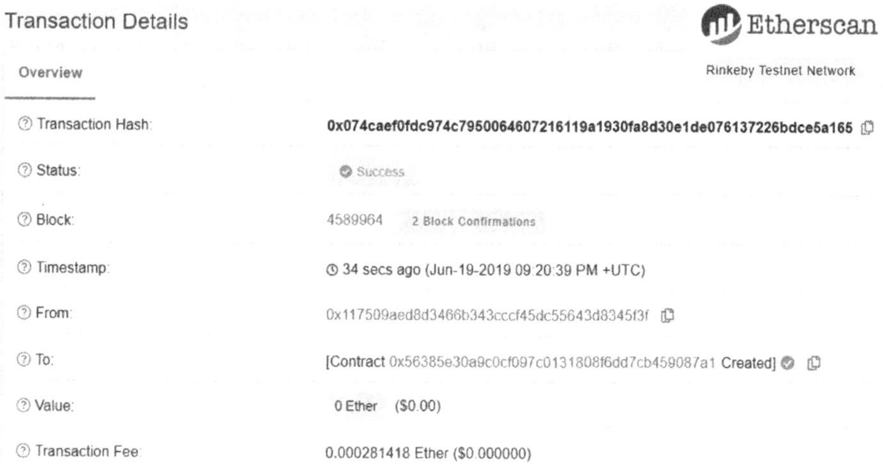

Transaction Details

Etherscan

Overview

Rinkeby Testnet Network

⑦ Transaction Hash:	**0x074caef0fdc974c7950064607216119a1930fa8d30e1de076137226bdce5a165**
⑦ Status:	✓ Success
⑦ Block:	4589964 2 Block Confirmations
⑦ Timestamp:	⏱ 34 secs ago (Jun-19-2019 09:20:39 PM +UTC)
⑦ From:	0x117509aed8d3466b343cccf45dc55643d8345f3f
⑦ To:	[Contract 0x56385e30a9c0cf097c0131808f6dd7cb459087a1 Created] ✓
⑦ Value:	0 Ether ($0.00)
⑦ Transaction Fee:	0.000281418 Ether ($0.000000)

Fig. 7. Generated smart contract deployment in the Ethereum Testnet

of smart contract capabilities over Blockchain network. The Blockchain integration effort varies from simple monitoring solution to blockchain-based process engines [5–8].

Weber et al. [5,6] are the first authors who use Blockchain for the execution of business processes. They demonstrate blockchain-based monitoring and execution of inter-organizational business processes. Afterwards, this work has been extended by other researchers. In particular, the tool Caterpillar [9,10] extends this work and builds a BPMN execution engine that runs on top of Ethereum. Caterpillar is the first open-source blockchain-based BPM system. It basically transforms a business process model into smart contract code.

A limited number of works take in consideration temporal constraints in blockchain-based BPM systems. Yasaweerasinghelage et al. [13] utilize process simulation to send transaction to a private Blockchain in order to evaluate its latency. Haarmann et al. [14] estimate duration through manual simulation techniques. Finally, Mavridou et al. [15] generate Solidity code from finite-state-machine based model while taking into consideration delayed processes. However, the latter works sill not mature enough and need more development to cover a richer set of temporal constraints for business processes.

In this paper, we extend the Caterpillar BPMN-to-Solidity work by various temporal constraints for business processes such as duration, temporal constraint over cardinality, temporal dependency and start/end temporal constraints.

7   Conclusion

In this paper, we introduced an extension for the first Ethereum-based process engine. More precisely, we enriched the process engine with the support of the following temporal constraints: duration, temporal constraint over cardinality, temporal dependency, start/end temporal constraints. Our approach is based on integrating time-guards inside the functions implementing the activities which have temporal constraints. In such way, the guards can replace the necessity for an explicit external timer service called through APIs. Moreover we explained the transformation from a simple process model to Solidity code through transformation rules, and we illustrate our approach with a use case, which we deploy in Ethereum Testnet.

In future work, we plan to present the monitoring of timed business processes and enable the enforcement of critical temporal constraints, based on monitoring the data exchanged via Blockchain. Furthermore, we plan to verify the execution of processes that span across organizational boundaries, i.e. inter-organizational business processes on Blockchain. Precisely, the goal is to ensure that these processes can meet global temporal constraints.

References

1. Li, Y., Luo, Z., Yin, J., Lida, X., Yin, Y., Zhaohui, W.: Enterprise pattern: integrating the business process into a unified enterprise model of modern service company. Enterp. Inf. Syst. **11**(1), 37–57 (2017)
2. Nakamoto, S.: Bitcoin: A Peer-to-Peer Electronic Cash System. Cryptography Mailing List (2008)
3. Wood, G.: Ethereum: a secure decentralised generalised transaction ledger. Ethereum project **151**, 1–32 (2014)
4. Mendling, J., et al.: Blockchains for business process management-challenges and opportunities. ACM Trans. Manag. Inf. Syst. **9**(1), 4 (2018)
5. Weber, I., Xu, X., Riveret, R., Governatori, G., Ponomarev, A., Mendling, J.: Untrusted business process monitoring and execution using blockchain. In: La Rosa, M., Loos, P., Pastor, O. (eds.) BPM 2016. LNCS, vol. 9850, pp. 329–347. Springer, Cham (2016). https://doi.org/10.1007/978-3-319-45348-4_19
6. García-Bañuelos, L., Ponomarev, A., Dumas, M., Weber, I.: Optimized execution of business processes on blockchain. In: Carmona, J., Engels, G., Kumar, A. (eds.) BPM 2017. LNCS, vol. 10445, pp. 130–146. Springer, Cham (2017). https://doi.org/10.1007/978-3-319-65000-5_8
7. Viriyasitavat, W., Da Xu, L., Bi, Z., Sapsomboon, A.: Blockchain-based business process management (BPM) framework for service composition in industry 4.0. J. Intell. Manuf. 1–12 (2018)
8. Sturm, C., Szalanczi, J., Schönig, S., Jablonski, S.: A lean architecture for blockchain based decentralized process execution. In: Daniel, F., Sheng, Q.Z., Motahari, H. (eds.) BPM 2018. LNBIP, vol. 342, pp. 361–373. Springer, Cham (2019). https://doi.org/10.1007/978-3-030-11641-5_29
9. López-Pintado, O., García-Bañuelos, L., Dumas, M., Weber, I.: Caterpillar: a blockchain-based business process management system. In: Proceedings of the BPM Demo Track and BPM Dissertation Award Co-Located with 15th International Conference on Business Process Modeling. CEUR Workshop Proceedings, vol. 1920. CEUR-WS.org (2017)
10. López-Pintado, O., García-Bañuelos, L., Dumas, M., Weber, I., Ponomarev, A.: Caterpillar: a business process execution engine on the ethereum blockchain. Softw. Pract. Exp. **49**(7), 1162–1193 (2019)

11. Cheikhrouhou, S., Kallel, S., Guermouche, N., Jmaiel, M.: The temporal perspective in business process modeling: a survey and research challenges. SOCA **9**(1), 75–85 (2015)
12. Bohnenkamp, H., Belinfante, A.: Timed testing with TorX. In: Fitzgerald, J., Hayes, I.J., Tarlecki, A. (eds.) FM 2005. LNCS, vol. 3582, pp. 173–188. Springer, Heidelberg (2005). https://doi.org/10.1007/11526841_13
13. Yasaweerasinghelage, R., Staples, M., Weber, I.: Predicting latency of blockchain-based systems using architectural modelling and simulation. In: Proceedings of the IEEE International Conference on Software Architecture (ICSA), pp. 253–256. IEEE (2017)
14. Haarmann, S.: Estimating the duration of blockchain-based business processes using simulation. In: Proceedings of the 11th Central European Workshop on Services and Their Composition (ZEUS), pp. 24–31 (2019)
15. Mavridou, A., Laszka, A.: Designing secure ethereum smart contracts: a finite state machine based approach. arXiv preprint arXiv:1711.09327 (2017)

Multi-scale Adaptive Threshold for DDoS Detection

Fatima Ezzahra Ouerfelli[1]([⊠])[iD], Khaled Barbaria[2], Belhassen Zouari[2],
and Claude Fachkha[3,4]

[1] Mediatron Lab, University of Carthage, Tunis, Tunisia
`fatima-ezzahra.ouerfelli@fst.utm.tn`
[2] Mediatron Lab, University of Carthage, Tunis, Tunisia
`khaled.barbaria@ensta.org, belhassen.zouari@fst.rnu.tn`
[3] University of Dubai, Dubai, UAE
`cfachkha@ud.ac.ae`
[4] Steppa Cyber Inc., Longueuil, Canada

Abstract. Distributed Denial of Services (DDoS) attacks are still among the top major cyber threats against online servers. One efficient way to defend against such threats is through adaptive threshold models, which can tune defense mechanisms according to network conditions and setup. However, the main challenge of such models is threshold selection which has a direct impact on detection accuracy and hence protection insurance. In this paper, we propose a new model to compute an adaptive threshold via distributed energy wavelet decomposition. Our model leverages consensus protocol to solve the single point of failure problem. The empirical evaluation, which is based on real DDoS attack traces, demonstrate that the proposed model is indeed capable to detect accurately and in real-time, DDoS threats.

Keywords: Distributed Denial of Service · Wavelet decomposition · Distributed systems · DDoS protection · DDoS detection

1 Introduction

In 2018, according to Kaspersky Lab [8], DDoS attacks spread at least 79 countries. Furthermore, the threat of these attack is significantly increased in terms of impact (e.g. targeting critical infrastructure), and size. In fact, recent attacks have generated malicious traffic that bypassed 1 Terra Bytes per second (TB/s) bandwidth. Such traffic can create network outage and damages to critical infrastructure such as transportation, health, power, energy, among others. Furthermore, some long-duration attacks are stealthy and can remain active for weeks [1].

In this context, it is highly desirable to design a system that promptly infers DDoS attacks, even in the situations where limited data is available at the observation points. In this paper, in order to achieve this goal, we propose a multiple

© Springer Nature Switzerland AG 2020
S. Kallel et al. (Eds.): CRiSIS 2019, LNCS 12026, pp. 342–354, 2020.
https://doi.org/10.1007/978-3-030-41568-6_22

time-series DDoS detection model that exploits wavelet decomposition and distributed algorithm to achieve its task. Specifically, we frame the contributions of this paper as follows:

- Exploiting decomposition wavelet technique to de-construct complex signals of DDoS attack into signals of finite bandwidth to find the adaptive threshold.
- Proposing a mask function that divides the signal into parts to simplify attack detection.
- Designing a collaborative distributed detection scheme by employing a consensus algorithm to leverage various resources, avoiding a single point of failure scenarios and reducing false positives.

The remainder of this paper is organized as follows:
In Sect. 2, we elaborate the related work and demonstrate how the proposed work is unique. In Sect. 5, we detail the proposed approach and discuss its components. In Sect. 6, we empirically evaluate the proposed scheme and demonstrate its effectiveness and promptness. In Sect. 7, we provide a discussion on distributed detection. Finally, Sect. 9 summarizes and concludes this paper.

2   Related Work

There are several contributions in DDoS attack detection including the use of energy decomposition and collaborative solutions. We list below some major contributions in these areas.

Li et al. [9] proposed energy distribution based on wavelet analysis to detect DDoS attack traffic. In fact, energy distribution over time would have limited variation if the traffic keeps its behavior over time. While an introduction of attack traffic in the network would elicit significant energy distribution deviation in a short time period. Their experimental results with typical Internet traffic tracing show that the variance of the energy distribution changes dramatically, causing a spike when traffic behavior is affected by a DDoS attack.

There are plethora of contributions [2,4,15] for detection DDoS attacks but only few of them focused on distributed detection, and none of them, to the best of our knowledge, employed wavelet decomposition techniques in such context. For instance, Nanadikar et al. [10] proposed a distributed defense scheme against DDoS attacks, which constructed a ring of intrusion prevention systems. These systems form virtual protection nodes surrounding the hosts to defend and collaborate by exchanging selected traffic information such as IP addresses, ports, and protocols. Furthermore, Wang et al. [14] proposed VicSifter, a distributed solution to fingerprint benign packets instead of retrieving attack packets from high-volume traffic.

Our proposed approach is complementary to the aforementioned literature work and further contributes, in fact, our approach is able to find the ultimate threshold value by exploiting energy distribution based on wavelet analysis in a distributed mode. Furthermore, it helps in coordinating the communication of threshold information among multiple and distributed observation and computation nodes leveraging consensus algorithm.

3   Wavelet Decomposition

We introduce in this part the wavelet decomposition and its advantages in attack detection. Wavelet analysis is an interesting new method for solving difficult problems in physics, mathematics, and engineering, with novel applications as diversified as signal processing, data compression, signal processing, computer graphics, pattern recognition, and also medical image technology [13]. Wavelets allow complex data such as speech, internet traffic, images, and patterns to be decomposed into basic forms at different scales and afterward reconstructed with high precision. This signal transmission is based on the transmission of a series of numbers. This wavelet representation of a function is a new technique and will allow the components of a non-stationary signal to be analyzed. This will allow us to analyze DDoS attacks in a distributed environment to increase the reliability of our system.

3.1   Wavelet Definition

The wavelet transform replaces the Fourier transform's sinusoidal waves by translations and dilations of a window called a wavelet. It takes two arguments namely time and scale. Discrete wavelet transform (DWT) deals with scaling parameter a and translation parameters b. The integral discrete wavelet transform of a function is:

$$Wf(a,b) = <f, \Psi_{a,b}> = \int_{-\infty}^{+\infty} f(t) \frac{1}{\sqrt{a}} \Psi * (\frac{t-b}{a}) dt \tag{1}$$

where the base atom is a zero average function, centered around zero with finite energy. The family of vectors is obtained by translations and dilatations of the base atom:

$$\Psi_{a,b}(t) = \frac{1}{\sqrt{a}} \Psi(\frac{t-b}{a}), a > 0, b \epsilon R \tag{2}$$

The original signal sequence x(n) can be expressed as the sum of the most components, that is:

$$S(n) = D_1(n) + A_1(n) = \sum_{j=1}^{J} D_j(n) + A_J(n) \tag{3}$$

Where $A_J(n)$ is the coefficients of wavelet decomposition signal at level J. The total energy of the signal can be expressed as:

$$\sum_{n=1}^{N} |S(n)|^2 = \sum_{n=1}^{N} |a_j(n)|^2 + \sum_{j=1}^{J} \sum_{n=1}^{N} |d_j(n)|^2 \tag{4}$$

Where N is the sample size, J is the total number of wavelet decomposition levels.

3.2   Example of Wavelet Decomposition

To better understand the wavelet decomposition, we present in the Fig. 1 proposed by the documentation Matlab an example of wavelet decomposition on a simple signal. We find on the left, the signal s and the curves a5, a4, a3, a2, and a1 which are the approximations at levels 5, 4, 3, 2, and 1. Here, we can say that the best approximation is a1; the next one is a2, and so on. We see clearly noise oscillations which are exhibited in a1, whereas a5 is smoother.

On the right, cfs represents the coefficients, s is the signal, and d5, d4, d3, d2, and d1 are the details at levels 5, 4, 3, 2, and 1.

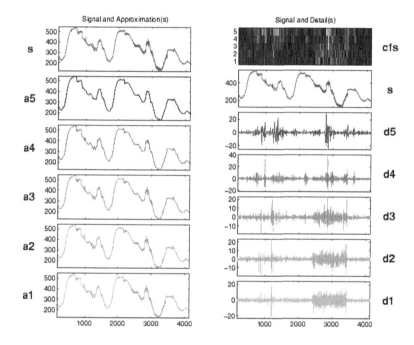

Fig. 1. Example of wavelet decomposition

4   Distributed Detection

4.1   Principle

Distributed systems are multiple computer systems working together effectively as a single unit [5]. Examples of distributed systems include supercomputers built out of multiple powerful processors or distributed databases used in many on-line systems. So, distributed systems can be more resilient, more powerful and speedier than single-computer systems. Further, there is a multitude of advantages to using a distributed system. In our case when our detection system

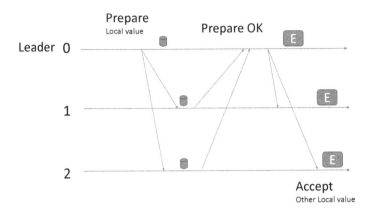

Fig. 2. Paxos protocol

is attacked, the protection mechanism may be able to stay up even if one server physically fails. Distributed systems can also be faster than single-computer systems. In the same context, once distributed systems are installed, they can also be easily scalable. When they're well designed, it is simple to add new hardware and telling the network to connect it to the distributed system.

4.2   Implementation of the PAXOS Consensus Algorithm

For the sake of the current work, we have integrated and implemented in Java language a variant of the Paxos algorithm of consensus [11] since it for suitable in building agreement among multiple hosts. Further, Paxos guarantees consistency across a group of unreliable replicas and attempts to come to an agreement even during periods when some replicas are unresponsive.

As shown in Fig. 2, the protocol is composed of two principals steps namely, preparation and acceptance. First, a leader node creates a proposal identified with a number. Then, it sends a Prepare message containing this proposal to the Acceptors (the others servers).

Second, an acceptor receives a message for a proposal N, it accept it if and only if it has not already promised to any prepare proposals having an identifier greater than N. In this case, it registers the corresponding value v.

In the following we will explain the implementation of PAXOS in our case.

5   Proposed Model

We propose in this part an innovative model that allows the detection of an attack in a simpler and more precise way without resorting to a large number of resources.

The principle of our method is to exploit wavelet decomposition to reduce the size of our signal. To achieve this task, we divide our signal into several parts through a method called "Mask" explained after. This method will allow us to analyze a minimal amount of traffic and decide whether there is an attack or not.

The initial parameters of our algorithm are chosen according to the best experimental results. More on threshold selection is discussed in Sect. 5.2.

5.1 The Use of MASK Technique

Let α_i a number of packets. The mask function is shown in Fig. 3 and it is defined by the following formula:

Mask(α_i) = 1 if s(i) < α_i and Mask(α_i) = 0 otherwise.

This function allows to partition a signal because it selects packets according to a predefined threshold.

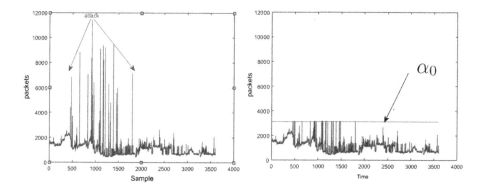

Fig. 3. Example mask(S)

5.2 The Local Algorithm

In flooding attack detection, the choice of the threshold value is very important. Threshold value needs to be estimated according to the packet traffic condition. If measured traffic exceeds a particular threshold it will be defined as an anomaly and distributed algorithm will be triggered.

The local algorithm is presented below:

Algorithm: Find adaptive threshold of signal S

Step 0 : Initialisation (chosen through experimentation)
(1) Initial number of packet $\alpha_0 = \text{mean}(S)$
(2) $\Delta = 20\%$ of α_0
(3) $\epsilon = [10..20]$
(4) Compute initial approximation energy $Ea_{\alpha max}$

Step 1
(1) $\text{Mask}(\alpha_i) = 1$ if $s(i) < \alpha_i$ and $=0$ otherwise
(2) Save part of signal $\text{save}(i) = s(i) * \text{Mask}(\alpha_i)$
(3) Wavelet decomposition of save(i) and energy compute Ea_{α_i}
(4) Update $\alpha_i = \alpha_i + \Delta$

Step 2 : Decision
IF $(Ea_{\alpha_i} - Ea_{\alpha max} < 0)$ **then** th_0 **is** the number of packets α_i and *Start legitimate traffic*

IF $(Ea_{\alpha_i} - Ea_{\alpha max} < \epsilon)$ **then** th_1 **is** the number of packets α_i and *Start attack traffic*

First, we take only a part of the original signal S (e.g., the mean of S) and we calculate its energy of wavelet decomposition.

Next, for each step, we add a number of packets determinate by the initial step and we continue until we reach the hole signal.

In Fig. 6, we note that the values of wavelet energy approximation increases until reaching a maximum value and decreases after. So, we suppose without losing generality that the maximum value corresponds to the end of normal traffic of region 1 and the beginning of the region 2 as legitimate traffic with large scale. Finally, the third region (region 3) is corresponding to high traffic indicates a DDoS attack.

Region 1: normal traffic $s < th_0$
Region 2: legitimate traffic with large scale $th_0 < s < th_1$
Region 3: high traffic (DDoS attack) $s > th_1$ Where th_0 is the threshold value of the number of packets corresponding to the maximum approximation energy Ea_{max} th_1 is the threshold value corresponding to the end of traffic with a large scale.
$th_1 = Ea_{max} - \Delta Ea$ with $10\% < \Delta Ea < 15\%$

5.3 Distributed Detection Algorithm

As mentioned above, the algorithm is composed of two phases, namely, prepare and accept. In our detection system (Fig. 4), in the first phase, when a node detects an exceeded threshold, it chooses to become the leader and selects a sequence number x and his threshold to create a proposal $P1(x, v)$ (Phase 1 in Fig. 4). Subsequently, it sends this proposal to the other nodes (named acceptors) and waits until a majority responds (Phase 2 in Fig. 4). At the second phase, it checks that everyone has received the value and expects the value of the other nodes. If this value exceeds the global threshold, which is the sum of the local thresholds, then a global attack is flagged.

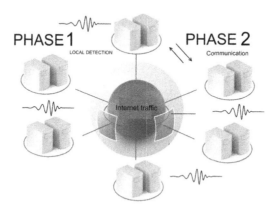

Fig. 4. Distributed detection system

6   Empirical Evaluations

In this section, we provide evaluation results which demonstrate the effectiveness of leveraging collaborative and decomposition wavelet techniques to infer DDoS attacks. In addition, we investigate temporal behaviors that are crucial for detecting the overall distributed attack. Our obtained results herein are based on recent Internet traffic traces from CAIDA [12].

6.1   Dataset Overview

To demonstrate the effectiveness of our method with any data source, we test our work on two completely different databases.

The CAIDA Anonymized Internet Traces 2008 Dataset, contains anonymous passive traffic from "Equinix-Chicago" OC192 link. The principal property of the dataset is that it is only one-way traffic as it has only responses from the victim node. DDoS traces block the victim by consuming the computing resources on the server and all of the bandwidths of the network connecting the server to the Internet.

Also, CAIDA 2013 dataset has high traffic rate as much as 50,000 packets/s that it contains SYN and UDP flood attacks.

6.2 Results at the Local Probe

In this part we will present the results recorded on the local probes.

We note the accuracy of the detection with faster calculation than other methods as explained in Sect. 8 (Fig. 5).

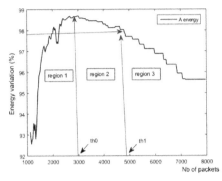

(a) Variation of the approximation energy Ea (%)

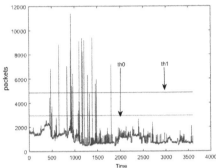

(b) Position of the threshold th_0, th_1

Fig. 5. CAIDA 2008 data set

By using the threshold value th_1 estimate before, we can classify the intervals time into set of the suspect intervals T_a or a set of the normal intervals T_{na}. We define a set of suspicious packets T_a as: $T_a = T_i$ such as values of $T_i > th_1$ Fig. 7 shows the classification of the different interval Ti by using the backscatter-2008 dataset. We note that T2, T3, T4, T5 are detected as DDoSs attack, but T1, T6, T7, T8 are classified as normal traffic. For the caida 2013 dataset, the intervals T1, T3, T4, T7, T8 are classified as DDoS attack (Fig. 8), while there are not attack during the intervals T2, T5, T6.

We note that the regions are clearly separated. The thresholds th_0 and th_1 determine exactly when the abnormal traffic starts. The calculation of the thresholds being simplified thanks to the decomposition by wavelet we gain in time of detection but also in time of computation.

6.3 Global Results

The existence of huge traffic in DDoS attacks is a reality in the operational environments in which DDoS detection systems have to cope. The purpose of this experiment is to demonstrate the effectiveness of the proposed distributed system for large traffic analysis, thus contributing to the reduction of the false-positive rate.

This is achieved through a distributed platform that allows to supervise the entire network. The results obtained previously locally allow us later to detect a global attack more easily.

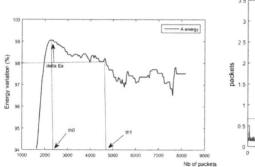
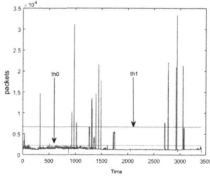

(a) Variation of the approximation energy (b) the position of the threshold th_0, th_1
Ea (%)

Fig. 6. CAIDA 2013 data set

Add to this, and as we will see in Sect. 7, the distributed system will allow us to detect the attack earlier.

6.4 Performance and Scalability

To estimate the accuracy of the detection, we estimate approximately the false Positive report (RPF), the false negative (FNR) and detection latency as performance metrics. The experiments we conducted on DDoS flows extracted from CAIDA demonstrated a 1% rate FNR with an average of 4% FPR. This is due to the variable sensitivity of the used thresholds.

It is important to note that the adopted Paxos protocol is able, in just 2 s, to coordinate, collaborate and alert an inferred DDoS attack. Further experimentation carried out previously to verify the scalability of the Paxos protocol

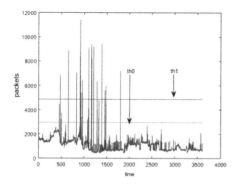
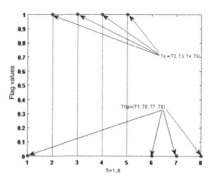

Fig. 7. Classification of the intervals time in the backscatter-2008 dataset.

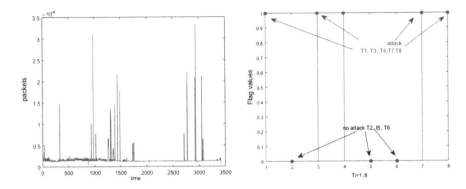

Fig. 8. Classification of the intervals time in the CAIDA-2013 dataset.

[6] demonstrated throughput of close to 1000 transactions/messages per second using a virtualized distributed system consisting of 30 hosts.

7 Discussion: Collaborative Attack Detection

The advantage of the PAXOS consensus protocol is the possibility to communicate with any machine. It is enough to agree on a value that will be exchanged and on a global threshold.

Also, the execution time of the PAXOS protocol depends on two parameters: the number of machines and the latency of the network. So, we have tested in our case the detection time of probes installed on virtual machines. We calculated the detection time (Fig. 9) on the second probe without the PAXOS protocol and then with the protocol. We observe that the first probe is able to detect an attack at the 53rd second, following the protocol the alert is triggered and probe 2 is alerted.

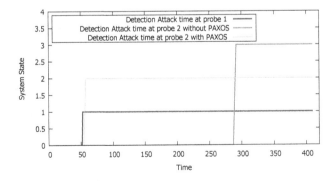

Fig. 9. Detection attack time

Instead of a delayed attack detection (second 292) as in the case of distributed architecture without consensus protocol, the second probe is notified of the attack at the 58th second. It saves a lot of time and can be decisive.

8   Comparison

Despite the difficulty to compare our work with other works because they use totally different methods we wanted to gather in the Table 1 the particularities of our method compared to the old research.

Table 1. Comparison with other models

	Our detection model	Fast entropy algorithm [3]	Chi-square detection [7]	Wavelet attack detection [9]
Traffic analysis	Mask function on the signal	All the signal	All the signal	Energy distribution of the signal
Attack estimation	Yes	No	No	Yes
Threshold reliability	Adaptive threshold	Entropy with adaptive threshold	Chi square threshold	No threshold specified

9   Conclusion

In this paper, we propose a multiple time-series DDoS detection model based on wavelet decomposition. The proposed model is able to mitigate particular attack signals effectively via distributed adaptive threshold metrics. Our results, which is based on real attack traces, are validated and our overall accuracy remained withing 1% FNR and an average of 4% FPR. Executed experimentation using various real DDoS traces from CAIDA have indeed validated the accuracy and scalability of the proposed architecture. Also, the proposed architecture (1) was validated in terms of detection accuracy and promptness at a single vantage point, (2) demonstrated its added-value in terms of detection promptness when operated in a distributed architecture using the consensus protocol, and (3) was validated when operated in a distributed architecture in the presence of legitimate traffic.

Finally, we are currently designing a large-scale DDoS experimentation testbed in collaboration with a leading industrial partner. The aim is to make the latter platform available for researchers and other stakeholders, to conduct massive experimentation related to various DDoS types, their detection mechanisms and mitigation capabilities.

References

1. Chen, A., Jin, Y., Cao, J., Li, L.E.: Tracking long duration flows in network traffic. In: 2010 Proceedings of the Infocom, pp. 1–5. IEEE (2010)
2. Chen, Z., Yeo, C.K., Lee, B.S., Lau, C.T.: Power spectrum entropy based detection and mitigation of low-rate DoS attacks. Comput. Netw. **136**, 80–94 (2018)
3. David, J., Thomas, C.: Ddos attack detection using fast entropy approach on flow-based network traffic. Procedia Comput. Sci. **50**, 30–36 (2015)
4. Du, Z., Ma, L., Li, H., Li, Q., Sun, G., Liu, Z.: Network traffic anomaly detection based on wavelet analysis. In: 2018 IEEE 16th International Conference on Software Engineering Research, Management and Applications (SERA), pp. 94–101. IEEE (2018)
5. El-Khattam, W., Salama, M.M.: Distributed generation technologies, definitions and benefits. Electr. Power Syst. Res. **71**(2), 119–128 (2004)
6. Ouerfelli, F.E., Barbaria, K., Bou-Harb, E., Fachkha, C., Zouari, B.: On the collaborative inference of DDoS: an information-theoretic distributed approach. In: 2018 14th International Wireless Communications & Mobile Computing Conference (IWCMC), pp. 518–523. IEEE (2018)
7. Feinstein, L., Schnackenberg, D., Balupari, R., Kindred, D.: Statistical approaches to DDoS attack detection and response. In: 2003 Proceedings of the DARPA Information Survivability Conference and Exposition, vol. 1, pp. 303–314. IEEE (2003)
8. Kosowski, D., Kołaczek, G., Juszczyszyn, K.: Evaluation of an Impact of the DoS attacks on the selected virtualization platforms. In: Borzemski, L., Świątek, J., Wilimowska, Z. (eds.) ISAT 2018. AISC, vol. 852, pp. 30–40. Springer, Cham (2019). https://doi.org/10.1007/978-3-319-99981-4_4
9. Li, L., Lee, G.: DDoS attack detection and wavelets. Telecommun. Syst. **28**(3–4), 435–451 (2005)
10. Nanadikar, K., Kachi, A., Karkhanis, A., Patole, S.: FireCol: a collaborative protection network for the detection of flooding DDoS attack. Int. J. Eng. Res. Technol. **3** (2014)
11. Ongaro, D., Ousterhout, J.: In search of an understandable consensus algorithm. In: 2014 USENIX Annual Technical Conference (USENIX ATC 2014), pp. 305–319 (2014)
12. Shannon, C.: CAIDA anonymized 2008 internet traces dataset. http://www.caida.org/data/passive/passive_2008_dataset.xml
13. Sifuzzaman, M., Islam, M.R., Ali, M.: Application of wavelet transform and its advantages compared to Fourier transform. J. Phys. Sci. **13**, 121–134 (2009)
14. Wang, F., Wang, X., Su, J., Xiao, B.: VicSifter: a collaborative DDoS detection system with lightweight victim identification. In: IEEE 11th International Conference on Trust, Security and Privacy in Computing and Communications, pp. 215–222. IEEE (2012)
15. Zheng, J., Li, Q., Gu, G., Cao, J., Yau, D.K., Wu, J.: Realtime DDoS defense using COTS SDN switches via adaptive correlation analysis. IEEE Trans. Inf. Forensics Secur. **13**(7), 1838–1853 (2018)

A Recommender System for User-Specific Vulnerability Scoring

Linus Karlsson$^{(\boxtimes)}$, Pegah Nikbakht Bideh, and Martin Hell

Department of Electrical and Information Technology,
Lund University, Lund, Sweden
{linus.karlsson,pegah.nikbakht_bideh,martin.hell}@eit.lth.se

Abstract. With the inclusion of external software components in their software, vendors also need to identify and evaluate vulnerabilities in the components they use. A growing number of external components makes this process more time-consuming, as vendors need to evaluate the severity and applicability of published vulnerabilities. The CVSS score is used to rank the severity of a vulnerability, but in its simplest form, it fails to take user properties into account. The CVSS also defines an environmental metric, allowing organizations to manually define individual impact requirements. However, it is limited to explicitly defined user information and only a subset of vulnerability properties is used in the metric. In this paper we address these shortcomings by presenting a recommender system specifically targeting software vulnerabilities. The recommender considers both user history, explicit user properties, and domain based knowledge. It provides a utility metric for each vulnerability, targeting the specific organization's requirements and needs. An initial evaluation with industry participants shows that the recommender can generate a metric closer to the users' reference rankings, based on predictive and rank accuracy metrics, compared to using CVSS environmental score.

1 Introduction

The Common Vulnerability Scoring System (CVSS) [4,8] defines a severity ranking for vulnerabilities. The base score does not take into account individual preferences of users. Instead, CVSS has an environmental metric which can be used to modify the base score such that it represents user dependent properties of vulnerabilities. It will rewrite the confidentiality, integrity, and availability metrics both to adjust them according to measures already taken by the organization, but also to capture the actual impact such loss would have on the organization. As this will differ between organizations, such a modified metric will better reflect the actual severity of a vulnerability to that organization.

The environmental metrics must be evaluated on a per vulnerability basis and are handled manually. This is both time consuming, error prone, and can lead to inconsistencies in case there are several vulnerabilities and they are handled by different analysts. Moreover, the environmental metric, though unique for

© Springer Nature Switzerland AG 2020
S. Kallel et al. (Eds.): CRiSIS 2019, LNCS 12026, pp. 355–364, 2020.
https://doi.org/10.1007/978-3-030-41568-6_23

the organization, only constitutes the sub-metrics available in the base score. Additional information that might affect the organization is not covered.

Recommender systems work by analyzing information about user preferences, and combine this with information about items, or with the history of other users. Their goal is to output recommendations targeting the specific user.

In this paper, we explore ways to improve measuring how a vulnerability affects an organization. Using machine learning techniques applied to recommender systems, we combine different properties and metrics in order to capture vulnerability data and map it to requirements of the specific organization. Compared to CVSS environmental metrics, our method provides several advantages.

First, the requirements for the organization is derived by combining explicit requirements with requirements learned from previous analysis of vulnerabilities. This data driven approach will not only use personal preferences, but also take into account how real vulnerabilities have been evaluated previously. Such learned data is able to capture information that might be overseen by analysts, or that are difficult to express. Second, our approach is general and is not restricted to a certain group of properties. It can be amended with new metrics if needed, focusing on metrics relevant for the given organization or device.

Our goal is to design a recommender that provides a personalized severity assessment based on a user profile. The profile is both explicit, based on the users' own choices, and implicit as the recommender learns from the users' previous actions. We also support inclusion of domain knowledge into the system, and discuss how the different parts can be weighted. Suitable similarity functions are used to form a utility function that outputs the personalized severity assessment. The recommender is also evaluated using participants from the industry. Though the evaluation is small scale, the results indicate that our recommender system is able to provide severity information that is closer to the users' actual preferences than the CVSS environmental score.

Compared to previous work such as [3,5–7,14], our approach uses more features, consider user preferences, learns from past user behavior, and/or provides scores instead of suggested actions (cf. [5]).

2   Recommenders and Vulnerability Severity Ratings

Generally, the goal of a recommender is to present recommendations of *items* to a set of *users*. An item can be for example a movie, a song, or a website. The idea is that the recommender should present a subset of items to the user, such that the user finds this subset relevant. The subset is found by matching user preferences or activity using a learned profile and sometimes other similar users' activity. In a shopping scenario, the added value for the user also leads to higher sales. In this paper, the goal of the recommender is to add value to an end-user by tailoring the severity score for vulnerabilities.

There are three major categories of recommender systems [1]: knowledge-based systems, content-based systems, and collaborative filtering. Other than these, recommendations can be generated from domain-specific knowledge. This

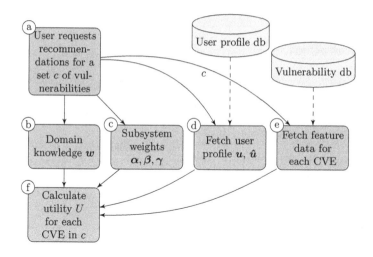

Fig. 1. Flow chart of recommendation generation

generates recommendations for a specific field of knowledge, and is designed specifically to handle data for that domain.

Many vulnerabilities are reported and given a CVE identifier. For each vulnerability, NVD provides a severity score. This score, denoted the base score, uses exploitability and impact submetrics in order to define a severity score between 0–10. This score is made to be reproducible and organization independent. Instead, the environmental score can be used to adapt the base score to an organization's requirements and needs.

3   System Model

We have identified the following requirements: (1) The recommender should give reasonable recommendations for new users of the system, avoiding the cold-start problem. (2) It should allow the user to select certain preferences that the system will honor. (3) It should expose a meaningful subset of user preferences to the user. (4) It should learn from user actions, so that future recommendations are as relevant as possible to the user. To avoid privacy concerns, only the user's own actions are considered.

No single class of recommender system can fulfill all requirements. Instead, we propose a hybrid recommender based on three parts. The first is a *domain-based* subsystem which provides domain-specific knowledge unique to a recommender for vulnerabilities. The second part is a *knowledge-based* subsystem which allows the user to select certain user preferences that they are interested in. Lastly, the third part is a *content-based* subsystem which learns from the user's previous actions to provide more meaningful recommendations for each user.

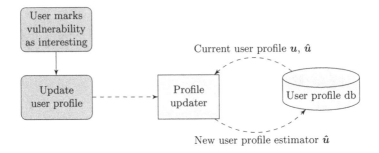

Fig. 2. Flow chart of user rating a vulnerability

3.1 Overall Recommender System Design

An overview of the recommendation generation process can be seen in Fig. 1. When a user requests recommendations for a set c of vulnerabilities, the feature data, domain-specific knowledge, user profiles, and weights are fetched from their respective storage. Each of these parts will be described in details in the following sections. These pieces will then be combined in the actual recommender, which then outputs recommendations in the range $[0, 1]$. A higher value means that a vulnerability is more relevant to the user.

Our hybrid recommender system learns user preferences based on the user's interaction with vulnerabilities. An overview of the rating procedure is shown in Fig. 2. First, the user rates a vulnerability based on their own preferences. Next, the current user profile is updated with the new information, so that a new user profile estimated called $\hat{u}$ is stored in the user profile database.

3.2 Feature Representation

A key task in designing a recommender is constructing a good feature extraction stage. In our case, this means that we wish to extract features from each vulnerability, to be used as input to the recommender, see block (e) in Fig. 1. First, a selection of features must be made, and later on their respective feature weight parameters must be decided. We will discuss actual features to use in Sect. 4.1. We consider the features of a vulnerability as a vector v, where each individual feature v_i denotes a specific feature value. Such a value could be of any type, such as a Boolean value, a real number, an integer in a specific range, categorical data, or hierarchical data.

3.3 User Profile Representation

There are two distinct parts of the user profile. First, there is the explicit user profile u, where the users explicitly select their own preferences. This is similar to the requirements that can be defined in the CVSS environmental metric. Second, there is the *estimated* user profile $\hat{u}$, which is determined from the user's interactions with the system. The system learns this profile about the user automatically. This allows the system to capture user preferences that are hard to explicitly express for users, either because the feature is complex, or because the user is unaware of them. The explicit user profile is the knowledge-based part of our hybrid recommender, while the estimated user profile is the content-based part.

Each of the two parts of the user profile is represented as a vector, where each element of the vector describes the interest the user has for each feature. The elements of the vectors are matched with the feature value from above, to find vulnerabilities to recommend to the user.

3.4 Domain-Specific Knowledge

The recommendations are not only based on the user profile, but also on a set of domain-specific knowledge, unique to the field of vulnerability assessment, and the same for all users. Such knowledge is required both to provide recommendations suitable for such a highly specific area of interest, but also serves as a component to solve the cold-start problem. The domain-specific knowledge w is represented in the same way as the user profile above.

3.5 Subsystem Weights

As described earlier, the recommender system is a hybrid system with three major parts. The three parts all contribute to the final result of the recommender, but they should be able to do so to different extents depending on the features, see Sect. 4.1. The subsystem weights are fetched at point (c) in Fig. 1.

The subsystems are given a weight between 0 and 1. Let the vectors α, β, γ describe the weights for the domain-based, knowledge-based, and content-based subsystems, respectively. For any given feature i, the sum $\alpha_i + \beta_i + \gamma_i = 1$. Note that relative weight of each subsystem can vary between different features.

3.6 Similarity Functions

A similarity function compares a value from the user profile, called the target value t_i, with the feature value extracted from the vulnerability v_i. We denote this function $\mathsf{sim}_i(t_i, v_i)$, where $0 \leq \mathsf{sim}_i(t_i, v_i) \leq 1$. Higher value means that the feature value is more similar to the target value. Here, we use the similarity functions given below. For examples of other variants, see e.g. [13].

First, we use $\mathsf{sim}_{\mathrm{dist}}$ which returns the absolute distance between t_i and v_i, scaled to be in the range $[0, 1]$ by knowing the minimum and maximum value. Second we use a scoring function $\mathsf{sim}_{\mathrm{mult}}$ which sees t_i as a multiplier to multiply the feature value v_i with. Third we use $\mathsf{sim}_{\mathrm{daydist}}$ which describes the distance in days between two values, implemented similarly to $\mathsf{sim}_{\mathrm{dist}}$. Fourth, we use $\mathsf{sim}_{\mathrm{cosine}}$ to calculate the cosine similarity between v_i and t_i, note that v_i and t_i are vectors in this case. Fifth, we use $\mathsf{sim}_{\mathrm{boost}}$ for Boolean values, where t_i is simply a constant which is returned if v_i is true.

3.7 Generating Recommendations

Combining the building blocks from the sections above, a complete recommender can now be described. The goal here is to describe a *utility function* U, which takes a given vulnerability v as input, and outputs the utility value, i.e. the user-specific severity assessment. As can be seen at point (f) in Fig. 1, the utility function U is the final step in a series of actions.

Utility U for a vulnerability can be described as:

$$U = \frac{1}{d} \sum_{i=1}^{d} \alpha_i \cdot \mathsf{sim}_i(w_i, v_i) + \beta_i \cdot \mathsf{sim}_i(u_i, v_i) + \gamma_i \cdot \mathsf{sim}_i(\hat{u}_i, v_i), \qquad (1)$$

where $\alpha_i, \beta_i, \gamma_i$ are the subsystem coefficients, sim_i is the similarity function for the ith feature, $w_i, u_i, \hat{u}_i$ are the target values for feature i for the different subsystems (i.e. elements of $w, u, \hat{u}$ respectively), and v_i is the feature value for feature i.

Because the similarity functions are limited to the range $[0, 1]$, and $\alpha_i + \beta_i + \gamma_i = 1$, the output of U will be a value between 0 and 1.

3.8 Updating User Profile

For estimating the user profile $\hat{u}$, we wish to combine the previous estimation with the new data about the user's preferences. We consider only input of vulnerabilities that the user *is interested in*, that is, positive training examples. Then, the update function update can be expressed as a function of the form $\hat{u}' = \mathsf{update}(\hat{u}, v)$, i.e., a function taking a new vulnerability v, the current $\hat{u}$, and returning a new estimation of the user preferences $\hat{u}'$.

We propose an approach inspired by [9], with some adaptions to make the update function applicable for any type of feature, not only text. The proposed update function is given by

$$\mathsf{update}(\hat{u}, v) = (\mathsf{mer}_1(\hat{u}_1, v_1), \dots, \mathsf{mer}_i(\hat{u}_i, v_i), \dots, \mathsf{mer}_d(\hat{u}_d, v_d)), \qquad (2)$$

where d is the number of features, and therefore elements in $\hat{u}$ and v.

For each pair $(\hat{u}_i, v_i)$, a *merge function* mer_i is applied. The merge function is similar to the similarity functions sim_i, but instead of comparing two elements, it merges them. The merging needs to be handled different for each feature type, and this construction is thus a generalization of [2,9].

In this paper we use two different merge functions, $\mathsf{mer}_{\mathrm{mma}}$ which is a merge function based on the Modified Moving Average, and $\mathsf{mer}_{\mathrm{add}}$ which simply performs an element-wise addition over two vectors $\hat{u}_i$ and v_i.

4 Implementation

Given the theoretical model described in the previous section, the actual recommender can now be constructed. This section describes such decisions for our implemented recommender. We stress that this is an example implementation of the model described in the previous section. Another implementation may choose different features, weights, or functions.

4.1 CVE Features

The implementation has used several sources for vulnerability information. A majority of the data is collected from NVD [11], but also other sites such as CVEdetails [10], and Google have been used. A list of features extracted is available in Table 1, and below we discuss the features in more detail.

Table 1. Feature selection in the implementation, feature types, weights of domain-based (α), knowledge-based (β), and content-based (γ) subsystems, and finally similarity and merge functions

Features	Data type	Subsystem weights			Functions	
		α	β	γ	sim	mer
Impact metrics	Categorical	0.0	0.5	0.5	sim_{mult}	mer_{mma}
Exploitability subscore	Numerical	0.0	0.8	0.2	sim_{mult}	mer_{mma}
Authentication	Categorical	0.3	0.35	0.35	sim_{mult}	mer_{mma}
Access vector	Categorical	0.3	0.35	0.35	sim_{dist}	mer_{mma}
CWE	Hierarchical	0.0	0.0	1.0	sim_{cosine}	mer_{add}
Published date	Date	1.0	0.0	0.0	$sim_{daydist}$	N/A
Metaspolit exploits	Boolean	0.3	0.7	0.0	sim_{boost}	N/A
Linked external resources	Numerical	1.0	0.0	0.0	sim_{mult}	N/A
Google hits	Numerical	1.0	0.0	0.0	sim_{mult}	N/A

Impact metrics includes the impact metrics in the CVSS score, namely confidentiality, integrity, and availability impact. These are categorical values where the impact can be NONE, PARTIAL, or COMPLETE. In our implementation, we map these values to numerical scores of 0.0, 0.5, and 1.0 respectively.

Exploitability subscore is the numerical exploitability subscore from the CVSS ranking, which estimates the ease of exploiting the vulnerability.

Authentication (CVSS metric) describes how many times an attacker needs to authenticate before performing an attack. It is a categorical feature with values NONE, SINGLE, or MULTIPLE. In our implementation, we map these values to numerical scores of 1.0, 0.5, and 0.0 respectively.

Access vector (CVSS metric) describes the attack vector for the vulnerability. It is categorical with the value NETWORK, ADJACENT, LOCAL. In our implementation, we map these to numerical values of 1.0, 0.5, and 0.0, respectively.

CWE ID categorizes vulnerabilities according to the type of the vulnerability.

Metasploit exploits is a Boolean value which describes if there is a Metasploit module [12] available for this vulnerability.

Linked external resources is a numerical value which counts the number of linked resources for a specific CVE on NVD.

Google hits is the number of Google search hits a specific CVE-ID has.

4.2   User Requirements Selection

When users start using the system, they should select what makes certain vulnerabilities more relevant to them. This is used to create the explicit user profile $\boldsymbol{u}$ for the recommender. The user profile is constructed by rating the importance of certain information about a vulnerability. The rating should be in the interval of $[0, 1]$, and will be used to construct the vector $\boldsymbol{u}$. User requirements can be selected in many ways, in our implementation the user can rate the following properties: confidentiality, integrity, and availability impact; exploit accessibility; access vector; and authentication.

4.3   Similarity and Merge Functions

The choice of similarity and merge functions are described in Table 1. In general, $\mathsf{sim}_{\mathrm{mult}}$ is the most common similarity function, since it maps a higher feature value to a more important vulnerability, by multiplying with some factor. In some cases, the $\mathsf{sim}_{\mathrm{dist}}$ distance similarity function is used instead, since this instead measures how close the feature value is to the user's preference. The Metasploit and publication date features have straightforward similarity functions based on their data type, while the CWE feature requires the use of the $\mathsf{sim}_{\mathrm{cosine}}$ similarity to correctly handle the comparison between CWE vectors.

If we instead look at merge functions, a modified moving average $\mathsf{mer}_{\mathrm{mma}}$ is used for most features, since it provides a simple way to converge towards to user's preference. For CWE, the special $\mathsf{mer}_{\mathrm{add}}$ function needs to be used such that the vector of previously seen CWEs are merged with the newly rated CWE. Finally, features with $\gamma_i = 0$ do not need merge functions, and are marked as N/A in Table 1.

5   Evaluation

In this section we present an initial evaluation of our recommender. For the evaluation, 8 users have been asked to participate. The users are working in the industry, for five different companies, and are people with high security awareness. These people are potential users of such a recommender.

Each user started by selecting their own user profile, with preferences described in Sect. 4.2. Then, 30 sample CVEs were selected, the CVEs were from different products, years, described different vulnerabilities, and were presented in a random order. The users were asked to rank these CVEs on a scale from 0 to 10, where a higher value indicated higher interest to the user. The users were asked to only consider properties of the CVE itself, rather than the product it affected. To avoid bias from the CVSS base score, this score, as well as the impact and exploitability subscores, were hidden from the user during the evaluation. The users could however see other information in the CVE to make an informed decision.

Then, CVEs were divided into training and test sets using k-fold cross-validation, using $k = 5$. We performed an evaluation where both the user profile and the training set were used to train the recommender, before generating recommendations. As a comparison, we also compared the results to using the CVSS2 environmental score, with explicit user profiles mapped to impact subscore modifiers. For both cases, the reference ranking was the manual ranking performed by the users.

The RMSE and NDPM [15] values were then calculated between the reference ranking and the recommender output, and between the reference ranking and the CVSS2 environmental score. The metrics can be seen in Table 2. We see that the RMSE values of the recommender system are lower compared to the CVSS environmental score. This indicates that the recommender has higher predictive rating accuracy for all users in comparison to just using the environmental score. The results also indicate higher rank accuracy in comparison to the environmental score based on the NDPM metric, for the majority of test users.

Table 2. RMSE and NDPM of recommender system and CVSS environmental score, relative the reference ranking, for different users. A lower value means higher accuracy.

	RMSE		NDPM	
	Recommender	Environmental	Recommender	Environmental
User 1	0.179	0.222	0.303	0.287
User 2	0.247	0.340	0.195	0.271
User 3	0.200	0.256	0.207	0.333
User 4	0.153	0.296	0.179	0.276
User 5	0.168	0.286	0.294	0.283
User 6	0.138	0.234	0.175	0.228
User 7	0.115	0.224	0.147	0.251
User 8	0.198	0.267	0.349	0.340

6 Conclusions and Future Work

We have defined, implemented and evaluated a recommender system providing severity assessments of vulnerabilities. The recommender system is specialized for vulnerabilities, and is designed to be useful specifically for the context of vulnerability assessment. Recommendations are generated by considering both users' explicit preferences, and by considering their previous interactions with the recommender. The system can be used with a variety of different inputs, and can easily be extended with new features if desired.

The evaluation shows that the system gives better recommendations compared to just using the CVSS environmental score. To be able to tune the parameters for optimized performance, data from more users is needed. However, the results from our evaluation with real users suggests that it is possible to improve the assessment using a recommender system approach. Other possible future work includes consider negative feedback in the learning phase, which may further improve the results when learning is enabled.

Acknowledgements. This work was partially supported by the Swedish Foundation for Strategic Research, grant RIT17-0035, and partially supported by the Wallenberg Autonomous Systems and Software Program (WASP) funded by Knut and Alice Wallenberg foundation.

References

1. Aggarwal, C.C.: Recommender Systems. Springer, Cham (2016). https://doi.org/10.1007/978-3-319-29659-3
2. Chen, L., Sycara, K.: WebMate: a personal agent for browsing and searching. In: Proceedings of the Second International Conference on Autonomous Agents, AGENTS 1998, pp. 132–139. ACM (1998)
3. Farris, K.A., Shah, A., Cybenko, G., Ganesan, R., Jajodia, S.: Vulcon: a system for vulnerability prioritization, mitigation, and management. ACM Trans. Priv. Secur. (TOPS) **21**(4), 1–28 (2018)
4. First: Common vulnerability scoring system v3.0: Specification document. https://www.first.org/cvss/specification-document
5. Gadepally, V.N., et al.: Recommender systems for the department of defense and the intelligence community. MIT Lincoln Laboratory (2016)
6. Lee, Y., Shin, S.: Toward semantic assessment of vulnerability severity: a text mining approach. In: 1st International Workshop on EntitY REtrieval (EYRE 2018) (2018)
7. Liu, Q., Zhang, Y.: VRSS: a new system for rating and scoring vulnerabilities. Comput. Commun. **34**, 264–273 (2011)
8. Mell, P.M., et al.: A complete guide to the common vulnerability scoring system version 2.0 (2007). https://www.nist.gov/publications/complete-guide-common-vulnerability-scoring-system-version-20
9. Van Meteren, R., Van Someren, M.: Using content-based filtering for recommendation. In: Proceedings of ECML 2000 Workshop: Machine Learning in Information Age, pp. 47–56 (2000)
10. MITRE Corporation: CVE details. https://www.cvedetails.com/
11. NIST: National vulnerability database. https://nvd.nist.gov/
12. Rapid7: Vulnerability and exploit database. https://www.rapid7.com/db
13. Smyth, B.: Case-based recommendation. In: Brusilovsky, P., Kobsa, A., Nejdl, W. (eds.) The Adaptive Web. LNCS, vol. 4321, pp. 342–376. Springer, Heidelberg (2007). https://doi.org/10.1007/978-3-540-72079-9_11
14. Spanos, G., Sioziou, A., Angelis, L.: WIVSS: a new methodology for scoring information systems vulnerabilities. In: Proceedings of the 17th Panhellenic Conference on Informatics, PCI 2013, pp. 83–90. ACM, New York (2013)
15. Yao, Y.Y.: Measuring retrieval effectiveness based on user preference of documents. J. Am. Soc. Inf. Sci. **46**(2), 133–145 (1995)

Distributed Detection System Using Wavelet Decomposition and Chi-Square Test

Fatima Ezzahra Ouerfelli[1]([envelope]) [ORCID], Khaled Barbaria[1], Belhassen Zouari[1], and Claude Fachkha[2,3]

[1] Mediatron Lab, University of Carthage, Tunis, Tunisia
fatima-ezzahra.ouerfelli@fst.utm.tn, khaled.barbaria@ensta.org,
belhassen.zouari@fst.rnu.tn
[2] University of Dubai, Dubai, UAE
cfachkha@ud.ac.ae
[3] Steppa Cyber Inc., Longueuil, Canada

Abstract. As of today, Distributed Denial of Service Attacks remain one the most devastating threats online. This paper presents an estimation model that integrates the discrete wavelet transform (DWT) and Chi-Square test (X_2) for detecting DDoS attacks. The present model presents a distributed architecture reducing the risk of single point of failure and increasing the reliability of the system. First, we uses the DWT to decompose the traffic data. Then, the obtained detail (high-frequency) components is used as input variable to forecast future traffic attack. To ensure a complete distribution of our system we test the PAXOS protocol which give a reliable communication between detection systems. The model is tested using real datasets of DDoS traces. So, our proposed system outperforms other conventional models that use a centralized architecture.

Keywords: Denial of Service · Wavelet decomposition · Distributed systems · DDoS · Chi-Square

1 Introduction

In 2018, the World Economic Forum (WEF) [16] ranked cyberattacks and Distributed Denial of Service (DDoS), at place four of its top 5 of the most threatening global risks for our society. In fact, DDoS attacks have become global phenomenon and a serious threat to any company or person with Internet exposure [12]. Also, research shows that DDoS attackers target any kind of organisation. Not only as part of a data breach, but also to receive a ransom, political problems or for competitive reasons. So we can see the impact of DDoS attacks on Bitcoin currency exchanges [4], or the impact on smart vehicles [14]. Whatever the motivation of these attacks, these are particularly devious and ultimately always damage those individuals that depend on their services. In this context,

© Springer Nature Switzerland AG 2020
S. Kallel et al. (Eds.): CRiSIS 2019, LNCS 12026, pp. 365–377, 2020.
https://doi.org/10.1007/978-3-030-41568-6_24

it is highly desirable to design a system that promptly infer DDoS attacks, even in the situations where limited data is available at the observation points.

In this paper, we propose a Multiple Time-series DDoS Detection Model that exploits wavelet decomposition and Chi-Square computations to achieve its task. The Wavelet Transform (WT) is a mathematical method used to represent a given signal in different scales and Chi-Square test is used to determine whether there is a significant difference between the expected frequencies and the observed frequencies in one or more categories. Specifically, we frame the contributions of this paper as follows:

- Exploiting decomposition wavelet to de-construct complex signals of DDoS attack into basic signals of finite bandwidth.
- Use Chi-Square techniques to infer DDoS attacks at local observation points.
- Designing a collaborative distributed detection scheme by employing a consensus algorithm to leverage various resources and avoiding single point of failure scenarios.

The remainder of this paper is organized as follows. In Sect. 2, we elaborate the related work and demonstrate how the proposed work is unique. In Sect. 3 we explain the foundations of our solution. In Sect. 4, we detail the proposed approach and discuss its components. In Sect. 5, we empirically evaluate the proposed scheme and demonstrate its effectiveness and promptness. Finally, Sect. 6 summarizes and concludes this paper.

2   Related Work

There are several contributions in DDoS attack detection including the use of energy decomposition, Chi-Square and collaborative solutions. We list below some major contributions in these areas.

Among the authors who propose the detection of attack, by decomposition of wavelet we propose the solution of Du et al. [2]. They propose to use wavelet analysis to extract information from the signal. Firstly, they extract the waveform features, and then use the support vector machine for classification.

Also Kaur et al. [6] propose to use wavelets as a signal processing tool to compute Hurst Index (H), it is used as a measure for computing degree of self-similarity in network traffic.

In an other context, Feinstein et al. [5] propose to use Pearson's Chi-Square Test for distribution comparison in cases where the measurements involved are discrete values. For each packet that arrives, they extract the value v, of the desired attribute (e.g., source address), they apply exponential decay to the stored frequency for v and do a current-traffic profile. This profile is compared with a baseline profile using the Chi-Square statistic.

In fact, the Chi-Square statistic does provide a useful measure of the deviation of a current traffic profile from the baseline.

In addition to this methods and others [1, 7, 11], there exists a plethora of solutions for detecting DDoS attacks, but only few of them focused on distributed detection, and none of them, to the best of our knowledge, employed information-theoretic techniques in such context. For instance, Nanadikar et al. [10] proposed a distributed defense scheme against DDoS attacks, which constructed a ring of intrusion prevention systems. These systems form virtual protection nodes surrounding the hosts to defend and collaborate by exchanging selected traffic information such as IP addresses, ports, and protocols. The weak point of this work is the lack of a reliable consensus protocol.

Indeed, our proposed approach is complementary to the aforementioned literature work and further contributes by (1) exploiting energy distribution based on wavelet analysis, (2) exploiting Chi-Square to detect attack in a local observation and (3) consolidating the previous methods by a fully distributed architecture Finally uniquely experimenting with various, real DDoS traces to evaluate and validate the outcomes of the proposed approach.

3 Foundation of Detection Model

We introduce in this section the fundamentals of wavelet decomposition, Chi-Square test and Paxos protocol. Based on the definitions, we present in detail why this methods can easily detect the attacks.

3.1 Wavelet Definition

The wavelet transform replaces the Fourier transform's sinusoidal waves by translations and dilations of a window called a wavelet. It takes two arguments: time and scale. Discrete wavelet transform (DWT) deals with a scaling parameter and b translation parameters. The integral discrete wavelet transform of a function is:

$$W f(a,b) = <f, \Psi_{a,b}> = \int_{-\infty}^{+\infty} f(t) \frac{1}{\sqrt{a}} \Psi * (\frac{t-b}{a}) dt \qquad (1)$$

where the base atom is a zero average function, centered around zero with a finite energy. The family of vectors is obtained by translations and dilatations of the base atom:

$$\Psi_{a,b}(t) = \frac{1}{\sqrt{a}} \Psi(\frac{t-b}{a}), a > 0, b \epsilon R \qquad (2)$$

For many signals, the low frequency content is the most important part of the origin signal. The high frequency content imparts flavor or nuance. In wavelet analysis, signal is decomposed in approximation and detail components [9]. Hence the wavelet algorithm based on the multi-resolution is to divide the signal into multiple components of different scales by orthogonal wavelet. its application is equivalent to the repeated use of a group of high and low pass filter, the time sequence signals were decomposed in several steps, the high pass filter generates signals of high frequency components, the low pass filter generates signals of low frequency approximation component. A DWT decomposition scheme is shown

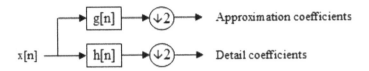

Fig. 1. Decomposition of signal in 2 levels

in Fig. 1 The outputs giving the detail coefficients (from the high-pass filter) and approximation coefficients (from the low-pass).

The filter output of the low-pass filter g in the diagram above is then subsampled by 2 and further processed by passing it again through a new low-pass filter g and a high-pass filter h with half the cut-off frequency of the previous one:

$$a[n] = \sum_{-\infty}^{+\infty} x[k]g[2n - k] \tag{3}$$

$$d[n] = \sum_{-\infty}^{+\infty} x[k]h[2n - k] \tag{4}$$

The original signal sequence x(n) can be expressed as the sum of the most components, that is:

$$S(n) = D_1(n) + A_1(n) = \sum_{j=1}^{J} D_j(n) + A_J(n) \tag{5}$$

Where $A_J(n)$ is the coefficients of wavelet decomposition signal at level J. The total energy of the signal can be expressed as:

$$\sum_{n=1}^{N} |s(n)|^2 = \sum_{n=1}^{N} |a_j(n)|^2 + \sum_{j=1}^{J} \sum_{n=1}^{N} |d_j(n)|^2 \tag{6}$$

Where N is the sample size, J is the total number of wavelet decomposition levels.

3.2   Chi-Square Test

A Chi-Square test [15] can be used to verify if the variance of a population is equal to a specified value. This test can be either a two-sided test or a one-sided test. The two-sided version tests against the alternative that the true variance is either less than or greater than the specified value. The one-sided version only tests in one direction. The choice of a two-sided or one-sided test is determined by the problem.

The Chi-Square hypothesis test is defined as:
H0: $\sigma^2 = \sigma_0^2$ Ha: $\sigma^2 < \sigma_0^2$ for a lower one-tailed test, $\sigma^2 > \sigma_0^2$ for an upper one-tailed test where N is the sample size and s is the sample standard deviation.

The key element of this formula is the ratio $(\frac{s}{\sigma_0})$ which compares the ratio of the sample standard deviation to the target standard deviation. The more this ratio deviates from 1, the more likely we are to reject the null hypothesis. Reject the null hypothesis that the variance is a specified value σ_0^2 if:

$T_s > \chi_{1-\alpha,N-1}^2$ for an upper one-tailed alternative,

$T_s > \chi_{\alpha,N-1}^2$ for a lower one-tailed alternative

$T_s > \chi_{\frac{\alpha}{2},N-1}^2$ for a two-tailed alternative or $T_s > \chi_{1-\frac{\alpha}{2},N-1}^2$ where $\chi_{.,N-1}^2$ is the critical value of the Chi-Square distribution with $N-1$ degrees of freedom.

3.3 Distributed Architecture with PAXOS Protocol

To ensure full distribution in our system, we have integrated and implemented a variant of the Paxos algorithm [8] since it is suitable in building agreement among multiple hosts. Further, Paxos guarantees consistency across a group of unreliable replicas and attempts to come to an agreement even during periods when some replicas are unresponsive. In Fig. 2, we present the multi-Paxos protocol.

The algorithm is composed of two phases, namely, "prepare" and "accept". In the first phase, a node chooses to become the leader and selects a sequence number x and a value v to create a proposal $P1(x,v)$. Subsequently, it sends this proposal to the acceptors (nodes 1 and 2 in Fig. 2) and waits till a majority responds. At the second phase, if a majority of acceptors fail to reply or "agree", the leader abandons the proposal and would initiate the protocol again. If a majority of acceptors agree, the leader verifies the values of the proposals and sends an "accept" request message with the proposal number and value. However, if the leader does receive an accept from a majority, the protocol can be considered terminated. It might be noteworthy to mention that the algorithm is practically resilient towards failures and has been shown to guarantee reliable agreements.

4   Proposed Model

The important performance metric of DDoS detection includes detection latency and detection accuracy. However it is impossible to reduce both and at the same time in a centralized system. We need to use a distributed architecture to increase the accuracy of our system but also to decrease the detection time.

4.1   Overall Algorithm Description

We explain the DDoS attack detecting algorithm based on detail data as follows:

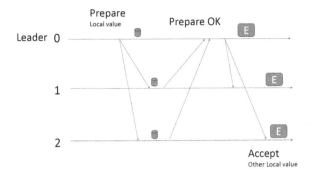

Fig. 2. PAXOS values exchange

Algorithm: Multiple times-series detection model

Local Detection
Step 0 : Initialisation
(1) Compute σ_0^2 that is the variance of the detail energy coefficients
(DW) of the traffic DDoS at level 3
Step 1: Capture traffic
(1) Capture traffic in a window time and store it in array
(2) Divide this DDoS traffic in 8 blocks : $T_1..T_8$
Step 2 : Wavelet decomposition
Decompose the block T_i with wavelet transform and store the detail
energy coefficients Dwi.
Step 3 : Chi-Square compute
(1) Compute Threshold Chi-Square $\chi_{0.5,i-1}^2$
(2) Compute value Chi-Square $= Ts = (Ti_{size} - 1)\frac{s^2}{\sigma_0^2}$
if Chi-Square value > Chi-Square threshold
        attack = yes
    else
        attack = no
Global detection
Step 4 : Decision
When the Chi-Square threshold is exceeded the system triggers the
Paxos protocol.

4.2 Local Detection: Wavelet Decomposition and Chi-Square Test

In order to accurately and timely detect the sudden change in the traffic, we adopt the wavelet decomposition in our approach. The basic idea of wavelet decomposition is to divide signal into high frequency and low frequency. High frequency components as Detail and Low Frequency Components as Approximation.

Intuitively speaking, anything that is 'high frequency' is something that is 'rapidly changing in time'. Anything that is 'low frequency' is something that is 'slowly changing in time'.

Consequently, any time we have 'detail' in a signal, it means that we have, very quick, rapid variations in time or space. This then becomes the 'detail' of our signal.

Therefore it is interesting to study the abrupt variations of a traffic because these variations will indicate simply that there is an attack.

To perform this study we use the Chi-Square test. The advantages of Chi-Square test are base on the fact that it is a no parametric test. It is extremely easy to calculate and interpret. Also it can be used on nominal data. So, we can adapt it to our attack detection case.

4.3   Global Detection: Consensus Protocol with Paxos

As mentioned above, the Paxos algorithm is composed of two phases, namely, prepare and accept. In our detection system, in the first phase, when a node detects an exceeded Chi-Square threshold, it chooses to become the leader and selects a sequence number x and his threshold to create a proposal $P1(x,v)$. Subsequently, it sends this proposal to the others nodes (named acceptors) and waits till a majority responds. At the second phase, it checks that everyone has received the value and expects the value of the other nodes. If this value exceeds the global threshold, which is the sum of the local thresholds then a global attack is flagged.

5   Simulation Results

We use actual datasets from the CAIDA Lab [13] to evaluate our approach. To improve the efficiency of our solution our system is tested on two different databases: CAIDA 2008 and CAIDA 2013.

5.1   Presentation of CAIDA Datasets: 2008 and 2013

The CAIDA: Anonymized Internet Traces 2008 Dataset, contains anonymous passive traffic from "Equinix-Chicago" OC192 link. The principle property of the dataset is that it is only one way traffic as it has only responses from the victim node. DDoS traces block the victim by consuming the computing resources on the server and all of the bandwidths of the network connecting the server to the Internet.

In the same context, CAIDA 2013 dataset has high traffic rate as much as 50,000 packets/s that it contains SYN flood attack and also UDP flood attack. An attack UDP flood can be started by sending a large number of UDP packets to random ports on a remote host. The attacker tries to occupy all available bandwidth of the victim so that it becomes unavailable for legitimate users. Flows of UDP flood contain many large-sized packets with the intention to overwhelm the destination.

Figure 4a shows a window of samples with during about an hour from CAIDA 2013 dataset. We note that the traffic rate is high reaching 35000 packets/s. So, the variance of the whole of the window is also high, which leads to a high value of the threshold $\chi^2_{0.5,N-1}$ for each interval Ti (in Table 3). The detection of DDoS attack for each interval Ti depends on the level wavelet decomposition.

5.2   Local Detection: Chi-Square After Wavelet Decomposition

CAIDA 2008: Figure 3b shows the variation of Chi-Square during each time interval T_i. We note that detection of attack depends on the level decomposition wavelet. There is a difference in accuracy of detection attack between the first, second and third levels. The third level decomposition wavelet gives a good result. That means, for the CAIDA 2008 dataset, we detect the anomalies for the time intervals T2 and T5 at the level three. This detection is an indication of a SYN flood attack during time interval T2, T3, T4 and T5.

We note in the Fig. 4 an observed peak during the time interval T4. This is due to the high value of the detail coefficients variance of sample s^2. In other words, this is due to the sharp increase of number of SYN packets and either the RST packets during T4. This is an indication for anomalies events in this portion of CAIDA 2008 dataset.

This high accuracy is achieved by finding the better combination of these parameter values.

In the same context, in Table 1, we note for the during time interval T3, the Chi-Square calculated value (665.5) at third decomposition level wavelet is greater than the Chi-Square tabulated value (273, $\alpha = .05$). Therefore we reject the null hypothesis H_0 and accept the alternative hypothesis H1. This means that at the time interval T3, an anomaly has been identified and we can say that there is DoS attack during the time interval T3.

Conjointly, we notice during the time interval T8 a non intrusive events in the CAIDA 2008 dataset. The calculated Chi-Square value is less than the critical value, so we cannot reject the null hypothesis H_0 for this particular time interval. The acceptance of the null hypothesis means that there is no intrusive traffic in CAIDA 2008 data during the time interval T8.

This is due to the fact that there is a little value of detail coefficients variance s_2 of time interval T8. The calculated Chi-Square values and their corresponding thresholds for the CAIDA 2008 dataset for all time interval from time interval T1 to T8 is shown in Table 1.

CAIDA 2013: Like for CAIDA 2008 dataset, we perform the same algorithm on CAIDA 2013 dataset.

We note that the values of the Chi-Square and the threshold $\chi^2_{0.5,N-1}$ depend on the level of the wavelet decomposition J. So, the threshold decreases when the level of the wavelet decomposition J increases. According to the Table 3 with

Table 1. Chi-Square values at different level decomposition wavelet (J = 3) in CAIDA 2008

Time intervals	T1	T2	T3	T4	T5	T6	T7	T8
Chi-Square value level 1	5,6	169	890	1992	542	27,7	48,1	21,9
$\chi^2_{0.5,N-1}$	286,1	239,5	273	420,7	545,1	359,3	506,1	585,1
Attack	No	No	Yes	Yes	No	No	No	No
Chi-Square value level 2	7,6	178,7	409,7	1761	307,5	40,3	57,7	44,8
$\chi^2_{0.5,N-1}$	286,1	239,5	273	420,7	545,1	359,3	506,1	585,1
Attack	No	No	Yes	Yes	No	No	No	No
Chi-Square value level 3	13,8	248	665,5	1572	754,9	51	164,4	71,5
$\chi^2_{0.5,N-1}$	286,1	239,5	273	420,7	545,1	359,3	506,1	585,1
Attack	No	Yes	Yes	Yes	Yes	No	No	No

Table 2. Chi-Square values at different level decomposition wavelet (J = 7) in CAIDA 2013

Time intervals	T1	T2	T3	T4	T5	T6	T7	T8
Chi-Square values caida 2013	1087	152,9	7969	7412	201,6	9,8	18613	1471
$\chi^2_{0.5,N-1}$	390,5	380,1	342,4	255,3	444,4	501,3	307,6	409,4
Attack	Yes	No	Yes	Yes	No	No	Yes	Yes

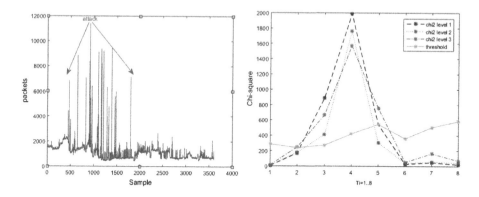

Fig. 3. The Chi-Square values at three levels decomposition wavelet in CAIDA 2008

a value of J = 3 for the both W and Ti, we notice that intervals T3, T4 and T7 present an anomaly while T1, T2, T5, T6 and T8 are normal traffic.

Furthermore according to the Table 2 with a value of J = 3 for the both W and Ti, we notice that intervals T3, T4 and T7 present an anomaly while T1, T2, T5, T6 and T8 are normal traffic.

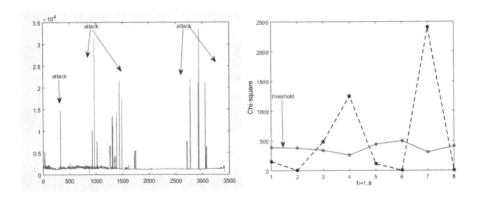

Fig. 4. The Chi-Square values at three levels decomposition wavelet in CAIDA 2013

We note that the chi square method added to the wavelet decomposition allows us to clearly separate the normal regions from the regions where there is an attack.

It is also interesting to specify that the only one is reliable and can detect the majority of DDoS attacks with a low false positive.

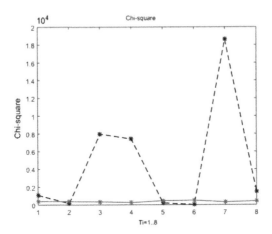

Fig. 5. The Chi-Square values at seven levels decomposition wavelet in CAIDA 2013

5.3   Global Detection

To appreciate the value of collaborative detection, we have study the detection time under a given distributed architecture in a previous work [3]. We test the time with and without the adoption of a consensus protocol. Under the attack, we observe in Fig. 6 that the first vantage point is capable of detecting the attack at the 53th second. Thanks to the consensus protocol, the first vantage point is indeed well capable at promptly sharing this information and notifying the second vantage point about the occurrence of the attack. More importantly, instead of a delayed attack detection (i.e., second 292) as in the case of the distributed architecture that does not employ a consensus protocol, the second vantage point gets notified about the attack at the 58th second. It is noticeable that the Paxos algorithm provides immensely prompt alertness by significantly reducing the detection time. Further conducted experimentation on the remaining DDoS attack flows by exploiting the consensus protocol have indeed demonstrated a similar ratio of detection attack time/delay between any two given vantage points (Fig. 5).

Table 3. Chi-Square values at different level decomposition wavelet $(J = 7)$ compared to threshold value in CAIDA 2013

Time intervals	T1	T2	T3	T4	T5	T6	T7	T8
Chi-Square values caida 2013	1087	152,9	7969	7412	201,6	9,8	18613	1471
$\chi^2_{0.5,N-1}$		390,5	380,1	342,4	255,3	444,4	501,3	307,6	409,4
Attack	Yes	No	Yes	Yes	No	No	Yes	Yes

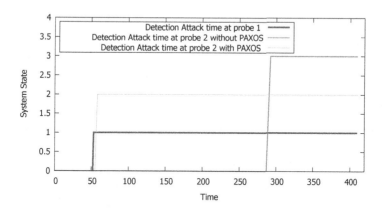

Fig. 6. Detection attack time

6   Conclusion

In this paper, we described a DDoS detection model based on wavelet and Chi-Square method. The rationale of our model is to promote that wavelets and Chi-square are able to filter the particular signals far better than conventional filters that are based on Fourier. Unfortunately Fourier analysis provides a frequency analysis but does not allow the temporal location of abrupt changes. Also, our experiment, shows a great accuracy of 2% FNR with an average of 3% FPR.

Executed experimentation using various real DDoS traces from CAIDA have indeed validated the accuracy and scalability of the proposed architecture. Also, the proposed architecture (1) was validated in terms of detection accuracy and promptness at a single vantage point, (2) demonstrated its added-value in terms of detection promptness when operated in a distributed architecture using the consensus protocol, and (3) was validated when operated in a distributed architecture in the presence of legitimate traffic.

Finally, we are currently designing a large-scale DDoS experimentation testbed in collaboration with a leading industrial partner. The aim is to make the latter platform available for researchers and other stakeholders, to conduct massive experimentation related to various DDoS types, their detection mechanisms and mitigation capabilities.

References

1. Cheng, R., Xu, R., Tang, X., Sheng, V.S., Cai, C.: An abnormal network flow feature sequence prediction approach for DDoS attacks detection in big data environment. Comput. Mater. Contin. **55**(1), 095–095 (2018)
2. Du, Z., Ma, L., Li, H., Li, Q., Sun, G., Liu, Z.: Network traffic anomaly detection based on wavelet analysis. In: 2018 IEEE 16th International Conference on Software Engineering Research, Management and Applications (SERA), pp. 94–101. IEEE (2018)
3. Ouerfelli, F.E., Barbaria, K., Bou-Harb, E., Fachkha, C., Zouari, B.: On the collaborative inference of DDoS: an information-theoretic distributed approach. In: 2018 14th International Wireless Communications & Mobile Computing Conference (IWCMC), pp. 518–523. IEEE (2018)
4. Feder, A., Gandal, N., Hamrick, J., Moore, T.: The impact of DDoD and other security shocks on bitcoin currency exchanges: evidence from Mt. Gox. J. Cybersecur. **3**(2), 137–144 (2018)
5. Feinstein, L., Schnackenberg, D., Balupari, R., Kindred, D.: Statistical approaches to DDoS attack detection and response. In: 2003 Proceedings of the DARPA Information Survivability Conference and Exposition, vol. 1, pp. 303–314. IEEE (2003)
6. Kaur, G., Bansal, A., Agarwal, A.: Wavelets based anomaly-based detection system or J48 and Naïve bayes based signature-based detection system: a comparison. In: Perez, G.M., Tiwari, S., Trivedi, M.C., Mishra, K.K. (eds.) Ambient Communications and Computer Systems. AISC, vol. 696, pp. 213–224. Springer, Singapore (2018). https://doi.org/10.1007/978-981-10-7386-1_19
7. Kuznetsova, A., Monakhov, Y., Nikitin, O., Kharlamov, A., Amochkin, A.: A machine-synesthetic approach to DDoS network attack detection. arXiv preprint arXiv:1901.04017 (2019)
8. Lamport, L., et al.: Paxos made simple. ACM SIGACT News **32**(4), 18–25 (2001)
9. Mallat, S.G.: A theory for multiresolution signal decomposition: the wavelet representation. IEEE Trans. Pattern Anal. Mach. Intell. **11**(7), 674–693 (1989)
10. Nanadikar, K., Kachi, A., Karkhanis, A., Patole, S.: FireCol: a collaborative protection network for the detection of flooding DDoS attack. Int. J. Eng. Res. Technol. **3** (2014)

11. Procopiou, A., Komninos, N., Douligeris, C.: ForChaos: real time application DDoS detection using forecasting and chaos theory in smart home IoT network. Wirel. Commun. Mob. Comput. **2019** (2019)
12. Sarre, R., Lau, L.Y.C., Chang, L.Y.: Responding to cybercrime: current trends (2018)
13. Shannon, C.: CAIDA anonymized 2008 internet traces dataset. http://www.caida.org/data/passive/passive_2008_dataset.xml
14. Siddiqui, A.J., Boukerche, A.: On the impact of DDoS attacks on software-defined internet-of-vehicles control plane. In: 2018 14th International Wireless Communications & Mobile Computing Conference (IWCMC), pp. 1284–1289. IEEE (2018)
15. Snedecor, G.W., Cochran, W.G.: Statistical Methods. Iowa State University Press, Ames (1989)
16. Soros, G.: Remarks delivered at the world economic forum (2018)

Correction to: *"I do it because they do it"*: Social-Neutralisation in Information Security Practices of Saudi Medical Interns

Saad Altamimi, Karen Renaud, and Timothy Storer

Correction to:
**Chapter ""*I do it because they do it*": Social-Neutralisation
in Information Security Practices of Saudi Medical Interns"**
**in: S. Kallel et al. (Eds.): *Risks and Security of Internet
and Systems*, LNCS 12026,**
https://doi.org/10.1007/978-3-030-41568-6_15

The book was inadvertently published with an error in the last name of the second author's name as Karen Renoud. The spelling of the second author's name was corrected.

The updated version of this chapter can be found at
https://doi.org/10.1007/978-3-030-41568-6_15

© Springer Nature Switzerland AG 2020
S. Kallel et al. (Eds.): CRiSIS 2019, LNCS 12026, p. C1, 2020.
https://doi.org/10.1007/978-3-030-41568-6_25

Author Index

Printed in the United States
By Bookmasters